New Perspectives on the Origins of Americanist Archaeology

The plaque reads "Model showing partial excavation of prehistoric Indian burial place, Orland, ME. Scale 3/8 in. = 1 foot. C.C. Willoughby." This plaster model by Willoughby was constructed at Putnam's request to display the "Methods of Archaeological Research by the Peabody Museum" for the 1893 World's Columbian Exposition in Chicago. Note the operations, such as stakes set out on the 10-foot square grid system, details of stratigraphic working faces, features, tape measures, camera, and other 'modern' archaeological procedures of the Peabody Museum method. Used by permission of the Peabody Museum of American Archaeology and Ethnology, Cambridge.

New Perspectives on the Origins of Americanist Archaeology

Edited by
DAVID L. BROWMAN AND STEPHEN WILLIAMS

THE UNIVERSITY OF ALABAMA PRESS
Tuscaloosa

Copyright © 2002
The University of Alabama Press
Tuscaloosa, Alabama 35487-0380
All rights reserved
Manufactured in the United States of America

9 8 7 6 5 4 3 2 1
09 08 07 06 05 04 03 02 01

Typeface: Trump Mediaeval

∞

The paper on which this book is printed meets the minimum requirements of American National Standard for Information Science-Permanence of Paper for Printed Library Materials, ANSI Z39.48-1984.

Library of Congress Cataloging-in-Publication Data

New perspectives on the origins of Americanist archaeology / edited by David L. Browman and Stephen Williams.
    p. cm.
"This volume grew out of the Second Gordon R. Willey Biennial Symposium on the History of Archaeology, held at the annual meetings of the Society for American Archaeology in Seattle, Washington, in 1998, where eight of the twelve papers in this volume were initially presented"—Pref.
  Includes bibliographical references (p.) and index.
  ISBN 0-8173-1128-9 (pbk. : alk. paper)
  1. Indians of North America—Antiquities—Congresses. 2. Archaeology—United States—History—Congresses. 3. Archaeology—United States—Methodology—Congresses. 4. Anthropology—United States—History—Congresses.
5. Indianists—United States—History—Congresses. 6. Women archaeologists—United States—History—Congresses. 7. United States—Antiquities—Congresses. I. Browman, David L. II. Williams, Stephen, 1926- III. Gordon R. Willey Biennial Symposium on the History of Archaeology (2nd : 1998 : Seattle, Wash.)
  E77.9 .N48 2002
  973'.01—dc21

2001003856

ISBN 978-0-8173-1128-5 (pbk. : alk. paper)
ISBN 978-0-8173-1325-8 (electronic)

Cover Photo Credit: Model of Orland Mound Excavation of 1892, Peabody Museum (courtesy of Stephen Williams)

Contents

List of Illustrations
vii

Preface
ix

Introduction
David L. Browman and Stephen Williams
1

1. The Strait of Anian: A Pathway to the New World
Stephen Williams
10

2. "From Whence Came Those Aboriginal Inhabitants of America?" A.D. 1500–1800
Stephen Williams
30

3. Roots of the Walam Olum: Constantine Samuel Rafinesque and the Intellectual Heritage of the Early Nineteenth Century
David M. Oestreicher
60

4. Toward a Science of Man: European Influences on the Archaeology of Ephraim George Squier
Terry A. Barnhart
87

5. Charles Rau: Developments in the Career of a Nineteenth-Century German-American Archaeologist
John E. Kelly
117

6. Europe's Prehistoric Dawn Reproduced: Daniel Wilson's
Magisterial Archaeology
Alice B. Kehoe
133

7. Maine Shell Midden Archaeology (1860–1910) and
the Influence of Adolphe von Morlot
Bruce J. Bourque
148

8. Frances Eliza Babbitt and the Growth of Professionalism
of Women in Archaeology
Hilary Lynn Chester
164

9. Henry Chapman Mercer: Archaeologist and Cultural Historian
David L. Browman
185

10. Frederic Ward Putnam: Contributions to the Development of
Archaeological Institutions and Encouragement of Women Practitioners
David L. Browman
209

11. Origins of Stratigraphic Excavation in North America: The Peabody
Museum Method and the Chicago Method
David L. Browman
242

12. George Grant MacCurdy: An American
Pioneer of Palaeoanthropology
Harvey M. Bricker
265

Notes
287

References
307

Contributors
367

Index
369

Illustrations

Figures

3.1 Verses 1–3 of the Walam Olum from the Rafinesque Manuscript
71

3.2 Construction of Rafinesque's compound signs from Chinese and Egyptian symbols
80

Tables

10.1 Summary of the list of 38 lectures on American Archaeology, listed by Putnam 1886
218

10.2 List of the date of enrollment as a member and election to Fellow status of women in AAAS from 1876 to 1901
223

12.1 ASPR Summer Field Schools
281

12.2 ASPR Field School Students in the Summer of 1930
282

12.3 Students in the ASPR Summer Field Schools
283

Preface

David L. Browman and Stephen Williams

This volume grew out of the Second Gordon R. Willey Biennial Symposium on the History of Archaeology, held at the annual meetings of the Society for American Archaeology in Seattle, Washington, in 1998, where eight of the twelve papers in this volume were initially presented. It seems only fitting that we should dedicate this collection of works on the intellectual roots of American archaeology to our old friend Gordon. He was a major professor and mentor for David Browman while he was a graduate student at Harvard and also a longtime friend and close colleague of Stephen Williams during his own nearly 40-year stay at Harvard's Peabody Museum. Gordon's interest in the history of the field has not abated, and we hope that he will find these efforts in that field both enlightening and important additions to an aspect of archaeology in which he has long had a strong interest.

We also wish to thank the members and staff of The University of Alabama Press for their efforts on our behalf in this exciting adventure into the history of Americanist archaeology. Nicole Mitchell, the Director, has led that effort for which we are grateful. Judith Knight is not only Acquisitions Editor, but was also our ever-present contact with the Press—she is also a cherished friend of Stephen Williams. Project Editor Jon Berry, copyeditor Jonathan Lawrence, and indexer Anne R. Gibbons have all helped our project in a most expeditious manner, for which we are most grateful.

That we are also able to thank two old friends, James B. Stoltman and Charles McNutt, for their careful readings of the volume and their perspicacious suggestions for useful changes in the text gives us great pleasure too. The two of them helped us make it a better volume. Other such help came from the many responses to our special research needs that came from Sarah R. Demb, Museum Archivist of the Peabody Museum. Her sources were a substantial aid to David Browman, especially in his Putnam research. Finally, some very important help of another kind came from a longtime friend of Stephen Williams—Albert H. Gordon of New York City, who, via a gift from the Gordon Foundation to the Peabody Museum, made a certain publishing enterprise possible: the hiring of the indexer of this volume.

New Perspectives on the Origins of Americanist Archaeology

Introduction

David L. Browman and Stephen Williams

This volume evolved out of a conversation the two of us had at a Society for American Archaeology (SAA) meeting in 1996. We observed that recent discussions on the history of Americanist archaeology as it was perceived to have evolved a century ago seemed to aggregate into predictable clusters: first, contributions from the early work in the American Southwest, and second, contributions from the work of researchers at the government agencies such as the U.S. National Museum, the Smithsonian Institution, and the Bureau of (American) Ethnology. While there is no question that these aggregates identify crucial components of the development of Americanist archaeology, other important early contributors not linked to these groups seemed to be consistently overlooked.

One solution to this issue that appealed to us was to directly address this oversight by recruiting a number of scholars interested in the history of Americanist archaeology to cover some of the institutions and individuals we thought were overlooked. The first step in developing a volume would be to get us all together to discuss the issues, and the simplest way to do that would be to organize a scientific session. Williams had participated in the SAA's History of Archaeology Committee for a number of years, sometimes as its chairperson, and Browman more recently had become a member. That committee proposed a biennial symposium on the "History of American Archaeology" at the SAA meetings, to be named for Gordon R. Willey in recognition of his longtime interest in the subject. The inaugural Willey Symposium was held in New Orleans at the annual SAA meeting in 1996. This symposium appeared to be the ideal forum to employ, and consequently the two of us organized a group of scholars for the Second

Willey Symposium in Seattle in the spring of 1998 as the mechanism by which we secured first drafts of manuscript chapters and had a chance to interact with the writers.

Intellectual Histories of American Archaeology

Interest in the intellectual history of the field of American archaeology, and volumes and articles on that topic, are hardly new. As early as 1856, Samuel Foster Haven (1806-1881), a Massachusetts scholar educated at both Harvard and Amherst, produced a lengthy and heavily researched volume on *The Archaeology of the United States*, published by the then recently founded Smithsonian Institution (Haven 1856). Haven's breadth of intellectual probing was startling—the running bibliography, not collected, is daunting. His subtitle—*Sketches, Historical and Bibliographical, of the Progress of Information and Opinions Respecting Vestiges of Antiquity in the United States*—gives some notion of the range.

Strangely enough, despite its fairly wide availability both in the original and reprint, this volume has never been thoroughly debriefed by modern scholars. Tackling the running, uncollected footnote bibliography would surely be a huge task, but one that would be of great value. Even detailed citation of Haven's information seems quite infrequent, but as will be seen, such treatment for this work and others like it is not uncommon in some areas of contemporary scholarship. There are some problems with the work; for example, Haven errs in suggesting that the Spanish missionaries Acosta and Garcia were in agreement on origins (1856:13). He also identifies them incorrectly as both being Jesuits, whereas only Acosta was. But these are minor problems in a sweeping overview very worthy of more study.

Haven was followed some 30 years later by another New Englander, also not surprisingly with a Harvard education, Justin Winsor (1831-1897). A longtime librarian at Harvard, Winsor published his eight-volume *Narrative and Critical History of America* (1884-1889) from that post. He was well known by his contemporary Harvard colleagues such as Frederic W. Putnam and others with an interest in archaeology. The first volume of the series was dedicated to *Aboriginal America*, and the authors cited range from Abbott and Acosta to Worsaae and Zeisberger. We can make such a detailed statement because the Winsor volume on archaeology and linguistics, which also originally had an uncollected bibliography, has now been reprinted with such a finding tool by John H. Ryan and Anne Paolucci (Winsor 1889/1995). This volume should be required reading for anyone posing as a scholar of North American archaeology, as also should the appended "Review Article" by Richard C. Clark and Henry Paolucci, who, though historians rather than archaeologists, have an interesting view of Winsor's accomplishment. We might add that knowledge of Winsor's work did seep out as far west as Ann Arbor, because James B. Griffin was well aware of it—perhaps through his long-term interaction with Philip Phillips of Harvard.

There is another gap, this one of nearly 40 years, until the next volume that deals extensively with the history of American archaeology, and it is even more rarely cited or read than Winsor's. This book is the 1930 Yale doctoral dissertation by Panchanan Mitra entitled *A History of American Anthropology*, published in Calcutta in 1933. Mitra was a student of Clark Wissler, and his scholarship is extraordinarily thorough. He was a late-1920s foreign exchange student who had done his undergraduate work at the University of Calcutta, to which he returned in 1930 as head of their anthropology department, regrettably to die a few years later. How thorough was he? The volume is over 200 printed pages, and the collected bibliography has more than 240 references, again from Acosta to Zeisberger.

Of course, Mitra thought highly of his mentor, and he discussed the "great synthetic schools" embracing Boas, Wissler, and even Dixon. There is also an extraordinary chapter, some 22 pages in length, on anthropologically important institutions and societies in the United States. Mitra was a careful scholar under Wissler's guidance, and there is no question that he really knew the sources. Yes, he does cite chapter and verse, and even often provides direct quotations. We certainly have learned a great deal from his work.[1]

Another 30 years would pass before the next major effort in the field of the history of American archaeology. Again, like Mitra, Alfred Irving Hallowell (1892–1974) would tackle the history of the *whole* field of anthropology. Hallowell's "The Beginnings of Anthropology in America" is the lead article of 90 pages in the *Selected Papers from the American Anthropologist: 1888–1920*, edited by Frederica de Laguna in 1960. Although certainly cited more frequently than Mitra's volume (which, by the way, is cited by Hallowell), it has never to our knowledge been the subject of any critical professional judgment in archaeology. Perhaps one reason for this, and we say this not in jest, is that it had reverted, for reasons known only to the author, to the non-collected footnote-style bibliography (as in Haven and Winsor). Thus there are many *ibid.*'s, some of which can only be tracked down by turning a dozen or more pages to find the referenced source.

All that aside, Hallowell's view is important for the postwar 1960s period. One critic has said it was not valuable for archaeology, but we do not share that view. Yes, there are some mistakes; for example, Hallowell (1960:4, n. 7) credits Acosta and Garcia with similar views on Indian origins. He apparently was using Haven's comment for this incorrect observation, but he does not cite him for this statement. We would certainly like to see the article reprinted with a collected bibliography and an index. It would be much more valuable and easier to use in that format, and would certainly be worth that effort.

When Hallowell's article appeared, Stephen Williams was beginning to take serious interest in the study of the history of the field (Willey and Sabloff 1993:11, n. 6). He was teaching the subject (Williams 1964, as cited in Willey and Sabloff 1974:9, 248) and even putting together classroom materials such as *The Foundations of American Archaeology* (Belmont and Williams 1965, cited in Willey and Sabloff 1974:9, 212). Thus began Williams's commitment to the history portion of the field that has only grown through some 35 years, and he has inoculated his former student, Browman, with the same passion.

Following Hallowell's important work by some seven years was another obscure work, at least to many students of the field—*Origins of the American Indians: European Concepts, 1492–1769.* This 1967 volume was the work of a University of Texas–trained scholar, Lee Eldridge Huddleston, who seems to have left this field of interest very soon thereafter. Huddleston was a historian with a substantial background in the European scholarship on the topic of Indian origins, and his work remains by far the most comprehensive study of this time period. While not well known in the field of archaeology, it is cited briefly in all editions of Willey and Sabloff (1974, 1980, 1993). Without attention to this work, questions about basic origins hypotheses during this period will not be well researched.

Although it appeared in a journal, not a book, Edwin Wilmsen's rather comprehensive article "An Outline of Early Man Studies in the United States" appeared during the same period, in 1965. It begins with early Spanish scholarship and quickly covers many of the important sources from Acosta and seventeenth-century Dutchmen to Thomas Gage and Pfefferkorn, the latter on the topic of the Bering Strait. Wilmsen's coverage on the later periods is also quite complete, from Jefferson and Benjamin Barton Smith to Atwater and Lyell. His sources include Haven and Winsor as well as minor journal articles, but not Mitra or Hallowell. This article is not often cited. Perhaps because Wilmsen was associated with Paleoindian field research, many recent scholars may have thought it was more about Clovis than arcane arguments of origins. It remains an important source on that topic. The 1960s were a period of foment in archaeology, with the "New Archaeology" set forth by Lewis Binford and colleagues almost taking over the national journal *American Antiquity*, which Wilmsen edited for much of the decade. Antihistorical attitudes were certainly part of that "new" view of the field, but clearly that did not include Wilmsen.

In more recent decades (1970 through 2000), study in the history of the field has flourished. First there was the small (in format) volume *The Development of North American Archaeology*, edited by James E. Fitting in 1973. Eight individual scholars, including Williams's student James B. Stoltman, wrote the separate chapters. Again it is an important source, but rarely cited in detail (perhaps the modest length of the chapters has something to do with that treatment). Fitting (1973:3) mentions that the individual authors were supposed to hold to a 30-page limit; apparently few or none followed that advice, and thus they were heavily edited to fit a 290-page printed text.

In his introduction, entitled "History and Crisis," Fitting notes that there was a current "crisis" in American archaeology which he expected to change the face of the field. From the perspective of 30 years, one can reasonably say "change," yes, but not a whole new paradigm for everyone, as some expected in the 1970s. Even archaeologists age, and their revolutions fade to less importance than when one stands on the battlements of a presumably dangerous conflict of ideas. These intellectual changes can be followed, of course, by looking at the widely read and cited Willey and Sabloff classic, *A History of American Archaeology*. For a specific view of these happenings, see "Consolidating and Broadening the New Archaeological Agenda" and "Mainstream Accommodations to the New Archaeology" (Willey and Sabloff 1993:242–297).

We have neither the courage nor the time to continue this review of the treatment of the history of American archaeology much further into more recent times. We will only note that there have been a number of recent treatments of various aspects of the history of the field by a group of well-known and prolific scholars, including, for example, Bruce Trigger, Curtis Hinsley, Jacob Gruber, and the Missouri duo of Michael O'Brien and Lee Lyman. Each has his own agenda and point of view. Perhaps it is best to lay aside further comment thereon until a later time. Less well known is the fine volume by Williams's friend and Peabody colleague Joan Mark, *Four Anthropologists: An American Science in Its Early Years* (1980), which discusses both Frederic Ward Putnam and William Henry Holmes. We commend it to your reading.

The Eighteenth- to Mid-Nineteenth-Century Pioneers, to the Civil War

Our initial stated focus in the Willey Symposium held in Seattle had been "Historical Views on American Archaeology's Connections to Europe before World War I." Thus the papers in this volume cover American scholars prior to 1915, and most of them focus particularly upon the European influences on early Americanist archaeology.

Especially important in setting up the influences are Stephen Williams's "The Straits of Anian" and "From Whence Came Those Aboriginal Inhabitants of America?" These two chapters provide the intellectual background of research on the origins of the Precolumbian American populations up to the beginning of the nineteenth century, and they include particular detail as well as a wealth of new information on the early perspectives of scholars from the seventeenth through the early nineteenth centuries.

The Walam Olum was a hotly debated document when it first appeared, and while continuing to be controversial, it was generally accepted through most of the nineteenth and early twentieth centuries. Although it is today no longer of much relevance to archaeological research, the origin of the manuscript and its influence on ideas regarding American archaeology in the nineteenth century are important for understanding the contexts of many early debates. David M. Oestreicher's exegesis of this "manuscript" in his chapter (along with his book in press) should finally put to rest any questions regarding the authenticity of this document. Rafinesque was a colorful character, and he made a series of important contributions in natural sciences of the Mid-South; his legacy should now be shifted to that venue.

Ephraim Squier is well known to most scholars of the history of American archaeology, but as archaeologists we have generally focused on the accuracy of the descriptions and illustrations of the mound complexes in his publications. Terry A. Barnhart, however, brings a historian's perspective in assessing Squier's work and its genesis. Barnhart considers Squier a transitional figure from the earlier types of research, perhaps as represented by Rafinesque, and the later, more scientifically focused studies as initiated by scholars in the last quarter of the nineteenth century. Diffusionism was a popular explanation in nineteenth-century archaeology, but Barnhart points out that contrary to the often-made assumption that Squier was a diffusionist, based on his perhaps best-known joint work with Davis on the Mound Builders, that this was not the case.

Charles Rau was a government archaeologist, one of the earliest of this genre, and in reviews of the origins of the discipline he is frequently dealt with in one or two sentences. John E. Kelly has dug into archival corners to provide a new perspective on the depth of Rau's contributions to Americanist archaeology. Kelly is best known for his work on Cahokia, and thus his chapter on Rau ferrets out the information most relevant to Rau's early career, which was the period of his major contributions to Midwest archaeology. Kelly traces Rau's movement from St. Louis to New York and ultimately to Washington, D.C.

Daniel Wilson should be best known for coining the term "prehistory" in 1851, although as Alice B. Kehoe points out, this contribution is often overlooked. Wilson began teaching the first archaeology in Canada, but because of his administrative abilities he was "lost" to archaeology, eventually becoming the president of the University of Toronto during its formative years. The archaeological works he produced after leaving Scotland for Canada were mainly syntheses; as is typical with syntheses, new research outdates them, and as with much of Wilson's work, such syntheses became obsolete and forgotten historical documents. In this article, Kehoe attempts to restore to Wilson the credit he deserves as an important scholar of prehistory by contrasting Wilson's work with that of some of his contemporaries, such as Lubbock, Morgan, and Powell.

Civil War to the Turn of the Century

One common thread that seemed to recur in our discussions on the papers that make up the second part of this volume was the underappreciated importance of Frederic Ward Putnam (1839–1915) of Harvard University's Peabody Museum. Either Putnam or the influence of his work at the Peabody Museum seems to be a significant part of the chapters by Bruce J. Bourque, Hilary Lynn Chester, Harvey M. Bricker, and David L. Browman. Hinsley (1999:144) recently characterized Putnam's interaction with individuals during the early period of his tenure at the Peabody Museum as "his correspondence school in archaeology that functioned simultaneously as a collecting arm for the Peabody Museum." The interactions among William Baker Nickerson, Frances Eliza Babbitt, and Albert Tarr Gamage discussed in the various chapters are excellent examples of this "correspondence school."

Bruce J. Bourque's chapter provides a summary of the beginnings of more methodological work in Maine archaeology, especially shell mound research. Bourque focuses on the great importance of the English translations of Adolphe von Morlot's summaries of European concepts and methodologies in doing prehistoric archaeology, which were published by the Smithsonian Institution (Morlot 1861, 1863). Bourque argues for a "second generation" of coastal shell midden work based on these pioneers.

Frances Eliza Babbitt, one of the important women practitioners of archaeology of the last quarter of the nineteenth century, has been rescued from obscurity in the chapter by Hilary Lynn Chester. Chester is interested in the context of the work of women in archaeology in general, so she focuses upon what she perceives as the reasons for the lack of visibility of women in archaeology during the formative years of the discipline.

Henry Chapman Mercer is best known to students of historical archaeology and of early-twentieth-century folk art restorations. Browman points out Mercer's important contributions to the development of prehistoric archaeology at Pennsylvania. In addition, in his evaluation of the new archaeological techniques Mercer championed, Browman suggests another avenue of European archaeological influence upon Americanist archaeology, through the contributions of Albert Gaudry and Marcellin Boule in their reinterpretation and expansion of the work of William Pengelly.

Several additional themes were suggested in our discussions at the Second Willey Symposium, but in the next two chapters Browman has elected to enlarge on only two of them. The first is the frequently overlooked issue of women's contributions to nineteenth-century Americanist archaeology. Many of the women involved in Americanist archaeology from 1875 to 1900 were either directly or indirectly recruited by Frederic W. Putnam's activities. Their number may be a surprise to most readers, as most histories of Americanist archaeology have overlooked their participation. Second is Putnam's underappreciated importance to several researchers of the nineteenth century and to the development of the Peabody Museum method of excavation. In doing the initial work on Putnam, Browman stumbled across an important linkage between Putnam's "Peabody Museum method" and Fay-Cooper Cole's "Chicago method," one that seems to have come about through Putnam's "correspondence school" strategy.

George Grant MacCurdy developed his archaeological interests in the context of the methodologies developed by Putnam and his colleagues. In the final chapter of this volume, Harvey M. Bricker does an exquisite job of detailing the development of MacCurdy's training, as well as the transfer back to Europe of an Americanized version of archaeology through the American School of Prehistoric Research.

Concluding Remarks

The history of Americanist archaeology is a critical topic for the practitioners of North American archaeology today. While the study of the history of the field goes back at least 150 years, it has been rather particularistic. As scholars in archaeology, we must know where we have been intellectually in our profession in the past at some deeper level of involvement, rather than just looking briefly at a list of scholars of the past and a sample of their ideas. As Croissant (2000:193) cogently observes, the "number, strength, and density of intellectual lineages and schools greatly affects the framing of research questions" in archaeology today.

Well-known discussions of the origins of Americanist archaeology such as Trigger (1989) and Willey and Sabloff (1974, 1980, 1993) cover so much background that they by necessity have become almost historical dictionaries or surveys of intellectual endeavors, rather than detailed inquiries into individual participants or concepts. We have felt it necessary to support a more comprehensive approach toward ideas, concepts, and intellectual positions through more detailed scholarship than has often been presented in past works. Our focus on several of the underappreciated contributors to the roots of Americanist archaeology prior to 1915 begins the process of a more thorough "sociology of knowledge" of our field. We hope that such an approach, exemplified by the chapters in this volume, will indeed move the studies of our intellectual disciplinary past forward in a positive fashion.

The Strait of Anian

A Pathway to the New World

Stephen Williams

The question of what the Strait of Anian[1] was and why it should be important to scholars interested in the history of archaeology must be answered at once. This strait, now called the Bering Strait, has played a central role in the discussion of the origins of the American Indians for many centuries (see discussion in chapter 2). This strait of Arctic water separates the two great continents, Asia and America, and seems surely to have been part of the major pathway into the New World for tens of thousands of years for the inhabitants who first colonized the Western Hemisphere. To begin, this chapter provides a brief history of our knowledge of this important geographical phenomenon though the ages of literacy and mapmaking as a background for the larger inquiry.

1500 B.C.–A.D. 1200: Geographic and Cartographic Beginnings

An understanding of the world and its organization must, for Europeans and the cultures descended from them, start with a Near Eastern foundation, beginning with the first explorations of the eastern Mediterranean, to be followed about 1000 B.C. by Phoenician navigators, and later by many developments in the Greco-Roman world. The careful mapping of the Mediterranean Sea was expanded in both lateral directions as far west as Britain and as far east as the Indian Ocean, as seen in Ptolemy's "world map" (ca. A.D. 150). This map also shows the extent of Roman knowledge of the Far East, as China was already known from its silk trade (Whitfield 1998:9–11). Less well known to many Europeans were the cartographic efforts conducted by their peers in the Middle East and China.

Important travelers to the New World late in the first millennium A.D. were the Vikings, but they have left us no cartographic data (Whitfield 1998:18–21), the Yale "Vinland map" notwithstanding (McNaughton 2000). However, the recent volume *Vikings: The North Atlantic Saga* (Fitzhugh and Ward 2000) provides new, up-to-date information on both the proven data from Iceland, Greenland, and Newfoundland (Fitzhugh 2000:11–25) and much suggestive information on even more North American contacts (Sigurdsson 2000:232–237, and companion chapters by other authors). It has been suggested by some researchers (Fitzhugh 2000:13) that explorers such as Columbus and the Cabots, after visits to Iceland, also knew about these earlier Norse trips before they too set off to "find" America.

A.D. 1200–1500: Openings to the East; Beginning of Major Voyages of Discovery

Important understanding of the Far East (China) and its culture began much earlier with overland trade between the Mediterranean and Chinese peoples via the ancient Silk Route. But it was not until after the rise of Genghis Khan around 1200 that many actual direct European contacts were made because of great interest in not only silk but the spices known from there. Among the earliest Mediterranean travelers (but not the first) were the Polo brothers—Niccolò and Maffeo—who visited China first from 1255 to 1269 and then returned in 1271 with Niccolò's son, Marco. They stayed in China for 17 years—hardly the brief visit many folks seem to think it was—and did not get back to Venice until 1295. Interestingly, the Polos, who had made most of their trips via land previously, came back this last time via a mainly sea voyage down through the Strait of Malacca and around India, adding the data they observed to European geographic knowledge.

During his stay, young Marco Polo worked directly for Kublai Khan, whom his father and uncle had gotten to know well during their first stay. Now, like all romantic heroes (and that is what Marco Polo has become), there are those who honor him and those who berate him as a liar. He is the subject of numerous books, but my take on him, prejudiced by the reading of Henry Yule's classic and revised volumes that span 20 years, is that Polo was a fine reporter of historical and geographic data, especially anthropological and natural history (Yule 1921). More recently, Whitfield (1998:22–30) lauds Polo with one hand and then throws in suspicions about his data with the other.

Yes, there were times when Polo's adjectives were a bit purple and extravagant, but read his reports on "Tartaria"—what we now call Siberia—and his descriptions ring true. He was the first to report on the great wealth of furs in this northern region, which he says he did not actually visit. His descriptions included the native lifeways, with sleds pulled by dogs and the use of skin houses, as well as semi-subterranean ones, and hunting with bow and arrow. He also reported that there were white bears seven feet tall. That last statement was clearly false, said many readers of his time, but then polar bears were not very well reported in 1300.

Marco Polo did not write his book directly. While he was in a Genoese jail as a result of a mischance in a local Italian war, Polo dictated his story to a fellow prisoner named Rusticello, who put it down in French in 1298–1299. It was best known in a Latin manuscript version translated around 1300. It was a very popular document, as over 140 copies are still recorded today. In 1477 the first printed version came out, and yes, Christopher Columbus had a copy and read it, making notes on it (Whitfield 1998:27).

Polo's volume, in its earliest version, had a great impact on cartography, despite the fact that there were no maps therein. One of the major cartographic efforts of this period was the "Catalan Atlas" (1375), rendered by the famous Majorcan Cartographic school. This atlas was strongly influenced by Marco Polo (Encyclopaedia Britannica 1999–2000). It made obvious use of Polo's descriptions of his own overall trip to China, and his return ocean voyage via the Strait of Malacca and around India to the Middle East, and then by land back to Venice. But also hidden in Polo's lengthy disquisition of peoples and places were some simple names of Chinese provinces, such as "Tollman" and "Anin." Yes, that is what this chapter is all about, as we shall see.

But it was surely Polo's description of other riches that really set off the great oceanic explorations in the Age of Discovery from 1450 to 1550: the Spice Islands had to be found. Early on, the Portuguese opted mainly for the long voyage around Africa, past India and its ocean, and then through the Strait of Malacca to the edge of China and even finally to Japan. The Spanish would much later try the western route across the Atlantic, but we all know about Columbus and his four trips from 1492 to 1499.

Now it is clear that Columbus had a good knowledge of the Spice Islands and of mainland China via Marco Polo's volume. What he did not know was the exact distance between Spain and those locations. Not until Magellan's circumnavigation from 1519 to 1522 did it become clear that the Pacific Ocean was of such great magnitude. As most readers will know, Columbus's fixation on the fact that he had "discovered" the legendary Spice Islands led him to name some of the Caribbean Islands after them, and he seems to have gone to his grave in 1506 still believing in this fiction. Dreams die hard.

A.D. 1500–1600: New Steps in Knowledge; the World Enlarged

So far our narrative has mainly looked at this wonderful expansion of world knowledge and challenge from the perspective of the Mediterranean area of Europe. Indeed, about this time, with the Treaty of Tordesillas in 1494, later ratified by a papal bull, the Spanish and Portuguese divided up the exploration of the world, with the Portuguese taking Africa and the eastern path to the Spice Islands and the Spanish opting for the western voyage to the same destination. But surely the inhabitants of those little British Isles on the western edge of Europe were not going to let such an opportunity go to waste. Shortly after Columbus, the English sent John Cabot (actually Giovanni Cabato from the Mediterranean) to see what could be found in the North Atlantic, far away from Spanish claims to the south. Cabot's voyages (1497, 1498)—the last one being a fatal one—did indeed show what the Vikings had known for centuries: yes, there was a North American continent not too far to the west (Harrisse 1896/1968; Morison 1971:157–209); but no, it was not China, although it might have profitable resources and other mysteries as well. Morison (1971:497) has even suggested that Cabot's voyages were also spurred by a desire to find "a short cut to the Indies."

Now, some of the maps of this period (1490 to 1510) are masterpieces of invention. In Johannes Ruysch's 1507 "World Map," the eastern Asia outline shows its heritage to Marco Polo, while its western Europe configuration benefits from centuries of on-site mapping. In between the two continents are scattered the Postcolumbian knowledge of the Caribbean and South America. For example, Cape Cod and Greenland are grotesquely attached to the Asian continent, while Iceland sits very properly to the northwest of Britain (Whitfield 1998:57). In Contarini's 1506 "World Map," we see a rather good representation of eastern Siberia, but if you run due south of the Kamchatka Peninsula you find yourself basking on the shores of the Caribbean islands (Whitfield 1998:55). Columbus's view of where he had landed was a mercifully short-lived misunderstanding of the scale of the earth, and most especially the size of the Pacific Ocean, the largest water mass on the planet.

The Portuguese mariners had primarily been engaged in coasting along the African shores into the Indian Ocean and on to the Pacific, from 1415 onward, long before Columbus set off across the Atlantic (Whitfield 1998:31-46). Thus they knew that route to the Orient well. It was one of these well-trained Portuguese navigators, Ferdinand Magellan, who "jumped ship" and went over to the Spanish in 1519 to carry out what Whitfield (1998:91) calls "the longest and most hazardous voyage in history"—his trip from Spain around the world with his fleet of five ships. In 1522 only one ship remained to sail into the Seville harbor, with only 20 survivors. Magellan had been killed in the Pacific well before the venture had made a successful landing in the "real" Spice Islands.

After this trip, the scale of the Pacific Ocean was really known, and the true global spread between the Asian and American continents was finally understood. Out of this geographical understanding would come the cartographic "need" of a strait or a land connection between these two great landmasses. Thus arose the concept of the "Strait of Anian," very probably named for Polo's adjacent northern Chinese province "Anin" with a coastline facing the New World. This Chinese coast and its northern extension into regions of eastern "Tartaria" were known in European terms first to Marco Polo in 1280, and much later by overland-traveling European Russians (Cossacks) in 1579.

The Age of Discovery led to an explosion of knowledge, coming from both the explorers themselves and the mapmakers who codified their observations. With all of these attempts to get to China one way or another in the sixteenth century, there was a burst of cartographic use of the concept of the "Strait of Anian," referring to the strait between the great landmasses of Asia and North America. My review of historical map sources (Kohl 1911 and Whitfield 1998, among others) suggests that the very first use of the term on a published map was by Giacomo Gastaldi in 1560, followed shortly by two other Italian mapmakers, Florani and Camocio (Whitfield 1998:87). Bolognini Zaltieri's lovely map of the New World, done in 1566, is widely known because it also shows what is now the western United States for the first time as a result of Coronado's trip there; it also shows the Strait of Anian (Whitfield 1998:87)

Northern European mapmakers such as Gerardus Mercator, the Flemish geographer, were soon to follow. Mercator's well-known map of the world in 1569 shows the Strait of Anian very clearly, as also did the map of Abraham Ortelius (the Dutchman Oertel) the next year (Kohl 1911:31). Whitfield (1998:101) refers to Ortelius with the adjective "Great," and indeed he was famous for his impressive 1570 atlas. His world maps show the Strait of Anian clearly and have the name "Anin" boldly in what is now known as western Canada (Van Ermen 1990:8–11). But less frequently referred to is Ortelius's 1570 very detailed map of the Strait of Anian region, which is said to be very unreliable (Van Ermen 1990:17). I would agree, as there is little or no resemblance between his "Tartaria" and Siberia. Interestingly, the place-name "Anin" is now back in Asia. Apparently, Ortelius was not a stickler for continuity.

Finally, in 1574 there was a little-known map published by Paulo de Fulani based on a document from a Spanish source, which has great detail on both sides of the Strait of Anian (Kohl 1911:302–303). It too has "Anian Regnum" in Siberia, and its geography seems to fit the real situation somewhat better than Ortelius's map does. Thus, despite little or no direct evidence, Continental cartographers believed in the Strait of Anian.

The sea voyages of this Age of Discovery were not just in the hands of the Spanish and Portuguese. I have already mentioned Cabot's voyages. We must remember that there were Norse settlements in Greenland from A.D. 980 on, just a few hundred miles from the North American continent. In the centuries following Cabot, both French and Basque fishermen also knew the Grand Banks very well (Morison 1971:220). Indeed, Basque whalers had a settlement on Red Bay, Newfoundland, in the mid–sixteenth century. However, most of this knowledge did not become widespread until much later.

Hence it should not be much of a surprise to find that other ways to the Spice Islands would be sought, especially by the English. Thus was born one of the most frustrating and costly geographic investigations of that era: the dual search for a North*west* Passage to the Pacific across the northern part of North America and a North*east* Passage to China over the top of Europe and Asia. There is no regular *usable* Northwest or Northeast Passage to the Pacific even today, but that was not known in the 1550s. Because the southern passages to China and the Spice Islands were in the hands of the Spanish and Portuguese, the English explorers decided to tackle these northern routes.

Thus in the time of Elizabeth I (1558–1603) and James I (1603–1625) there were many seafaring Britishers willing to risk life and limb in this strange entanglement with the Strait of Anian. Both routes would putatively have made use of that Strait to reach their final destination—China. Although Martin Frobisher and Sir Humphrey Gilbert may not be well known to the reader, both of them caught "Strait fever." These gentlemen were in a circle of scholars surrounding John Dee (1527-1608), a Cambridge-trained geographer, who later was a member of Elizabeth's court (Cormack 1997:81). Dee had studied with the great cartographer Mercator, so he was well informed as to the current views of the world.

In the 1550s, some members of this circle, with advice from Dee, were ready to seek the impossible for much-sought fame and possibly great financial gain as well (Cormack 1997). Frobisher, with aid from the government and other London sources, made three unsuccessful attempts (1576, 1577, and 1578) to find a passage north of Newfoundland that would let him reach the Pacific. His investigations around Baffin Bay led him to think in 1577 he might have found gold instead. His third exploration, in 1578, proved that his find was merely "fools gold" (Fitzhugh and Olin 1993).

There was one positive result from Frobisher's overall investigations, however. In 1578, George Best, one of his shipmates, published his own report of the explorations, including a map of the region showing the Strait of Anian in its proper westerly position (Whitfield 1998:50) but connected across the continent by the imaginary "Frobisher Straits" that they had hoped to find. Both the Northeast and Northwest Passages to Cathay are boldly shown leading to the "Straight of Anian" (Morison 1971:546; Whitfield 1998:50). Because this map came out after the three Frobisher failures, its purpose was not promotion but to illustrate Best's volume on the Frobisher expeditions.

But Frobisher's lack of success did not stop other members of Dee's gang of true believers. Thus in 1576, as Sir Humphrey Gilbert, a close friend of Queen Elizabeth's, was preparing to undertake his search across the Atlantic, he produced an interesting heart-shaped map showing Anian and its strait on the left and Europe, Africa, and Asia on the right (Whitfield 1998:79). Now that we know more about Gilbert's background (Cormack 1997), it is clear that this is a direct effort by Gilbert himself to promote funds for his project. In 1578, Gilbert made his first attempt to make a late-summer crossing of the North Atlantic in his search for the Northwest Passage, but he turned back after bad luck and many problems with his other would-be fleetmates. In June 1583, after having raised a lot of money (including his own inheritance), Gilbert set out on his second attempt. He made a rough but successful crossing to Newfoundland and Nova Scotia (Morison 1971:561-582).

The Strait of Anian / 17

Gilbert was pleased with what he had found in these northerly lands, despite not finding the route to China, and he set sail with his now smaller fleet to return to England. However, they were hit by a very strong storm, and his smaller ship, the *Squirrel*, sank with all aboard, ending Gilbert's dream forever. Morison (1971:578) saw him as a brilliant but controversial pathfinder for the British's later colonization of North America.

But then there was that "other" way to reach China, and the English (along with some Dutch explorers as well) led the way in searching for the North*east* Passage. These attempts occurred from 1553 to 1580, with a considerable loss of life: the "frozen sea" was a relentless adversary. Failure did not daunt them, and the British tried repeatedly to go over the top of the Scandinavian countries and into the Russian White Sea and then further east. The British Muscovy Company did make a sea-river-land connection to Moscow from 1553 to 1560 and even to the Caspian Sea with some mercantile success, the latter carried out by Anthony Jenkinson (Encyclopaedia Britannica 1999–2000). This last effort was almost the only bright result in all this unusual seafaring to the north by the British. However, the Dutch were also in a relationship with the Russians via overland trade, and one of them, Olivier Brunel, made coasting voyages to the mouth of the river Ob (Whitfield 1998:49–52, 78–84, 177–184).

Another spectacular map generated by the Northeast Passage explorations was by the Dutch scholar Willem Barentz in 1598 (Whitfield 1998:48). It has finely delineated shorelines where the Dutch expeditions had worked, leaving those portions beyond their voyages very generalized. The Strait of Anian is carefully defined. Barentz was following up the earlier Dutch work in that area, which coincided with the British Muscovy Company efforts mentioned above.

We must not forget Sir Francis Drake's 1577–1580 ultimate circumnavigation of the world. According to Whitfield (1998:101), Drake was supposed to enter the Pacific via Magellan's Strait and then turn north to return to England via the Strait of Anian. Wisely, he did less than that and more, in that once in the Pacific he does not seem to have gone much further north than California in search of the elusive strait. Then he wisely turned to the southwest across the Pacific, skipping China altogether, with a path south of Java and around Cape Horn back to England, contributing greatly to British geographic knowledge (Whitfield 1998:102–103).

During the late sixteenth century, one other tantalizing bit of data about "Anian" comes from the extraordinary Portuguese historian

Antonio Galvano (1490–1563) in his 1563 *Tratado*. That volume is amazing in its broad coverage of "Discoveries of the World" and is given credibility by its translation into English for Hakluyt in 1601. There is also a positive modern citation by Morison (1971:100). Galvano mentions "where the Island of *Aynan* standeth, which also they say did joine hard to the land of China" (Galvano 1601:27, emphasis added).

To put some closure on these dogged attempts to find the elusive Northeast and Northwest Passages, let it be said that apparently nothing could stop presumably sane human beings (all male as far as I know) from trying to make these northern voyages successfully. More than a dozen leaders and many seamen joined together over a period of many centuries (from 1600 to 1900) to attempt these passages, with a great loss of lives. Final resolution to both such voyages was only finally attained in the twentieth century with modern iron vessels and the possibility of global warming aiding in the successful transitioning through these ice-clogged passages, which did indeed exist after all (Britannica 1999–2000).

A.D. 1600–1800: Others Look at the Strait of Anian Region

It is hardly rational to think that all our knowledge of the Strait of Anian should come entirely via scholars from Western Europe rather than from the locals. I admit that my research does not include any Chinese sources, but I am aware of Russian data that will help understand this region better. As early as 1580, Cossacks crossed the Urals and began to push Russian control of the land into "Tartaria." This military and commercial expansion soon won the attention of the Czars, and more focused attempts to explore the potential of this nether region were undertaken.

The economic reason for this action was the clearly seen future of the fur trade, which did indeed, as we shall see, capture the interest of people in many parts of the world during these two centuries (A.D. 1600–1800). Despite the difficulties of travel across this huge region, not to mention its rugged terrain and extremely cold winters, the Russians were able to establish the far eastern village of Yakutsk by 1637, and by 1638 to reach the nearby Sea of Okhotsk, with its opening on the northern Pacific Ocean. This body of water is sheltered by the Kamchatka Peninsula and provided an excellent taking-off place for explorations. However, surprisingly, the northern coast of eastern Siberia was used for such early explorations as well, because it was easily reached by rivers such as the Lena or Kolyma to enter the Arctic Ocean in the summertime.

"By 1645, the first trading ships were plying between the Kolyma and the Lena along the Arctic Coast" (Encyclopaedia Britannica 1999–2000, Arctic:1). Thus we can now turn directly to the Strait of Anian at last. In 1648, Semyon Ivanov Dezhnyov (or Deshnef) (1605–1673), a Cossack, led a fleet of seven vessels east from the Kolyma along the northern edge of Siberia. They were apparently headed for the Gulf of Anadyr because its interior basin was said to be rich in furs. The fleet ran into difficulties, and only three vessels reached the Strait of Anian and turned south past "East Cape," the place where the two continents are closest together. This cape is now designated Cape Dezhnyov (or Deshnef) on many maps for self-evident reasons, although some maps retain the simpler "East Cape" designation. More of the Russian fleet was lost along the way; the Strait of Anian was obviously not an easy passage. Indeed, this Cossack-led group sailed right by the Gulf of Anadyr, their objective, and landed quite far to the south at Cape Olyutorsky. The party then proceeded overland to the Anadir Basin.

Thus the records as now known show quite clearly that Vitus Bering's well-publicized Russian-sponsored trip in 1728 was the second, not the first, investigation of the Strait of Anian. How does this historical omission happen? Well, part of the solution can only be answered with a simple reply: bureaucrats. The best we can say at this point is the following: Dezhnyov apparently went back by land via the usual routes of communication, first to Yakutsk on the Lena River and then southeast following the Lena valley to Irkutsk, near Lake Baikal. Irkutsk had been an important trade and travel center since before 1600 because of its location. It naturally became a governmental center during the Russian expansion into Siberia, but not until 1652.

I can only posit that when Dezhnyov finished his trek from the Anadir Basin back to Yakutsk, the nearest major settlement, he wearily deposited his documentation of his great voyage there in 1648–1649. Again the *Encyclopaedia Britannica* (1999–2000) comes to our aid with a short declarative sentence: "his report lay buried in the archives at Yakutsk until German historian Gerhard Friedrich Muller found it in 1736." Thus the higher-ups in St. Petersburg apparently never saw the report, although it is hard to believe that documentation of this large voyage of exploration never existed there.

Hence, by 1650 the ground truth voyage to prove that the Strait of Anian really existed had occurred, it just was not widely known. Thus it is no surprise that one of the last maps showing the Strait of Anian, albeit in French (D'estroit d'Anien), is that of Father Hennepin in 1683. But we will have to wait until the next century and Peter the Great to sponsor "new" investigations that would catch everyone's eye. The Russians were not shy about hiring outside help for their important and still quite private investigations of the great treasure house that was Siberia.

Thus in 1724 Peter the Great appointed the Dane Vitus J. Bering to lead an expedition to northeastern Siberia and to investigate the division of the two continents. One can only suppose that Peter was not aware of Dezhnyov's successful trip through the Strait, due to the fact that documents were then in the Yakutsk "archives." The expedition, however, did not leave St. Petersburg until February 1725. Bering proceeded slowly across the continent, under orders not to discuss the nature and wealth of the land he passed through. He apparently took his time getting to the Kamchatka Peninsula, where he built his ships, and finally in 1728 he headed north through the Strait that now bears his name. However, he did not see Alaska, and he returned to Kamchatka to make the same overland trip, arriving in St. Petersburg in March 1730. Whatever lack of speed he might have shown, his name would then forever be given to the old "Strait of Anian."

Bering was not yet done with "his" strait: he was unsatisfied with the results and turned again to those then in charge. Catherine the Great thus sent him on a second voyage to go through the Strait again in 1733. This venture was no speedier than the first. They arrived in Okhotsk on the shore of the Okhotsk Sea and puttered about for six years, finally sailing out in 1740 with two ships. After a stop along the way, they finally succeeded in reaching the Gulf of Alaska in the summer of 1741. On the return trip to Okhotsk, Bering fell ill and died upon a small island, where he was buried.

By 1750 the Strait of Anian question had been pretty well settled. Dezhnyov had gone through there in 1648–1649, and then Bering would make his two visits. The Russians would begin to chart the region, and soon its name would change to "Bering." However, as late as 1720 the German mapmaker Zurner would show the Pacific with the "Fretum Anian" north of California and with no guesses as to the Asian side (Whitfield 1998:115).

But all that would change in the next half century thanks to a rather motley crew: a world-renowned English sea captain, a soon-to-be American president, a Dartmouth College dropout, a quite unknown English navigator/astronomer with a strong penchant for travel, and a small marine mammal. Very much later, another American president would succinctly sum up the whole situation in one sentence.

Of course, the British sea captain was James Cook, of whom it has been said that he "explored more of the earth's surface than any other single man in history" (Whitfield 1998:125). Cook made three important Pacific voyages between 1768 and 1779, dying in Hawaii as a result of a small conflict with its inhabitants. Cook's third voyage (1776–1780) is of most interest here, because once again the British were concerned about the possible connection between the Bering Strait and Hudson Bay. Spurred by the potential of the fur trade, the British government was offering a reward of 20,000 pounds to any British ship that would discover such a passage (Whitfield 1998:124). Obviously, Cook decided to give it a try. He came north from Tahiti to the Hawaiian Islands in 1778, then headed to the northeast to follow closely the northwest coast of North America to Alaska, observing sea otters along the way. Then they went far to the north through the Bering Strait until he ran into pack ice. Cook then turned south again to winter in Hawaii before making a further investigation of the area in the early part of 1779.

Following a misunderstanding with the local population, Cook alone was killed as he attempted to return to his ship (February 14, 1779). The crew, still interested in a possible share of the reward if they found the connection to Hudson Bay, did not immediately return to London. Instead, they headed back north as Cook had intended and again went carefully through the Strait, seeking the elusive Northeast Passage. Failing that objective, the ship then coasted down past the Kamchatka Peninsula and by Japan and returned via the Strait of Malacca to London in 1780. So much for British hope for a quick northern passage to China. You have to give them credit: they were persistent!

There is little doubt that one of the really important things about the area covered by Cook in his last voyage was the presence of a much-sought-after resource in the northern Pacific: the precious fur-bearing sea otter, a native of only this region in the world. That beast, now hovering on the edge of extinction near the West Coast of the United States due to many adverse conditions in its habitat, was a very highly valued marine animal that was once very plentiful throughout the northern Pacific waters south of the Bering Strait.

Current inhabitants of the North American continent which centuries before was the fur-trading capital of the world may now have little knowledge and in some cases great contempt for the harvesting of animal pelts for wearing apparel. They may not want to know about the worldwide fur trade that for centuries made fortunes for some, and widely treasured coats and headwear for the elites of Eurasia from London to St. Petersburg, and even further east to China. While silks and finely made cloths were part of the Chinese elite clothing, fur garments were also held in high esteem in Cathay. Thus when Marco Polo was there in the thirteenth century, he reported extensively on the high quality of furs available in Tartaria, stating that the further north one went, the better the quality of the furs. While Polo did not see that area himself, his details relating to the inhabitants and environment are very accurate, as we now know.

A few centuries later, as the European Russians pushed further east into what we now call Siberia, they had a special interest in the riches in furs that this area contained and later made it a "state secret." The Chinese were also not particularly forthcoming with information on this subject. If you know the location of a gold mine, you do not put it boldly on a map for all to see. So far I have been speaking mainly of the land mammals and their fur-bearing attributes. My research on sea otters has been rather minimal, but it is clear that by the time Cook carefully surveyed the northern Pacific region in the 1770s, sea otters were much sought after for their lovely fur.

But to get back to our query about that strange group of individuals I introduced a few paragraphs back: the first was Captain Cook, whom you have already met; the second one was the Englishman Joseph Billings, who was the navigator/astronomer for Cook's third and final voyage. The Russians, under the auspices of Catherine the Great, subsequently chose Billings to lead an eight-year trek from St. Petersburg to the Arctic Ocean and the Bering Strait region and back. Much of it was overland to Siberia, and then various ocean trips were made from ports on both the Arctic Ocean and on the Sea of Okhotsk and the Kamchatka Peninsula. The trip began in August 1785 and lasted until 1793.

The trip was documented by Gavriil Sarychev (also transliterated as Gavrila Sarychew and Gawrila Sarytschew), a Russian officer. He reported that at Okhotsk on Kamchatka Bay, Russian ships owned by a trading company and, supported by the government, regularly left that harbor for expeditions to the Aleutians and North America "for the purpose of collecting furs" (Sarychev 1806/1969:17). These voyages often lasted 10 years, Sarychev said.

However, long-distance trade was also on Sarychev's mind as he wrote in 1789, while at the town of Kamchatka, that the products of the region could also help establish trade with China, Japan, and even the East Indies. Among the materials for this trade would be furs of "sea-beavers, sea lions, otters, foxes, minevers and above all the fangs of the walrus or river-horse" (Sarychev 1806/1969:70). Thus it is no wonder that outsiders might have an interest as well; hence Cook's 1776–1779 voyage, which took such great care to investigate this region not once but twice.

One of the main reasons for presenting data from this Russian expedition is to confirm the great value of fur-bearing animals in this part of the world, which certainly was part of Captain Cook's special interest and care in his investigation of the northern Pacific region. But the other is that this knowledge, shared by his navigator, Billings, also involved the third person who took part in some of these adventures. This was the American John Ledyard, a young man from Connecticut who dropped out of Dartmouth College at the end of his freshman year, made his way across the Atlantic as a seaman, and finally was taken on board Captain Cook's ship in London as a crew member of the third voyage. Ledyard was hardly the typical Ivy League chap, although he came from an old New England family, and yes, there is a town named Ledyard, Connecticut. He was also hardly irrational, although he did leave the Dartmouth campus in his freshman year and canoed down from Hanover to the Atlantic. I understand freshmen still repeat this feat each year.

After an Atlantic crossing, Ledyard shipped out as a corporal of marines as Cook's ship left London on July 12, 1776. We know little of his time aboard Cook's vessel, except that he certainly got to know Joseph Billings quite well, and Billings also Ledyard, during their four years together at sea. The *Dictionary of American Biography* (Ghent 1933) suggests that Ledyard immediately saw the value of fur trade in northwestern America as they arrived in Nootka Sound. Arriving back in London in 1780 at the end of the voyage, Ledyard spent two years in jail because he refused to fight against his own country. Later shipped to America as an English soldier, he escaped to his family in Connecticut, where he tried to interest business people in the Nootka fur trade, but without success.

Ledyard returned to Europe in 1784 and soon made contact with none other than Thomas Jefferson, then resident in Paris caring for American affairs of state. Jefferson met Ledyard and learned of his almost fanatic desire to get to the North Pacific area. Ledyard suggested that he would walk across Russia to the Pacific and then possibly "catch a boat" to Nootka Sound, and then trudge back to Virginia. It would be a good way to get a real fix on all this possible fur-trade operation. What a bold idea for the young adventurer from Connecticut! (As to a possible source for this idea—Jonathan Carver—see chapter 2 of this volume.)

Now we do know that the conversation actually took place because Jefferson discusses this rather wild notion in a letter (Jefferson to Charles Thompson, September 20, 1787; Boyd 1955, 12:159-161). Jefferson was anxious to know more about the inhabitants of Siberia and their customs and especially their languages, since he was just completing his significant work *Notes on Virginia*. Therein Jefferson did discuss the very possibility that the ancestors of the American Indians had come from Ledyard's own Siberian area of interest.

Ledyard made several attempts to get Catherine's permission to go to this area, with no success, even though he was supported by Jefferson. However, Ledyard was not to be put off. When he went back into Russia in the fall of 1786 and found that the Empress was absent from St. Petersburg, he soon began his journey across the thousands of treacherous miles that separated him from the Pacific Coast he sought to visit. He had planned to walk, but our Russian source, Sarychev, sneers at this effort. He instead indicates that Ledyard reached Yakutsk in the late fall of 1787 via the "civility of the Russian travelers, whom he met on the road, who carried him from place to place without any recompense" (1806/1969:43).

Yakutsk was still some distance from the Pacific, but it was a good place for Ledyard to spend the winter. The Russians gave him warm clothes and treated him with kindness, but his temperament was such that "the only return which Mr. Ledyard made for this extraordinary hospitality was to calumniate and abuse everyone; and to finally challenge his benefactor for remonstrating with him on the impropriety of his behavior" (Sarychev 1806/1969:43). This description of Ledyard is not at variance with other sources; he was indeed a strong-willed and headstrong person, not to mention lacking in courtesy at times.

But fate had another answer for John Ledyard in far-distant Yakutsk, for the leader of the Russian exploring expedition was of course none other than our English navigator/astronomer Joseph Billings, from Cook's last Pacific voyage. Billings returned shortly to their main base in Yakutsk, recognized the unruly American, his former shipmate, and put him under house arrest for being in the area without proper papers. Billings personally took him back to Irkutsk, where Ledyard was clapped into irons in February 1788 and sent back to St. Petersburg. So died his wild dream; and fate was not good to him in his very next adventure, which was to search for the source of the White Nile. Tragically, Ledyard died of a local fever in Cairo in January 1789 at age 38 before he could undertake this mission.

Thomas Jefferson, when he became president, would take up the fallen torch of John Ledyard and hand it to a couple of Virginians named Meriwether Lewis and William Clark, who would venture forth from near Monticello (Ledyard's final overland objective). Their trip really began at St. Louis on the Missouri River and extended to that very North Pacific Coast of America that Ledyard had hoped to reach. I hope that when these two neighbors of his (Lewis and Clark) successfully returned to Monticello and/or the White House in 1806 with the details of this rich American area for the fur trade, Jefferson had them raise a glass to the memory of the undaunted John Ledyard.

Thus we have all the characters of our narrative but the last: the sea captain, the American statesman, the young American adventurer, the British navigator, and the much-sought-after sea otter. The other American president was William Jefferson Clinton, who was wont to exclaim: "It's the economy, stupid!" And he was right—it was all about the fur trade and the moneys that could be made from exploiting that fur trade on both sides of the North Pacific, below the Strait of Anian.

A final coda to the Ledyard story is that there are to be found in several related documents materials that would or could have been of great interest to Jefferson and his concerns for what Ledyard might see on his projected journey. Sarychev's account, translated into English and published in London in 1806, includes a wealth of data on the aboriginal inhabitants of Siberia, including five illustrations (two in color) that show ethnographic data in great detail, including dress, bows and arrows, housing, dogsleds, and so forth (Sarychev 1806/1969:inserts). There is even a shaman doing a curing. I do not know if Jefferson ever had access to this volume. Of equal interest is what I take to be a rather rare map of the region by none other than Vitus Bering from his 1725–1729 expedition. This presumably rare item is in the British Museum. Besides showing a rather simplified outline of the landmass and some topography, it also has both tribal locations and some Russian villages, as well as quite detailed ethnographic illustrations of clothing, and finally, yes, a dogsled (Whitfield 1998:136–137). Again, Marco Polo is shown as a good reporter!

A.D. 1800–1900: The Tide Has Turned; Bering Strait It Is

Although I confess that I seem to have spent an inordinate amount of time and energy on what appears to be a small topic—the Strait of Anian—I still feel that such a subject can and did turn up new information and has allowed me to add to some of the intellectual aspects of archaeology and history as well. I certainly feel that such research can enlarge our knowledge of our intellectual past and of how both archaeology and geography grow and change through time.

I would suggest that by 1850, American archaeology was beginning to swing toward a better understanding of the "origins of the Indians," but certainly not with any better chronology than that used centuries before. The Strait of Anian had been completely superseded by the Bering Strait, and my acid test for that usage is found in Samuel Haven's definitive 1856 publication of *The Archaeology of the United States*, published by the Smithsonian. Therein the question of Indian origins is specifically discussed under the index topic "Behring Straits, a probable route of migration to America, [page] 147." Enough said. And so it would be from then on. No Russians need apply.

However, strangely enough, I can state that according to some sources, Dezhnyov's name was put on Russian maps for the "East Cape" he rounded so many years earlier. After all, it was indeed the most easterly reaching cape in Asia. My 1929 *Encyclopaedia Britannica*, in naming that important point of land, uses "Cape Deshnef," and the 1999 *National Geographic Atlas* has gone to "Deshneva Mys. (East Cape)"! So one way or another there is still some reference to that very early European explorer of the Arctic.

But there were other scholars in the nineteenth century who still had a very strong and broad interest in the Strait of Anian problem from a mainly historical point of view. This was the work presented in a little-known "Disquisition" written in 1857 by the German scholar Johann Georg Kohl (1808–1878), quite obviously a cartographic specialist. Kohl came to America in 1854 at the age of 46. He remained in America only three years, working in the Washington area, partly with a government subsidy. Kohl focused on a comprehensive study of maps of America in its broadest sense. He prepared while here a paper with the main title "Asia and America" (Kohl 1911). Despite this enigmatic short title, his lengthy subtitle gives away his real intent: "An Historical Disquisition Concerning the Ideas Which Former Geographers Had about the Geographical Relation and Connection of the Old and New World." It was all about the Strait of Anian, of course—a study of all the early maps on the subject. Unfortunately, this 1857 paper, which is exhaustive and contains many maps not used by later scholars, was not published until 1911.

How and why did this long delay occur? Funding for this visiting German scholar apparently ran out due to a financial crisis in this country. Kohl then returned to Bremen, Germany, in 1857, where he died in 1878. He seems to have had support from the Smithsonian during his visit to America. His important collection of early American maps, many of which he had brought with him, ended up in the Library of Congress, while his manuscript went to Joseph Henry at the Smithsonian Institution. Justin Winsor, Librarian at Harvard and a noted historian, studied and cataloged these maps.

Somewhat later, with the support of Samuel Haven of the American Antiquarian Society of Massachusetts, it was decided to print the article in the *Proceedings* of that society. But there were some very unfortunate delays, and thus Kohl's work finally reached publication in 1911, some 54 years after completion. Except for the modest reference by Nunn (1929), it remained in further obscurity for many more decades until finally cited by Morison (1971) and, of course, herein.

A.D. 1900–2000: The Last Century on the Strait of Anian

The most surprising thing to this writer is that, so far as I have been able to determine, no archaeological or anthropological scholar of the twentieth century who has dealt with the Bering Strait hypothesis has ever even mentioned this older terminology for this important stretch of water.[2] On the other hand, historians have spent plenty of time and ink on the subject. I have been led into this area of Anian research via the writings of my late Harvard colleague, Professor Samuel Eliot Morison, in his two extraordinary volumes on *The European Discovery of America* (1971, 1974). The Strait of Anian appears frequently both in the text of the volumes and in the footnotes. It is in his work that I found the mother lode of citations on this topic (Morison 1971:515).

The most recent (1929) and most comprehensive work I know of is a modest-sized volume (35 pages) entitled *Origin of the Strait of Anian Concept*, written by George E. Nunn and privately published. I know nothing about Nunn except that, judging from his little volume, he cared enormously about this topic. His first footnote includes fifteen references on Anian, only two of which I have read. Like most students of the subject, he follows Ptolemy and Marco Polo as basic and important early geographical sources. He also identifies Gastaldi and Zaltieri as the first cartographers to place the Strait of Anian in the proper location. Nunn then turns to the genesis of the name itself (Anian), and he feels confident that Dr. Sophus Ruge, a nineteenth-century German scholar, was correct in citing a passage from a rather obscure edition of Marco Polo's *Travels* as the source (Ruge 1873). This edition was in Italian and of the period that could have influenced the two Italian cartographers mentioned above. Nunn is unwilling to say whether he would favor Gastaldi over Zaltieri as the geographer initially responsible for using this concept, but he has another important pro–Marco Polo insight concerning Anian. He has a sketch of Gastaldi's earlier (1566) map "Tertia Pars Asiae" showing Polo's journey that has "Ania Pro[vince]" in a far northeast position near the location of the Strait (Nunn 1929:24–25).

While Nunn's work is an extraordinary piece of scholarship, it is, like all such constructions, a personal view. It seems strange to me that while citing Kohl's little-known "Disquisition" (1911) in the very first footnote in his little volume, which covers a large number of pertinent sources, Nunn makes no further use of the information provided by Kohl. I grant you that Kohl himself is not well known in America, despite having written more than half a dozen books on American subjects that are published in English.

It is quite clear that within the German academic community, which included Kohl, the fact that Bering was not the first discoverer to sail through the Strait must have been well known for many decades. I have not searched for any more German sources, however. Perhaps scholars and cartographers stuck with the Bering story and name because it was, by the late time of Muller's 1736 discovery, just too well known and accepted. Don't spoil a great story with a new Russian Cossack hero instead.

However, there are some cracks in this splendid symmetry of leaving the Russians directly out of the naming of the Strait for the long-suffering Danish navigator Vitus Bering. For example, in the 1929 *Encyclopaedia Britannica* (3:347) there is a short discussion of Mr. Bering and his exploits in the region in a biographical format. However, just following it there is a much longer discussion of "Bering Island, Sea and Strait." Herein the anonymous author clearly indicates that the Russians had been busy in that area for some time, and specifically states: "Isai Ignatiev went east from the Kolyma river in 1646, and Simon Dezhnev in 1648 followed his route and prolonged it, rounding the East of Dezhnev cape and entering the Strait. The post of Andyrsk was founded on the river Anadyr, and an overland way gradually opened up." This article also cites several German scientific sources, so the unknown writer may indeed have known of Muller's 1736 discovery of Dezhnyov's documents in Yakutsk.

Certainly this information has fully come down through the *Britannica* pathway to their great discussion of the Russian Arctic explorations now presented on their web-based version of today (Encyclopaedia Britannica 1999–2000). And yes, the research of "the German historian Gerhard Friedrich Muller" in 1736 on this subject is indeed cited therein. Perhaps the shadow of Johann Kohl is quietly rejoicing, with just a little angst at how long it took others to learn what he knew almost 150 years before.

So there are some happy endings in this long trek through the literature and the history of geography of the Strait of Anian and the very human attempts to understand both the shape of the landmasses of Asia and America and how these studies could and would have an impact on the basic questions of the "origins of the American Indians." It has been a very interesting trip. However, in closing I want to add that two older colleagues of mine, now deceased, William G. Haag and Robert Wauchope, both discussed the Bering Strait, the first geographically (Haag 1962) and the second historically (Wauchope 1962), but neither mentioned the "Strait of Anian" concept.

2

"From Whence Came Those Aboriginal Inhabitants of America?"

A.D. 1500–1800

Stephen Williams

Introduction: Some Primary Questions and Answers

The questions of who were the first occupants of the New World, where they came from, and when are more than 500 years old, since they began to be asked from the time the Western Hemisphere was being encountered by European explorers.[1] I am going to discuss the background of this topic in the time period from A.D. 1500–1800.

Some basic parameters can be set for this discussion of the answers that have been given to this oft-spoken query of "Whence?" The question was first posed following Columbus's "discovery" of the New World. He surely was not the first European to visit the Western Hemisphere; the Norse had done that 500 years earlier. Nor was he traveling into what was completely terra incognita, or fearful of falling off the edge of a "flat" world. Some pre-1492 European knowledge of the distant continent may well have existed among the Icelanders, for example. The concern of a non-round earth was certainly an old wives' tale by the end of the thirteenth century. Classical scholars had centuries before recognized the world as a sphere and had constructed "globes" and also estimated quite accurately the earth's circumference (Whitfield 1998:54–59).

However, for a proper understanding of the worldview in the 1490s we must go back as far as the thirteenth century and the travels of Marco Polo, whose impact on later cartography was immense. Polo's long trip and visit to China from 1271 to 1295 and his later description of that region were hardly hidden from medieval scholars. More than 100 versions of Polo's manuscript description of his travels are extant today. While it is true that Polo himself did not construct a map based

"From Whence Came Those Aboriginal Inhabitants of America?" / 31

on his lengthy stay in the East, his narrative is clear enough that more recent scholars have been able to trace his travels quite accurately (Yule 1921). Much earlier Portuguese cartographers, some of the best of their time, were able to add East Asia, India, and the location of the Spice Islands to their "Portolan" charts using Polo's data (e.g., Laurentian/Medicean Portolano 1351 and Catalan Atlas 1375; see Whitfield 1998: 31–41).

Actually, Columbus was very likely not even ignorant in general terms of the oceanic distance to the New World (his Cathay) but probably underestimated it due to Ptolemy's incorrect figures. Following Columbus's first voyage, in 1492, not to mention his other three trips to the "West" Indies, as they would soon be called, the most amazing thing is the rapidity with which further discovery of the new hemisphere took place between 1492 and 1550.

One of the best sources from the period were the "Decades," as his chapters were called, by Peter Martyr, whose book *De Orbe Novo* (1511–1530), written in Spain, was the first "history" of these exciting events (Anghiera 1912). Martyr's successive "Decades" provided up-to-date information in a manner that almost equals today's websites. Exploration, trade, and mapmaking went hand in hand, and the delineation of the New World in a cartographic manner was done amazingly quickly and with considerable accuracy (Whitfield 1998:53–89).

As Samuel E. Morison (1974:3–161) and Whitfield (1998) have clearly set forth, the raison d'être for Columbus's voyages was obvious: the search for a shorter path to the Spice Islands. Ever since Marco Polo's descriptions of Cathay, and with the rise of the Muslim Empire blocking the European/Asian overland trade (the ancient Silk Route), other paths to the Orient were sought. Some were rather irrational (at least to our eyes), but they were still tried over and over again. For the English it was via the North*west* Passage across the top of North America by Martin Forbisher (1576–1578) and many others. Other Europeans tried the North*east* Passage, going over the top of Europe and into Russia that way. None was really successful until the twentieth century, a bit late! (See chapter 1 for more details on these attempts.)

Another aspect of possible Old World contacts with the New that has not received much attention until recently is the fact of long-term occupation of western Greenland by Icelandic/Norse settlers many centuries prior to 1492. Of course, there was also the now-proven but short-lived settlement of North America (Vinland) by Vikings around 1000 in Newfoundland (Fitzhugh and Ward 2000). However, less spectacular but of much greater duration were the extensive occupations on the southwest tip of Greenland (the so-called Eastern and Western settlements) just some 400 miles across the Davis Strait from the New World. For some centuries (900s through the 1400s), these Europeans were living in well-built houses, with barns, churches, and fields of crops. Trade with these settlers was carried out by both Icelanders and other Europeans, so it was not a secret matter. It has even been suggested that quite regular trips might have been made to the west in search of wood and other materials scarce in Greenland, but no physical evidence now exists, as far as I know, to prove such continued contact (Fitzhugh and Ward 2000; Seaver 1996).

The Strait of Anian Question

Another major geographical query about the New World rested on whether there was a physical connection between Asia and this newly found continent. By 1560, an Italian, Giacomo Gastaldi, first showed the Strait of Anian[2] (aka the Bering Strait) on a map showing a narrow gap separating the two continents. Many other mapmakers soon followed this delineation (Morison 1971, 1974; Whitfield 1998:86-87). The Bolognini Zaltieri map of 1566 also is particularly clear in its definition of those straits. On this same map there is an area called "Quivira" in the American Southwest that was sought by many Spanish explorers, including Coronado. The sixteenth-century cartographic view was therefore that a strait of not very great width separated Asia and the New World. This map feature would then strangely disappear for quite a long time, at least based on my own cartographic study (see discussion in chapter 1).

This new cartographic treatment of an area crucial in the "origins" hypothesis argument was not then based on any direct exploration.[3] Instead, it seems to come strictly from literary sources, especially Marco Polo. Polo had never gotten very far north, never into Siberia proper, so he had no firsthand knowledge of the area. However, he does describe the northland with considerable accuracy. There are large white bears, great quantities of fabulous furs, sledges drawn by dogs, people living in leather tents with bows and arrows, and so forth. Not to mention the midnight sun! No, he never went there, but Marco Polo did have good informants (Yule 1921).

The word "Anian" does appear on some of the earliest maps in the area that can be guessed as being northern China or eastern Siberia. Later it appears in the Strait. It would be centuries before the Dane Vitus Bering actually officially explored the strait for the Russians (trips in 1728 and 1741). He proved that the earlier cartographers were correct in their "invention" of the Strait of Anian, and got his name on this "discovery." However, there are also positive data which prove that Russian explorers had gotten there first, before 1700 (Fisher 1977; and see chapter 1 in this volume). I would suggest that the reason for such governmental security about this region involved the simple fact that the region was a gold mine of fabulous furs, one of the most highly regarded items in royal regalia for centuries.

Thus, as we shall see, it was clear that by 1580, Spanish navigators and some of the intelligentsia were quite secure in the notion that Asia and the New World were only separated in the north by a relatively narrow strait they called Anian. Hence at that time in the mid-sixteenth century and later it was not a piece of secret information. However, to make things easier for the readers, I will use the term for immigrations across this Arctic strait that is more familiar today—the "Bering Strait hypothesis"—although with some reluctance.

The Inhabitants of the New World: What to Call the Immigrants?

Now that we have the geography in hand, I will turn to the peopling of the New World. Although the origins of the American Indians have been ascribed to many different groups and many locations, I will simplify the terminology for this paper with some covering terms. Most of the Asian immigrants were usually called "Tartars" or "Tatars." These names referred to many tribal groups from northeast Asia, especially those adjacent to the Strait of Anian. Again we are indebted to Marco Polo for most of this usage. Although he did not get to this area himself, Polo wrote two short chapters in his report specifically on the "northern" Tartars (Yule 1921:Bk. 4, Chs. 20–21). These non-agricultural people subsisted on the milk and flesh of their cattle and had quantities of domestic animals (camels, horses, sheep, etc.). This is where the large white bears and wonderful fur-bearing animals lived. Some of their houses were underground or semisubterranean. Not a bad precis of this northern land.

According to Polo, one region in this quarter was called the "Land of Darkness." Although the commonly used French translation of Polo's works suggests that he meant "perpetual" darkness, Henry Yule (1921:485, n. 1), suggests that this is a misunderstanding, and that Polo knew that this was a seasonal event, not a year-round condition. Another early testament of the significance and broad spread of the information about the Tartars is to be found in a revised edition of Richard Eden's 1555 volume on Peter Martyr's *Decades* (Adams 1992). Therein Richard Willes's lead-off "epistle" is a paean of praise to the study of geography in which he casually throws in the following miscellaneous knowledge: "The wylde and rogishe Tartares might for famine perishe in the winter, if they in the sommer skyfully followed not the sonne" (Willes in Adams 1992:n.p.)

As demonstrated by this broad usage, these northernmost Tartars, as a whole, entered European knowledge through Polo's book and become the obvious candidates for migrants to the New World via the Strait of Anian. Their name, Tartars, would appear on many early maps as well in the region now referred to as Siberia from the sixteenth century on. So Tartars they shall be.

From the very first writings on *origins*, the other major population source for the New World was thought to be from the Old World, either from Europe or from Mediterranean-area cultures: Norse, Irish/Celts, Romans, Egyptians, the Lost Tribes of Israel, and so forth. They mostly shared the traits of civilization—writing, metal tools, and so forth, and necessarily ships and navigation. I will term these voyagers "Transatlanteans."[4]

There is one final small grouping of possible immigrants that I will term "Transpacificans." They purportedly came from eastern Asia, like the Tartars, but from further south in China proper, and made it to the New World by crossing the Pacific in boats. They were often thought to have landed even as far south as Peru.

Now, turning directly to answering the origins question, my presentation will follow the chronological order of the publication of pertinent documents. The reader will find mini-biographies of the involved scholars at the end of this chapter (in a section termed "Cast of Characters"), where it will be noted whether their contributions were based on firsthand accounts or literary sources.

The First Spanish Authors: A.D. 1500–1600

It all began with Columbus, of course. But because he apparently never really gave up the notion that he had discovered the East Indies, not a "new world," Columbus was not involved with this query. To him they were just "Indians" of the Indies, pure and simple. The first author to write extensively on the real aspect of the topic was Fernandez Oviedo, who published his findings between 1535 and 1550. Oviedo had lived in the Caribbean area and was knowledgeable about most of the significant writings of his period. The question of a possible land connection to the New World from Asia had already been raised by this time, but he would have none of it (Huddleston 1967:14–21). Instead, he favored a Transatlantean view, with the possibility of several quite different groups, including Carthaginians, coming to the New World across the Atlantic in the past. Not a very good start!

However, the next scholar to tackle the origins question was much different. He was José Acosta, a Spanish Jesuit scholar with a fine education and a breadth of firsthand knowledge. Like Oviedo, he spent time in the New World, some 18 years (1570–1589?); not only that, but he worked for 16 years in Peru with the Indians. He came over as a missionary and began to write a lengthy *History of the Indies* while still in Peru. He later stopped off for a year (1586) in the Valley of Mexico with another Jesuit, who also worked with Indians. The following year he returned to Spain and worked on completing his major work, *The Natural and Moral History of the Indies*. He published this broad and masterful work in 1590, and it was available in English by 1604, where it got some notice, as we shall see.

Acosta's version of the answer to the origins question is so up-to-date as to be a little scary. We know from recent works (Burgaleta 1999) that Acosta came from a well-to-do Spanish family and was a dedicated scholar, joining the Jesuits at age 12. His scholarship shows: Acosta strongly espoused the Bering Strait hypothesis a century and a half before the Strait of Anian was actually shown to exist. Not only that, but he clearly suggested that these early settlers of the New World came over as hunters and gatherers and only later achieved agriculture. Finally, they even achieved more advanced cultures; he had indeed seen impressive ruins in both Peru and Mexico. It was a truly significant intellectual achievement.

Certainly one aid to Acosta's adoption of this view stems from his own lengthy personal experiences in the New World. He had seen and lived with Peruvian Indians. He also published the first book in Peru: a catechism in the native language. In terms of a broader knowledge of the world, he had also made two Atlantic crossings, presumably with Spanish mariners. When he came back to Spain, he landed at Seville before making his way north to the Jesuit College at Salamanca, where he resided while he finished his book.

As to Acosta's geographic knowledge, we know that in Seville there was what was to become the Archives of the Indies, certainly a source of great value. Also, one must understand that as a Jesuit scholar he had easy access to much information. He certainly knew about his Jesuit colleagues who had been in the Far East (Burgaleta 1999:15). The Jesuit Francis Xavier was in Japan in 1551, and then in China when he died in 1552. Thus in 1580 members of the order certainly would have known that part of the world quite well. What maps were in their own libraries is not clear, nor do I know directly whether there was a copy of Marco Polo's *Travels* available to Acosta. However, it is not unlikely, because it had been available in printed form since 1477.

One can state that Acosta's scholarship and knowledge were very broad. In his volume on the New World, he deals carefully with both biblical and classical sources with regard to the occupants found there. He finds those sources wanting in providing data to answer the origins question. The fact that he had firsthand knowledge of native Americans in Peru and Mexico certainly cleared his vision from using any Transatlantean answers. Acosta felt he knew who had built the monuments in South America and Mexico. His work was a startling answer to our query. Sadly, despite its early availability to other scholars in both Latin and English, it did not have as strong an effect as one could wish (Huddleston 1967:48–55). However, a recent English study (Cormack 1997) indicates quite clearly that the Acosta volume (translated into English by E. Grimstone in London in 1604) was in many of the most important college libraries in Britain in the seventeenth century.

However, when we now turn to another Spanish scholar of the period, Gregorio Garcia, one finds a very different answer. Garcia was a Dominican friar who had also been in the New World. Just after the turn of the century, in 1607, he tackled the question of Indian origins in a large volume devoted, unlike Acosta's, to nothing but this subject. One would have to say that Garcia had a very open mind. He discussed virtually every possible hypothesis, but he did not apply any criteria to distinguish the far-fetched from those based on reasonable data. It was a hopeless, mainly Transatlantean, mishmash. Startlingly, Garcia does not even mention Acosta's work, as far as I can tell.

One of Garcia's most careful critics (he has had but few, unfortunately) was the American scholar Lee Huddleston, who wrote as follows after saying that Garcia's book had been "misunderstood": "This situation arises largely from the failure of his readers—especially modern ones—to grasp the fact that his purpose was not to prove any one opinion as against any other, but *to prove them all*" (1967:74, emphasis in original). Thus Garcia casually opens the floodgates forever to all who want to use the Bible and other ancient European histories to explain the origin of the Indians and their cultures in the New World (Williams 1991:189–285).

So, shortly after the beginning of the seventeenth century the lines were firmly drawn in Spanish scholarship: Acostan followers, who were essentially pro-Tartars and believers in the Strait hypothesis, versus Garcians, to whom Transatlantean voyagers, even Spanish, were seen as the source of the inhabitants of the New World. This controversy was not a minor intellectual debate; it involved dozens of scholars for much of the seventeenth century, with, unfortunately, more adherents on Garcia's side than Acosta's (Huddleston 1967:48–76).

The Debate in Northern Europe: A.D. 1600–1650

While Spanish scholars were wrangling over the origins topic, there would be a comparable set-to in northern Europe. Here scholars, while not ignorant of the Spanish works, found plenty to argue about among themselves. It is significant, I think, to see that this topic mattered to so many well-trained intellectuals at this time. For example, between 1580 and 1620 there were in England a number of scholars whose attention turned to the New World, a century after John Cabot's early voyages there. Although Cormack (1997) has classed them as geographers, their interest was both historical and promotional. Principal among them was Richard Hakluyt, a Welshman educated at Oxford. He spent time also in Paris and then proceeded to turn out a series of erudite volumes on New World explorations and discoveries (Hakluyt 1582, 1589). They would have an immense impact on European scholars and adventurers.

In the 1620s Hakluyt was followed by Samuel Purchas, who, on his own, published a posthumous volume collected by Hakluyt and others. These books helped focus English interest on colonization and were extraordinary in their breadth of scholarship. Yes, the Spanish works by Acosta and others were included among their sources. These Hakluyt volumes are still admired and used by twentieth-century scholars such as Morison (1971, 1974) and Huddleston (1967).

In the early part of the seventeenth century, another English scholar, little known to anthropologists today, Edward Brerewood, took up the Acostan tradition and wrote strongly toward Tartar sources for the settling of the New World. His work was primarily based on linguistic evidence, but he does cite Acosta directly. Brerewood was trained at Oxford with both B.A. (1587) and M.A. (1590) degrees. His interest in the past is exemplified by his membership in the Society of Antiquaries in London (Cormack 1997:197). He became a professor of Astronomy at the Gresham College in London, but he remained connected to his circle of friends in geography at Oxford.

Brerewood's 1614 book, *Enquiries Touching the Diversity of Languages and Religions, Through the Chief Parts of the World*, has not been directly available to me. However, Benjamin Smith Barton's 1798 volume provides a very long quotation therefrom, of which this is but a part:[5] "It is very likely that *America* received her first inhabitants, from the East border of Asia: So it is altogether unlike[ly] that it received them from any other part of all that Border, save from *Tartary*. . . . [A]fter the neer vicinity of *Asia* to *America*, this reason above all other, may best establish and perswade . . . for those parts of *Asia* and *America*, are continent one with the other, or at most, dis-joined but by some narrow Channel of the Ocean" (Brerewood 1674, quoted in Barton 1798:iv–v). Brerewood both supports the Strait connection and attacks many of the Garcian suggestions. His *Enquiries* was of great interest and was translated and republished for the next 60 years. Purchas knew this work by Brerewood and in his last volume supported his conclusions on origins (Huddleston 1967:114–117). Thus English scholars too joined in the origins argument, mercifully on the Acostan side.

In this very same period, another debate on Indian origins was raging in the Netherlands. Jan de Laet, a Flemish merchant, had by 1640 written histories and other intellectual treatises. He had published in 1625 a volume entitled *L'Histoire de Nouveau Monde ou description des Indies Occidentales*. De Laet was very familiar with Acosta's *Historia* as well. His debate opponent, Hugo Grotius, a fellow Dutchman, was internationally known for his legal writings and political stance—well enough known to be exiled by the Dutch government. This debate arose as a result of the fact that after 1600, the English, French, and Dutch had begun to go to the West Indies in greater numbers (Huddleston 1967:111).

Grotius was acting as Sweden's ambassador in Paris in 1640, and for reasons not clear to me, he set to writing a pamphlet on the subject of the "Origins of the American People" (*De Origine Gentium Americanarum*). He had a draft copy sent to de Laet, who responded with some suggested help on the topic. Grotius subsequently published his treatise in 1642; it suggested Transatlantean (especially northern European) origins of all of the Indians north of Panama. He made no mention of the work of either Acosta or de Laet on this subject, and overall his position was much like Garcia's.

Grotius was a widely known intellectual, and his opinion carried a lot of weight. De Laet and, soon, a younger colleague of his, Georg Horn, attacked Grotius's work strongly and with some bitterness. Their position, and that of some of their followers in the 1650s, was strongly

"From Whence Came Those Aboriginal Inhabitants of America?" / 39

that of Acosta, whom they quoted frequently. The value of this mid-century debate is to underline that American Indian origins were certainly then a topic worthy of strong intellectual discourse among well-educated antagonists (Huddleston 1967:118-128).

During roughly this same period (1607-1729), the old Acostan versus Garcian debate continued vigorously among Spanish scholars. Huddleston (1967:77-107) has carefully delineated the nuances of the disagreements. Although it is impossible to condense his careful scholarship, one can say that the Acostans certainly sought new data, which included further support of the Strait of Anian theory and even linguistic data (the number of different languages). On the Garcian side there was even stronger support by some that Transatlantean crossing were so easy and that even ancient Spaniards should be included with the Carthaginians, Romans, and Greeks as Precolumbian settlers. It seems that nothing had changed.

However, one cannot finish this century without another piece of positive evidence on the Acostan position from a rather strange source. Thomas Gage was perhaps an unlikely character for such a useful bit of insight, since he was the black-sheep son of a rather noted English family. However, he had a number of things going for him, including a 12-year stay (1625-1637) in Central America. Gage went to Mexico and Guatemala as a Dominican friar, and he saw these countries as well as many others on his way to and from England. We will see that he had intellectual ties to the Acostan position, although there is no evidence to indicate that he had actually read Acosta's volume.

J. Eric S. Thompson, an Englishman and Mayanist archaeologist, edited and wrote the Introduction to a twentieth-century republication of Gage's volume. As was sometimes the custom in that era, Thompson forthrightly tells us that he has "cleaned up" the text somewhat, especially removing slurs made by Gage against the Catholic Church. This action Thompson felt was necessary in that Gage had left the Church of Rome and turned into a Puritan Protestant *after* returning to England and before he wrote his important travel volume. No one reading his volume (Thompson 1958) can doubt that Gage was a good observer, and that he must have taken quite careful notes while in the New World. Gage's knowledge of geography, resources, and politics is both detailed and broad in scope. Here is his brief discussion of a part of northern Mexico:

> Quivira is seated on the western part of America, just over against Tartary, from whence being not much distant, some suppose that

the inhabitants first came into this New World. Indeed the Indians of America seem in many things to be of that race and progeny of the Tartars, in that Quivira and all the west side of the country towards Asia is far more populous than the east towards Europe, which showeth these parts to have been first inhabited. Secondly, their uncivility and barbarous properties tell us that they are most like the Tartars of any. Thirdly, the west side of America, if it be not continent with Tartary, is yet disjoined but by a small strait. Fourthly, the people of Quivira nearest to Tartary are said to follow seasons and pasturing of their cattle like the Tartars. All this side of America is full of herbage and enjoyeth a temperate air. (Thompson 1958:92)

The year before the publication of the Gage volume, Thompson wrote a brief note in *American Antiquity,* "The First Peopling of the New World," in which he cites the then-recent footnote by Ralph Beals in the same journal on José Acosta (Thompson 1957). Also in this note, Thompson suggests that Gage may have been the first one to suggest in English the "Bering Strait thesis." The latter is not the case, as I hope this chapter proves. I might add that in the Gage volume, Thompson mentions in a footnote (1958:92) that the Mexican archaeologist Pablo Martinez del Rio was the one who first told him of Acosta and his views on Asian connections. Thus some Latin American field-workers seem to have known about the Acosta position long before other North American archaeologists were.

Overall, this period (A.D. 1600–1800) was one of continued controversy over the basic origins question, with a rather balanced result: the Acostans and the Garcians were still tilting at the question with precious little new data. After Acosta and Garcia, only Gage had looked at the question with a fully New World perspective based on direct experience in the area. But there were interesting stirrings in another important region, the Strait of Anian itself, as described below, and in more detail in chapter 1.

The Eighteenth Century: A.D. 1700–1800

With the important expansion of European settlement of North America in the latter half of the seventeenth century, especially by the French and English, there would be in this next century many more travelers and even some residents who were documenting Indian culture, including their languages. Not that linguistics had not already played a part in many of the earlier discussions of origins, for better and for worse, but now better data directly from more tribes were being collected.

So too would better geographical information add to the cause of the Acostans and their literary descendants. The discovery of the Strait of Anian (aka Bering) would be made. Vitus Bering, a Dane, after a trip to the East Indies, would join the Russian Navy in 1728 and take off overland for Siberia. He would then sail from Okhotsk, past Kamchatka, and north to the Strait that now bears his name. He went north to 67° N, far above the Strait—quite an accomplishment. However, there is clear evidence that Bering was not the first to make this voyage.

In the previous century, in 1648, Russian ships under the command of Semyon Dezhnyov first explored the strait, but with little result. Many years later, in 1741, after many delays, Bering made a second trip to the Strait and this time sighted Alaska. He died as he was returning from that voyage. The Acostan and Anian believers had been right all along. There was only a modest strait between Asia and America.

Captain James Cook, the famed British navigator, while on his third and final Pacific voyage in 1778, would also scout out the whole northern Pacific rim from western Canada to the Kamchatka Peninsula. He also sailed north in the Bering Strait as far as the pack-ice barrier would allow. So now it was "really" known for certain that the two vast continents were nearly joined at the north, and maps would soon show these data. Indeed, so strong was the English interest in this area that even after Cook's death in Hawaii in 1779, his ship, under new command, made a return swing to the Kamchatka region before going back to England. Thus one can see that it was an area of great interest and concern for the British, too. Scholars in America, like Jefferson (1784), soon had this Bering Strait data as well.

Turning now to eighteenth-century scholars concerned with the questions of origins, we have yet another Jesuit in Pierre Charlevoix. He came to New France, first to teach there (1705–1709) and then to travel more extensively (1720–1722) through the colonies. Charlevoix produced a large two-volume work based on these travels, published in French in 1744 and in English in 1761, in which he wrote extensively on the question of Indian origins; the first chapter, some 40 pages long, was devoted to that topic. It remains one of the few documents that equals that of Acosta, his brother in the cloth, in scale and careful analysis (Mitra 1933:23–24).

Yes, Charlevoix had consulted almost every source I have so far mentioned, and many more that I have skipped over. His conclusions were simple and straightforward: he was in the Acostan camp with the Bering Strait hypothesis, and yes, Tartary was the source of the earliest New World settlers. He said presciently that the Eskimos came later. Charlevoix strongly believed in using linguistic analysis to determine how long the Indians had been in the New World. And going a bit out on a limb for a cleric, he also suggested that these settlers in this hemisphere might have arrived *before* the Noachian flood—a very long time ago. Quite a remarkable tour de force; quite worth copying, as we shall see.

Another of the period's writers on origins, also a Jesuit priest and scholar, was Ignaz Pfefferkorn. Less well known than Charlevoix, he was from Germany and, like Acosta, had been a resident in the New World. He served as a missionary in the state of Sonora, Mexico, from 1756 until he was subjected to expulsion in 1767, as were all Jesuits at that time. He returned to Europe and finally ended up back in his native Germany after some years of imprisonment in Spain with other Jesuits. There he completed his volume entitled *Description of the Province of Sonora* in 1794, shortly before his death.

Pfefferkorn strongly supports the Bering Strait hypothesis for the origin of the Indians, although he does not mention Acosta. He says that he had been strongly convinced of that idea and had prepared a treatise on that subject which he intended for his volume. While in the progress of completing the work, he learned of Captain Cook's third voyage and of his proof of the "Strait." Pfefferkorn then states that he would "not wish to delay my reader with my conjectures. To me it is almost certain that the first inhabitants of America really came across from Asia by way of this strait." Perhaps not wishing to sound too dogmatic, he adds: "It is possible, however, that people also came from Greenland or from a northwestern part of Europe" (Pfefferkorn 1794/1949:161).

One of the first Americans to join in this argument was John Bartram of Pennsylvania, best known as a pioneering botanist of some note. His son, William, would also study botany and the Indians. In 1751 the elder Bartram made an interesting trip north through New York and into Canada. Some "friends" in London then published his "raw" notes without his permission. The "editors'" preface has some demeaning comments about the author in this strange publication, which need not detain us now. However, in this preface (p. vii) there is also reference to the Grotius/de Laet debate, discussed above, indicating quite a broad audience for this origins question.

John Bartram observed members of the Iroquois Nation on this trip, but his comments are for the most part superficial. However, seeing these "original inhabitants" caused him to reflect on their origins at the end of his narrative. Bartram seems to be aware of Charlevoix's writings because he adds details, including a specific anecdote, that are to be found in the Frenchman's volume. The modest eight paragraphs on origins are a very mixed bag. On the one hand, he indicates the ease of crossing the Atlantic, either across the North Atlantic via Greenland or to South America by vessels of "Egyptians, Phoenicians, or Carthaginians." On the other hand, he also states, "Again it is not unlikely but there may be land most of the way from America to Japan, at least islands, separated only by narrow channels, and in sight, or nearly so, of one another" (Bartram 1751/1798:vii). Thus a wild mixture of the worst aspects of Transatlantean ties with some geographic data upholding the possibility of support for the Bering Strait hypothesis. Bartram seems unwilling to choose. His son, William, would make more important contributions to understanding the Indians of the southeastern United States.

At about the same time as Bartram's trip and narrative, a foreign traveler named Peter Kalm appeared on the New World horizon. A well-trained scholar from Sweden, Kalm was an economist with a strong interest in botany. He spent three years in North America (1748–1750), visiting the eastern parts mainly in New England, Canada, and the Great Lakes, but he also had time to go as far south as the Mid-Atlantic States. His concerns were broad in terms of both natural history and anthropology. He saw and studied everything from a Catholic nunnery in Quebec to Eskimos, and even managed to marry a widow in New Jersey. He investigated past and present farm practices, and even tried his hand at looking into the origin of American Indians, but with small success.

Kalm saw few Indians, since he stayed primarily in the more heavily European-occupied coastal areas, except for a trip to Niagara Falls. For example, he specifically says he asked the "French, who travel far into the country," about the food of the Indians. It was while in Quebec in the fall of 1749 that he considered briefly the question of Indian origins and any archaeological remains that might give evidence of earlier occupations. He was disappointed; he saw none of the ruins that dot Europe and made it so pleasant. "We can enjoy none of these pleasures in *America*" (Kalm 1771:419, his emphasis).

One must recall that Kalm was talking about the archaeology of the northeastern United States. Had he by chance visited the Ohio Valley, he might have seen some mound structures worthy of awe. It is by a quirk of fate, not intention, that the map accompanying John Reinhold Forster's London version of Kalm's *Travels* is a remarkable piece of cartography that does indeed show "antique sculptures" near what is now called Wheeling, West Virginia. About a century later, someone could have handed Kalm a copy of Squier and Davis's (1848) volume and put him on a steamboat to Pittsburgh for a trip that would have indeed dazzled even his jaded European eyes.

But one must admit that Peter Kalm did not give up easily on archaeology. He had scraped the barrel for any prehistoric bits. He saw these in some poorly reported "furrowed fields" now deserted on the edge of the Great Plains, some "great pillars of stone," and finally one pillar "covered with unknown characters." It was sent to France and now lost. However, some Jesuits in Canada saw the stone before it was sent over and declared the letters to be *Tartarian* characters. Kalm was quite convinced that none of this evidence pointed to American Indian craftsmanship (Kalm 1771:420-421). I feel sure Kalm was correct, but for the wrong reasons. In substance, Kalm makes a very small contribution to our "whence" concerns, but he tried.[6]

Another European visitor was Le Page du Pratz, who spent 16 years in lower Louisiana (1718-1734). He was a Dutchman who came to New Orleans as a very young man. Apparently du Pratz had an alliance with a young Indian girl during much of his stay both near New Orleans and later in the Natchez region. His major contributions to anthropology are his comments on the Natchez and their history. We do know that he met Charlevoix very briefly in 1722, though whether they discussed Indian origins is not known. Du Pratz seems to have had a rather catholic view of the topic, partly favoring Transatlantean ties to Phoenicians or Carthaginians, but then he also throws in possible connections to China or Japan. To complete the picture, he then turns to an Acostan view indicating "a great resemblance between them [Indians] and the Tartars in the north-eastern part of Asia" (Dethloff 1972:6-7; Mitra 1933:21-22). Du Pratz sounds a bit like some of our contemporary politicians, wanting to cover all sides of an argument.

We turn next to a contributor who came from across the English Channel to Ireland and who would spend a considerable amount of time among the southeastern Indians, especially the Choctaw. James Adair was a trader with the Indians working out of South Carolina for the English over a period of 40 years (1735-1775). He is thought by some to have been the first Englishman to have gone all the way west across Tennessee to the Mississippi River. We know little about his education, but his great work *A History of American Indians*, published in the year he died, certainly displays considerable learning in many directions. Adair made significant contributions to our understanding of the lifeways of many Southeastern tribes, and John Swanton, for example, made great use of his knowledge.

However, when one approaches Adair's view on the origin of the Indians, there are some difficulties. He would come to be thought of by many as one of the strongest supporters of the Lost Tribes of Israel hypothesis, a position thought to be held by many as early as the sixteenth century (but see Huddleston 1967:33–47). There is little question about Adair's commitment; his documentation runs for 206 pages, according to Mitra (1933:38). Yes, there are lots of connections between Jews and Indians according to Adair. But one must also recognize that in this period in the eighteenth century there were also many who felt that there were ethnic and linguistic ties that ran eastward all the way from the Mediterranean to the northern Pacific. That is, one could actually tie these Jewish people together via Scythians to the Tartars!

Why is that important? Because of the very rational way that Adair then completed his discussion:

> Ancient History is quite silent concerning America, which indicates that it has been since time immemorial rent asunder from the African continent, according to Plato's Timaeus. The northeast parts of Asia [Siberia] also were undiscovered until of late. ... But the Russians, after several dangerous attempts, have clearly convinced the world that they [Asia and America] are now divided and have a close communication by a narrow strait, in which several islands are situated; through which there is an easy passage from the north-east of Asia to the north-west of America, by way of Kamaschatka, which probably joined to the north-west point of America. By this passage, supposing the main continents were separated, it was very practical for the inhabitants to go to this extensive new world; and afterwards to have proceeded in quest of suitable climes, according to the law of nature, that directs every creature to such climes as are most convenient and agreeable. (Adair 1775:219, quoted in Mitra 1933:40–41)

With such a forthright presentation by Adair, it is unfortunate that most recent scholars of the history of Americanist archaeology (Hallowell 1960:5; Willey and Sabloff 1993:16; and others) have only spoken of his strong commitment to the "Lost Tribes" theory, not to his careful delineation of the Bering Strait hypothesis. Mitra, on the other hand, saw these data and also championed Adair's contributions to American ethnology. Adair cannot, therefore, be cast wholeheartedly into the Transatlantean camp for his Jewish-Scythian-Tartar connections; his Acostan position on the Strait negates that.

Finally, we turn to another contributor to this question of origins from North America. Of course, Thomas Jefferson was one of the most prominent figures in the origins discussion. He is well known for his early excavations, about 1770, into an Indian burial mound shortly after completing college at William and Mary. He did not write about his concerns on this topic until after the Revolution, in 1782. His *Notes on Virginia*, written in response to an inquiry by the French, is crucial to this discussion, but with some difficulties. Jefferson states his origins beliefs but does not let us know how he reached them. This mode is in marked contrast to Charlevoix, for example. However, it can perhaps be understood in terms of the nature of Jefferson's document, a series of responses to specific numbered queries.

Jefferson's position on origins is very Acostan: he believes strongly in the Bering Strait connection. Indeed, in his later letters he shows that he must have known something of the Russian data, and he cites directly Cook's 1778 voyage to the Strait region. To be forthright, one must also indicate that Jefferson also first mentions the possibility of transatlantic connections, but with no great emphasis. Other sources on this topic that were available to him include the book by Jonathan Carver, which was indeed in his library.

In terms of data, Jefferson was very well informed on linguistic materials. Based on the great diversity of Indian languages, he felt that the original occupants of the New World had been here for a very long time. He also correctly indicated that the Eskimo were of a different origin, as did many other early scholars. He continued his interest in the topic, as is noted in later work. We know that Jefferson met John Ledyard in Paris and hoped that Ledyard might obtain new linguistic and ethnographic data on his planned trip to Siberia, which unfortunately ended at Yakutsk. Jefferson was also later bolstered in his view of the antiquity of the Indians by data from pioneering work in tree-ring counting that was done in the 1790s in Ohio.

But Jefferson was not the only early American president to have an interest in the topic of "Whence came the aborigines?" George Washington, rarely spoken of intellectually in the same breath as his younger friend Jefferson, did receive a copy of *Notes on Virginia* directly from Paris, where some editions of the work were published. In 1788 Washington had also received a gift copy of a volume on the language of a

Connecticut Indian tribe from its author, Jonathan Edwards, son of the Yale University president.

In his letter of thanks, Washington wrote:

> I have long regretted that so many Tribes of the American Aborigines should have become almost or entirely extinct, without leaving such vestiges, as that the genius and idiom of their language might be traced. Perhaps from such sources, the descent or the kindred of nations, whose origins are lost in remote antiquity or illiterate darkness, might be more rationally investigated, than in any other mode. The task that you have imposed upon yourself, of preserving some materials for this purpose, is certainly to be commended. (Cushing 1997:53)

One might suggest that these words follow in thought and conclusion much of what Jefferson (1784) had written in his response to Query XI (Aborigines: A description of the Indians established in that state). But that is not said to suggest plagiarism, merely that Washington held similar views. As I have indicated elsewhere (Williams 1991:213-214), Washington too had a long-term interest in Indian history and had observed ancient Indian pictographs while in the "west" during the French and Indian Wars.

We next turn to a rather different sort of character in many ways, Jonathan Carver. But as we will see, Carver is almost as complex and difficult to understand fully as our last two subjects. Like only Bartram, Jefferson, and Washington, Carver was also born and raised in America. He grew up in Connecticut and received a good education there, which included surveying. He joined the Army at the beginning of the French and Indian Wars, enlisting in Massachusetts. Afterward, Carver went west in 1766-1767 on an exploring trip through the Great Lakes to the Mississippi Valley. He even went farther west up the Minnesota River valley and wintered over there, near the edge of the Great Plains. While on this adventurous trip he saw and studied many Indians. His long trek involved political and monetary problems, but they need not delay us here (Holmes 1930).

Upon Carver's return to the East, he sought to publish a volume on his travel narratives and his researches on the Indians. He was unsuccessful in this attempt in America, and in 1769 he then went to London to try to achieve his goal, leaving his wife and family behind. It was a very desperate time for Carver. Years passed as he unceasingly worked on his manuscript in great poverty. Finally, after nearly 10 years, some Fleet Street editors in London came to his aid. His book *Travels through the Interior Parts of North America* was published in 1778, not long before he died a pauper in 1780.

Why do we care? Because Carver's book would become, according to most sources, far and away the best-seller of the century for books of this sort. Everyone read it; it was also published in New York in 1779. As I have noted, Jefferson had a copy. Why is that important? Following an account of his trip and fairly detailed notes on the Indians he had encountered, Carver devoted a lengthy chapter to the topic of Indian origins. Space will not allow a full discussion of the question of authorship of that segment of this well-known but often castigated volume.[7] After careful study, I am sure that Carver did indeed plagiarize much of it from Charlevoix's writings. Carver's origins chapter covered authors from Acosta through the Dutch arguments to the French, with Charlevoix's data clearly mentioned.

Thus certainly via Carver's book, the Acostan view, within which Tartar origins and the Bering Strait hypothesis were upheld, was then widely disseminated to many contemporary scholars, including Jefferson. One must note that the naysayers were quite quick to attack Carver. Even though dead or dying at the time, he was considered fair game. Even in these attacks, though, there were problems. First of all, there was the out-and-out charge that Carver was a liar—that is, that he had not done and seen what he had reported on his trip to the West, but had simply made it up. Careful study shows that this was not true. A recent author, Timothy Severin (1967:197–98) has suggested that a London ghostwriter added to Carver's original text many fanciful notions about his travels and what he saw, a notion I cannot verify or contradict.[8]

On the other hand, I am on much firmer ground when it comes to the chapter on Indian origins. A careful analysis of the 40 pages therein suggests quite clearly that this is all Carver's own work in one sense. He has taken Charlevoix's discussion of the topic in hand and followed it page by page, even copying some of the phrasing. It is pure and simple plagiarism (or is it just copying?) from a very good source. He makes one major addition; he remarks on the more recent work of James Adair—not available to Charlevoix, of course. Herein he is quite careful to denote Adair's own remarks, to some of which he provides useful comments.

Finally, Carver returns to the first-person singular to set forth his own views on origins. He uses recently discovered data on the geogra-

"From Whence Came Those Aboriginal Inhabitants of America?" / 49

phy of the North from many sources to conclude that it was by the Strait of Anian that the first aborigines came: "There appearing to be a cluster of islands that reach as far as Siberia, it is probable from their proximity to America, that it received its first inhabitants from them. This conclusion is the most rational I am able to draw, supposing that since the Aborigines got footing on this continent, no extraordinary or sudden change in position or surface of it has taken place" (Carver 1778:210).

Carver's some additional nine pages on this specific topic indicate his use of a variety of sources, including Russian ones, and also the hope that further linguistic study would show the nature of the connections between the Siberian inhabitants and those of America. He, then a man in poor health and nearly 70 years of age, makes one further gesture of commitment to the cause of knowledge. As he is about to end his volume, he states:

> The limits of my present undertaking will not permit me to dwell any longer on this subject, or to enumerate any other proofs in favour of my hypothesis [Strait of Anian]. I am however so thoroughly convinced of the certainty of it, and so desirous have I been to obtain every testimony which can be procured in its support, that I once made an offer to a private society of gentlemen, who are curious in such researches, and to whom I had communicated my sentiments on this point, that I would undertake a journey, on receiving such supplies as were needed, through the north-east parts of Europe and Asia to the interior parts of America, from thence to England; making, as I proceeded, such observations both on the languages and manners of the people with whom I should be conversant, as might tend to illustrate the doctrine I have here laid down, and to satisfy the curiosity of the learned or inquisitive; but as this proposal was judged to require a national than a private support, it was not carried into execution. (Carver 1778:215–216)

One could characterize this as just the blather of a crazy old man, but let's not forget what he had done years before on his trek across almost half of America. Of course, he couldn't do it then in 1778, but was he a fool to dream of such a journey in support of a personal conviction? Almost an idée fixe, one would have to admit. Now one could only wish that there had been an audiotape system in Mr. Jefferson's

Paris office so that we could hear exactly what a young man from Connecticut (Carver's natal state) named John Ledyard would, not too much later, say to Jefferson on this very same topic.

Mr. Ledyard was a character larger than life too. This son of a well-known Connecticut family (yes, there is a coastal town near Groton by that name) went briefly to Dartmouth and then to sea, making several Atlantic crossings. He finally showed up in London and presented himself to Captain Cook, who was preparing for his third voyage. Ledyard was almost six feet tall and powerfully built. Cook hired him, and the ship sailed on July 12, 1776. It was an epic voyage that covered the Pacific and provided the English with great knowledge of western America from California to above the Arctic Circle. Cook's vessel went through the Bering Strait and returned to Hawaii, where Cook was killed. The ship, rather than heading immediately back to London, returned, now under Edward Clarke, to the Russian coast near Kamchatka. Why? It was the fur trade, of course. And young Mr. Ledyard smelled a fortune waiting to be made. He arrived back in London in 1780.

Now the story becomes complex. Ledyard is in London in 1780, just two years after the publication of Carver's volume and the year he died. Our interest is whether Ledyard ever read the lengthy quotation by Carver, cited above. The reason is that when Ledyard finally gets to Paris four years later, in 1784, and talks with Jefferson, he presents a very similar notion. He will cross Europe and Asia to the Pacific Coast, presumably near Kamchatka. On the way he will both look at the possibilities for the fur trade and also collect information on the "natives" for Mr. Jefferson. And yes, he was then willing to try to catch a boat ride to North America, preferably near where the Nootka resided. He would then make the modest hike across America to Virginia, or thereabouts. Where did Ledyard get this extraordinary notion? This itinerary matches Carver's almost exactly.

Well, no, indeed there is a Jefferson letter from Paris (Jefferson to Charles Thompson, September 20, 1787; Boyd 1955, 12:159–161) that confirms Ledyard's proposed trip, of which Jefferson wonders how the trip is going. In one of the wonderful quirks of research, I know more of the answer than one could hope. While investigating the larger question of Siberian explorations and the Strait of Anian, I came across an English translation of a late-eighteenth-century expedition to Siberia. Often called by European scholars the "Billings Expedition," instead of "Sarychev's Voyage to the Northeast of Siberia," surprisingly it provides important data and coincidences for our John Ledyard.

I detailed Ledyard's amazing journey in chapter 1, so I will merely repeat that, yes, Ledyard did cross the Eurasian continent, and almost got to Kamchatka. However, he was found to be an illegal traveler and was sent back to Europe in 1788. He died shortly thereafter in Cairo, Egypt, in early 1789. As far as I know, there are no surviving personal documents of Ledyard's trip through "Tartaria." Jefferson would have to look elsewhere for his linguistic data, despite two grandiose plans to elicit such information from the native peoples of Siberia.

Our final source on the origins question, just before the turn of the century, the temporal cut-off point of this inquiry, is another American, Benjamin Smith Barton. He was a fine scholar with a strong education and broad interests. Born in Lancaster, Pennsylvania, he was educated in Europe in natural science and medicine until 1789. He practiced medicine in Philadelphia and became a professor at what is now the University of Pennsylvania in 1791. Because of his ties to Europe, he became a conduit of American archaeological information to interested parties there.[9]

While still in Europe, in Edinburgh, Barton wrote in 1787 his first published paper: "Observations on Some Parts of Natural History; to Which Is Prefixed an Account of Several Vestiges of an Ancient Date, Which Have Been Discovered in the Western Country." He was but 21 years of age—and he knew it, for his text includes the statement that it was "the effort of a very young man." However, Barton had already had some experience in the field, unlike some famous authors on the topic of origins. Barton was orphaned at an early age with his mother's death when he was 8 and his father's when only 12. He grew up with family help, however.

His mother's brother was the well-to-do and well-known Philadelphia scientist David Rittenhouse, whose work in astronomy and mathematics had made him widely respected in intellectual circles. Rittenhouse was also an accomplished surveyor, and he took on governmental projects such as land survey in the West (i.e., west of the Appalachians) and elsewhere. Thus it was in May 1785, at the age of 19, that the young "Ben" Barton joined his uncle, David Rittenhouse, on a surveying trip to western Pennsylvania. They returned in October of that same year. Here, as his cousin William Paul Crillon Barton wrote many years later, "he first had an opportunity of mixing with the savage natives of this country—then he first turned his attention to their manners, their history, their medicines and pathology, and to other interesting points of inquiry, all of which he pursued with great zeal for the remainder of his life" (1816:276).

Barton spent those nearly six months in the field "west of the Appalachians" with Rittenhouse, but our direct knowledge of those events is limited to a few sentences in his short paper "Observations on Some Parts of Natural History, to Which Is Prefixed an Account of Several Remarkable Vestiges of an Ancient Date, Which Have Been Discovered in Different Parts of North America, Part I," published in London in 1787 and dedicated to his older brother, William. Barton wrote this paper while in Europe getting a medical degree. It attempts to answer the question, "Who made these monuments?"

Barton prefaced his work with "great diffidence," and well he might, as the contents range widely with only modest literature support. His primary sources are well known: Jonathan Carver, Peter Kalm, Thomas Jefferson, and most importantly, "Abbe" Clavigero. However, his major contribution is the description of several mound sites he apparently visited in the summer of 1785 on the Ohio River: the Grave Creek mound near Wheeling, West Virginia, and the mounds on the Muskingum (Marietta). There is also an early map, thanks to William Tilton of Philadelphia, of the very soon-to-be-well-known Marietta mound group, first published elsewhere in 1787–1788 (Willey and Sabloff 1993: 25–26).

That is all well and good—a positive contribution—but then 21-year-old Barton gets caught up in wild speculations as to the origins of the builders of these monuments. With the "help" of mainly Clavigero's data, but not his views, Barton suggests that these earthworks and others in the eastern United States were not erected by the Indians. He considers them too complex for their skills, and instead argues that they were the work of far-ranging Danes, who tramped from Labrador to the Valley of Mexico, where they became the ancestors of the Toltecs (Willey and Sabloff 1993:224).

What a youthful extravagance by Benjamin Smith Barton! Yet we do know via W. P. C. Barton's careful research that less than a year after this publication he wrote a letter (probably to his brother William) as follows: "I am already ashamed of many parts of it [the book]; and I am confident my language will make you smile." But this ink was spilled privately without a public retraction. However, Barton then did also say: "but then the facts [his firsthand view of the mounds] would have been all this time unknown" (Barton 1816:278).

There is little question that this early trip to the West was a very important event in Barton's life. He saw things and places that would change the direction of his interests forever. Not that he wouldn't continue toward natural science and medicine, which were his major interests, but he could never avoid data and concerns about the aborigines of America as long as he lived. Indeed, although the coverage of this chapter stops at 1800, Barton would continue writing on the topic to his dying day in 1815—an early death, at age 49, due to a nearly lifelong affliction of gout and arthritis that first appeared while he was a student in Edinburgh (Barton 1816:282).

Certainly Barton's major contribution on the origins topic was that entitled *New Views of the Origin of the Tribes and Nations of America*, published in 1798. This was based primarily on a study of Indian languages that Barton had begun soon after his return from his schooling in Europe. Barton was a member of the American Philosophical Society, whose purview was broad enough to engage his strong interest in both the natural sciences (especially botany, for which he was probably best known) and archaeology. However, if one surveys his long and extraordinary bibliography, there are many articles in medical subjects as well.

In 1789, upon his return from Europe with his medical diploma from Göttingen, Germany, following study in Edinburgh and London, Barton was given a professorship in Natural History and Botany at the College of Philadelphia, now the University of Pennsylvania, at the age of 24. Certainly this was a very young age for such an appointment. Through the American Philosophical Society, of course, he would meet and know Jefferson, another scholar interested in looking at Indian languages for their ability to provide information on the time and dispersions of the Indian tribes.

A careful reading of this 1798 volume will quickly show that Barton's linguistic analysis is very simple. He has some 80 pages of words he had collected from sources all over the world. There are 56 different words that include categories of everything from heaven and god to body parts, weather, and time, as well as elements such as earth, land, and water. Each entry begins with the word in Delaware (Lenni-Lenape), then goes through numerous other eastern and southeastern tribes, then to those in Mexico, and finally those in Siberia. And yes, it is all based on the similarity in sounds (phonetic look- or sound-alikes) because, of course, he himself had heard but a few of the words spoken. At least from my point of view, it is pretty much a waste of time given the quality of the data. And one must admit that Barton himself seems to understand some of the weaknesses of this approach.

However, in the first half of the book Barton does take on Jefferson forthrightly on some linguistic matters. He disagrees with Jefferson's notion (in Query XI) that more American Indian languages are "radical" than in Asia and elsewhere. By "radical" Jefferson means "root," or as it would be said now, there are more basic language families in America than in Asia. Barton feels that this is not the case. Indeed, he ends up putting a great many of the Indian languages in the eastern United States together in an *omnium gatherum* of "Delaware," for example. But it is hardly worth arguing further, as most of Barton's comparative linguistics is so flawed by problems of sources, spellings, comparability of meanings, etc., that there can be no reasonable discussion about these data. Nonetheless, the simple scale of his attempt, the great coverage of the literature, and his ability many times to view it critically make Barton's *New Views* deserving of our attention today.

Barton's last work of the eighteenth century is an extraordinary piece of work, both in the breadth of materials and notions considered and in his ability to look more broadly at the subject matter, linguistics, and what information a study thereof might provide. In his final note of this volume of more than 200 pages, he concludes with these thoughts of what his study of languages tells us:

> Knowledge is gradually revealed to us; and it becomes mankind to be grateful for the revelation. Time, which has scattered abroad the nations of the earth; which has crumbled into dust the proud monuments, destroyed the written histories, and the traditions of mankind, still preserves fragments of *languages*, those least perishable medals. It is worthy of science to collect these medals, and to preserve them, as much as possible, from the ravages of time. They teach us great and interesting truths: that there was a time when the ancestors of all the present races of mankind were centered in some narrow spots; and that they are all, if not brothers, most nearly related. (1798:80–81, emphasis added)

Barton's view of the history of humankind was rather more limited than ours today, and it is also true that his notion spoke in a very clearly biblical sense; however, a single center for the origin of all human language is not truly an absolutely crazy thought, is it? It was a long way from Philadelphia to East Africa even then.

Final Comments

Thus we have gone many centuries from Marco Polo to Benjamin Smith Barton, and across the world from Venice to Philadelphia. The individuals discussed herein never all met each other along these centuries, but most of them did know many of the others committed to this inquiry by the imperishable ideas wrapped in the covers of the volumes they wrote. No, they didn't all agree, but they did each other the courtesy of finding out, in most cases, what others had said on the topic. That is what intellectual discourse is all about, according to Mr. Jefferson in 1784: "Great question has arisen from whence came those aboriginal inhabitants of America?"

As a coda to this lengthy disquisition on origins from 1500 to 1800, we might close with a view from the middle of the nineteenth century, when in 1856 Samuel Haven wrote as follows, in what is really the first book on the history of American archaeology, that as to origins of the inhabitants of Americas, "The probability of permanent settlements from the Pacific side of the eastern hemisphere [Asia], near Behring Strait, has the support of more positive indications" (1856:156). He then goes on for more than 10 pages on why it was then so difficult to make that statement with greater certainty. The sum of all these many pages of my own on this topic gives strength to a position that must still be held today: we are quite correctly continuing to search for data, whether it be Kennewick man[10] or others, to now solve the question of origins that has at least a half a millennium of history behind it.[11]

Cast of Characters (or Biographical Repertory)

(I have labeled the following individuals "F.R." if they did field research on their topic, or "D.B.," for deskbound, if they did mainly literary research.)

Acosta, José de (1539–1600). Acosta was a Spanish Jesuit; his 1590 volume (English edition 1604) was the first significant treatise on origins. He espoused a Bering Strait hypothesis and a development of Indian culture through time. He spent nearly two decades (1570–1586) in Peru and Mexico. F.R.

Adair, James (ca. 1709–1775). An English trader with the Indians, Adair was born in Ireland. He traveled out of South Carolina (1735–1775) and covered the Southeast as far west as the Mississippi. His large volume (1775) is best known for his support of the Lost Tribes of Israel, but actually contains other, more important ideas on origins, including the Bering Strait and Choctaw ethnography. F.R.

Barton, Benjamin Smith (1766–1815). A Philadelphian, both a professor (University of Pennsylvania) and a medical doctor, Barton was a friend of Jefferson's and an American Philosophical Society member with a great breadth of interests. He was a very well read scholar, and his *New Views of the Origin of the Tribes* made extensive use of linguistics. D.B.

Bartram, John (1699-1777). An American botanist, Bartram was the father of William Bartram (1739-1823), who followed in his footsteps. He lived in Philadelphia, but in 1743 he made a trip to the western part of the state and New York and Canada. His 1751 *Observations* contains a short closing section on origins. F.R.

Bering, Vitus Jonassen (1681-1741). A Danish navigator, Bering joined the Russian Navy in 1704. Following Russian exploration of Siberia in the seventeenth century, he made his first voyage into the straits from Kamchatka in 1728, deciding that the continents were not connected. Not satisfied with that finding, he returned to the area in 1741 and sighted Alaska during that voyage, only to die on his return trip. F.R.

Brerewood, Edward (1565?-1613). Brerewood was an important early English scholar whose *Enquiries* of 1614 was very valuable (see note 5). D.B.

Cabot, John (Giovanni Cabato) (ca. 1450-1499). Probably born in Genoa, Italy, Cabot moved to Venice in 1461, and later to Bristol, England, in 1495 (Harrisse 1896/1968). In 1497, with support of the king, he sailed successfully across the North Atlantic in his ship *Matthew* to North America and planted the English flag. A contemporary letter (1498) by Englishman John Day to Christopher Columbus described the trip. In 1498, Cabot tried another such western voyage, but all were lost at sea. His son, Sebastian, continued in his father's occupation. F.R.

Carver, Jonathan (1710-1780). Born in Weymouth, Massachusetts, but educated in Connecticut, Carver joined the army and served in the French and Indian Wars. He made a trip to the West in 1766-1767, going as far as the Minnesota River valley, where he studied the Indians. He went to London in 1769 to try to publish his journal, dying there in 1780, just a year after his famous book was published. F.R.

Charlevoix, Pierre (François Xavier de) (1682-1761). A French Jesuit, Charlevoix came to Canada to teach, 1705-1709, and returned again in 1720-1722 when he traveled through New France from St. Lawrence to New Orleans. His masterful two-volume journal (French 1744; English 1769, 3 vols.) begins with a lengthy and scholarly review of origins. F.R.

Clavigero, Franciso Javier (1731-1787). The son of an Italian who was a royal agent, Clavigero was born and educated in Mexico. He entered the Jesuit order in 1748 and spent much of his time teaching in Indian schools. In June 1767 he and all other Jesuits were banished from the Spanish Empire. From 1773 until his death in 1787 he served as a priest in Bologna. While there he wrote both his 1780-1781 *History of Mexico* and a lesser-known 1789 *History of California*. F.R.

Cook, James (1728-1779). An English naval captain born in Yorkshire, Cook joined the Royal Navy in 1755 and by 1759-1767 was busy doing coastal surveying on the North Atlantic Coast of America with exemplary results. In 1768 he began the first of his three major voyages to the Pacific, which can only be described as extraordinary in their compass of space and newly found territories. The third and last voyage (1776-1779) interests us here because it was Cook who confirmed Bering's discovery of the Bering Strait in 1778. F.R.

de Laet, Joannes (1593-1649). De Laet started the argument on origins in Europe that flourished in the 1640s and 1650s. A man of considerable intellectual stature, he had been a director of the Dutch West India Company, hence his interest in the Americas. D.B.

du Pratz, Le Page (Antonine Simon) (1695-1775). Born in Holland, du Pratz lived in Louisiana from 1718 to 1734 as a settler, spending eight of those years with the Natchez. He even traveled very briefly with Charlevoix. His work *History of Louisiana* (French 1758, English 1763) devoted much of its contents to the Indians. F.R.

Gage, Thomas (1603?-1656). Gage was an Englishman whose clerical background saw a change from a Dominican friar to a freethinking Protestant. He was a careful and well-educated observer who, thanks to his years in the New World (primarily Mexico), was a strong voice on Indian origins. F.R.

Garcia, Gregorio (d. 1627). A Spanish Dominican, Garcia spent nine years in Peru in the late 1590s. His volume, solely centered on Indian origins, is an *omnium gatherum* of all the notions, careful or crazy, that he could put his hands on. The "Garcian tradition," as Huddleston has put it, is thus a fertile source for confirming any notion that had been set forth. F.R.

Grotius, Hugo (1585-1645). A prominent Dutch scholar with a law degree from Leyden, Grotius was later exiled to France for his political beliefs in 1621. He spent the next two decades in Paris, where he wrote many important works, including a 1643 attack on de Laet's 1625 article on Indian origins. D.B.

Hakluyt, Richard (1552-1616). A London-born scholar of Welsh descent, Hakluyt went to Oxford in 1570 and received an M.A. there in 1577. He joined the clergy, but his great interest was in world exploration. He first spent time in Paris and then returned to England, finally with a post in Bristol. His first book, in 1582, was *Divers Voyages Touching on the Discoverie of America,* followed by the 1589-1590 *Voyages and Discoveries: The Principal Navigations, Voyages, Traffiques and Discoveries of the English Nation.* He strongly supported English colonization of the New World. D.B.

Horn, Georg (1620-1670). A younger friend and supporter of de Laet, Horn joined in the Grotius/de Laet debate in the 1650s. His peers respected his scholarship and strong views. D.B.

Jefferson, Thomas (1743-1823). Jefferson was the best-known participant in the question about the origin of Indians. Although he is most often touted as America's first archaeologist, one cannot forget his lifelong interest in linguistics, too, for that field contributed importantly to his judgment as to the age of the Indians' occupation of the New World. He was a strong believer in both the Bering Strait hypothesis and ties to the near-Asian ancestors. D.B.

Kalm, Peter (1716-1779). A Swedish professor of economics with a strong interest in botany, Kalm made a trip to North America in 1748-1750, visiting much of eastern North America. Although most often reporting on botanically related subjects, he found time to report on the Indians also. His volumes were quite quickly translated into English by John Reinhold Forster in 1770-1771. F.R.

Ledyard, John (1751-1789). Born in Connecticut, Ledyard attended Dartmouth College briefly, then went to sea at age 22 and joined Captain Cook's third voyage in 1776. While on that voyage he noted the fur trade potential in the Bering Sea region. He saw Jefferson in Paris in 1784 and talked of going to Siberia and then possibly to North America. In 1787, without Russian permission, he traveled to Yakutsk. F.R.

Martyr, Peter (1457-1526), also known as Pietro Martire d'Anghiera, P. M. d'Aughier (Morison 1971), or Pedro Matir de Angleria (Huddleston 1967). He was a contemporary of the events of New World discovery and knew Columbus. Although he was born and educated in Italy, Martyr spent most of his life in Spain, closely involved with Queen Isabella. He published *De Orbe Novo;* the best English translation, by F. A. McNutt in 1912, has a lengthy and very informative introduction. D.B.

Oviedo, Fernandez de (1478-1557). Oviedo was the author of the first work (1535-1550) on the inhabitants of the New World, a book based on personal experience in the Caribbean area as well as knowledge of all the significant writings of the other commentators on America. He specifically rejected the land-bridge hypothesis and favored the "Trans-

"From Whence Came Those Aboriginal Inhabitants of America?" / 59

atlantean" view that would gain much favor in the centuries to follow. He made repeated use of Aristotle's views and the possibility of Carthaginian voyages. F.R.

Pfefferkorn, Ignaz (1725-1796). A well-educated Jesuit priest from Germany, Pfefferkorn, like Acosta, benefited intellectually from his stay in the New World. His eleven years in Mexico as a missionary in Sonora (1756-1767) were very informative. He was a well-documented member of the Strait of Anian group, who waffled slightly toward some European connections too. F.R.

Polo, Marco (ca. 1254-1324). Born in Venice, Marco was the son of Niccolò Polo, who, along with his brother Maffeo, first visited China in 1260, spending almost a decade there. In 1271 the two Polo brothers returned to China, this time with young Marco. They did not arrive in China proper until 1275. The Polos left China in 1292 and arrived back in Venice in 1295. In 1298, Marco Polo was captured during a sea battle between Venice and Genoa, and he spent nearly a year in a prison in Genoa, where he met Rusticano of Pisa, who took down the lengthy narrative of Polo's years in Cathay. F.R.

Purchas, Samuel (1576-1626). An English compiler of works on travel and discovery, Purchas was educated at both Cambridge and Oxford. He brought together a number of works of some value, but he is best known for his publication of *Purchas his Pilgrimes*; the final amended five-volume version appeared in 1625. D.B.

Washington, George (1732-1799). Born in Virginia, Washington was home taught, and it was there where he learned surveying and became quite well-read. His military experiences in the French and Indian Wars took him to the West and brought him to where he observed Indians firsthand but not always in battle. While never the scholar that Jefferson was, he had a recognized interest in Indians (Williams 1991:213-214). D.B.

3

Roots of the Walam Olum

Constantine Samuel Rafinesque and the Intellectual Heritage of the Early Nineteenth Century

David M. Oestreicher

> Cuvier ... took bones of extinct animals and restored them out of many or even a few! *I take scattered words of extinct Nations and Languages, and out of a few or any number, I restore them to our historical knowledge.* Therefore I imitate or rather emulate Cuvier; he has been greatly praised! shall I be?
> —Rafinesque (1840:69)

Introduction

In December 1834, a hastily written letter was sent from Philadelphia to a distinguished committee of scholars in Paris. Penned by the well-known naturalist Constantine Samuel Rafinesque (1783–1840), the letter announced the discovery of an ancient North American epic that would ultimately excite, confound, and captivate the anthropological world. "There is in Philadelphia," Rafinesque wrote, "among several fragments of Neobagun[1] and Wampum figures ... a manuscript on tablets of cedar wood (the sacred tree of the Linnique peoples).[2] ... The whole of it ... offers new philological and also graphic materials. ... The name of the manuscript merits attention, it is WALLAM OLUM" (Rafinesque 1834b:266).[3]

The Wallam Olum, Rafinesque explained (hereafter spelled Walam Olum),[4] was a series of wooden tablets inscribed and painted with the "hieroglyphics" of the Lenape or Delaware Indians.[5] Although he stated that the symbols were at first inexplicable to him, Rafinesque also claimed to possess a series of epic songs that had been transcribed from the Lenape tongue which accompanied the glyphs. Each verse in the epic corresponded to a pictograph on the tablets. Rafinesque claimed that after a decade of diligent work, and with the help of Lenape dictionaries compiled by Moravian missionaries, he had at last succeeded in translating the songs and unlocking the mystery of the tablets.

His efforts seemed to reveal an astonishing saga. Reaching deep into antiquity, the Walam Olum related a creation myth, a deluge story, and the sweeping migration of ancient Lenape people out of Asia into North America. It told of their journey across America, their conquest of the Mound Builders' civilization, their fracturing into the various Algonquian-speaking peoples who spanned the North American continent, and the ultimate settlement of the main body of the tribe along the Atlantic coast.

Rafinesque hoped the Walam Olum would furnish important evidence about the peopling of America to the scholarly committee and win him the International Volney Essay Contest, over which the committee presided. A prize of 1,200 francs was to be awarded the author of the most informative paper on the languages of the "Leni-Lennape, Mohegan et Chippaway" (Boewe 1988:14; Rafinesque 1834a).

Although Rafinesque failed to win the prize, he refused to give up on the Walam Olum. In 1836 he published a translation of the epic in his book *The American Nations*, unleashing a controversy that would perplex some of the most renowned scholars over the ensuing century and a half. Ephraim G. Squier (1849a) and Daniel G. Brinton (1885), both pivotal figures during the formative years of anthropology, published their own translations and commentaries of the epic. Cyrus Thomas, who conducted the Smithsonian Institution's classic study of the Mound Builders, regarded the Walam Olum as a critical piece of evidence in his determination of the identity and fate of the Ohio Valley Mound Builders (Thomas 1889, 1890, 1891). Horatio Hale, Mark R. Harrington, James Mooney, Frank G. Speck, Clinton A. Weslager, and other noteworthy scholars endorsed the document's validity in their writings. Although an increasing number of scholars would question the Walam Olum's historical reliability and antiquity (the development of radiocarbon dating in the mid–twentieth century, for example, contradicted the time frame of ancient history presented in the epic), most continued to accept the Walam Olum as genuine Lenape folklore.

Among the most ambitious efforts to determine the credibility of the Walam Olum was an interdisciplinary 20-year study funded and directed by pharmaceutical tycoon Eli Lilly under the auspices of the Indiana Historical Society. Lilly employed a team of more than a dozen scholars to authenticate the document on linguistic, ethnographic, historical, and archaeological grounds. In 1954 the Lilly team published *Walam Olum, or Red Score—The Migration Legend of the Lenni Lenape or Delaware Indians*, a lavishly bound and gilded volume with a new translation by the linguist, Charles F. Voegelin, and commentary by Erminie Voegelin, Glenn Black, Paul Weer, Lilly, and others. However, this work, like its predecessors, proved inconclusive.

Other scholars had noted contradictions and were skeptical of the Walam Olum or believed it to be a hoax,[6] but no conclusive evidence was advanced proving it a fraud. Some cited the dubious circumstances under which the epic was purportedly obtained[7] or pointed to the inexplicable disappearance of the original tablets. Indeed, scholars have had to rely solely upon Rafinesque's notebook "copies" to study the pictographs and Lenape text. No eyewitness to the actual Walam Olum has ever come forward to verify Rafinesque's story.

Other investigators—even some who believed that the Walam Olum was authentic—noted that Rafinesque was a controversial and perhaps unscrupulous figure. Born in Constantinople in 1783 and reared in Italy and France, Rafinesque settled permanently in the United States in 1815. He was a man as colorful as any of Mark Twain's fictional frontier characters, and his interests were as varied as are opinions concerning his credibility. He delved into botany, zoology, ethnology, philology, archaeology, and history, among numerous other pursuits. In his ideas concerning the origin of species, he has sometimes been credited with anticipating Darwin and modern evolutionary theory, but such credit is out of context and inappropriate (Brinton 1885:150; Fitzpatrick 1982:53).[8] He also attributed Latin names to thousands of plant species and genera, several hundred of which are accepted today (Charles E. Boewe, personal communication 1994). From 1819 to 1826 he was a professor of historical and natural sciences at Transylvania University in Lexington, Kentucky, and thereafter he made a living in Philadelphia, mainly through buying and selling books, lecturing, and publishing his own works.

Yet Rafinesque's penchant for wild exaggeration, his outrageous and self-aggrandizing declarations, and his sloppy and undisciplined methods led his contemporary Henry Rowe Schoolcraft to declare that he "spoiled historically and scientifically, everything he touched" (1849/1972:470). A shameless self-promoter, Rafinesque on one occasion offered a critique of his own poetry, which was written under the guise of a pseudonym, Constantine Jobson, extolling it in a glowing review as bearing "the stamp of genius . . . such as is but seldom expected on this side of the Atlantic . . . superior to Pope and [Erasmus] Darwin in moral tendency, variety of subjects and sublimity ... in some respects ... superior" to Milton (Rafinesque 1836b/1956:5-6)!

In addition to his poetical prowess, Rafinesque claimed to have concocted a "cure" for tuberculosis, which he marketed in his book *The Pulmist, or Introduction to the Art of Curing and Preventing the Consumption, or Chronic Phthisis* (1829). He arrived at an investment program "never to be liable to losses," which he promoted in another book, *Safe Banking* (1837:59); attempted to sell plans that would "prevent any boat from ever sinking" (1832-1833:202); and offered to sell the public an unpatented "secret discovery"—"incombustible varnish and paint" that would "save the lives of 100,000 persons doomed to be burnt alive" (1832-1833:183-186, 202).

Rafinesque also claimed to have "undertaken to learn the Latin and Greek, as well as the Hebrew, Sanscrit, Chinese and fifty other languages" before his seventeenth year (Rafinesque 1836c:9). His linguistic writings, however, are so riddled with errors and misconceptions that they are worthless, as much of his information is based upon the mere comparison of word lists, with little or no understanding of the respective grammars. Rafinesque "is doubtless a man of immense knowledge—as badly digested as may be & crack-brained I am sure," wrote one of his contemporaries, the naturalist Lewis David von Schweinitz (in Stuckey 1986:31).

Though Rafinesque has frequently been hailed as a neglected genius and a pioneer far ahead of his time in numerous fields (a view encouraged by Rafinesque himself), many of those who knew him personally shared the opinion of his contemporary Charles W. Short, that Rafinesque was "an unprincipled charlatan." Short (in Stuckey 1986:37) observed: "Now every body knows that poor Raffy was a most bare-faced liar, not to say a rogue; and the only possible way of apologizing for his gross frauds and deceptions is by Mr. Durand's charitable supposition that he was deranged."

In 1994, textual evidence was advanced demonstrating that the Walam Olum is indeed a hoax and that Rafinesque, its alleged discoverer, was in fact its author (Oestreicher 1994). Rafinesque had fabricated the "original" Delaware Indian verses of the epic out of the very sources he claimed to have used as translation aids; the pictographs were also all derived from various published sources (Oestreicher 1994: 3-12, 16-21, 1995a:10-72, 101-231). Additional evidence demonstrated that the document was created in the hopes of securing the prestigious Volney Prize and attaining for Rafinesque a lasting and long-coveted place in history (Oestreicher 1994:12-15, 1995a:73-88).[9]

It is ironic that a text promoted as the most ancient of American epics is neither ancient nor American. In the theories that inspired it and even in much of its content, it might accurately be described as a European import. It is the work of a European émigré; it was crafted in part to fool a committee of European savants; it was modeled largely after a noted European forgery; it attempted to resolve the major scientific dilemmas of the age which European and Euro-American scholars were grappling with; it incorporated the latest theories and research—and even plagiarized specific examples—of European scholars; and it attempted to preserve intact the traditional Western worldview in the light of an increasing flood of contradictory scientific evidence. In a final, ironic twist, the Amerindian people whom the epic purportedly describes are often portrayed in an unflattering and decidedly Eurocentric light.[10] This chapter shall explore the influence of Europe upon Rafinesque's great American hoax.

Rafinesque and His Era

To better understand the Walam Olum in context, it may be helpful to consider the age in which it arose and some of the questions it hoped to resolve. The early decades of the nineteenth century were a period ripe with scientific discovery. After years of mystery, lost scripts such as Old Persian cuneiform and Egyptian hieroglyphics were being deciphered; ancient civilizations, beginning with Herculaneum and Pompeii, were being unearthed; and exotic peoples across the globe, from the Chinese to the American Indians, were captivating the imagination of the Western world. On both sides of the Atlantic, scholars turned to the infant sciences of comparative ethnology and philology to corroborate the biblical account of human origins.

In America, much of the debate centered around the origin of the American Indians, a people not accounted for in the Bible, and upon the genesis of the fantastic earthen mounds that greeted Euro-American settlers exploring the Midwest. Deep-rooted beliefs regarding human origins were increasingly questioned: Was there one creation of humanity, as depicted in Genesis, or were there separate creations on different continents? If there was a single creation, on which continent did it occur? Did Noah's flood reach the New World, and did American Indians arrive before or after it? If they were truly descendants of Noah, and had therefore arrived after the flood, how did they reach a continent entirely surrounded by oceans? Equally intriguing, was there once a primordial universal language antedating the biblical Tower of Babel, and could traces of that first tongue be found in American Indian languages? Similarly, was there a single primordial writing system linking Amerindians and Old World peoples that could also reveal the secret of human origins?

As for the mysterious earthen ruins scattered throughout the Ohio and Mississippi Valleys, most scholars and laymen concluded that a primitive people could not have erected such structures—some in the shape of animals, and the largest (the Great Serpent Mound in Ohio) extending nearly a quarter mile in length—and there was continual debate over the nature and fate of the supposed lost civilization that had built them. Numerous theories were advanced to identify the Mound Builders; some claiming they were Vikings, others ancient Hindus, still others, Israelites.

In attempting to address these questions, most American antiquarians tended to look to the works of prominent European scholars for guidance, shaping their conclusions in accordance with the Old World establishment. Because most scholars of the period regarded the biblical account of human origins as the most ancient and authentic account, they generally attempted to harmonize whatever new scientific and ethnographic information was uncovered with the scenario presented in Scripture (a task that would prove increasingly daunting in the decades preceding Darwin's *Origin of Species*). Let us review some examples of how the Walam Olum bears the unmistakable influence of European scholarship and the vexing issues of the day.

Biblical Origin Influences

As noted, the connection of Amerindians to the rest of the human race was among the most puzzling questions of the era. Apparently, a primitive people had lived for untold centuries on a continent completely surrounded by oceans. Was there a means of determining whether they had arrived from the Old World, and consequently, whether the account of a single origin in Genesis was correct? Many scholars felt that there was. They reasoned that because there had been a single origin of humanity, it was probable that peoples across the globe might retain dim cultural memories of the most ancient events. Discerning similar mythologies among disparate peoples could go a long way toward confirming the veracity of the Western worldview. To be sure, different nations might recognize the biblical figures by different names. Nevertheless, it was widely believed that the most ancient history of mankind—the era from Creation until the dispersion of nations following the flood—was a universal one.

The importance of resolving this issue was underscored in a pioneer essay comparing the mythologies of Greece, Italy, and India by the eminent British philologist Sir William Jones: "Either the first eleven chapters of Genesis, all due allowances being made for a figurative Eastern style, are true," Jones maintained, "or the whole fabrick of our national religion is false; a conclusion, which none of us, I trust, would wish to be drawn" (Franklin 1995:350; Jones 1788a/1979a:191).[11] Jones argued further that mythological parallels were found not only in the "strange religions" of the old Greeks, Italians, and Hindus, but in "that of *Egypt, China, Persia, Phrygia, Phoenice, Syria* . . . and even islands, of *America*" (Jones 1788a/1979a:188).

American scholars were quick to seize upon such arguments. As the ethnologist Sir Edwin James wrote:

> That these people [the American Indians] have customs and opinions closely resembling those of the Asiatics, particularly of the Hebrews, previous to the christian dispensation, will not be denied; but the final result of all inquiries into this subject will, perhaps, be the adoption of the opinion of *Bryant*, of *Sir William Jones*, and other men of profound research, that Egyptians, Greeks, and Italians, Persians, Ethiopians, Phenecians, Celts and Tuscans, proceeded, originally, from one central place, and that the same people carried their religion and sciences into China and Japan, to Mexico and Peru, and, we may add, to the banks of the Mississippi, and the coasts of Hudson's Bay. (James, in Tanner 1830: 352–353)

Equally intriguing was the widely accepted notion that American Indian languages, like all languages, descended from an original "primitive language of mankind"—a language spoken before the destruction of the Tower of Babel.[12] The well-known British scholar Jacob Bryant, for example, attempted to link scores of place-names and mythological characters with their alleged biblical counterparts by comparing similar-sounding syllables in their names. In his influential work *A New System, or An Analysis of Ancient Mythology* (1774–1776), Bryant wrote:

> There are in every climate some shattered fragments of original history; some traces of a primitive and universal language. And these may be observed in the names of Deities, terms of worship, and titles of honour, which prevail among nations widely separated: who for ages have had no connexion. The like may be found in the names of pagodas and temples; and of sundry other objects,

which will present themselves to the traveller. Even America would contribute to this purpose. The more rude the monuments, the more ancient they may possibly prove; and afford a greater light upon inquiry. (1774-1776, 3:600-601)

Rafinesque was so taken by this passage in Bryant that he included much of it in his preface to *The American Nations*, with the sentence concerning American affinities to Old World languages in italics.

The French scholar Antoine Court de Gébelin went even further than Bryant. In his unfinished nine-volume work, *Monde Primitif* (1787-1788), Court de Gébelin actually attempted to reconstruct the "primitive language of mankind" by identifying what he believed were the "universal roots"—similar-sounding syllables with purported universal meanings—in words from various languages around the world, including American Indian languages. Court de Gébelin's work became enormously popular in its time and was considered by many to contain the key to resolving the riddle of human origins.

Of such endeavors, the renowned philologist Peter Stephen du Ponceau—president of the American Philosophical Society and himself of European background—would caution: "It is astonishing to see what efforts have been made by men of superior as well as those of inferior talents, to discover the origin of human speech, to trace an original or primitive language in those which now exist, to invent a universal or philosophical, idiom, a universal grammar, a universal alphabet, and so many other *universals*, while the *particulars* are yet to be learned" (1827:13).

Unswayed by Du Ponceau's argument, Rafinesque was convinced of his ability to reconstruct the so-called original primitive tongue, original religion, and ancient universal history. Indeed, not only did he attempt to do so in the Walam Olum, but he grafted into the text the very etymologies, myths, and historical examples discussed by his predecessors. In this supposedly Native American epic, strange words and myths with little or no connection to Delaware language and culture often appear. When examined, such anomalies may usually be traced to Rafinesque's European and Euro-American sources. The following are several of numerous examples.

Biblical Creation in the Delaware Walam Olum

The first song of the Walam Olum places in the mouths of the Indians themselves a historical scenario that harmonizes the biblical creation account with other newly discovered creation mythologies from around the world. Ironically, it scarcely draws from any Amerindian mythology—Delaware or otherwise. Some verses are derived from Genesis, others from partial translations and summaries of ancient Chinese classics, especially as elucidated in a chapter by Le Roux des Hautes-Rayes entitled "Extracts from the Chinese Historians," which was included in Goguet and Fugere's *The Origin of Laws, Arts, and Sciences, and Their Progress among the Most Ancient Nations* (1761, 3:300–325).[13]

Why the preponderant reliance upon Old World sources to craft an American Indian epic? To be sure, Rafinesque had only a minimal amount of mythological material on the Delaware and other Algonquian tribes at his disposal, but this seems to be the least of his reasons. Rather, overwhelming evidence suggests that he wished his epic to be an accurate reconstruction of actual events in remotest antiquity. Because he staunchly believed that all nations arose from a single primordial culture in central Asia (a thesis sparked especially by Jones's research),[14] he was certain that the most ancient stories, like the language and pictographs, would have been known to all. By this logic, the mythology of virtually any culture could provide accurate material for a Native American epic. Inevitably, Rafinesque turned to the two cultures commonly thought to have preserved the oldest and most reliable records of antiquity—the Hebrew and Chinese accounts. In language and examples blatantly plagiarized from one of his idols, the French paleontologist Georges Cuvier,[15] Rafinesque would write:

> It is in vain that we seek complete light on the fact and early deeds of mankind, in the obscure American traditions. They [Amerindian traditions] can only offer corroborating proofs or concurrent details [of the history recorded in more accurate sources]. We must therefore search for these deeds of the American ancestors, among the nations which have preserved the earliest records.
>
> ... [T]wo of the oldest, and best accounts of ancient history, deserve peculiar attention: as they appear founded on truth, and less involved in fables, or hidden style than any other. They are the Mosaic [biblical] account and the Chinese account. (Rafinesque 1836a, 2:66–67)

Not only did both traditions preserve written records "in books dating from 3 to 4,000 years past," Rafinesque noted, but both accounts described human origins in central Asia. Albeit located at opposite ends of the Asian continent, the traditions of both cultures "appear to meet in the early period [of history] at the centre of Asia, and offer the same events, nations, tribes and deeds of this central cradle of mankind, *and of the Americans also, whose traditions often point to that cradle"* (1836a, 2:67-68; emphasis added).

Thus, the odd synthesis of Chinese and Hebrew mythologies that shapes the beginning of the Walam Olum should not surprise us; it is a reflection of Rafinesque's view of an ancient universal history as elucidated by his predecessors and contemporaries. As Rafinesque, feigning both scientific discovery and surprise, informs us in an endnote to the Walam Olum: "This account of the creation is strikingly similar to the mosaic and oriental accounts" (1836a, 1:151).

Indeed it is. The Walam Olum describes a single, transcendent "God-creator"—"the first being, an eternal being, and invisible although everywhere"—who rules alone at the dawn of time and fashions the universe. The creator is depicted in a fog above the primordial waters that cover the earth. A sudden brightness appears before he removes the water to create "islands" (i.e., continents) (Rafinesque 1836a, 1:125-126 [hereafter WO], 1:1-3, 7-8). These events—and the very chronology in which they occur—conform precisely with Hebraic tradition, in which God, the author of the universe, hovers over the face of the primordial deep that covers the land, creates light, and then separates the waters, causing dry land to appear (Genesis 1:1-10). Even the wording in the Walam Olum replicates the early verses of Genesis.

Of course, Rafinesque also had on hand an extract of the Hindi *Ordinances of Menu*, which appeared in the *Asiatic Researches* (Asiatic Researches 1979-1980, 5:iii-xi). The extract compared the ancient creation account in the *Ordinances* alongside its biblical counterpart in parallel columns. Rafinesque did not have to look far to locate important details to further incorporate into his epic. If the *Ordinances* describe God as "the first cause," as lacking "visible parts," as "existing everywhere" from "eternity," and as "moving over the waters" at the beginning of creation, the Walam Olum likewise depicts God as "the first being, an eternal being, and invisible although everywhere" who exists in the fog over the water (WO I:1-3). If the *Ordinances* relate that God is the "soul of all beings" who "framed every creature" and "gave being to time . . . to the stars also," the Walam Olum similarly states that God made "first beings also, Angels also, Souls also" (WO 1:10). (As we shall see, Rafinesque's symbols for "beings," "angels," and "souls" are variants of the ancient Chinese symbol for "star," making this Walam Olum passage nearly identical to the Hindi text.) It is important to underscore that the biblical/Hindi concordances that later appeared in the Walam Olum were first explicitly spelled out in the *Asiatic Researches,* a work Rafinesque considered paramount in gaining his knowledge of history.

The account of God's fashioning the universe was only the beginning of the Walam Olum's biblical borrowings. Exactly as in the story of Adam and Eve, the god depicted in the Walam Olum created the first man, then "gave" the first woman to the first man and placed at man's disposal all other creatures (WO 1:12–13). In addition, Genesis relates that mankind's first food comprised "the fruit of the trees of the garden" and that Paradise was lost due to the influence of an evil serpent. This too is paralleled in the Walam Olum, wherein the "first food" of humanity was "fruit," (WO 1:19) and where a time of universal concord and happiness (i.e., Eden) existed until an evil serpent, a "snake god," brought "wickedness, crime, and unhappiness" into the world (WO 1:14–15, 21–23) (See Figure 3.1).

The Creation of Jin-wis, the Adam of the Lenape

As noted, some biblical borrowings were synchronized with Chinese language and lore, and further fashioned to accord with Amerindian vocabulary. The fantastic construction of Jin-wis, whom the Walam Olum describes as the first human ancestor, is such an example.

The Delaware text of WO I:11 reads: *"Wtenk-manito Jinwis lennowak-mukom"* (Indian Historical society 1954:19). In his English translation, Rafinesque informs us that the verse means "And afterwards he [God] made the man-being JIN-WIS, ancestor of the men" (Rafinesque 1836a 1:126). Although virtually every part of this sentence is riddled with preposterous errors in the Delaware language (as is the whole of the Walam Olum), one word—Jin-wis—is entirely anomalous. No such word exists in Delaware, and investigators were at a loss as to whether the term was derived from an extinct Delaware dialect, was of foreign origin, or was merely a poorly transcribed but well-known Delaware word. Because we now know that Rafinesque was the author of the Walam Olum, and not its "translator," his professorial "analysis" of Jin-wis in *The American Nations* (together with an examination of his source materials) enables us to understand this pseudo-construction and its raison d'être.

In fashioning the Walam Olum, Rafinesque needed a Lenape name for biblical Adam, the first man. Because Court de Gébelin had asserted that all languages, including Hebrew, were descended from the original "primitive" tongue, and that all languages still bore traces of that first

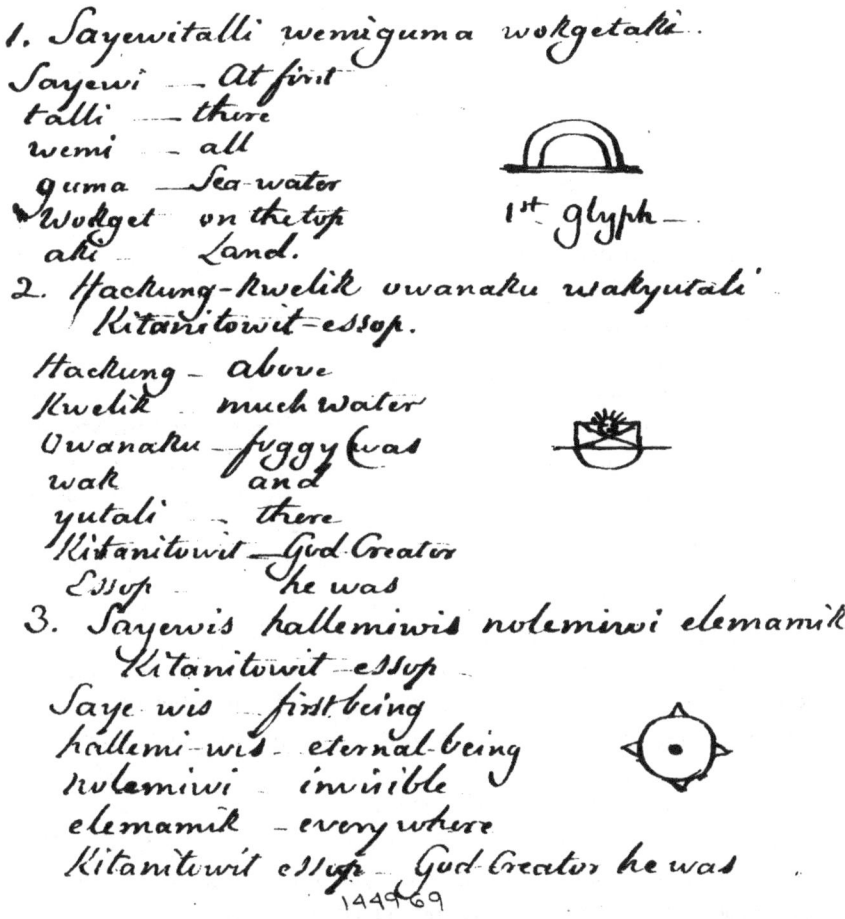

Figure 3.1
Verses 1–3 of the Walam Olum as they appear in the Rafinesque manuscript. At left is the pseudo-Delaware text; in the center is Rafinesque's English "translation," and on the right are the pictographs allegedly copied by Rafinesque from the "original" wooden tablets. Courtesy of the University of Pennsylvania, Department of Special Collections.

speech (i.e., universal "roots" supposedly embedded in every word), Rafinesque believed he could "restore" original meanings to the words of any language by locating and translating their supposed universal roots. In order to ascertain Adam's Lenape name, Rafinesque was certain that if he compared the universal roots signifying the first human ancestor in Asiatic languages, and that if he then were to find "affinities" (i.e., cognate "roots"; similar-sounding syllables) in the Delaware language, he would thus be able to identify Adam's original Lenape name.

Long before he constructed the Walam Olum, Rafinesque had read that the Hebrew name Adam ('ādām) simply means "man" or "mankind" (Clarke 1825-1826, 1:35; Fabre d'Olivet 1815/1921, 2:56), and saw that Fabre d'Olivet,[16] his favorite biblical commentator, sometimes referred to humanity as the "Adamic race." "Adam," Rafinesque argued, must have been an allegorical Hebraic reference to an original race of humans, the "Adamic race," rather than to a single person. But what name would this "race" have originally been known by in the "primitive tongue"?

In Court de Gébelin's *Monde Primitif*, Rafinesque found what he was looking for. *Gin*, the Chinese word for "man," had universal implications older than either Hebrew or Chinese. Court de Gébelin argued that *gin* was cognate to Latin *gens*, Hebrew *CHN* (i.e., kōhēn the word for "priest"), and English "king" (1787-1788, 2:579, 3:304; see also Bryant 1774-1776, 1:40-43, where some of the same identifications are made). He read further in Le Roux that the *Gine-hoang* (*Jên Huang*), or *Gin*, were the first men according to Chinese legends (Goguet and Fugere 1761, 3:301-302; Rafinesque 1832-1833:22, 24, 1836a, 2:110, 117-119). Surely, Rafinesque believed, these *Gine-hoang*, or *Gin*, comprised the Chinese tradition of the "Adamic tribes." Rafinesque chose to spell this word as *Jin*, following John Barrow's spelling in his *Travels in China* (1806:243).[17]

Adding a few "proofs" of his own to those already supplied in *Monde Primitif* (but as usual, not citing Court de Gébelin as his initial source of etymologies), Rafinesque contended that the Chinese term *Jin*, "man," was cognate to the "Jins or Genis of the primitive Arabs and Persians," "the Jains of India," "Gens in Latin," English "King," biblical "KIN," or Cain, a "Ruler of men" (which he confused with Court de Gébelin's CHN [priest]), and so forth. All had sprung "from the ancient source of JIN, the primitive men of Asia from Arabia to China" (Rafinesque 1832-1833:24, 1836a, 1:152, 2:30-31, 118).

Later, when Rafinesque was crafting the Walam Olum and his ideas regarding the *Jin* or "Adamic race" were fully shaped, he needed to find a similar-sounding Amerindian word that would demonstrate his theory. In Barton's *New Views of the Origin of the Tribes and Nations of America*, he discovered that the "Indians of Penobscot and St. Johns" referred to "god" as *Jeenoois*—a word that appeared to Rafinesque strikingly similar to *Gine-hoang* and to *Jin* (Barton 1798:1; Rafinesque 1836a:Appendix, 20). Barton had identified the "Indians of Penobscot and St. Johns" as members of the "Delaware-Stock"—tribes allegedly descended from the Delaware—and Rafinesque was therefore certain that the Delaware proper would once have used the word *Jeenoois*. So far as Rafinesque was concerned, Penobscot *Jeenoois* was identical to the Chinese *Gine-hoang* and to *Jin*; it was an "archaic" term that the "Delaware-Stock" must have imported from Asia. If Amerindians interpreted *Jeenoois* as "god" rather than "man," Rafinesque rationalized, this was because the gods of ancient mythology must be understood as deified historical figures—an idea expressed by many of his favorite writers.

As for the final syllable *-oois* of *Jinoois* (which Rafinesque respelled *-wis*), a translation seemed to be readily available in Court de Gébelin's *Monde Primitif*, that ever-reliable source of "universal" etymologies. According to Court de Gébelin, the Latin verb *esse*, "to be," was cognate to Hebrew *ish*, "'īš," another word besides 'ādām meaning "man," and that whenever the syllables *es, issi, ishi*, and so forth occurred in American Indian languages, they should be regarded as containing "primitive roots" for both "man" and "to be" (Court de Gébelin 1787–1788, 2:179–181, 8:522).

For Rafinesque, the matter was settled. The *wis* of *Jinoois* could only mean "being," and so it was translated wherever he inserted this disembodied syllable into his epic. Without citing the source of his information, he explained to his readers in professorial tones that *wis* was "identical" to Hebrew *ish* (which, following the French scholar Fabre d'Olivet, he sometimes misspelled *aish*). "Jin-Wis is the AISH or Adam of all the Linapi tribes," Rafinesque wrote. "[The Lenape Indian suffix] W'IS is identic with [Hebrew] ISH ['man']" (1836a, 1:152). In this manner he "reconstructed" the original Lenape name of the Adamic race, and the fantastic Chinese/Hebrew/Latin/Penobscot *Jin-wis*, or "Man-Being," entered the mythology of the Walam Olum.

For Rafinesque, the "discovery" and presentation of such etymologies involved far more than mere word games. It represented an attempt to settle some of the most important questions of the day. By mangling Delaware words to approximate words (and mythological characters) found in his sources, Rafinesque demonstrated the descent of all humanity from one common stock, just as described in the Bible, and "proved" the former existence of an ancient universal primitive tongue. Here at last was evidence challenging the arguments of the polygenists, who advocated that mankind and animals had been created on multiple occasions on different continents.

Such "discoveries" also provided an occasion for Rafinesque to flourish his pseudophilological prowess. His "analysis" of "archaic words" in the Walam Olum—compounds of his own making, modeled after his sources—feign both surprise and discovery: "It must be noticed that many words of these two ancient songs [of the Walam Olum] are often obsolete now in some modern dialects; but preserved in others. This with the peculiar ancient style, and the many words suppressed in the narrative, and the constant compound words, have rendered this translation a difficult task" (Rafinesque 1836a, 1:152).

The Manes of the Romans; Manito of the Lenape

The inclusion of *Jin-wis* and other supposedly archaic words in the Walam Olum were intended, as Rafinesque's own notes testify, to establish the specific Asian origins of the American Indians. Similar examples in the text abound. For example, in WO I:14, the impossible truncation *makimani,* "bad spirit," appears. Rafinesque's writings make clear that the word is not merely a careless misspelling of the widespread Algonquian designation *matchee mannitou,* "bad spirit," which John Heckewelder (1820:291), John Johnston (1820:291), John Long (1791:264), Constantin-François Volney (1804:500), and other travelers had transcribed. Rather, Rafinesque truncated *matchee mannitoo,* "bad spirit," and altered it to *makimani,* "bad spirit," because he believed that the element *mani* (of *mannitoo*) was synonymous with the so-called *Mani* (various deities and tribes) of Asia and Africa (as for the alteration of *matchee* to *maki,* this change simply reflects the orthographic system Rafinesque used in the Walam Olum [see Oestreicher 1995a:439–442]).

Rafinesque's conclusions once again reflect his European sources: Volney (1804:500) had written that the Algonquian *Manetoua,* or "spirits," were "analogous to the *Manes, Mani-um* of the Romans"—the spirits of the dead. Court de Gébelin (1787–1788, 8:518) had asserted that the Algonquian word *Manitou,* "deity," was the same word as *Man*—the designation for "deity" purportedly once universally bestowed upon the sun and moon.

Bryant (whose etymologies on the subject seem to have inspired both Volney's and Court de Gébelin's) had argued for a string of far-flung associations that linked the Roman Manes, the lunar deity Moon or Mon, the Canaanite god Baal Maon, the Isle of Mona or Man, the Menæi of Sicily, the Minyæ of Greece, the Minnæi of Arabia, and other disparate peoples, gods, and places (Bryant 1774–1776, 2:414–422, 441–443, 454–457, 471, 499, 507–515). The different peoples, Bryant believed, bore the name of their common ancestor—the *Man, Mani,* or a similar variant. As for the gods or spirits with the same designation, Bryant maintained that primitive peoples simply deified their ancestors.[18] "Most [Greek and Roman] Deities were formed out of titles [of ancestors]," Bryant expounded, "and the whole of their worship was confined to a few deified men [such as *Manes*]. . . . They were no other than their Arkite ancestors [who emerged from Noah's ark, and who were later worshiped as] the Baalim [pagan gods] of the Scriptures: to these they offered; and to these they made vows" (1774-1776, 2:441-446, 454-457).

Rafinesque was well aware of the postulations of Bryant, Court de Gébelin, and Volney, which flood the text of his *The American Nations* (Rafinesque 1836a, 2:213, 220, 240-241), and it is no coincidence that the same mistaken etymologies and theories appear in the text of the Walam Olum. Rafinesque wished to show that the ancient *mani* were known to the American Indians, further proving a common past in Asia; and that, just as Bryant had said, "primitive peoples" regarded their ancestors and various ancient nations as deities (hence the alleged connection in the Walam Olum between *mani* and *mannitoo,* "spirit").

The presence of the *maki mani,* or "bad spirit," in the Walam Olum would also achieve another purpose: it would assume the mythological equivalent of the devil or serpent in the biblical Garden of Eden story. To prove his point, Rafinesque's pictograph for *maki mani* is a snake—intended to signify the same serpent that appeared in Paradise, the same "devils" in the form of "snakes" described in McKenney's Ojibwa flood legend (1827:303), and various other serpents and devils described in the numerous disparate mythologies he had gleaned.

Again, Rafinesque believed that all ancient deities, good or bad, were simply mythologized human beings—the evil ones, of course, being devils.[19] "Human devils are met everywhere in primitive history," he explained, "and may have suggested many of our Satanic or demoniacal notions. Devil and Snake is also synonymous in many languages" (1836a, 2:223). In this manner, the early songs of the Walam Olum are deliberately ensconced in cryptic language, conforming with the nineteenth-century view that the ancients typically related history within the allegorical framework of mythology. Rafinesque has, nevertheless, left abundant clues as to how his work is to be interpreted. One note, for example, reads:

Animalization [the representation of historical human figures or tribes as animals] pervades the whole of the fabulous periods of history. . . . Whenever we meet in history or fables, animals acting like men and conversing, they are surely men, and often tribes individualized by an animal appellation: such as might be emblematic or patronymic, adopted honorable names, as lion, tyger, eagle; or else nicknames given in derision by foes, such as snake. (Rafinesque 1836a, 1:150)[20]

Thus the early sections of the Walam Olum are filled with metaphorical allusions to animals, animal ancestors, and gods designed by the author of the hoax to be "primitive" representations of actual historical events, people, tribes, and places. As we have seen, such interpretation of ancient myth had all been elucidated in Court de Gébelin's popular *Monde Primitif*, Bryant's *Analysis of Ancient Mythology*, and other noted works of the period.

In his introduction to the Walam Olum, Rafinesque warns us that "We must learn to appreciate this primitive form of speech and style, as allegorical names of men &c. *It is very needful in order to understand the following narratives* [of the Walam Olum]" (1836a, 1:121–122; emphasis added). In other words, the enlightened reader should accord the Walam Olum the greatest attention, for its seemingly primitive metaphors, when properly interpreted—and Rafinesque tells us exactly how they are to be interpreted—actually describe the factual history of the earth.

The Three Races of Mankind

In keeping with the tenor of his time, Rafinesque devoted nearly the whole of the first three songs of the Walam Olum to presenting his "universal history." He specifically referred to this portion of the epic as describing the "Asiatic period"—the era when the ancestors of all mankind supposedly dwelled in central Asia until the dispersion of mankind following Noah's flood.

As noted, numerous biblical concordances have been inserted into the verses of the hoax. Indeed, even Noah and his three sons appear in the Walam Olum, albeit with Amerindian names. Together with Nanabush (the Ojibwa flood hero whom Rafinesque believed was identical to Noah),[21] three groups of humans survive the deluge. Verse 13 reads: "Nanabush, Nanabush, became the grandfather of the beings [*owini*], the grandfather of the men [*linnowi*], and the grandfather of the turtles [*tulapewi*]" (Rafinesque 1836a, 1:128). Any ambiguities the verse might contain are cleared up by Rafinesque's commentary: "The men were then called *Linowi* and *Linapi:* two other races of men were saved, the *Owini* (beings) and the *Tulapewi,* turtlings or atlantes [Atlanteans]" (1836a, 1:92). Rafinesque is even more specific elsewhere, informing us that the "3 sons of Noah are evidently as many tribes. The THBE [*tēbāh,* 'ark'] of Noah contained therefore 4 tribes, including his [Noah's] own" (1836a, 1:92).

Thus an alleged American Indian epic, the Walam Olum, has been made to conform precisely with the narrative in Genesis, in which the three sons of Noah—Shem, Ham, and Japheth—become the patriarchs of three distinct families of mankind that repopulate the earth. The biblical scenario had for millennia been the prototype of the linguistic and cultural classification of the world's peoples by Westerners. Even Sir William Jones, whose philological discoveries were of truly great magnitude, had nevertheless been bound to its confines, arguing forcefully that all the world's languages belonged to three linguistic families—"Tartar," "Indian" (Indo-European), and "Arabian." We should hardly expect Rafinesque to have presented a different scenario.

Pictographic Palingenesy

To construct the pictographs of the Walam Olum, Rafinesque once again relied mainly upon the theories and research of European scholars. Authentic glyphs from various published sources were appropriated by Rafinesque, truncated into what he believed were the "roots" or "simple signs" of each picture, and then rejoined to form a variety of new combinations or "compound signs" in the Walam Olum.

Lacking examples of authentic Delaware pictographs from which to model his glyphs, Rafinesque turned to other sources long in his possession which he refers to frequently in various books and articles. Among the pictographic sources grafted into the Walam Olum are characters from the ancient Chinese *Ku-Wên* script, gathered mainly from the first volume of *Mémoires Concernant L'Histoire, Les Sciences, Les Arts, Les Moeurs, Les Usages, &c. Des Chinois* (Missionaries de Pekin 1776); several glyphs from the fraudulent "Bust of Isis," also included in the *Mémoires;*[22] Egyptian hieroglyphics, derived mainly from Jean François Champollion's *Précis du Système Hiéroglyphique* (1827), but also from the *Mémoires;* Ojibwa *Midewiwin* pictographs, obtained from Part II, Chapter III of *A Narrative of the Captivity and Adventures of John Tanner* (Tanner 1830); and to a lesser extent Mayan glyphs gathered from Del Rio and Cabrera's *Description of the Ruins of an Ancient City* (1822); and North African symbols from "A Discourse of the diversitie of Letters used by divers Nations of the World" (Table 47, p. 184) in *Purchas His Pilgrimes* (Purchas 1625:Part 1, Book 1, Chapter XVII, pp. 176–186).

Such an eclectic and bizarre fusion of truncated pictographs purporting to be of Delaware origin was not incongruous for Rafinesque. On the contrary, he deliberately constructed such a synthesis to prove that American Indians had Old World origins and that their writing system was directly descended from an allegedly universal and ideographic "primitive system" of writing. The "Lenape" pictographs would therefore contain numerous Old World glyphs that were once supposedly part of the original universal system. Indeed, Rafinesque asserted that the Walam Olum glyphs were "probably once imported from Asia" (1836a, 1:123), and he openly compared the Walam Olum pictographs with various American Indian, Chinese, and Egyptian signs in order to demonstrate their common background (1834b:266–269, 1834c, 1840: 76–81). Far from feeling that he needed to hide the pictographic sources from which the Walam Olum was composed, Rafinesque was convinced that a comparison of carefully selected (and often tampered-with) signs would demonstrate the veracity of his claims.

Again, Rafinesque's ideas regarding an ancient and globally diffused system of writing were by no means original. Following the example set by Court de Gébelin, as well as by the Jesuits in the *Mémoires* and by other European writers, Rafinesque brought together lists of different pictographs from various cultures in an effort to link them and prove affinities. However, unlike most of his predecessors, he often relied upon unscrupulous means to create his lists. Some glyphs have been truncated from their published sources almost beyond recognition in an effort to isolate the supposed "roots" and demonstrate far-flung connections. Others are entirely spurious and are clandestine attempts to re-create glyphs he was lacking and to force analogies.

It is indicative of Rafinesque's concern with "authenticity" that he took such pains to locate glyphs from ancient Old and New World sources in his construction of the Walam Olum. Had he been unconcerned with "reconstructing" what he believed was an accurate ancient system of writing, he might simply have invented the glyphs ex nihilo. Regarding the pictographic materials he had collected (i.e., sliced, diced, and "adapted" from published sources), he wrote: "Out of these materials . . . might be formed or restored a peculiar graphic system of north America . . . probably once imported from Asia" (1836a, 1:123).

Throughout the first song, as elsewhere in the Walam Olum, Rafinesque's pictographs play a clever and subtle role in expressing his meaning and proving the theories he found in his sources. For example, he had read discussions in the Jesuit writings and elsewhere that the primitive Chinese and Tartars worshiped heavenly bodies and had "celestial Rulers" (Kircher 1987:133; Rafinesque 1832–1833:23, 1836a, 2:6). Because he was convinced that American Indians had originated in central Asia, and therefore that the religion of the earliest American Indians was also "celestial," he crafted the Walam Olum pictographs to demonstrate these concepts. For instance, WO I:9 reads: "It was then, when again the God-Creator made the makers or spirits" (1836a, 1:126). Accordingly, the pictograph for this verse is derived (with several minor modifications by Rafinesque) from the ancient Chinese symbol for constellation. The pictograph would thus demonstrate that the gods of the Indians were, in fact, heavenly bodies.

In addition, this same glyph, with its three stars embedded in a triangle, also implied the triune aspect of some of the major gods of the Far East. The Jesuit writings, which figure among Rafinesque's favorite sources, frequently relate such beliefs in China and India; some missionaries were even convinced that the devil had introduced to the Far East a mockery of the Trinity to confound potential converts (Kircher 1987:125). Indeed, Rafinesque had long argued that American Indians worshiped the same divine triads of China and India but under different names (1832–1833:54–56), a concept already advanced by two of Rafinesque's contemporaries in the Ohio Valley, John D. Clifford and Caleb Atwater.[23]

Rafinesque's ideas on how to render his "hieroglyphics" for the Walam Olum were almost certainly influenced not only by Kircher's works on Egypt and China (see Rafinesque 1836a, 2:2–3), but also by Horapollo's immensely popular work, *Hieroglyphica*, which for centuries defined the Western world's interpretations of Egyptian hieroglyphics before the discoveries of Champollion. For example, Horapollo writes: "When a star is painted by the Egyptians, they mean a *god*, twilight, night, and time, as well as a man's *soul*" (Horapollo 1993:73, emphasis added). Horapollo further notes that the sun is one of the symbols for "eternity" (1993:43). Accordingly, Rafinesque adapted and modified various Egyptian hieroglyphic and Chinese *Ku-Wên* depictions of the sun or stars to signify a number of identical concepts in the Walam Olum, including the "God Creator," an "eternal being" (WO I:3); celestial god-kings (WO I:17); "beings," "angels," and "souls" (WO I:10; see also Rafinesque 1836a, 2:151, n. 3); and the "Bad Spirit" who created evil. Such adaptations, in which the symbols for star or the sun have been accorded a variety of definitions connected with the

80 / David M. Oestreicher

Walam Olum III: 19

northern manly
Eastern manly
Southern manly . . .
with wives or women of man
daughters of man
and with dogs of man

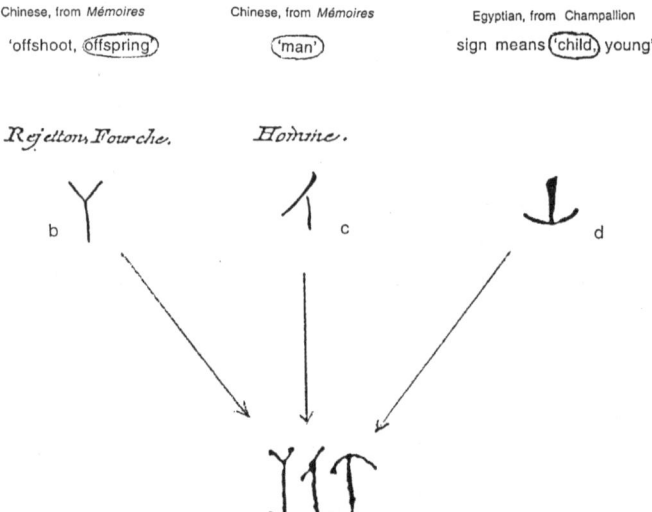

Figure 3.2
Construction of Rafinesque's compound signs from Chinese and Egyptian symbols. Example from Walam Olum III:19.

term "spirit," neatly prove Rafinesque's long-championed theories (again, of European origin) concerning the religious perceptions of the early American Indians and their links with the Far East.

Similarly, a portion of the pictograph for WO III:19 (see Figure 3.2a) incorporates both Egyptian and Chinese materials. The "root" or "simple sign" that makes up the left side of the pictograph is a Chinese *Ku-Wên* symbol derived from the *Mémoires* (Plate VI; see Figure 3.2b), wherein it is entitled *Rejetton, Fourche* (*Rejetton* translates as "shoot, sprout, offshoot" and is a metaphor for "offspring"; *Fourche* simply denotes "fork"). The "simple sign" in the center is also derived from the

Mémoires (Plate VIII; see Figure 3.2c) and is entitled *Homme* ("man"). The "simple sign" to the right is taken from Champollion's work and is the Egyptian Demotic determinative for "child, young" (Champollion 1827:Appendix: "Hiéroglyphes Phonétiques: Alphabet Harmonique" No. 104; see Figure 3.2d). Rafinesque has drawn this last character upside down, apparently to conform with the contours of the rest of the pictograph.

It is no coincidence that the central sign of this Walam Olum pictograph is "man" and that it is accompanied on both sides with symbols for "young" and "offspring." We are informed in WO III:19 that nine Lenape clans, each containing the word "man" ("[N]orthern manly, Eastern manly, Southern manly," etc.), crossed the Bering Strait together with their wives and progeny. This pictograph demonstrates beyond any doubt that Rafinesque not only derived many of his pictographs from diverse Old World materials but sometimes attempted to preserve the meaning of the symbols just as he found them in his sources. Similar examples abound (Oestreicher 1995a:172–183, 190–192, 205–206, 209–211).

Historical Help from Humboldt

Among the European scholars Rafinesque most idolized was the influential scientist and explorer Alexander von Humboldt. Indeed, Rafinesque's *Annals of Kentucky* was dedicated to Humboldt—"in token of the high value set upon his Researches on America" (Rafinesque 1824:ii). In Humboldt's *Researches Concerning the Institutions and Monuments of the Ancient Inhabitants of America* (1814),[24] the famed scholar suggested that the legendary Toltec immigration to Mexico might be connected with the downfall of the "Tsin" (i.e., Chin/Jin) empire in China and noted that the Toltec tribe had brought with it "paintings, indicating year by year the events of its migration" (1:169–170). He further argued that if "tribes of the Tartar race have passed over to the northwest coast of America" migrating "south and east" across the continent—a scenario that "etymological researches seem to indicate"—we should expect to find in America "a hieroglyphical writing . . . and traditions respecting the first state of the world, recalling to our minds the sciences, the arts, and the religious opinions of the Asiatic nations" (1:146–147).

Humboldt's discussion would become a veritable blueprint for Rafinesque's hoax. The scenario presented in the Walam Olum—with its Old World hieroglyphs, etymologies, cosmogonic traditions, ancient history, and religious beliefs, including its depiction of the breakup of the Jin empire and the migration of central Asian tribes via the northwest coast of America (i.e., the Bering Strait) to the southern and eastern portions of the continent—is drawn directly from this and other discussions in the works of Humboldt and other writers which Rafinesque, according to his own testimony, relied upon intimately for his research on American Indians. If anything, Rafinesque's forgery is an elaboration of the ideas of his predecessors and contemporaries.

Rafinesque and Macpherson

Rafinesque did not draw only from the work of noted European scientists and scholars for the construction of the Walam Olum—European forgeries also played an important role. The fraudulent "Bust of Isis" has been noted as a source of Rafinesque's pictographs, but we would be remiss if we failed to mention one of the most controversial European forgeries of all—James Macpherson's epic songs of Ossian.

Like most of his generation, Rafinesque had long been profoundly influenced by Macpherson's spurious work. Macpherson's Ossian hoax was published in a number of separate installments and, like the Walam Olum, was largely based upon earlier literary sources. The first installment, published in June 1760, was entitled *Fragments of Ancient Poetry, Collected in the Highlands of Scotland, and Translated from the Galic or Erse Language*. It made the bold claim that the various "fragments" of poetry included therein were probably "episodes of a greater work" that had originally been uttered by Celtic bards living in antiquity (Blair 1760:v; Saunders 1968:79). According to Macpherson and Dr. Hugh Blair, the literary critic and theologian who furnished a preface, the "fragments" of this epic poetry had survived not only in ancient manuscripts (in which the Scottish public was manifesting an ever-growing interest) but in the songs of living bards in the highlands.

Thus Macpherson and his followers contended that an entire epic, purportedly as great as Homer's and relating events equally dramatic (with far-reaching implications for the national glory of the Scottish people), was said to be extant in the highlands of Scotland. All that was needed was a man with enough talent to locate the bards and manuscripts and to translate, assemble, and restore the "fragments" to their original glory—Macpherson himself, of course. Such claims are remarkably similar to those Rafinesque would later make of his own work.

Although some critics, most notably Samuel Johnson, would brand

Macpherson a forger, the work was enthusiastically received, and Macpherson was sufficiently emboldened to produce additional works, including *Fingal* and *Temora* (Macpherson 1762, 1763). In these works, Macpherson claimed to present not unconnected "fragments," but entire epics he had supposedly been able to reconstruct. To fend off critics, Macpherson (1763:226-247) appended a "specimen" of the "original" Gaelic text to *Temora*, which scholarship has since demonstrated is spurious (Saunders 1968:189-190; Trevor-Roper 1984:18). The incident was later paralleled by Rafinesque, who, with virtually identical wording, appended a "specimen" of the "original text and poetry of these annals" (i.e., the pseudo-Delaware text) to his publication of the "translation" of the Walam Olum in *The American Nations* (1836a, 1:160-161).

In short, it is no coincidence that the Walam Olum comprises "poetical annals," "historical songs," and "fragments" (i.e., the John Burns "fragment" and other "fragments" that Rafinesque appends), just as the Ossian epics do. Nor should we be surprised that a "king" in Macpherson's *Temora* is named "Mild and Tall" while a "king" in the Walam Olum bears the name "Long and mild" (Macpherson 1763:69; WO IV:62).[25] (The Lenape word for "tall" is listed in Rafinesque's sources as being built upon the root for "long"; ungrammatical though it is, Rafinesque's version is thus nearly an exact replication of Macpherson's.)

In addition, the very name of Rafinesque's hoax, Walam Olum, bears the stamp of Macpherson's endeavor. Although both *Walam* and *Olum* are impossible truncations of Delaware names derived from a list compiled by a Moravian missionary, John Heckewelder, and intended by Rafinesque to mean "Painted Record,"[26] the term *Olum* is far more than a meaningless Delaware truncation. Rafinesque considered this disembodied syllable a linguistic cognate to the name of the purported Celtic bard "Olen" (i.e., *Ullin*, whom he had read of in Macpherson's epics). He further linked his truncation with the ancient Irish *Ollamh* (spelled "Olam" by Rafinesque), the highest grade of bard, as well as with the *Ogham*, the earliest writings of the Druids and Irish (Rafinesque 1836a, 1:151).

Similarly, the authentic Delaware name *Olumapies* (Heckewelder 1834:384), from which Rafinesque first derived the truncation "Olum," also figures as a chief in the Walam Olum (i.e., "Olumapi") (WO IV:23; Rafinesque 1836a, 1:133). Heckewelder informs us that this Delaware name signifies a person "well bundled up." Rafinesque, however, has twisted the definition in the pages of the Walam Olum to mean "manly recorder or bundler [of ancient record sticks]." Like the Celtic bard *Ullin* and the Irish *Ollamh,* the Walam Olum chief *Olumapies* was a keeper of ancient records recited in epic song; the very name of the hoax, Walam Olum, allegedly signified the records themselves.

Indeed, it would be surprising had Rafinesque not imitated Macpherson's poems. Not only had Rafinesque, a voracious reader, been aware of one of the most influential literary works of the late eighteenth and early nineteenth centuries, but his poetry had been published in close proximity to excerpts from Ossian in the *Western Review and Miscellaneous Magazine* when he was a resident in Kentucky. Even more telling, Rafinesque informs us in that journal that some of his own poetry was created in conscious imitation of the "beautiful kind of style, which was the PRIMITIVE POETRY of mankind" to be found in such works as Ossian (Rafinesque 1820:232), which he listed together with the Bible and the Koran.

Although the spurious Scottish epics served as a model for the Walam Olum, it is worth noting that the Walam Olum also bears the influence of an American forgery, *The Book of Mormon* (Smith 1830/1977), which, ironically, was as much a product of the era of the great decipherments and the effort to resolve the riddle of Amerindian origins as the alleged Delaware epic. The parallels between *The Book of Mormon* and the Walam Olum are striking: both claim to be epics explaining the presence of the American Indians in the New World; both claim to reveal the identity and fate of the Mound Builders; both were allegedly written in glyphic form, in languages either extinct or unknown to the vast majority of Euro-Americans; both needed to be translated by extraordinary means, either by divine aid or scientific genius; and both sets of "original" tablets vanished without a trace (Oestreicher 1994:13, 1995a:73-76; a more extensive discussion on the connection between the two works is found in my forthcoming book).

Conclusions

This chapter has noted some examples of how Rafinesque was influenced by European scholarship, and how the Walam Olum—an alleged Amerindian epic that would wield disproportionate influence in the history of American archaeology—was in reality transplanted from the soil of the Old World. Not only is there a plethora of examples proving the influence of European luminaries and theories upon the Walam Olum, but on numerous occasions throughout his career, Rafinesque openly compared his scholarly efforts with that of his great contemporaries. For example, in his extravagant and erroneous claim to have made an original breakthrough in the decipherment of the Mayan hieroglyphs,[27] Rafinesque published an open letter to Jean François Champollion, the famed decipherer of ancient Egyptian:

> You have become celebrated by decyphering, at last, the glyphs and characters of the ancient Egyptians, which all your learned predecessors had deemed a riddle, and pronounced impossible to read. You first announced your discovery in a letter. I am going to follow your footsteps on another continent, and a theme equally obscure; to none but yourself can I address with more propriety, letters on a subject so much alike in purpose and importance, and so similar to your own labours. (Rafinesque 1832–1833:4)

It is unlikely that the great cryptographer ever saw the letter addressed to him by Rafinesque in the latter's American periodical, the *Atlantic Journal* (which was in any case evidently intended mainly to bedazzle a local Philadelphia audience). A second letter to Champollion would follow (Rafinesque 1832–1833:40–44),[28] and both letters, as well as an 1827 letter to Du Ponceau published in the *Saturday Evening Post* entitled "Important Historical and Philological Discovery" (Rafinesque 1827), comprised a deliberate attempt to parallel Champollion's famous *Lettre à M. Dacier relative à l'Alphabet des hiéroglyphes phonétiques*, in which Champollion first announced to the public his decipherment of Egyptian in 1822. In addition, Rafinesque was doubtless well aware that A. I. Silvestre de Sacy of the Prix Volney committee, to whom he addressed his announcement regarding the Walam Olum, was the same leading Orientalist who had recognized Champollion's decipherment of Egyptian.

Indeed, even when Rafinesque's work was lampooned by contemporaries, he took refuge in lamenting (through the public venue, in characteristic fashion) that he was surrounded by ignorant buffoons unappreciative of his genius: "My historical and philological discoveries are called insane! Thus was Champollion insane when he restored the Egyptian Antiquities as I do the American" (Rafinesque 1832–1833:3). Elsewhere he railed: "It is only in Europe that my discoveries may be fully appreciated: here I am like *Bacon* and *Galileo*, somewhat ahead of the age and my neighbors; but a time will come, and perhaps within a short period, when such labors as mine will meet with general approbation" (Rafinesque 1821:73).

Such statements are most revealing of Rafinesque's view of himself, but they also reflect a broader American concern with crafting a national identity comparable to that of the Old World: the "monuments" or earthen mounds of America were as venerable as the Parthenon or the ruins of Rome; the Mound Builders had a past as hoary as that of Europe (and even appeared to have been an Old World people, perhaps ancient Europeans); the American "ruins" sometimes boasted hieroglyphic writings; and the accomplishments of America's decipherers were equal to those of their counterparts in the Old World.

Ascertaining which European scholars Rafinesque both emulated and clandestinely grafted information from is not difficult, as his works are filled with ubiquitous comparisons of himself with his heroes. Claiming, for example, to have fulfilled the hopes of leading scholars (as well as biblical prophets and Greek philosophers!), Rafinesque declared in the preface of *The American Nations:* "The worthies who have been taken for models or guides in this arduous undertaking, are Solomon, Moses, Job, St. Paul, St. Augustine, Plato, Niebuhr, Humboldt, Malcolm, Gebelin, D'Olivet, Bryant, Adelung, Drummond, Pritchard, Champollion, Klaproth, Jones, Wilford, Akbar, Price, Bailly, Russell, Beattie, Herder, Carli, Barton &c." (1836a, 1:3-4). Excluding the biblical and classical figures, nearly all the "guides" cited by Rafinesque are noted European scholars. These and other authorities provided the framework of human origins that Rafinesque incorporated into his Walam Olum. Although Rafinesque typically presented himself as a lone defender of science and a perpetual discoverer of "new facts," his was not an original mind, nor may he be placed beside the scientific luminaries of his day. Rather, the originality of his anthropological work was confined largely to the cleverness with which he expressed other people's ideas—often passing them off as his own. To a startling degree, Rafinesque's thoughts, philological and historical examples, and even words arose from his favorite published authorities—the great savants of the European Enlightenment.[29]

4

Toward a Science of Man
European Influences on the Archaeology of Ephraim George Squier

Terry A. Barnhart

American archaeology's connections to Europe from the mid- to late nineteenth century are nowhere more evident than in the archaeology of Ephraim George Squier. Ideas about prehistory and topics of research under discussion in Europe had a significant impact on Squier's archaeological investigations, as they did on those of several of his contemporaries. Those influences are present whether one examines his mound explorations and surveys with Dr. Edwin Hamilton Davis in Ohio from 1845 to 1847, his early monographs and minor writings, or his activities in the American Ethnological Society in the 1850s and 1860s. While historians have recognized Squier as "the first definitive voice in American archaeology" (Stanton 1960:82, see also Bieder 1986:104–145; Tax 1973:173–223), the extent to which his investigations were informed by a transatlantic conversation about human origins, antiquity, and theories of cultural development remains imperfectly known. That climate of opinion owed much to the archaeological and ethnological researches conducted by European learned societies and savants. The views of Alexander von Humboldt, Edme François Jomard, the expatriated English Egyptologist George Robins Gliddon, Luke Burke of the London *Ethnological Journal*, and French physical anthropologist Paul Broca were engrafted upon Squier's archaeological thought at distinct junctures of his long and productive career as a scholar.

The manner in which Squier incorporated the theories and opinions of European scholars into his own approach to American prehistory is an important consideration in any appraisal of his archaeological career. His correspondence with European scholars, his membership in several European learned societies,[1] and his familiarity with the progress of ethnological researches conducted in different parts of the globe exposed him to ideas and techniques that became significant features of his own scholarship. Those influences were important in his efforts to replace the older, more fragmented, and more general ethnology practiced in the United States with a more comprehensive, specialized, and integrated concept of anthropology as practiced in Europe. Nor was Squier alone in that effort. Samuel George Morton, Josiah Clark Nott, and George Robins Gliddon—all members of the so-called American School of anthropology—consciously attempted to recruit American archaeologists and ethnologists to a new conception of ethnology throughout the 1840s and 1850s, and one that more nearly conformed with anthropological investigations being conducted in Europe. As Nott and Gliddon stated matters in 1854, Morton was the founder of their "cis-Atlantic school of Anthropology" (1854:ix).

An integrated approach to the study of man did not emerge in the United States until later in the nineteenth century, when "scientific anthropology" replaced the older and more fragmented "ethnology." But Squier and his associates in the American School were already moving in that direction at midcentury, however tentatively and ineffectively. Squier exemplifies an anthropologically oriented approach to American prehistory that was consonant with later developments, especially in his use of ethnological and historical analogies to interpret archaeological artifacts and sites. He is, indeed, a transitional figure in the history of American archaeology in many regards, such as in his attempt to transform the American Ethnological Society into the short-lived Anthropological Institute of New-York in 1871. It in no way detracts from the originality of his researches to point out that European ideas and developments exerted significant influences on his archaeological thought. Some of those influences were direct and others of a more generalized nature, but all were significant.

Squier's career as an archaeologist began abruptly in 1845 after earlier experiences as a teacher, civil engineer, poet, and journalist. Shortly after he assumed duties as editor of the *Scioto Gazette* in Chillicothe, Ohio, he made the acquaintance of Dr. Edwin Hamilton Davis. Ten years Squier's elder, Davis was a practicing physician, surgeon, and self-declared "moundologist" who contracted "the antiquarian malady" at an early age.[2] Through his association with Davis, Squier was received into a fraternity of Ohio antiquarians who had made the study of archaeology an impassioned avocation. All about him were prehistoric earthworks, cabinets of curiosities, and individuals like Davis who possessed an incurable enthusiasm for an absorbing field of inquiry. Davis paid for the mound excavations, sometimes assisted Squier with making surveys, and accompanied him in the field whenever his medical practice allowed. Although the Davis of Squier and Davis has largely remained a nonentity, Davis's contributions to the Squier-Davis investigations merit more recognition than they have generally received (Barnhart 1983, 1986a, 1989).

When Squier and Davis began their investigations, little was known about the prehistoric Indian mounds and geometric enclosures that rose conspicuously from the Ohio landscape. They had been the subject of frequent comment since the beginning of Euro-American settlement in the Ohio Valley in the late eighteenth century, but with few exceptions, little regard was given to classifying the structural differences of these remains or the possibility that they were built by different peoples, in different eras, and for different purposes. Descriptive accounts based on actual surveys and excavations were far too sporadic and few in number to support a systematic and comprehensive study. The state of knowledge on the subject of American antiquities had little changed since 1820, when Caleb Atwater of Circleville, Ohio, under the auspices of the American Antiquarian Society, made the first general survey of Ohio's mounds and earthworks. In large measure, the mooted questions concerning the origin, era, and assumed purposes of these works remained "lost in a labyrinth of doubt" and idle speculation (Atwater 1820:110, 110 n, 111, 121). Those who would decipher the riddle of the mounds through the often erroneous and contradictory literature on the subject were often more bewildered than enlightened. There were many investigators who eschewed speculation for close description and restrained comparison in the eighteenth and nineteenth centuries, but their contributions to American archaeology have gone largely unappreciated (see chapter two in this volume).

By the mid–nineteenth century, however, circumstances were rapidly changing. Romantic and fanciful speculation about the mounds continued to be certain, but idle conjecture was beginning to give way to a more scientifically exacting approach (the beginning of Willey and Sabloff's "Classificatory-Descriptive Period" [1980:34–82]). With the founding of the American Ethnological Society in 1842, the emerging field of archaeology began to take on the trappings of a scientific discipline. Its development was stimulated by the assimilation of new sources of ethnographic information. As the United States expanded beyond the Mississippi and as American merchants, missionaries, and explorers penetrated foreign markets and cultures, more aboriginal peoples and antiquities were brought under study. Particularly notable were the ethnological collections, vocabularies, and publications resulting from the first United States Exploring Expedition of 1838 to 1842. A further impetus to archaeological investigation was the publication of Edward Kingsborough's nine-volume *Antiquities of Mexico* (1830–1848), John Lloyd Stephens's *Incidents of Travel in Central America, Chiapas, and Yucatan* (1841), and Frederick Catherwood's *Views of Ancient Monuments in Central America, Chiapas, and Yucatan* (1844), works that revealed a new chapter in the history of aboriginal America. Who would come forward and do for the rude monuments of the Mississippi Valley what Stephens and Catherwood had done for the monumental architecture of Mesoamerica?

Nowhere were those discoveries more earnestly discussed than among the ardent members of the American Ethnological Society of New York. The society became the clearinghouse of information about archaeological, ethnographic, historical, geographical, and linguistic researches around the globe. The investigations of Squier and Davis came to the society's attention in 1846, when Squier presented examples of the artifacts recovered in his excavations with Davis, along with maps, plans, and sectional views of the mounds and earthworks of the Scioto River Valley. Since its founding, the American Ethnological Society had promoted the study of ethnology in its widest accepted meaning: "inquiries into the origin, progress, and characteristics of the various races of man." Archaeology, philology, and ethnography were all embraced by the papers read before its eclectic members. The first volume of the society's highly regarded *Transactions*, published in 1845, contained an article by Henry Rowe Schoolcraft on the excavation of the Grave Creek mound in western Virginia and another by Gerard Troost on the antiquities of Tennessee. The society specifically encouraged further investigations into the origin and character of the earthworks of the Ohio and Mississippi Valleys, noting that "there are few individuals in our western country who may not obtain interesting materials for their elucidation" (Anonymous 1845:ii, ix, x, 1848:vii, viii). Few individuals were then better situated to pursue the investigations of those remains than Messieurs Squier and Davis.

Understandably, Squier's presentation of the preliminary results of the Squier-Davis investigations generated considerable interest among its members, so much so that the secretary of the society, New York publisher John Russell Bartlett, and the society's venerable founder and president, Albert Gallatin, offered to publish a full account of their researches in the next volume of the *Transactions*. They also endorsed Squier's plan for extending his explorations with Davis into other areas of the Mississippi Valley. With the encouragement of Gallatin and Bartlett, Squier's scholarly career would be firmly established. Both men used their influence to promote interest in his researches among other members of the eastern scientific community and the public at large. Furthermore, through his relationships with Bartlett, Gallatin, and other members of the American Ethnological Society, Squier would be introduced to a transatlantic conversation about human origins, antiquity, and theories of cultural development.

It was at the conclusion of the Squier-Davis investigations in May 1847 that Squier first met the expatriated Englishman and popular lecturer on Egyptology, George Robins Gliddon. Gliddon's polygenist views on human origins and antiquity greatly influenced Squier's emerging archaeological thought. A former U.S. consul at Cairo and a 23-year resident of Egypt, Gliddon established himself as an American authority on Egyptian archaeology with a course of seven lectures delivered at Boston in the winter of 1842–1843. Those lectures formed the basis of his *Ancient Egypt*, published in 1844. Eighteen thousand copies of this work sold in the United States within three years, and it eventually appeared in at least thirteen editions. It was Gliddon who provided the 137 Egyptian and Nubian skulls that formed the basis of Samuel George Morton's highly regarded *Crania Aegyptiaca*, published the same year. Encouraged by the success of *Ancient Egypt*, Gliddon launched a new lecture series on Egyptian archaeology in 1846.[3]

Gliddon and Squier were introduced through correspondence by their mutual acquaintance, John Russell Bartlett. Bartlett suggested that Squier invite Gliddon to speak at Chillicothe, and upon learning of this, Gliddon wrote Squier that he would welcome an opportunity to explain his "hieroglyphical discoveries" to the citizens of Chillicothe. He eagerly accepted Squier's invitation and in early May gave a course of four well-received lectures on Egyptian history, religion, arts, sciences, and customs as revealed by their archaeological remains. Gliddon's lectures were high drama conducted by a practiced hand. His canvas tableaux covered the four walls of a lecture hall, enveloping his audience within a panorama of pyramids, temples, hieroglyphic inscriptions, and portraits illustrating Egyptian costume and physical type. Within this setting, the animated Gliddon discussed the latest findings on the chronology and ethnography of ancient Egypt. He was a popularizer and not an original investigator, but the effectiveness of his lectures made a deep impression on those in the United States, like Squier, who concerned themselves with the vexed question of human origins. Gliddon's audiences learned that European Egyptologists were then carrying the era of Menes to four and even five thousand years before Christ, an antiquity that could not be accounted for within the restrictions of biblical chronology. Moreover, through the osteological evidence offered in Morton's *Crania Aegyptiaca* and by the various representations of physical types found on Egyptian monuments, Gliddon demonstrated that the physical type of the Egyptians, Negroes, and other ethnic elements in Egyptian society were radically distinct in 2000 B.C., and had not changed since.

Gliddon treaded lightly on the implications of those evidences in his public lectures, but they were clear enough for those willing to pursue them to a logical conclusion. The time necessary for Egyptian civilization to reach the stage of development it had attained by 2000 B.C. could not be reconciled with the Hebrew chronology. Nor could the ancient diversity of mankind be derived from a single pair of human beings. The various races of man, therefore, must have originated in separate creations. The theory of separate origins was certainly not a new one. The monogenist-polygenist debate dates back to European sources in the sixteenth and seventeenth centuries and the ideas of separate origins promoted by the racial theory of Blumenback (Haven 1856:3-16; Winsor 1889a). By the mid-nineteenth century, however, the theory took on new trappings of respectability in some quarters of American ethnology, based on the supposed evidences offered by physical anthropology and archaeology. The separate origins theory became known as the doctrine of polygenesis and was endorsed by many eminent scientists in the United States and Europe, including Louis Agassiz in the United States. Advocates of polygenesis argued that each of the human races had separate origins and was a distinct species. Did not the racial distinctiveness of the American Indian and the apparently remote antiquity of the mounds lead to similar conclusions? To Gliddon and others they certainly did. Gliddon would later introduce Squier's work to Edme François Jomard and fellow iconoclast Luke Burke, editor of the London *Ethnological Journal*. Through his relationship with Gliddon, Squier became associated with what the *Ethnological Journal* referred to as "the school of American Ethnologists" (Burke 1848:173). Historians have come to know this group as the American School of anthropology, whose fascinating and seemingly incongruous members were bound together by the theory of separate origins (Nott and Gliddon 1854, 1857; Stanton 1960:82-89). The impious son of a clergyman, Squier was a curious member indeed.

By the conclusion of his Chillicothe lectures, Gliddon and his "Mound Digger" Squier had become fast friends and confidential correspondents. In Gliddon, Squier met a personality fully as audacious, gregarious, and irreverent as his own. Gliddon's enthusiasm for all branches of anthropological inquiry and his rather sycophantic attentions to the results of Squier's researches formed the basis of their friendship. Squier positively reveled in Gliddon's self-conscious paganism. Although Gliddon's lectures were ostensibly touted as confirming "Bible History," that was certainly not true of the Book of Genesis or of Bishop Usher's widely received chronology of human antiquity based upon that source. Privately, Gliddon took an impish delight in "knocking the Bible into a cocked hat."[4] Gliddon, Josiah Clark Nott of Mobile, Samuel George Morton of Philadelphia, and the yet impressionable Squier came to form a veritable coterie of iconoclasm. Although Squier was far too cautious to openly align himself with the controversial racial theories of the American School, his implicit endorsement of its major tenets (a somewhat qualified embrace, as we will see) is apparent in some of his lesser-known writings.

Unquestionably, Gliddon's racial theory and correspondence with Squier were major influences on his anthropological thought.[5] Gliddon also did more than anyone else to promote interest in Squier's researches in Europe, where they attracted the attention of Edme François Jomard, president of the Geographical Society of Paris and the sole survivor of Bonaparte's scientific corps in Egypt. Jomard published a detailed notice of the Squier-Davis investigations in the *Bulletin de la Société de Géographie* as early as December 1846, based upon a letter written by Benjamin Silliman to Dr. G. A. Mantell of London and published in Silliman's *Journal of American Arts and Sciences*. Jomard's account also cites a letter written to him by Squier on October 12, 1846, regarding the position of human remains and different types of burials found within the mounds. Jomard continued to give detached notices of the subsequent progress of Squier's investigations (Barnhart 1986b; Jomard 1846, 1848a, 1848b, 1848c).

Jomard took particular interest in Squier's "sound" opinions on the state of American civilization at the time of the European conquest, and on the similarities exhibited between some archaeological remains in the Old and New Worlds. Jomard believed that the archaeological remains in the New World indicated that a higher state of civilization had once existed there than that encountered by the first European explorers. At the time of the European conquest, Jomard asserted, groups in North America were found living in an uncultivated and semi-savage state, where the arts were forgotten and tradition itself was dead. Even Mexico and Peru he regarded to be but pale reflections of their former states of civilization. Squier's discoveries in the mounds seemed to add yet further evidence in support of Jomard's theory of cultural decline. A higher state of civilization was suggested by the materials found in the mounds, some of which had been transported from distant locations through extensive commerce or migrations. In either event, their presence in Ohio mounds established the fact that a contemporaneous communication had occurred between the Great Lakes, the Allegheny Mountains, and the Gulf of Mexico during the era in which the mounds were constructed (Jomard 1848c).

It was the "coincidences in forms" between archaeological remains and ethnological characteristics in the Old and New Worlds that most intrigued Jomard. Those similarities did not appear to Squier as proof that the American race derived from Asia, as many assumed, an opinion in which Jomard fully concurred. Jomard and Squier both accepted the Humboldtian principle that human societies everywhere exhibited certain analogies. German naturalist and explorer Baron Alexander von Humboldt (1769–1859), perhaps the most respected scientist of his day, succinctly stated the promise and peril of cross-cultural analogies in a series of questions that were well known to nineteenth-century investigators. As Humboldt noted in the first volume of his *Researches:*

> It would no doubt be absurd to suppose the migration of Egyptian colonies wherever pyramidal monuments and symbolical paintings are found; but how can we avoid being struck with the traces of resemblance offered by the vast pictures of manners, of arts, of language, and traditions, which exist at present among nations at the most remote distance from each other? Why should we hesitate to point out, wherever they occur, the analogies of construction in languages, of style in monuments, and of fictions in cosmogonies, although we may be unable to decide what were the secret causes of these resemblances, while no historical fact carries us back to the epoch of the communications, which existed between the inhabitants of different climates? (1814:147–148)

Discovering "the secret causes" of those resemblances was an archaeological and ethnological problem to which Squier would dedicate several years of research and reflection. He greatly admired Humboldt and would later cite him in support of his own views on the similarities that naturally arose between peoples remotely separated by time and place.[6]

It was in the essence of man to seek progress, Jomard believed, and progress was always achieved in human societies under favorable circumstances. Thus one may see similarities between the industries, fundamental ideas, and symbols of the African, the American, and the Asian without deriving the American race from the former or the latter. Throughout time and in all parts of the globe, man, a born imitator, had copied natural forms and phenomena as a means of self-expression. Nature presented human societies with certain constant forms and identical phenomena that impressed themselves upon human imagination, furnishing it with the same raw materials or analogous models for self-expression and creativity. Thus one should not be surprised at finding similarities among people at the most distant points of the globe.

Even differences among human cultures, which Jomard admitted were more numerous than similarities in many instances, could be explained by the same line of reasoning. Whereas nature presented uniformity in certain phenomena and forms throughout the globe, it by no means did so in all forms and all phenomena. Nature also manifests diversity across various localities. Thus we find differences in the arts, customs, and languages of peoples on different continents which point to what is truly distinctive about human societies within those locations. But the single most important cause of similarities between men, despite their physical differences and diverse languages, was humankind's aptitude and need to know, the faculty of reflecting, and of combining ideas in order to form a judgment. It was that psychic unity or "divine breath" that animated and distinguished mankind from the brute. With this divine gift to all humanity, why would it not have everywhere produced certain elementary results? Where, therefore, was the necessity of explaining similarities between the nations of the globe through improbable theories that are repugnant to good sense? Jomard lamented that the branch of natural history which examined human varieties in the light of these considerations had been neglected for too long.

Jomard's observations introduced Squier to a new line of inquiry. We can trace his interest in developing and explaining cultural analogies in some of the theoretical aspects of *Ancient Monuments of the Mississippi Valley,* and in observations made in the appendix to his *Aboriginal Monuments of the State of New York,* his minor writings on the historical and mythological traditions of the Algonquins, and most extensively in *The Serpent Symbol.* These linkages are among the least-understood aspects of his major writings. Squier considered *The Serpent Symbol,* the most speculative of his works, to be an elaboration of questions and archaeological problems relating to similarities among archaeological remains that he had more circumspectly raised in his Smithsonian monographs. Those problems appear to have first taken shape during his correspondence with Jomard in 1846 and 1847, and they became something of a preoccupation with Squier for several more years.

The development of cultural analogies became a salient feature of Squier's archaeological thought that first emerged in *Ancient Monuments of the Mississippi Valley*. The use of analogy informed Squier and Davis's classifications of mounds and earthworks, their comments on the Serpent Mound, and those made in regard to the sculptured-stone rattlesnake tablets recovered from a mound at Clark's Work (today known as the Hopewell site). This part of *Ancient Monuments* clearly owes more to Squier than to Davis, but Davis was likewise convinced that many of the mounds and their contents were of a religious origin. Both investigators were satisfied that the form and position of several of the geometric enclosures in the Mississippi Valley established that they had not been constructed for defensive purposes. Because many of the presumably sacrificial or altar mounds were frequently found inside or near "sacred enclosures," the authors concluded that the areas within them had been set off as "tabooed" or consecrated ground:

> We have reason to believe that the religious system of the moundbuilders, like that of the Aztecs, exercised among them a great, if not a controlling influence. Their government may have been, for aught we know, a government of the priesthood; one in which the priestly and civil functions were jointly exercised, and one sufficiently powerful to have secured in the Mississippi valley, as it did in Mexico, the erection of many of those vast monuments, which for ages will continue to challenge the wonder of men.... It is a conclusion which every day's investigation and observation has tended to confirm, that most, perhaps all, of the earthworks not manifestly defensive in their character, were in some way connected with the superstitious rites of their builders,— though in what precise manner, it is, and perhaps, ever will be, impossible satisfactorily to determine. (Squier and Davis 1848: 47–48)

The lamp of analogy offered Squier and Davis a way to infer, however indirectly, what the general principles of those religious rites and conceptions may have been—at least to the extent that one could infer them from the design and assumed symbolism of the works themselves. Squier and Davis's discussion of the numerous rectangular, circular, and elliptical enclosures of the Ohio Valley is an important case in point. The authors classified these remains as "sacred enclosures," and the mounds found within them are likewise attributed to a religious purpose. The magnitude and obvious design of these works gave Squier and Davis pause for reflection and comment on the possible symbolic meaning of their various forms and combinations. "We can find their parallels only in the great temples of A(ve)bury and Stonehenge in England, and Carnac in Brittany, and must [by reason of analogy] associate them with sun worship and its kindred superstitions" (Squier and Davis 1848:49). As indicated in this brief but suggestive passage, Squier had seized upon "sun worship and its kindred superstitions" as the underlying principle of the various religious and mythological systems of the American Indian. He was convinced that a comparative analysis of those systems and those found among the early nations of the Old World would lead to important results. This inquiry would involve the examination of archaeological remains in the Old World, the principles upon which they were constructed, and the degree to which a symbolic meaning could be deduced from their designs. He believed that such an approach would provide a rationale for interpreting the symbolism of archaeological remains throughout the American continent.

Squier's early interest in such analogies is further evident in his observations on the Great Serpent Mound of Brush Creek. The discovery of the Serpent Mound in 1846 engendered in Squier a cultlike fascination with serpent symbolism and the problem of explaining its presence in the New World. John Russell Bartlett, secretary of the American Ethnological Society, regarded the "great serpent and egg" to be one of the most important discoveries yet made in American archaeology. "You are perhaps aware that the 'serpent and egg' are very prominent in the Hindu mythology. But even with this striking analogy, I would not be so ready to jump to conclusions in connecting the American and Asiatic races as some are. I can only say, it is the most striking of any analogies yet discovered."[7] Gliddon also took interest in "that Serpent's Egg-business," but he expressed concern about what Squier would make of it. He regarded it "as a very dangerous subject for theorizing upon, lest it should not be the Serpent and the egg!—so be cautious."[8]

Squier enlisted Gliddon's knowledge in oriental mythology and classical history in investigating the archaeological problems suggested by the serpent-and-egg effigy at Brush Creek. He asked Gliddon: "Do the *Serpent* and the *Egg,* separate or in combination, occur among the *Egyptian* symbols, and if they occur what signification was assigned to them? Was the *Serpent* in Egypt in any way associated with the worship of the sun and its attendant worship of the Phallus[?]" Gliddon responded with a 15-page disquisition on serpent symbolism in ancient Egypt, asking Squier "to excuse brevity." But again he sounded a note of caution. "No one has recognized more thoroughly than yourself, ... this harmonizing furor of uncritical observers to confound things distinct in origin as in nature, if presenting at first sight a suppositious resemblance to the vestiges of other Nations, other countries, other centres of man's civilization."[9] Gliddon worried about the conclusions that would follow the announcement of Squier's "Serpico-Ovine discoveries." Uncritical observers, and certainly monogenists, would surely embrace the discovery as evidence that the Mound Builders originated in Asia. The problem with serpent symbolism in antiquity, Gliddon noted, was its ubiquity: "the serpent is everywhere in the mythologies and cosmogonies of the East, and one cannot be assured that the Serpent of the Ophites (any more than that emitting [from] or encircling the *Mundane Egg*) was Egyptian rather than Jewish, Persian, or Hindustanic."[10] Gliddon could not find the serpent and egg in combination on a single Egyptian monument, so he abstained from speculation. Neither could he find hieroglyphic evidence directly connecting phallic worship with the solar symbol of the serpent.

Gliddon's stricture that Squier not make too much of the serpent-and-egg effigy lest it prove not to be "*the* egg" was a sound one, for some later students of the Serpent Mound have questioned whether the egg of the serpent-and-egg effigy is an egg at all or the representation of something else. Squier and Davis, however, harbored no such doubts based upon their survey of the site. They were nonetheless cautious in the observations made about the Serpent Mound in *Ancient Monuments:*

> The serpent, separate or in combination with the circle, egg, or globe, has been a predominant symbol among many primitive nations. It prevailed in Egypt, Greece, and Assyria, and entered widely into the superstitions of the Celts, the Hindoos, and the Chinese. It even penetrated into America; and was conspicuous in the mythology of the ancient Mexicans, among whom its significance does not seem to have differed materially from that

which it possessed in the old world. The fact that the ancient Celts, and perhaps other nations of the old continent, erected sacred structures in the form of the serpent, is one of high interest. Of this description was the great temple of A(ve)bury, in England,—in many respects the most imposing ancient monument of the British islands. (Squier and Davis 1848:97)

Gliddon remained curious about Squier's "philosophy of Eggs & Serpents," which he characterized as "the most beautiful and dangerous subject of your discoveries."[11]

Squier's interest in serpent symbolism was further piqued by the recovery of sculptured-stone rattlesnake tablets from Mound No. 1 of Clarke's Work in the Scioto Valley (today known as the Hopewell site). As Davis observed to John Russell Bartlett shortly after the discovery of the tablets in 1846, "My friend, Mr. Squier, is so enthusiastic upon this subject, that he goes off half-cocked sometimes (as the Western phrase is)."[12] Squier interpreted the find as evidence of the Mound Builders' "higher grade of art" and of their probable religious conceptions. Squier little doubted that the tablets were highly venerated within the proscriptions of the Mound Builders' religion, and he became enthralled in speculation concerning the possible significance of their serpentine design:

The serpent entered widely into the superstitions of the American nations, savage and semicivilized, and was conspicuous among their symbols as the emblem of the greatest gods of their mythology, both good and evil. And wherever it appears, whether among the carvings of the Natchez (who, according to Charlevoix, placed it upon their altars as an object of worship), among the paintings of the Aztecs, or upon the temples of Central America, it is worthy of remark that it is invariably a rattlesnake. . . . As such it appears in the crown of Tezcatliopoca, the Brahman of the Aztec pantheon, and in the helmets of the warrior priests of that divinity. The featherheaded rattlesnake, it should be observed, was in Mexico the peculiar symbol of Tezcatliopoca, otherwise symbolized as the sun. (Squier and Davis 1848:276)

The serpent symbol, associated here with sun worship, seemed to link the mythological system of the Mound Builders with those of the Natchez, the Aztecs, and the aboriginal inhabitants of Central America. Such analogies, if fully investigated, were certain to shed much light on the development of "the primitive superstitions of remotely separated people, and especially upon the origin of the American race" (Squier and Davis 1848:98). Just how it was that the serpent symbol had "penetrated into America" and how its presence here was significant in terms of "the origin of the American race," Squier did not then say. Tracing the origin of universal ideas and symbols is one thing; tracing the origin of races of people is quite another. If the former did not necessarily suggest a common origin or more-than-accidental communication between the Old and New Worlds at a remote time, the latter certainly did. Squier never adequately addressed the implication of that comment in any of his subsequent writings, although he was still grappling with the problem several years later in *The Serpent Symbol*. Such analogies could be made more easily than they could be proven, even when they seemed to be more than mere coincidence and were subjected to the severest tests of critical scrutiny. Those analogies were both an allusive and illusive subject of inquiry.

By the conclusion of his investigation with Davis, Squier had become so preoccupied with this line of inquiry that he contemplated writing a book on the subject. He could not ignore, he wrote Joseph Henry, the "connections existing between our Western Monuments and those of Central America, and incidentally with those of Southern Asia." His investigations in Ohio had led him to "an analysis of the religion and mythology of the Savage and Semi-Civilized nations of this continent, in connection with those primitive beliefs which have undergone so many modifications (yet retain their original features) in Asia." He regarded the results of those investigations to be "truly remarkable," and again stated his certainty that once completed they would bring new evidence to bear upon the "the origin and antiquity of the American race." The confidence and enthusiasm he expressed in those findings are worthy of note: "I speak with almost absolute certainty when I say that I have the key to the whole system of our aboriginal religion, North and South, and that I have identified not only the original purpose of the imposing monuments of Central America, but the very nature of the worship and the divinities to which they were dedicated."[13] Squier was uncertain whether he should embody those findings in the volume he was preparing for the Smithsonian, for they were based upon the discoveries that he and Davis had made jointly in Ohio and were legitimately connected with them. But owing to his open feud with Davis over their respective contributions to those investigations and authorship of the Squier-Davis manuscript forthcoming from the Smithsonian, he wanted it known that conceptually those ideas were exclusively his own (Barnhart 1983, 1989). His "best friends" had advised him to reserve those considerations for a separate volume under Squier's name only, but he was reluctant to do so since he feared that he might never again have the opportunity to present his views on the subject before the public.

Squier's growing interest in pursuing these investigations beyond casual mention can also be seen in his dispute with Joseph Henry, secretary of the Smithsonian Institution, over the elimination of certain "theoretical matter" from the Squier-Davis manuscript just prior to its printing. Determined to establish the highest standard of scholarship for the works published by the Smithsonian, Henry asserted himself with Squier by insisting that theorizing be eliminated, or at least kept in a subordinate position to facts. He also eliminated several engravings that Squier had garnered from other sources, restricting him to original illustrations relating directly to the Squier-Davis surveys, excavations, and artifacts, and those of their collaborators.[14] Henry's editorial prerogative in this matter incensed Squier, who denied that he had any theories to propound and angrily declared himself to be just as competent as Henry in deciding what should and should not be eliminated from the manuscript. Chiding Henry's timidity, he asserted that "It will be time enough to get frightened and cry 'wolf' when the wolf is seen."[15] Although the theoretical matter alluded to was not specified, it most certainly related to Squier's preoccupation with inferring the religious conceptions and practices of the Mound Builders through cultural analogies with other aboriginal peoples in America and with the early nations of the Old World. Apparently, Squier had inserted illustrative materials into the manuscript that would enable his readers to make the necessary comparisons.

Squier complained to Samuel George Morton that *Ancient Monuments of the Mississippi Valley* had been "emasculated" by Henry's editing. He would thereafter remain free and clear of all "entangling alliances" with institutions: "I have danced to one turn in fetters—for the first and last time."[16] He was further angered at the Smithsonian for its reluctance to underwrite the cost of extending his investigations into other portions of the Mississippi Valley. He complained that he had not received a "red cent" of remuneration or reimbursement for the cost of his explorations, even though the Smithsonian had been willing enough to publish the results. "Rich men may possibly afford to be patronized," but not he. Squier was determined that once his business with the Smithsonian was concluded, "our paths will diverge at a very large angle"[17] Squier's attitude toward the Smithsonian was unfortunate if somewhat understandable, for his reputation as an archaeologist rested squarely upon the originality and disciplined nature of his two Smithsonian monographs. Nonetheless, he did part company with the Smithsonian immediately after completing work on his second Smithsonian monograph.

Aboriginal Monuments of the State of New York was accepted for publication by the Smithsonian in October 1849, but it was not published until 1851.[18] Squier continued to take an enlarged view of his subject when describing his fieldwork in western New York (Barnhart 1996), but in an elaborate appendix (which is longer than the monograph proper) he further develops the cultural analogies raised in *Ancient Monuments*. It is here that Squier placed much of the comparative and speculative materials that Joseph Henry had excised from his first Smithsonian monograph. He compares the defensive structures of American aborigines with those of the Pacific Islanders and Celts; the sepulchral monuments in Mexico and Central America and those of the Old World; the aboriginal sacred enclosures or "temples" of North American Indians to those of Mexico, Central America, and Peru; similar religious sites of the Polynesian Islanders and Hindus; and the primitive temples of the British Isles. He also includes an all-important discussion of the symbolism of temples.

In making these extended comparisons, however, Squier hastened to note that no connection or common origin between the aboriginal remains of the Old and New Worlds should be thereby inferred. Such analogies were logically explained as "the inevitable results of similar conditions" existing among distinct and widely separated peoples. Once again the ideas of Jomard and Humboldt are clearly evident in his formulation.

> Human development must be, if not in precisely the same channels, in the same direction, and must pass through the same stages. We cannot be surprised, therefore, that the earlier, as in fact the later monuments of every people, exhibit resemblances more or less striking. What is true physically, or rather monumentally, is not less so in respect to intellectual and moral development. And it is not to be denied that the want of a sufficient allowance, for natural and inevitable coincidences, has led to many errors in tracing the origin and affinities of nations. (Squier 1851b:99)

That observation expresses a fundamentally important concept in Squier's archaeological thought. One need not look for common origins and mysterious cultural dependencies to explain the similarities existing between the aboriginal remains of America and those found in other parts of the world. Comparisons of archaeological sites could suggest common underlying principles—Squier would call them universals—but did not necessarily suggest more. That thread of logic, although certainly not original to Squier, runs through all of his early anthropological writings, and it explains his interest in developing cultural analogies as a means of explicating the probable origin and meaning of mute archaeological evidence. More importantly, his interest in tracing supposed universals in "the intellectual and moral development" of man explains why he was so intent upon comparing religious ideas, symbolism, and customs from around the globe, especially those of the aboriginal peoples of the Americas.

The pursuit of that objective led to Squier's cognate researches into Native American mythological and historical traditions, which remains a comparatively obscure but important aspect of his investigations. He pursued this line of inquiry in his study of the supposed traditions of the Lenape Indians contained in the Walam Olum manuscript of Constantine Rafinesque, and the Algonquian legends related to him by the Ojibwa chief, historian, and Wesleyan missionary George Copeway, or *Kah-ge-gagah-bowh* ("Firm Standing") (Squier 1849a:273, 292). His approach to the study of these traditions was greatly influenced by McCulloh's *Researches*, Prescott's *Mexico*, Barton's "Origin of the American Nations" published in the *Transactions of the American Philosophical Society*, and Schoolcraft's *Algic Researches* and *Notes on the Iroquois*. All of these writers noted the importance of religious and mythological conceptions in tracing the origin and affinities of ancient peoples, and their views were points of departure for Squier's own research into the myths and traditions of aboriginal America. But it would be European writers who would ultimately lead him to a rationale for explaining religious symbolism and seeming cultural dependencies.

The results of these inquiries were published in the *American Whig Review* in 1848 and 1849 (Squier 1848a, 1848b, 1849a, 1849b). Squier argued for the importance of this collateral department of inquiry in helping to determine the origin, affinities, and connections of the American race on its own terms, without identifying it with known peoples of the world. The mythological and historical traditions of the various Indian groups, he was convinced, would go far toward solving these problems and establishing the rank of the American race in the "scale of human development" (Squier 1849a:274–275). If such original materials could be collected, "they would open to the world a new view of the aboriginal mind" (Squier 1848a:256). Squier also saw in these traditions further evidence of parallels in the intellectual development of early peoples throughout the world. He concluded that the religious, mythological, and historical traditions of the American Indians showed "not only a wonderful uniformity and concurrence in their elements and more important particulars, but also an absolute identity, in many essential respects, with those which existed among the primitive nations of the monumental and traditional periods" (Squier 1849a:275).

Squier's explanation for this "absolute identity" goes to the very heart of his archaeological theory. The "predominant" religious ideas of aboriginal America were based on what was usually known as "Sun Worship," but which he thought should more properly be called "the adoration of the powers of Nature." He believed this to be the underlying principle of early religious or mythological systems throughout the world, and argued that in aboriginal America it was found in its simplest and most vague forms through all intermediate stages of development. Squier had no difficulty in accounting for these similarities "without claiming a common origin for the nations displaying them." As he noted, mankind was everywhere the same in regard to certain fundamentals of intellectual development:

> Alike in the elements of their mental and moral situations; having common hopes and aspirations, . . . moved by the same impulses, and actuated by similar motives, is it surprising that there exist among nations of men the most widely separated, a wonderful unity of elementary beliefs and conceptions? All have before them the suggestions of Nature, the grand phenomena of which are everywhere the same; and all from the observance would be apt to arrive at similar results. (Squier 1849b:393)

Similarities in religious symbolism among widely separated peoples, therefore, were a natural and predictable phenomenon. Since the development of a symbolic system to convey abstract religious ideas was a necessity among all nonliterate peoples, the presence in aboriginal America of religious symbols and associated observances that were essentially the same as those that existed among early peoples in the Old World could be logically explained. Such similarities were entirely attributable to universals in human reasoning and could not be used in support of popular theories that derived the American Indian from Tartary, Hindustan, or the Mediterranean. Analogies among the beliefs and practices of distinct peoples could thus be developed "without sinking the Atlantides in an overwhelming cataclysm, or leading vagrant tribes 'through deserts vast, and regions of eternal snow'; or invoking the shadowy Thorfinn, or the apocryphal 'Madoc, with his ten ships,' to account for the form of a sacrifice, or the method of an incantation" (Squier 1849b:394). That rationale for explaining parallels in cultural development runs throughout Squier's early writings. Once again, the influence of Jomard and Humboldt is clearly evident in that formulation.

Squier finally gave full expression to these ideas in *The Serpent Symbol, and the Worship of the Reciprocal Principles of Nature in America*, published in 1851. The work is quite appropriately dedicated to Edme François Jomard, whose interest in the comparative study of archaeological remains and correspondence with Squier ultimately led to its production. It was the first and last volume of Squier's self-styled American Archaeological Researches series.[19] Although the comparatively obscure *Serpent Symbol* is decidedly of a different character from Squier's Smithsonian monographs, it is intimately connected with them in many ways. Freed from the restraining hand of Joseph Henry, Squier indulged in speculation that previously had been kept within proper limits. *The Serpent Symbol* is at its worst a cut-and-paste elaboration of his earlier writings, and at its best Squier's boldest, most philosophical, and most original conception of aboriginal America. Squier himself had ambivalent feelings about the work. As he confided to Samuel George Morton, "*Snake* 'drags its slow length along,' and when published will probably be bought by three persons, read by two, and understood by one!"[20] The work has largely remained a footnote to his career.

The Serpent Symbol is Squier's attempt to discover the underlying principles of the aboriginal religions of America, as revealed through mythological conceptions and historical traditions, the iconography of archaeological remains, and the study of analogous beliefs and antiquities in the Old World. The significance of the work, in contrast to his Smithsonian monographs, lies not in its original contributions to knowledge but in the boldness of its approach and the ambitiousness of its goals. The primary purpose of his researches was to establish the "essential identity" in some of the fundamental religious conceptions of ancient peoples in the Old and New Worlds, and to illustrate similarities in their manner of expressing them through symbolical systems—to wit, "the machinery of creation, the multiplication of gods, and the investing of them with attributes" (Squier 1851a:viii). Squier investigated these subjects in the spirit of Humboldt, who remarked in the introduction to his *Researches* that "we shall be surprised to find, towards the end of the 15th century, in a world which we call new, those ancient institutions, those religious notions, and that style of building which seem in Asia to indicate the dawn of civilization" (1814, 1:2). The occurrence of those similarities had led many to conclude that they were based upon "an original connection—especially as such a conclusion is in strict harmony with popular prejudice" (Squier 1851a:ix).

But before that conclusion could be accepted, it was first necessary to ask how similar conditions and similar mental, moral, and physical "constitutions" might result in institutions, religions, and archaeological remains of an analogous or "cognate type." Received opinion on the subject could not be accepted as conclusive, for at no previous time were the materials for the comparative study of man more abundant. Many of the "great collateral questions of natural science" had been answered in recent years, while geographic exploration had advanced knowledge about the religions, institutions, histories, and customs of nations around the globe. Archaeologists could now make systematic comparisons among groups greatly separated by time and place, and evaluate "the relations" they sustained one to the other. "For no sciences are so eminently inductive," said Squier, "as Archaeology and Ethnology, or the Sciences of Man and Nations; none which require so extensive a range of facts to their elucidation" (1851a:ix).

In elucidating those facts, Squier revealed an extensive breadth of learning and an avowed disposition to favor no established theories or opinions. "In pursuing my investigations, I have sought only to arrive at truth, however much it may conflict with preconceived notions, or what are often called 'established opinions.' I have no system to sustain, no creed to defend; but entertain as many hypotheses as there are possibilities, and claim to be ready to reject or accept according to the weight of evidence and the tendency of facts" (1851a:ix). There was clearly no concession to monogenism and biblical ethnology in that statement, but neither was there an endorsement of polygenism. Yet Squier's sympathy for the doctrine of separate origins seemed clear enough to some. The Reverend Dr. Francis L. Hawks, a founder of the American Ethnological Society and a biblical ethnologist, reportedly considered *The Serpent Symbol* "a most adroit and dangerous attack on the Christian religion."[21] Squier found that assertion "rather cool in consideration of the fact that the Bible and Christianity were not even discussed."

Squier doubted that the unity and distinctiveness of the American race would have ever been called into question were it not for the efforts of scholars to rationalize the existence of the American Indian with the Bible (which required all branches of the human species to be derived from a single pair). But as it was, many persisted in the belief that American Indians were descendants of one or more of the nations known in ancient history, and directed their inquiries toward establishing which group or groups had been the progenitors of the American Indian. Squier, like other members of the American School of anthropolgy, saw no need to rationalize the Bible and the American Indian, nor to derive them from the lost tribes of Israel or any other hypothetical ancestors in the Old World. Those who persisted in doing so based upon the alleged proofs of analogy ignored a more plausible explanation, such as that made by the English theologian William Warburton (1698-1779) in his *Divine Legation of Moses* (1738-1765). They had, said Warburton, committed "the old, inveterate error, that a similitude of customs and manners, amongst the various tribes of mankind most remote from each other, must needs arise from some communication. Whereas human nature, without any help, will in the same circumstances always exhibit the same appearances" (Warburton 1741, 3:991, cited in Squier 1849b:390).

As a result of his own investigations into the religious conceptions of the American Indian, Squier was certain that the predominant religious ideas and symbols of American Indian groups were rooted in sun worship, or Sabianism. The worship of the sun or fire, to Squier the universal symbol of the procreative power in nature, should be more properly called the worship of the reciprocal powers of nature—a universal form of worship that predated history to the earliest periods of man's social development. The worship of nature was the basis of all ancient mythological systems, as was found among American Indians in all parts of the continent. These were inherent psychological principles deeply ingrained in man's early religious beliefs, and they did not, according to Squier, denote common origins for the various nations sharing them. The reciprocal principles of nature were not exclusively expressed in sun worship, for they often took the form of phallic worship in the Old and New Worlds. He deduced the essential elements of phallicism from the ancient religions of Asia and Europe—Ouranus and Gia, Osiris and Isis, the Ligham and Yoni of Hindustan—and explained the rationale of its existence in the Old World.

Evidence of phallic worship in America is also presented. The comments of Dulaure were called to witness, as well as what Squier regarded as conclusive evidence of its practice in America based upon the work of Stephens and Catherwood. He identified phallic designs in Peru and Central America and their probable existence in the monoliths at Copan, presented evidence of phallic worship in the Mississippi Valley, and thought it likely that the worship of reciprocal principles in their various forms had also occurred in the Yucatán and in Nicaragua. Illustrations of the principles in Hindu mythology, extended notices citing Prichard on the connection of the reciprocal principles with the religious systems of Greece and Rome, and the existence of related ideas in the cosmologies of the aboriginal nations of America added further testimony to the universality of the reciprocal principles of nature.

Squier had discussed the rudiments of these ideas in his earlier works, but in *The Serpent Symbol* he elaborated upon them and extended them with supplemental materials drawn from an eclectic array of sources. To attempt such a synthesis was as courageous as it was naive, as impossible as it was suggestive. Squier had taken the eighteenth- and nineteenth-century preoccupation with cultural analogies and given it his own twist, using the observations of Warburton, Jomard, Humboldt, and others as his points of departure. The work also owes much to literary romanticism, which left a deep impression on American archaeology in the mid–nineteenth century. Squier well illustrates the connection between romanticism and American archaeology, perhaps none better, and in *The Serpent Symbol* it was given free rein. His reading of oriental literature, much in vogue among the literary salons of the period, led him to see a "psychic unity" in human thought, and what he perceived to be the universal principle that explained it. He ransacked Coleman's *Hindu Mythology*, Tod's *Rajast'han*, and Savary's *Egypt* in search of symbols and associated beliefs and practices that might aid him in that endeavor.

What Squier concluded at the end of his sampling of world religions was that the serpent symbol, as an expression of reciprocal powers of nature, had figured prominently in the religious systems and symbolic representations of aboriginal America, particularly among the populations of Mexico and Central America. The significance of the serpent symbol in America was "essentially the same with that which attached to it among the early nations of the old continent" (Squier 1851a:251). The parallelism and uniformity he had identified in the elementary religious ideas and corresponding symbols of the Old and New World led him irresistibly to ascribe to

> the emblematic *serpent and egg of Ohio* a significance radically the same with that which was assigned to the analogous compound symbol among the primitive nations of the East. This conclusion is further sustained, as we have seen, by the character of some of the religious structures of the old continent, in which we find the symbolic serpent, and the egg or circle represented on a most gigantic scale. Analogy could probably furnish no more decisive sanction, unless by exhibiting other structures, in which not only a general correspondence, but an absolute identity should exist. Such an identity it would be unreasonable to look for, even among the works of the same people, constructed in accordance with a common design. (Squier 1851a:251)

It was then that Squier delivered his boldest stroke, one that gave monogenists a glimmer of hope and that polygenists doubtless looked upon with disapproval. He set caution aside for a moment in order to "hazard the suggestion that the symbolical Serpent and Egg effigy of Ohio are distinctly allusive to the specific notions of cosmogony which prevailed among the nations of the East, for the reason that it has been impossible to bring positive collateral proof that such notions were entertained by any of the American nations" (Squier 1851a:251–252). What, his readers might well ask, was the point of that suggestion? Squier answered that rhetorical question in no uncertain terms. If one assumed an Asiatic origin for the American Indian, the presence of the serpent and egg in America was not a difficult matter. But if one accepted the view that these rudimentary ideas were "inherent and absolute, or not necessarily derivative," then the "rationale of symbolism" reasonably explained "a general coincidence in symbolic representations, if not in religious rites" (1851a:253). In that case, it was not necessary to derive them from anywhere and to point to any remote period of communication or connection with the ancient peoples of the Old World. Squier refused to state a preference for either of these hypotheses, disappointing those who may have looked to him to decide between them.

If the emphasis Squier placed upon uniformity in man's mental, moral, and physical faculties suggested to some that he leaned toward the latter position, he noted, it was only to counterbalance the inordinate amount of unsound speculation and errors that feeble analogies had often occasioned. The uncritical acceptance of similarities and coincidences, real or imagined, as proof of connections depending upon "communications remote or recent" was a fallacy that had to be expunged. Humboldt had cautioned wisely when remarking upon this very problem, and once again Squier called upon him in his concluding observations in *The Serpent Symbol*. "How rash to point out the group of nations on the old continent to which the Toltecs, Aztecs, Muyscas, and Peruvians present the nearest analogies; since these analogies are apparent in the traditions, the monuments, and customs which perhaps preceded the present divisions of Asiatics into Chinese, Hindus, and Mongol" (Humboldt 1814, 1:25).

But the presence of the serpent symbol in America, said Squier, presented no easy solution. He was clearly at a loss to explain it, even upon the principles he had so diligently and consistently enunciated in his works. He easily understood how the annual shedding of a snake's skin might symbolize reproduction, time, or even evil forces, but most of its occurrences were not readily accounted for unless they were essentially arbitrary. The fact that serpent symbolism in aboriginal America appeared to be essentially arbitrary imparted a special interest to its predominance on the American continent, especially in Mexico and Central America. Squier was treading upon dangerous ground here, just as Gliddon had said. Gliddon must have been troubled greatly by Squier's final conclusion:

> This fact also tends to establish a community of origin, or a connection or intercourse of some kind, between the primitive nations of the two continents; for it can hardly be supposed that a strictly arbitrary symbol should accidentally be chosen to express the same ideas and combinations of ideas, by nations of diverse origins and totally disconnected. Hence it is that the serpent claims so large a portion of our attention; for the more numerous and decided the coincidences between its various symbolical applications, the more plausible the hypothesis of a dependence, at some period or other, between the people of the old and new worlds. (Squier 1851a:254)

Those who take interest in Squier's affiliation with the polygenists in the American School of anthropology would do well to reflect upon the meaning of that passage. That he was receptive to the doctrine of separate origins is undeniable, but he was not so doctrinaire a supporter as to reject the possibility that certain analogies, if submitted to the proper tests, might show connections more or less intimate between the Old and New Worlds during the remote recesses of prehistory. Squier clearly regarded the serpent symbol in America as being suggestive of just such a connection, but he readily admitted that such speculation did not meet the requirements of absolute proof. But he was at least willing to entertain the possibility that serpent symbolism indicated a common origin, connection, or intercourse of some kind, even when submitted to the critical scrutiny he himself required. Squier quoted the British oriental scholar and antiquary Sir William Jones (1746-1794) in support of his own position. As Jones had once observed, even the most rigid proofs required of analogies did not preclude the possibility of a least some common origin:

> We cannot justly conclude by arguments, preceding the proof of fact, that one idolatrous people must have borrowed their deities, rites, and tenets from another; since gods of all shapes and dimensions may be framed by the boundless powers of imagination, or by the frauds and follies of men, in countries never connected; but when features of resemblance too strong to have been accidental are observable in different systems of polytheism, without fancy or prejudice to color them and improve their likeness, we can scarcely help believing that some connection has in immemorial time subsisted between the several nations which have adopted them. (Sir William Jones, *On the Gods of Greece, Italy, and India*, 1785, 1:229, cited in Squier 1851a:254 n)

Squier believed this to be a reasonably safe position to maintain. The hypothesis of a remote connection did not necessarily prove monogenism or disprove polygenism, for a people of entirely distinct and separate origins could theoretically have had a period of influential contact at some point in their remote pasts. The fact that Squier openly entertained that possibility is precisely why the doctrinaire Gliddon regarded such speculations as "dangerous." They did not refute the separate origins theory, but introduced untidy anomalies that were not easily explained. Squier may well have been a convert to polygenism, but he was first and last a freethinker. There was no room for biblical ethnology in his vision of aboriginal America, but he was too cautious by far to openly ally himself with all the tenets of the polygenists.

Not all of Squier's interests, ideas, and influences are attributable to European sources. Some were of a more homegrown variety, such as his relationship with other members of the American School of anthropology. But not even the American School was isolated from related developments in Europe, as the works of Morton, Nott, and Gliddon readily attest. Gliddon's self-conscious invocation of a "cis-Atlantic school of Anthropology" must be taken into account. The American School's interest in promoting a more comprehensive and integrated approach to ethnology should be viewed in that light. Squier articulated that concern in his article "On American Ethnology," which appeared in the *American Whig Review* in April 1849. The study of man, he intoned, was "the noblest" of all endeavors, and one that embraced the study of the physical environment, philology, physiology, and history. Ethnology in this comprehensive sense was "essentially the science of the age; the offspring of that prevailing mental and physical energy which neglects no subject of inquiry." As a field of study, he further noted, it presupposed the need to accumulate a large body of concurrent data from several scientific disciplines (Squier 1849b:385). That approach to the study of man was a distinguishing characteristic of all those identified with the American School of ethnology, although it is better known for its racist tenets and endorsement of the doctrine of separate origins.

Squier's relationship with the American School is intriguing. He at no time came out in support of polygenism, but he was clearly open and even sympathetic to its claims to attention. But there can be no doubt about the low opinion he held of those members of the American Ethnological Society who opposed even the discussion of unorthodox views. As a means of circumventing their influence, Squier proposed the establishment of an American "Archaeological and Ethnological Journal" on the model of the London *Ethnological Journal:* "The public mind is very nearly prepared to receive the unqualified Truth; and if the doses are skillfully administered it will one day come to be very well purged of chronic prejudice and malignant ignorance."[22] Squier believed that the conservative doctors of divinity in the American Ethnological Society were not prepared to take the medicine, and understandably balked at the suggestion that his proposed journal be merged into the *Transactions of the American Ethnological Society*. Only an independent journal could be a medium of "sound opinion and truth," one that would be prepared to contradict popular prejudice and "shock long visaged divines." As he confided to Morton, "Every Society and every Institute has its Procrustean bed upon which every thing comprehensive, bold, and manly must suffer mutilation." Even though he regarded the American Ethnological Society as by far the most liberal of any similar organization in the United States, it still had those members "who really believed in a devil [and] that the world was made in six days of twenty four [hours] each."

Squier did not abandon the American Ethnological Society, notwithstanding his strictures about some of its members. He was its more active and important member throughout the 1850s and 1860s, but he continued to struggle with biblical ethnology's hold upon several of its members. He finally attempted the reorganization and revitalization of the American Ethnological Society as the Anthropological Institute of New-York in 1871.[23] Squier was joined in that effort by Charles C. Jones, Jr., William H. Thomson, John G. Shea, Henry T. Drowne, Josiah Clark Nott, Alexander J. Cotheal, and Charles Rau. The American Ethnological Society was established in 1842 essentially under the auspices of Albert Gallatin, whose home became a salon for ethnological discussions, and whose purse paid for the first two volumes of the *Transactions of the American Ethnological Society*, published in 1845 and 1848. Its reputation as a learned society rested primarily on the authority of those two volumes. During the early years of its existence the society made significant contributions to ethnography generally, and especially in American ethnography, but it entered into a period of decline in the early 1850s. It published the first part of the third and final volume of its highly regarded *Transactions* (1853) but never completed it,[24] one volume only of some disjointed numbers of its *Bulletin* (1860–1861), and a few fugitive papers.

Matters became even worse for the society by the late 1860s. Of the society's forty-seven resident members in the last published membership list, twenty-five were either deceased or had moved from the city. The number of the society's corresponding or honorary members was unknown, its archives had largely disappeared, and it was without means. It was behind all similar societies in the world and had lost the authority it once commanded. It had become preoccupied, said Squier, "with 'holy stones' and such rubbish ... and [the] apparent sanction of bold impostures" (Squier 1872:18). Those wishing to end that state of affairs met at a regular meeting of the American Ethnological Society held on May 11, 1869. Squier, Alexander J. Cotheal, J. A. Spencer, Josiah Clark Nott, and Charles C. Jones, Jr., were appointed a special committee to report on the best means of reorganizing the society along lines more in accord with developments in anthropological, ethnological, and archaeological science in Europe.

The committee took the newly consolidated Ethnological and Anthropological Societies of London as its model in presenting the Anthropological Institute of New-York to the world. "By the consolidation of the Ethnological Society of London with the Anthropological Society of the same capital, the designation 'Ethnological' had ceased to apply to any society of importance in Europe, and the term 'Anthropological' had been accepted instead." The new name was more comprehensive and better reflected the fact that the study of man required "the cooperation of naturalists as well as archaeologists, anatomists as well as antiquaries" (Squier 1872:20). Squier submitted the committee's report and resolutions on November 17, 1869, and the American Ethnological Society was formally dissolved and succeeded by the Anthropological Institute of New-York on March 9, 1871, and incorporated on March 20. Squier was president of the new institute, George Gibbs and Josiah Clark Nott vice-presidents, and Edwin Hamilton Davis a member of the executive committee.

The new organization was needed, said Squier, because "Anthropology, which is only a more comprehensive name for the Science of Man than Ethnology, has really risen to the rank of a recognized science. It is no longer hazy speculation; its area is no longer the waste field into which pretenders, half-schooled philosophers, vague theorists, and Jonathan Oldbucks of all sorts, may shove their inconsequent rubbish" (Squier 1872:16). Sadly, the American Ethnological Society had contributed nothing to these developments. What was needed was an organization that could promote "a wider and deeper investigation of the character and true relations of the varieties and races of mankind than had ever existed before. . . . But this investigation must be made *ab initio*, or rather in a purely abstract scientific sense. It can not be done by men who, for any reason or motive, bring into the study the element of faith, or adhesion to dogmas or creeds of any kind whatever. These subtle elements of depression of scientific inquiry have been, to a certain degree, the ruin of this Society" (Squier 1872:16). Squier could remember when the question of human unity could not even be discussed without offending some of the society's members, and when introduced it became a matter of protest. In matters pertaining to scientific inquiry, Squier asserted, "the item of faith must be entirely eliminated" (1872:17).

Those developments were further explained by Dr. Paul Broca, secretary-general of the Anthropological Society of Paris and professor of medicine at the University of Paris, in an address given before the Anthropological Society of Paris. Squier published the address in the *Journal of the Anthropological Institute of New-York* as a further elaboration of the new institute's purposes (Broca 1872). It was the physical characteristics of man that most interested Broca, who sought the guidance offered by anatomy and craniology in studying the natural history of man. He regarded anatomy as "the only sure foundation of natural history" (Broca 1872:27, 29, 34, 35). The comparative osteology of human races required representative collections, thus pointing to the importance attached to craniological museums in Europe. Savants in Europe were methodically advancing their researches in prehistoric archaeology and paleontology, and each new discovery further demonstrated the antiquity of man and suggested new lines of investigation. The Anthropological Society of Paris, for example, added prehistoric, paleontological, and zoological anthropology to the branches of study that defined the emerging discipline of anthropology in Europe. "Now, what is the chief aim of anthropology," Broca asked, "if it be not the natural history of man—that is to say, the anatomy and biology of man?" (Broca 1872:35).

Broca also noted, significantly, that there were parallel developments between the American Ethnological Society in New York, founded in 1842, and the Ethnological Society of London, established that same year. Neither society had distanced itself from the older and more fragmented ethnology in the face of new developments. As Broca noted of those societies, by "dividing ethnology from natural history" they deprived themselves of the aid of scholars schooled in the rigorous methods of observation (Broca 1872:29). In both societies, the rise of anthropological science appealed to some members and repelled others who tenaciously cleaved to the old ethnology. The introduction of anatomy and natural history into the time-honored pursuits of the Ethnological Society of London eventually resulted in a schism, one not unlike that which occurred within the ranks of the American Ethnological Society. The dissenting members of the Ethnological Society of London founded the Anthropological Society of London on February 24, 1863, and subsequently launched the *Anthropological Review*. Those rival entities consolidated in 1870 as the Anthropological Society of London. Those parallels were not lost on Squier, who had participated in similar events and discussions within the American Ethnological Society throughout the 1850s and 1860s. It is not surprising that he modeled the Anthropological Institute of New-York on the recently consolidated Anthropological Society of London.

Anthropological studies in Europe received further impetus from the establishment of the International Congress of Anthropology and Prehistoric Archaeology. The idea for such a congress originated with Gabriel de Mortillet, who, at a meeting of the Society of Natural Sciences held at Spezzia in September 1865, proposed to the society's antehistoric section the creation of an International Paleontological Congress. The proposal was adopted, and the congress first met at Neufchatel in September 1866. The next congress was held in Paris in August 1867 under the new name of the International Congress of Anthropology and Prehistoric Archaeology. The Paris congress coincided with the Exposition Universelle, to which many American and European countries sent delegations. Both Squier and John Russell Bartlett attended, Squier serving as a vice-president of the congress and a delegate of the American Ethnological Society, while Bartlett attended as a delegate of both the American Ethnological Society and the American Antiquarian Society (Bartlett Autobiography, 1868, manuscript pages 80–94, JRB). Squier's participation in the congress had doubtless been a spur to his attempted reorganization of the American Ethnological Society.

Squier's aspirations for the short-lived Anthropological Institute of New-York were never realized. It would be left to the next generation of anthropologically trained archaeologists to institute the kind of studies he had endeavored to promote at an earlier date. Squier began his archaeological researches in 1845 firmly within the tradition of romantic antiquarianism, but his archaeological thought continued to develop over the next 30 years. The influence of European ideas and approaches to the study of prehistory played an important part in the process, as he made a concerted effort to keep abreast of archaeological and ethnological investigations in Europe. Squier struggled to free American archaeology from what Bruce G. Trigger (1989:70–72) has called "the impasse of antiquarianism"—the need to connect prehistoric remains to written records and the known people of the past. He is a transitional figure in the history of American archaeology in many ways.

5

Charles Rau

Developments in the Career of a Nineteenth-Century German-American Archaeologist

John E. Kelly

Introduction

I first became aware of the underappreciated importance of Charles Rau's pioneering work in archaeology during archival work I conducted as part of the archaeological investigations on the East St. Louis mound group (Kelly 1994). My preliminary assessment of Rau is that locally he had an impact on several individuals and their involvement in archaeology. One of those individuals was Dr. John J. R. Patrick, a renowned collector, who, with the St. Clair County surveyor Gustavus F. Hilgard and several assistants, undertook the first systematic mapping of the various mound groups opposite St. Louis. These included not only the mounds in East St. Louis, but also the groups of Cahokia, Fairmont City, and the Snyder group, now known as the Pulcher site (Kelly 1993).

Intrigued by Rau's writings, I became interested in determining the contacts and interactions that affected the development of his career. In fact, it is a basic premise that Rau was influenced by several factors, including his German educational background in the sciences; his exodus with numerous other well-educated Germans to St. Louis; his subsequent residence in the German-dominated community of Belleville, Illinois, where he amassed a large artifact collection; and his later residence in New York City, where he began to publish numerous articles. My goal has been to find evidence for some of these factors.

Previous Research on Rau

Curtis Hinsley's (1994) volume on the development of anthropology within the Smithsonian Institution has recently reintroduced the nineteenth-century German-American scholar Charles Rau to the archaeological world. Prior to this, Rau was briefly referenced in Willey and Sabloff's (1974:83) *A History of American Archaeology* in regard to his classificatory work at the Smithsonian and his early publication (Rau 1879) on the tablet from Palenque that had made its way into the Smithsonian Institution collections. Meltzer (1983:6–7) also discusses Rau's insightful perspective on discrepancies in the parallels between North America and Europe, especially those of the Paleolithic and Neolithic. The rapid developments in archaeology toward the end of the nineteenth century, shortly before Rau's death (a period dubbed Eastern North American archaeology's "golden age" by Williams [1991:71]), in effect literally covered Rau's early achievements in the 1860s and 1870s. Justin Winsor (1889a:403) did provide praise for some of Rau's thorough compilations. As noted by Hough (1935:389) in his short biography of Rau, "he was a painstaking and methodical scholar, reaching conclusions from which he could not be shaken. His analytical and orderly mind grasped readily and completely the subject of classification. The first in America to recognize the importance of the study of aboriginal technology, he had great and beneficial influence on pioneer anthropology." Nearly 60 years later Hinsley (1994:42–47) discussed Rau in terms of his career as an individual who tried desperately to find a position in his adopted discipline after his immigration to America at the age of twenty-two. Since Rau's work and role at the Smithsonian Institution have been covered by Hinsley (1994), only the highlights will be summarized.

My primary focus is on the development of Rau's career prior to the Smithsonian position: How did he become involved in archaeology? What were the underlying reasons behind his interest in archaeology? Which individuals contributed to his development? When this research was initiated, I considered Rau's education in Europe to be critical to any understanding of his interest in archaeology. Earlier, Hough (1935: 388) also suggested that Rau's education at the University of Heidelberg served to stimulate his interest in European archaeology and eventually "formed the basis of his work in the American field." I also thought it likely that additional stimulus was provided by his interaction with the German professionals in the St. Louis area, especially those involved with institutions such as the St. Louis Academy of Science.

The European Discoveries

The impact that archaeological discoveries in Europe prior to 1860 had on Rau's thinking are only beginning to be understood. European prehistory has a long developmental history prior to its emergence as a discipline in the nineteenth century. The numerous scientific developments and findings being made during the early decades were focused on the origins of humanity and its antiquity, and they are thoroughly discussed in a number of recent volumes (Grayson 1983; Trigger 1989) on the foundations of European prehistory. The beginnings of European and North American archaeology were uniquely distinct, especially in subject matter. Prior to 1860 most scholars in the eastern United States were examining the origins of the numerous mounds, while discoveries in Europe prior to 1860 were centered around a number of subjects that included the association of humans with Pleistocene megafauna and the discovery of more recent materials such as the Swiss Lake Dwellers (Morlot 1863) and the Scandinavian kitchen middens. These new findings were readily woven into the geological and evolutionary paradigms that effectively established the temporal and processual dimensions so critical to the study of the past. The European results eventually had some impact on the course of study in North America, especially the search for early humans in association with Pleistocene megafauna.

Certainly a number of discoveries in Europe may have influenced Rau during his early years. For example, a few years after Rau's birth, Dr. Philippe-Charles Schmerling (1791–1836) was intensely pursuing fossil remains from more than 40 caves near Liège (de Laet 1981). Schmerling's 1833 publication provided some of the earliest documented associations of extinct Pleistocene species with human remains. These discoveries, along with other similar finds by Boucher de Perthes in France and Father MacEnery in England, added to the intense debate that had been raging in geology between the Catastrophic Diluvialists and the Fluvialists regarding the earth's geologic history (Daniel 1950). Charles Lyell's classic on this debate, *The Principles of Geology*, was published between 1830 and 1833. In addition to Schmerling's investigations on the antiquity of humans, there was Worsaae's (1847) study on the *Primeval Antiquities of Denmark*, in which he outlined the three-age system. Rau (1876) later discussed in depth the significance of these data, but it is not clear when he became acquainted with them. Much of the aforementioned work in Europe had considerable historical roots (see Daniel 1950; Grayson 1983; Trigger 1989). We know that information on archaeological discoveries in the Americas was published in French by David Warden in 1827, and Rau eventually contributed to this literature in the late 1850s and early 1860s with articles in *Die Natur*. By the middle of the nineteenth century an evolutionary framework had emerged from the numerous European discoveries.

The Formative European Years

Rau was born in 1826 in Verviers, Belgium, 15 kilometers upriver along the Meuse from the university city of Liège and nearly the same distance from Germany to the east. At the time of his birth, Belgium had been united politically with the Netherlands for nearly a decade, but in 1830 the Belgians revolted and declared their independence. Little is known about Rau's early life or that of his parents; however, his probate will indicated that he had a brother who resided in Prussia at the time of his death. Based on Rau's correspondence with Joseph Henry in the 1860s, he also had an uncle Gehard Rath Rau who was "Professor of the National Economy" at the University of Heidelberg.[1] There is mention made in the Smithsonian biographical notes of another possible uncle, the prominent German scholar Karl Heinrich Rau.

Occasionally, glimpses into Rau's earlier years appear in his writings. For example, one aspect of his upbringing is revealed in his (1864a) translation of the German Jesuit, Jacob Baegert's, manuscript on the ethnography of the California Peninsula Indians. Here Rau reveals his religious upbringing as a Protestant (he attended the Protestant-based University of Heidelberg).

Gustave Koerner, an earlier German émigré to America who knew Rau later as a teacher in Belleville, Illinois, indicated that Rau's real profession was that of a geologist, chemist, and mineralogist (McCormack 1909:Vol. 1). Presumably these fields were the focus of Rau's studies at Heidelberg, because he was to teach these subjects at one of the medical schools in St. Louis in 1855. The Smithsonian Institution archival notes from his early letters indicate that he had left his studies at the University of Heidelberg for an apprenticeship in the iron industry at Siegen, some 100 kilometers north of Heidelberg, and later assumed the role of a mine superintendent at Remagen along the Rhine.

At the time of Rau's youth and education, the political landscape of western and central Europe was in a constant state of flux. A significant body of archeological and geological literature had been compiled even before Rau left Germany for St. Louis in 1848, and it is likely that his interest in geology and archeology may have been sparked by Schmerling's investigations, Lyell's publications, and Worsaae's three-age system, among others. However, we have no definitive evidence at this time as to what specifically may have sparked his interest in the past, and when. A careful examination of the University of Heidelberg curriculum and instructors at the time of his attendance may eventually provide some of the necessary insights.

The Midwestern Years

Rau's immigration to the United States in 1848 was part of the general exodus by thousands of young German liberals. These young revolutionaries were embroiled in the political upheaval that was ongoing with the unification of Germany and the creation of a German republic. Many of those leaving were well educated. In fact, some 15 years earlier there had been a similar flight that included individuals such as botanist George Engelmann, physician Adolphus Wislizenus, and lawyer Gustave Koerner, who arrived in the St. Louis and settled in communities such as Belleville, where they became known as the "Latin Farmers" (Gentsch 1963). Thus, when the new wave of émigrés arrived, there was already an in situ German community.

Rau's entry into the United States in October 1848 was through New Orleans and, presumably, up the Mississippi River on a paddle wheeler. In one of his later publications, Rau (1884:39) recounts seeing some of the houses on stilts in the town of Balize near New Orleans. While we lack details on his experiences in Germany, a little more is known of his life in the Midwest between 1848 and 1861. By 1850 he had settled in Belleville, Illinois, located in the dissected upland prairies some 24 kilometers from St. Louis. This small farming community, the county seat of St. Clair County, was founded in 1814 and incorporated in 1850 (Gentsch 1963). The community was composed of a mixed population from a variety of backgrounds, including a large number of German immigrants.

The German intellectuals who had settled in the Belleville area after the first revolt in 1833 had by 1839 established the German Library Society of St. Clair in the home of Anton Schott. In 1853 this facility was transferred to the Odd Fellows Hall in Belleville. Eventually this library formed the nucleus of the Belleville Public Library, established in 1889. Rau served as the librarian in 1853 (Anonymous 1853).

The Germans and other residents of Belleville valued education, and during this period a number of different private schools emerged in this community. As early as 1850, Rau taught in one of the first schools for German and English students formed by the Belleville School Association (Gentsch 1963:111; Raab 1898). Until 1852, he taught German as well as history, geography, and natural sciences. Rau and another teacher were heavily criticized in the *Belleville Zeitung* by John Kraus, an immigrant teacher from Frankfort, for not being trained elementary school teachers (Raab 1898:8).

After his librarian position, Rau was hired in August 1855 to lecture on mineralogy, geology, and general botany in Dr. Adam Hammer's newly chartered medical school, the St. Louis College of Medicine and Natural Science. This facility closed the following winter because several faculty members from Europe did not arrive. Hammer had also been educated at the University of Heidelberg and had arrived in 1848. Also on the faculty was another Heidelberg graduate, J. Schiel, who was to teach natural philosophy and chemistry. This institution later reopened as the Humboldt Institut in 1859, but Rau was not involved. What was important in part about Hammer was his insistence on a more rigorous medical education (Bull 1909). This rigor prevailed in most of the German-educated scholars, including Rau.

In 1857, Rau established a boys' school in Belleville with C. F. Noetling, a Pennsylvania German; however, this school folded in 1860 after Noetling left and classes decreased in size (Raab 1898). The classes were conducted in the second story over Feickert's Bakery on North Illinois Street. In his memoir, Illinois politician Koerner (McCormack 1909:562) speaks quite highly of Rau as an individual with an excellent university education who taught history and geography. Koerner further notes Rau's inability to find employment in his field of expertise and remarks that "he was somewhat eccentric, but a very conscientious teacher." Another perspective on Rau was provided by Belleville educator Henry Raab. One of Raab's articles presents the only evidence of how Rau became involved in the collection of Indian artifacts, as well as further insights into his personality:

> Mr. Rau had pursued his studies in the University of Heidelberg and had prepared himself for academic instruction. He came of "good family," and had never practically became acquainted with the tricks of American youth and was rather deficient in school government. His general knowledge was comprehensive and in the domain of archaeology he has added considerably to that science. At that time, Indian relics were frequently found on the farms; these tomahawks, spades, arrowheads, etc. were brought to school by the boys and exhibited in the most tempting manner. Mr. Rau was anxious to acquire these objects, so precious to him for his collection, and when he was unable to obtain these by begging and flattery, he would have recourse to stratagem, even to violence. His parsimony would not permit him to obtain these specimens by the expenditure of a few cents, but he must have them to complete his collection. He was a diligent student of the history of the aborigines, and in consequence of his comprehen-

sive knowledge in this branch, he was appointed curator in the Smithsonian Institution in Washington in 1861. He died only a few years ago in that city. In spite of his odd fancies and weaknesses—he was or became an old bachelor—his labors in the schoolroom were not unsuccessful. (1898:8)

From this description we can see the beginnings of Rau's collection in the United States. It is during his stay in Belleville that Rau writes Joseph Henry regarding several items. Henry responds by sending one of the Smithsonian Institution publications. What appears to be Rau's first publication, "Die Graeber von Panama," appeared in 1859 in the relatively new German periodical *Die Natur.* This publication was under the editorship of Drs. Otto Ule and Karl Mueller of Halle, Prussia. It was this outlet that Rau employed in his early writings, with 22 articles on North American antiquities by 1863.[2]

After the Belleville school closed in 1860, Rau returned to St. Louis to reside at Fourth and Almond (Kennedy and Company 1860; Rau 1872). He is listed in the city directory as a teacher, but his place of instruction is not known. This residence actually put Rau closer to the St. Louis mounds, including the Big Mound, which was slowly being destroyed (Kilgo 1994; Marshall 1992; Williams and Goggins 1956). Unfortunately, Rau never mentions this mound; in fact, he rarely discusses the mounds at all. This omission seems odd given the fact that the Mound Builder debate was the focus of much discussion at this time, although it is possible that Rau presented his perspective in his articles published in *Die Natur.* In his later Smithsonian article on trade, he states up front that

> a number of archaeologists make a distinction between the builders of the extensive mural earthworks and tumuli of North America and the tribes whom the whites found in possession of the country, and consequently separate the relics of the mound-builders from those of the later inhabitants. Such a line of demarcation certainly must appear totally obliterated with regard to the relations which I am about to discuss, for which reason I shall by no means adhere to this vague division in my essay, but shall only advert to the former Indian population in general. (Rau 1872:349)

To place Rau and the mounds into perspective locally, it is important to note first that in the 1850s a number of intellectual institutions began to emerge in St. Louis. Among these were Washington University and the St. Louis Academy of Science in 1856 (Bruton 1992). It was in the meetings of the latter that the origins of Big Mound were debated. Never mind that some thought that a race of Mound Builders had constructed this large earthen monument; geologists such as Worthen (1866:314–315) argued that Big Mound and the other mounds in the American Bottom to the east were "simply outliers of loess and drift." Others, such as Nathaniel Holmes, a St. Louis lawyer and academy member, brought in pottery and other artifacts eroding from its faces, indicating that it was a Native American construct. By 1868, several years after Rau had left the area, this St. Louis monument had been razed. For some reason, Rau never became involved in these academic debates; his focus was solely on the study of material culture.

The move to St. Louis put Rau within three kilometers of the East St. Louis group, which was still extant. The city of East St. Louis had been incorporated in 1859 and was beginning to undergo much development. In 1860 he visited an area of Cahokia Creek that he indicated (Rau 1867a) was just north of Illinoistown. During his sojourn Rau discovered ceramics in the creek bank; he eventually described this material in an article published by the Smithsonian Institution in 1867. The specific location of this ceramic sample is not known, although Moorehead (1923:39–40) suspected that it was upstream from his 1922 testing. Moorehead was directed to this area by William Seever, a local collector, who knew Patrick, who in turn was familiar with Rau.

The following summer, Rau visited Monroe County, Illinois, southeast of St. Louis, and excavated several stone box graves. In October 1861 he presented a paper entitled "On Some Ancient Indian Graves in Monroe and St. Clair Counties, Illinois" at the St. Louis Academy of Science. This paper was to be published in the academy's proceedings, but it never appeared. The unpublished manuscript describing the results of his investigations is presumably the one on file at the Smithsonian Institution. Parts of this manuscript were used in a later article in the *American Naturalist* (Rau 1882) that he had presented at the Montreal meeting of the American Association for the Advancement of Science in 1882. The eminent Georgia prehistorian Charles Jones (1873) had earlier described Rau's finds in his *Antiquities of the Southern Indians*. In fact, the two were acquainted during their residence in New York City.

On April 2, 1861, the shots fired at Fort Sumter set into motion the Civil War. Locally, many of the German exiles from the revolt of "forty-eight" came to the aid of the Union. This resulted in a successful campaign to thwart the efforts of the secessionist-minded governor of Missouri (Primm 1983; Rowan 1983), who intended the surreptitious takeover of St. Louis. Whether Rau was involved in this conflict is unknown at this time, but his brief reference (1864b) to a stone hoe recovered in 1861 during General John C. Fremont's construction of an earthen embankment in the German settlement of New Bremen in north St. Louis is suggestive of his presence. Whether Rau recovered the hoe while the walls were being constructed or it was later given to him by an individual participating in this construction is at this time unclear.

Rau's departure for New York City occurred between the fall of 1861 and 1863. There is mention in one of his letters to Joseph Henry that he had returned to Europe two years earlier.[3] This may have been between his leaving St. Louis and moving to New York. While he was in Germany he spoke with a number of prominent archaeologists who were impressed with the *Smithsonian Contributions to Knowledge* series.

Rau's years in St. Louis were important ones. While artifact collecting was common for this time, it was the actual study of these materials and the subsequent publication of the results that set Rau apart from many of his contemporary collectors, such as William Snyder and John Patrick, in Belleville. During this period of development, we discover how he began to accumulate a collection of materials. A portion of these data formed the basis for articles he wrote once he left the area, as well as for some of the German-language articles he wrote while in the area. In addition to collecting data that were used in his analyses and publications, Rau must have also influenced individuals such as Patrick. An Irish immigrant, Patrick established a dental practice in Belleville in 1853 and began collecting shortly after returning from the Civil War. He made it his life's work to map the mounds in St. Clair County, a task he had completed by 1880 if not sooner. Rau and Patrick corresponded over the years, and it was Patrick's collection that Rau sought and displayed at the 1876 Centennial Exposition in Philadelphia. Ultimately, Patrick provided Rau with the hoes that ended up in the latter's collection and publication (Rau 1869b).

The New York Years

The date of Rau's arrival in New York City is somewhat vague, as are his reasons for leaving St. Louis. As noted earlier, he may have left St. Louis for Germany, to then return to New York where he took up residence and assumed the position as a teacher of Irish youths in the city's

Seventh Ward (Rau 1867b). An anonymous article in the *New Yorker Staats-Zeitung* in 1862, apparently written by Rau, suggests his presence there that year.

While in New York, Rau joined or was elected to a number of learned societies, such as the American Ethnological Society. He also lectured before the New York Liberal Club. He became acquainted with two noted collectors, Dr. Edwin Davis and Colonel Charles C. Jones, who were also residents of the city. Davis was the coauthor of the classic mound volume, *Ancient Monuments of the Mississippi Valley* (Squier and Davis 1848). Another acquaintance was a German, Charles C. Claus, who had a collection of German and Danish flint implements. Rau eventually assisted Claus in selling this collection to the newly created Peabody Museum at Harvard University.[4]

From New York, Rau began to publish articles in a number of venues. As noted earlier, his initial publications on archaeology were in the German periodical *Die Natur*. Of importance is the fact that by the time Rau corresponded with Henry in 1863 regarding the publication of articles by the Smithsonian Institution, he had already published some "twenty-two articles on North American Antiquities, . . . containing descriptions and drawings of our earth-works and the implements found in connection with them." He further notes in this letter that these articles have "been so favorably received in Germany, that I feel encouraged to prepare a larger work (in German) on the above named subject. As you know, there is at the present time a universal interest for archaeological researches prevailing in Europe, and a work of this kind having for its subject the Archaeology of the United States, never has been published in Germany."[5]

Rau's earliest English publication, entitled "Agricultural Implements of the North American Stone Period," appeared in the 1863 *Annual Report of the Smithsonian Institution* (Rau 1864b). This article provides some insights into his writing style and method of presentation as regards the study and classification of artifacts. For example, he relies on his collection of several large stone tools from Belleville and St. Louis to describe two types of agricultural implements. His types were based on the shape of the artifacts. The large ovate forms were classified as shovels, while those with notches were designated hoes. He felt compelled to publish this article, since there was an absence of any modern description.

Although in the 1858 minutes of the St. Louis Academy of Science the term "hoe" is used but not described, Rau's interpretation of these artifacts as agricultural implements employs several lines of evidence:

their shape, traces of wear or polish, and the orientation of the striations indicating the direction of use. From his examination of Davis's collection, Rau concludes that these implements are restricted to those states bordering the Mississippi River. He then discusses the ethnohistoric literature of DuPratz, Garcilaso de la Vega, and Marquies de Nonville for analogies regarding the hoe and the importance of maize agriculture.

In his concluding paragraph, Rau (1864b:380) places Native Americans within an evolutionary framework in which they were "warriors by disposition, and hunters by necessity," having "made some steps toward an agricultural state. But the arrival of the whites instead of adding to their improvement, served only to lower their condition, and reduced them, finally, to the position of strangers in their own land." This recognition of the impact of the Europeans on Native Americans is a theme repeated throughout his writing.

Many of Rau's subsequent articles on cultural material (1867a), technology (1869a), and trade (1872) had a distinct organizational structure. For example, the description of the materials and their context were presented first, along with quantitative information on size. This information was followed by a discussion of his interpretation of the materials, which often relied on parallels with Europe, and then the use of the ethnographic literature. Rau had an excellent grasp of the literature, both in the United States and abroad. In fact, the recent Neolithic and Bronze Age finds of the Swiss Lake Dwellers and the earlier Mesolithic Danish kitchen middens were some of the European discoveries that he used for comparison (Rau 1865, 1876). He visited Europe, corresponded with European scholars, and also amassed a collection of European artifacts that were left to the Smithsonian upon his death (Wilson 1890c).

There were two other articles again published in the annual reports of the Smithsonian that described, first, pottery (Rau 1867a), and second, a cache of hoes (Rau 1869b) in his collection from the area of the East St. Louis mound group (Kelly 1994). These presentations represent the first clear, concise description of materials from the region. More importantly, they were later republished in the French periodical *Matériaux pour l'Histoire Primitive et Naturelle de l'Homme*.

In addition to descriptions of material culture, Rau had an interest in the area of technology, which he explored in the article "Drilling Stone without Metal" (Rau 1869a). In this essay he employed keen observational skills, supplemented by the results of the experimental work he had conducted.

Rau's English publications were augmented by articles in the German periodicals *Die Natur, Archivs für Anthropologie,* and *Correspondenz-Blatt der deutschen Gesellschaft für Anthropologie.* The extent to which he influenced European archaeologists at this time has not been pursued. In 1875, shortly before leaving New York for the Smithsonian, Rau also prepared a series of essays on the European Stone Age for *Harper's New Monthly Magazine.* These vignettes were then compiled into a book, *Early Man in Europe* (Rau 1876). While this work appears to have been little cited among professionals of the time, it was nonetheless intended to inform the public of the numerous discoveries being made in Europe and their evolutionary context. Meltzer and Sturtevant (1983:328–332), in their discussion of the Holly Oak Pendant, suggest that Rau's illustration of the La Madeleine mammoth in the aforementioned volume may have served as the basis for this forgery.

As Hinsley (1994:44) notes, Rau was keenly interested in the parallel developments between Europe and North America. It was Rau's organization and examination of material culture and its contexts that provided the data necessary for studying these parallels. His interest in the parallel developments may have been precipitated by the guide to the archaeological exhibits at the 1867 Paris Exposition, in which "[de] Mortillet declared that prehistoric studies revealed human progress to be a law of nature, that all human groups passed through similar stages of development, and the great antiquity of humanity" (Trigger 1989:100).

Some basis for de Mortillet's influence on Rau's writings can be found in a number of instances, including a brief note on the conference in *The Historical Magazine* (Rau 1867b), a subsequent letter on this exposition, and later discussion of Rau's interest in the parallelism between the two continents.[6] Rau was also familiar with Gabriel de Mortillet, having had de Mortillet reprint some of his Smithsonian Institution articles (1867a, 1869b) in *Matériaux pour l'Histoire Primitive et Naturelle de l'Homme.*

Rau's interest in the parallels between Europe and North America were presented in a letter to Henry suggesting a publication by the Smithsonian.[7] Essentially, Rau wanted to prepare a "comparative view of the Stone Age in Europe and America." Henry was receptive to this idea initially,[8] thinking that this was a "sketch of the present state of American Archaeology, making such comparisons with that of Europe as the material at present would warrant, and that this would be suitable for an annual report or miscellaneous collection."[9]

However, George Gibbs, with whom Rau corresponded, showed Henry a letter he received from Rau that apparently outlined a much more extensive volume than had been suggested to Henry. Henry was not completely opposed to such a volume, but noted that such an undertaking, of which Rau was capable, entailed "a large amount of original research, not in the line of printed matter, but in that of investigations, explorations, the comparison of an extended series of aboriginal implements, etc.."[10] In the same letter, Henry goes on to express his doubts that the time had not arrived for such a work, and that although "a lively interest is now awakened as to the subject of archaeology, and much attention is given to the collection of implements and facts relating to the aboriginal inhabitants of this continent," what was required at this time was "sketches of progress, suggestions of hypotheses to direct lines of research, and instructions as to the method of making explorations, and the preservation of relics, etc." Although Rau never followed through on Henry's proposal, he continued to pursue until his death his idea for a publication comparing the Stone Age of both continents.

Throughout his stay in New York, Rau's purpose was to gain employment as an archaeologist in some institution—particularly the Smithsonian, since it was the most prominent institution at the time. The publications he put out, particularly those through the Smithsonian's annual reports, were one means for achieving this goal. In an effort to reach that objective, he maintained a prolonged correspondence with Joseph Henry, secretary of the Smithsonian Institution, over possible positions.

In the meantime, Rau continued his employment as a teacher of Irish youths in the schools of New York. As he indicated in a letter to Henry, it was a task he greatly detested.[11] In 1866 he applied for the position of director of the newly formed Peabody Museum at Harvard University. Unfortunately, he lost out to Jeffries Wyman, whom Rau considered a fine anatomist but not an archaeologist. However, Wyman already held a professorship at Harvard (Appel 1992), and with his Crimson credentials he was chosen the first director. Wyman did conduct archaeological fieldwork, especially into the shell mounds along the Atlantic coast; and as noted by Williams (1991:68), Wyman's 1875 publication on the shell mounds of the St. Johns River in Florida was a "virtuoso performance." In his correspondence with Wyman, Rau, based on his knowledge of the European results, encouraged Wyman to seek out evidence for early antiquities in caves as well (Hinsley 1992). Rau (1864c) also conducted investigations into a shell midden near Keysport, New Jersey, in 1863.[12] Again, he does a credible job describing the material recovered, its context, and its significance. Ironically, he relies on Charles Lyell and Charles Darwin, not for their contributions to stratigraphy and evolution, but for the ethnographic data they had collected along the coast of Georgia and Tierra del Fuego.

In the Loop: The Smithsonian Years

In 1875, apparently on the verge of joblessness, Rau obtained a one-year position with the Smithsonian Institution to organize the archaeological collections for the 1876 Centennial Exposition in Philadelphia.[13] This job eventually turned into a full-time position with the Smithsonian, and Rau subsequently became the curator of antiquities in the National Museum, a position he held until his death in 1887.

Although secure in his job at the Smithsonian, Rau continued to publish. Of particular ethical interest was his divestiture of further personal collecting of materials (Wilson 1890c). In part this was initiated by Henry in his letter offering Rau a position in 1875.[14] The focus of Rau's publications shifted to important items that had made their way into the museum. Again, many of these items were described in brief articles in the annual report. Rau also maintained the catalogs, organized the collections (a task for which he was well suited), and published a catalog of the materials in the museum. His theoretical focus continued to be on the parallel developments between Europe and America (Hinsley 1994). In 1882, Rau received an honorary Ph.D. from the University of Freiberg in Germany. He had additional plans to publish on the antiquity of humans in the New World, but his death in July 1887 cut this effort short.

Summary

As with many careers, there are developmental stages that are affected by different influences. Rau's development as an archaeologist consists of four stages, including his European education, his period of collecting in the Midwest, the analysis and publication of the collections, and his career within the Smithsonian. The suppositions put forth at the beginning of this chapter regarding the development of his career remain unresolved. Rau's educational background in geology and mineralogy at the University of Heidelberg effectively laid the groundwork. However, it is unclear whether he had already developed an interest in European archaeology at that time, as proposed by Hough (1935).

Rau's 13 years in the St. Louis area as a teacher and librarian provided him with an opportunity to conduct some "excavations" and collect materials that formed the basis of a number of later publications. In fact, he had already begun to publish in a German periodical on New World antiquities before he left St. Louis. Rau did not begin to publish in English until he arrived in New York City. Again he was confined to teaching; however, the next 13 years in New York City represented a period of analysis and publication on the materials acquired in St. Louis, as well as other topics of interest. Upon leaving New York City for the Smithsonian Institution, his analysis and writing continued until his death. Rau's focus was classification and description, and eventually he focused his attention on the parallel developments of cultural evolution in North America and Europe. He maintained that all humans passed through the same technological stages, and thus he searched diligently in the Americas for these parallels. Rau was probably influenced by the numerous evolutionary works that emanated from Europe in the 1850s and 1860s.

In the end, Rau had achieved what was presumably his goal, to become a respected archaeologist. He was dedicated to his profession, even when he was unable to find work. He continued to publish on his earlier collections, and while he contributed little in the way of fieldwork, he did conduct excavations and understood the importance of stratigraphy from a geological standpoint. However, there are no records of his excavations, although he alludes to some maps in one of his unpublished manuscripts. He was a keen observer of materials and their context. As such, he pursued the parallel levels of development between the Old and New Worlds, and this was an important conduit for the exchange of ideas and materials (Hinsley 1994).

With the emergence of the Bureau of Ethnology under the direction of John Wesley Powell and his Mound Survey under the tutelage of Cyrus Thomas, the Smithsonian emerged as an archaeological powerhouse. The contributions of this agency and those within, such as Holmes, and the emergence of the Peabody Museum at Harvard, under the new direction of Frederic Ward Putnam, simply overwhelmed Rau's contributions.

While there was nothing revolutionary about Rau's contributions, they were nonetheless some of the best descriptive work for the period. His connections to scholars in Europe were extremely important, and this is an area of research that needs more attention. The collections and the work he conducted in the St. Louis area were the first of their kind, and they still stand as the only source of information on sites destroyed by the development of a metropolitan area. In many respects it is unfortunate that Rau left the area and did not continue his writings on the unique resources there. However, he was interested in larger questions, ones that have only begun to be addressed.

Acknowledgments

Attempts to understand the history of archaeology require the assistance and perceptiveness of other individuals also engaged in this endeavor. I would like to first acknowledge the assistance provided by personnel at the Smithsonian Institution's National Anthropological Archives and the Smithsonian Institution Archives over the last decade. It was here I first met David Meltzer, who provided some initial guidance and more recently took the time to read and provide comments on an earlier draft of this chapter. His encouragement and suggestions have been greatly appreciated. As always, Scott Bruton has provided assistance in tracking down and forwarding some critical archival materials from the Smithsonian. Jim Kraaker of the Smithsonian Institution was also helpful in examining the Smithsonian catalog initially created by Rau. Lucretia Kelly has continued to read and reread the various drafts with many useful suggestions. Finally, I would like to thank the editors, Stephen Williams and David Browman, for including me in this volume. Their constant dialogue and feedback on what has been a unique adventure into the dark closets of our discipline's early development has provided an important glimpse of the complexity and level of sophistication already achieved by the mid–nineteenth century.

6

Europe's Prehistoric Dawn Reproduced
Daniel Wilson's Magisterial Archaeology

Alice B. Kehoe

Introduction

The standard histories of archaeology (Daniel 1967; Trigger 1989; Willey and Sabloff 1993) credit John Lubbock, Lord Avebury, with establishing the science of prehistoric archaeology. In this chapter, I will show that Lubbock's claim does not stand against the clear priority of Daniel Wilson (Kehoe 1991, 1998). Wilson constructed the science of prehistoric archaeology, for English speakers, in two books, his 1851 *Archaeology and Prehistoric Annals of Scotland* (the first use of the word "prehistory" in English [OED]) and his 1862 *Prehistoric Man*, and in the principal article on "Archaeology" in both the eighth (1853) and ninth (1878a/1900) editions of the *Encyclopaedia Britannica*. Sir James Simpson, addressing the Society of Antiquaries of Scotland a decade after the publication of *Archaeology and Prehistoric Annals of Scotland*, declared that it transformed archaeology "from the Archaeology of our forefathers, [with] as little relation to their antiquarianism as modern chemistry and modern astronomy have to their former prototypes" (1861:5). Wilson's *Prehistoric Man*, especially its 1876 third edition, presented American Indian archaeology within a Eurocentric world perspective. Like water to a fish, this framework seems so comfortable to archeologists that it was generally unremarked until NAGPRA (Native American Graves Protection and Repatriation Act) opened the Pandora's box of multiple pasts.

©Alice B. Kehoe

Daniel Wilson and the Construction of a Science of Prehistoric Archaeology

Daniel Wilson (1816–1892) was born in Edinburgh to a tradesman's family (Ash et al. 1999; Kehoe 1998:14). With his younger brother George, who would become the first director of the National Museum of Technology in Edinburgh, Daniel as a boy explored widely around his hometown. Too poor to matriculate at Edinburgh University, he trained as an art engraver and in the mid-1840s published a thoroughly researched history of Edinburgh buildings and neighborhoods, illustrated by his own engravings. This work gained him the patronage of Robert Chambers, reformer, publisher (W. & R. Chambers Ltd.), and author of the anonymously published 1844 best-seller *Vestiges of the Natural History of Creation*. In that book, Chambers proposed a deist evolution with two fundamental laws, the law of gravity for inorganic matter and the law of variety-production for organic matter.[1] (Peter Roget had first proposed the law of variety-production in 1830.) Chambers was a monogenist and insisted that in every race, from time to time, innovative genius appears, and that those populations in more frequent contact with others profit from the diffusion of useful innovations.

Under Chambers's leadership, and following an 1846 visit solicited by Chambers from the Dane Jens Worsaae, Wilson organized the collections of the Society of Antiquaries of Scotland. Chambers was an avocational geologist studying ancient shorelines of the North Sea, hence he visited Denmark, met Worsaae, and determined to bring the Thomsen three-age system to Scotland. For Chambers and his protégé Wilson, geology was the model as well as sister science for prehistoric archaeology. Chambers's efforts culminated in 1851 with the establishment of the National Museum of Scotland, housing the Antiquaries' collection organized by Wilson on the four-age system (Christianity is the fourth age) (Kehoe 1998:16). Wilson expanded and published his catalog of the collections the same year as *Archaeology and Prehistoric Annals of Scotland*.

Wilson's introduction of the term "prehistoric" into English, his active collegial engagement, and his continuing exposition of prehistoric archaeology led successive editors to select him to write the principal article on archaeology for the eighth (1853) and ninth (1878a/1900) editions of the *Encyclopaedia Britannica*. This reference work was subsequently published in American editions. In close to 14,000 words, Wilson established archaeology within Quaternary studies as the link between geology and history. Like geologists, archaeologists lack written texts and must depend upon inductive logic to interpret stratigraphically sequenced data; unlike paleontologists, archaeologists study humans through their works, less clearly and definitively linked to originating behavior than are the fossils of organic beings. Archaeologists' proximate goals are local and national culture histories, ultimately the entire evolutionary history of humankind. "Nearly all the phenomena which pertain to the natural history of man, and to the historic development of the race, may be witnessed in their various stages in contemporary races of our own day" (Wilson 1878a/1900:335). Under the unilinear and Eurocentric schema, national histories are subsumed under humanity's common evolution. Any one of the more evolved nations (e.g., Britain) can serve as an exemplar of the full trajectory of evolution, just as indigenous American societies can exemplify less-evolved stages.

Because northern Europe had been outside the Roman Empire, its prehistoric epoch was prolonged compared to southern Europe and England. This circumstance dramatized the distinction between antiquarians (like Walter Scott's [1816] Jonathan Oldbuck), who were always seeking material aspects of canonical classical texts, and prehistoric archaeologists, who were obliged to construct scientific argument from mute data. Wilson emphasizes the "scientific accuracy" resulting from "an intelligent system of chronological sequence," that formalized by Scandinavian archaeologists "who from their very geographical position were happily freed from the confusing element of classical prejudices" (1878a/1900:334). Moving from northern Britain to America, Wilson saw the life of Indians on the Anglo-American frontier illuminating the material remains recovered in Scotland from his remote ancestors roaming similar forests (1876, 1:5). By 1878, Wilson, feeling obliged to accept Lubbock's modification of the Stone Age, presented the four-stage sequence of Paleolithic, Neolithic, Bronze, and Iron Ages, the last confined to Eurasia and markedly stimulating "social progress."

The 1878 encyclopedia article "Archaeology" encompasses Wilson's entry under that title, plus a separate one on classical archaeology directly following Wilson's and twice as long, written by A. Stuart Murray of the British Museum. A bibliography is appended to the entire two-part "Archaeology" after Murray's article, but it pertains entirely to Wilson's entry, Murray listing his sources in the text. Thus readers quickly seeking additional material on archaeology might assume that the best or most relevant publications deal only with prehistoric archaeology. Under "The General Subject," one sees Lubbock's

Pre-Historic Times (London, 1865); Tylor's *Researches into the Early History of Mankind* (London, 1870); Steven's *Flint Chips, a Guide to Prehistoric Archaeology, &c.* (London, 1870); Fergusson's *Rude Stone Monuments in All Countries, Their Ages and Uses* (London, 1872); Lyell's *Antiquity of Man* (2nd ed., London, 1873); Southall's *Recent Origin of Man* (Philadelphia, 1875); and Wilson's *Prehistoric Man* (3rd ed., London, 1876) (Wilson 1878a/1900:367). Lubbock (a synthesizer of archaeological publications for his friend Charles Darwin), Tylor (armchair researcher after a youthful visit to Mexican ruins), and the geologist Lyell are today credited with foundational work in anthropology. The other books cited by Wilson are virtually forgotten. Note that the "comparative method" using ethnology to interpret archaeology is well represented in Wilson's list. Discussion of archaeological method per se, excavation, is absent.

The bulk of the bibliography is given to sets of references by country: England, Scotland, Ireland, Denmark, Sweden, Norway, Germany, Belgium, France, Spain, Switzerland, Austria, Italy, Russia, Greece–Asia Minor–Palestine–Egypt ("See the articles under these heads in recent volumes of the *Matériaux pour l'Histoire Primitive et Naturelle de l'Homme*"; this source is also listed for France under "Mortillet and Cartailhac"), India, and America. For America, Wilson lists John Lloyd Stephen's *Central America and Yucatan* (London, 1842); Mayer's *Mexico as It Was and Is* (New York and London, 1844); three volumes by Squier; Schoolcraft's *Indian Tribes of the United States*; and Bancroft's *Native Races of the Pacific States*, volumes 4 and 5 (Wilson 1878a/1900:368). Of these American sources, only the Mayer is no longer known: Stephens, with its illustrations of Mayan ruins by Catherwood, is a classic still in print, and Squier, Schoolcraft, and Bancroft are consulted today by scholars. Wilson's list reveals his active engagement with the professional literature in archaeology even when his leadership at University College, Toronto, occupied ever more of his time and energy (Killian 1998:17–19).

Methodologically, scientific archaeology was presented in both Wilson's encyclopedia article and his books as a subfield of quaternary geology that uses comparative ethnology instead of zoology to interpret its data. The copious ethnography of Wilson's *Prehistoric Man* amplified this approach. Its underpinning would be an understanding of stratigraphy and enough basic civil engineering to carry out field surveys and mapping, skills fostered by the popularity of geology fieldwork in nineteenth-century Britain (Rudwick 1985:3–4, 40); Wilson's lengthy exposition, in his encyclopedia article, of the glacial-geology context of prehistoric archaeology underscored its dependence on geology. Not until the 1880s did even leading archaeological researchers (e.g., Flinders Petrie) explicitly problematize excavation procedures and typologies created toward inducing seriation (Daniel 1967:233, 236; Sklenár 1983:111).

Wilson's second edition of *Prehistoric Man* was printed before Lubbock's *Pre-Historic Times* appeared. Even in his 1876 third edition, instead of Lubbock's erudite jargon "Palaeolithic" and "Neolithic," Wilson discussed a primeval "Stone period" and noted the persistence of crude stone artifacts alongside quite elegant ones among, for instance, the Shoshone (Wilson 1876, 1:178). He never questioned the superiority of his own British culture, yet as an artist, painter, and engraver he had a keen eye for beauty and genuine appreciation of the arts of non-western nations. His prolix Victorian literary style befitted his broad-ranging discussion of civilizations. The respected English historian Henry Hallam had praised *The Archaeology and Prehistoric Annals of Scotland* as "the most scientific treatment of the archaeological evidences of primitive history that had ever been written" (quoted in Hale 1893: 259). *Prehistoric Man* built on that reputation. It is chock-full of artifacts and sites and literary references, and it is organized in a logical series of chapters focused on artifact material or site features. Its science lies in adducing empirical data from fieldwork and provenienced collections to support generalizations about human capacities and cultural development—for example, the validity of a "Stone period" is demonstrated through comparison of artifacts from the Paleolithic deposits in Brixham Cave, Grime's Graves, and Colonel A. Lane Fox's (later General Pitt-Rivers's) explorations at Cissbury, all in England, with Wilson's observations during an 1874 visit to Flint Ridge, Ohio: the common interpretation of toolmakers of primitive intelligence is critiqued by noting that "the ruder implements of the [glacial] drift" may be quarry blanks rather than indices of their knappers' mental or manual capacity (Wilson 1876, 1:64–79).

Lack of a university degree had frustrated Wilson's efforts to land a professional position in Scotland, so in 1853 he accepted the post of professor of history and of English literature at the new University College, Toronto. Lord Elgin, son of the Elgin Marbles raptor, member of the Antiquaries of Scotland, and governor-general of Canada, had favored Wilson's appointment. Settled in Ontario, Wilson developed wide connections with a number of leading American researchers, including Dr. Edwin C. Davis (Ephraim Squier's collaborator), Lewis Henry Morgan, and Louis Agassiz, his discussions with these cited in

Prehistoric Man (Davis: Wilson 1876, 2:104; Morgan: 2:276–278, 297; Agassiz: 1:119–120, 2:199). At the same time, Wilson maintained membership in European learned societies and correspondence with British scholars, including Charles Lyell,[2] hosting some, notably his mentor Robert Chambers, during their visits to Canada (Wilson 1878b, 2:148).

In Canada, Wilson met educated American Indians in Toronto and used academic vacations for "repeated visits" (Wilson 1876, 1:201) to observe bush Ojibwa on summerlong wilderness canoe trips with Ojibwa guides around Lake Superior: these forest-dwelling Ojibwa were to him the personification of the ancient ancestors of the Scots. He also traveled to study collections in the Smithsonian, Philadelphia, and Harvard and undertook extended tours of the American Midwest, for example in 1874, to visit its monumental sites and examine collections with regional avocational archaeologists such as Edwin H. Davis and Charles Whittlesley. Since his *Archaeology and Prehistoric Annals of Scotland* was widely known, as was his *Prehistoric Man* after 1862, it is likely that these trips engaged the American avocationals in discussions of cutting-edge archaeological theory with Professor Wilson.

Only a year after his 1853 arrival in Toronto, Wilson presented a paper, abstracted in the *Canadian Journal of Industry, Science and Art (Proceedings of the Canadian Institute, Toronto)*, "Remarks on Some Coincidences between the Primitive Antiquities of the Old and New World"; this topic he returned to in 1879, "A Comparison of the Succession of Archaeological Periods in America with Those of Europe" (abstract only published). The next year, 1855, he published in *Canadian Journal* "Observations Suggested by Specimens of a Class of Conchological Relics of the Red Indian Tribes of Canada West [Ontario]," and in 1856, "Antiquities of the Copper Region of the North American Lakes," in *Proceedings of the Society of Antiquaries of Scotland*. Archaeological reports continued, in the *Canadian Journal*, of "The Ancient Miners of Lake Superior" (1856), "Southern Shores of Lake Superior" (1856), "Discovery of Indian Remains, County Norfolk, Canada West" (1856), "Indian Remains (Simcoe County)" (1856), and "Historical Footprints in America" (1864) discussing Norse in America and questions of hoaxes and forgeries, a topic continued in an 1869 paper. In the 1887 proceedings of the Canadian Institute, he reported "Some Stone Implements from Lake St. John." Again in the proceedings of the Scottish Antiquaries in 1875, he published "Notices of Sculptured Rocks and Boulders Recently Observed in Ohio and Kentucky, United States of America, and of the Probable Origin of the Cup-Markings Which Occur on Stones There and in Other Countries." Besides these occasional archaeological contributions, Wilson published a series of papers on archaeological crania and reviews of a number of major archaeological studies. Most of his archaeological reports and information from books he reviewed, as well as his researches on contemporary Canadian Indian and mixed Indian-Eurocanadian populations, were incorporated in editions of *Prehistoric Man*.[3]

Prehistoric Man, published in two volumes by Macmillan in London in 1862, incorporated Wilson's experiences with Ojibwa as exemplar of ancient peoples, and also gave extensive descriptions, illustrated by Wilson's own engravings of artifacts, of American antiquities, Mesoamerican and South American as well as midwestern. The diversity basically exemplified the Law of Variety-Production, that precursor to Darwin asserting a fundamental natural process of speciation through adaptation to differing environments. A monogenist like his mentor Chambers, Wilson held that American Indians were like other humans in having an innate capacity for developing or assimilating to civilization. He pointed out, in *Prehistoric Man*, that Asian races, like the American, had both civilized and uncivilized branches, the uncivilized either choosing to live a less trammeled life or occupying an environment such as desert steppe that cannot support denser sedentary populations: "The Arab sheikh, wandering with his flocks over the desert, is not greatly in advance of the Indian of the American forests, either in mechanical skill or artistic refinement; yet the Idumean Job was just such a pastoral Arab, but, nevertheless, a philosopher and a poet, far above any who dwelt amid the wondrous developments of mechanical and artistic progress in the cities of the Tigris or the Euphrates" (Wilson 1876, 1:36). These discussions reiterated the monogenist principle that Eurasian and American races are no more than variants—indeed, sets of variants—of the fundamental human condition.

Wilson studied Samuel Morton's crania collection, among others, but rejected Morton's (1839) relatively facile racial stereotypes. Admiring the Mound Builders, Wilson equivocated on whether historic First Nations in the Midwest were their direct descendants. Contra Lewis Henry Morgan, Wilson fully accepted, on material evidence, the indigenous civilizations of Mesoamerica and Peru. For all his Victorian grandiloquence, Wilson was committed to inductive science and diligent in pursuit of direct empirical observations; Morgan took a priori positions and instead of examining material evidence, even secondhand through publications such as Stephens (1841, 1843) or Tylor (1861), boldly proclaimed the Spanish chronicles "nearly worthless" (Morgan 1985/1877:187) and ignored the English travelers' descriptions (Kehoe

1998:172–178). (Wilson's 1876 edition of *Prehistoric Man* referenced Stephens seven times and Tylor's *Anahuac* twice.)

Wilson (1876, 2:343, 347) postulated three routes by which the Americas became inhabited: Bering Strait, trans-Pacific, and trans-mid-Atlantic, the latter two necessarily by boat. By 1876, Bering Strait was, as Wilson (1876, 2:343) noted, "the most favoured theory." A South Pacific (i.e., Polynesian) migration had been suggested by Gallatin on linguistic affinities, Wilson (1876, 2:342, 347) informed his readers, while the fact that the mid-Atlantic islands the Canaries, Azores, and Cape Verde were inhabited centuries before the European Age of Discovery implied voyaging westward that logically could have terminated in the Antilles. Wilson then insisted that the Americas had subsequently become isolated from the other continents and our indigenous civilizations had developed sui generis. This was a necessary corollary to his insistence on American Indians' innate capacity for civilization: American civilizations demonstrated monogenesis, the essential humanity of all the living races. One can note that although he does not cite the classical philosopher, Wilson's position follows Aristotle's claim that human nature is normally realized in the polis.

Macmillan printed 2,000 copies of the enlarged 1876 third edition of Wilson's *Prehistoric Man*. Copies turn up in local U.S. and Canadian libraries, as well as in college libraries, although I have been unable to find a way to trace the 2,000 copies. Bruce Trigger (1992) has argued that Wilson's work was eclipsed by Lubbock's 1865 *Pre-Historic Times*, not only because Lubbock, as a banker, politician, and "FOD"—Friend of Darwin—in England greatly outranked the poor exile Wilson, but also, Trigger believes, because Lubbock's blatantly racist propaganda was more in tune with the times than Wilson's Scottish Enlightenment tenets. Trigger is undoubtedly correct on this point, but I think it is precisely because Wilson carried the Scottish culture that he was welcomed in America.

Scottish immigrants had a dominant influence on nineteenth-century bourgeois American culture (Bozeman 1977; Hovenkamp 1978; Noll 1994:85–88). The U.S. education system is a copy of the Scottish system, from free schooling underwritten by local communities (parishes in Scotland) and public day secondary schools through four-year college baccalaureate programs. Scottish Common-Sense Realism, expounded by Thomas Reid in the eighteenth century and proselytized by his disciple Dugald Stewart at the turn of the century, was a pragmatic philosophy which postulated that truth was likely to lie in consensus (i.e., in English, "common sense"). The philosophy was highly congruent with democracy, as was the Scots' respect for intelligence whatever one's social class: for example, the ditchdigger's son Robert Burns became an acclaimed poet and the stonemason Hugh Miller a famous geologist. Joseph Henry, first Secretary of the Smithsonian, was the son of Scottish immigrants to America. Henry envisioned thousands of ordinary Americans using their limited leisure as he had done, in experiments or collection of specimens, thereby creating a democratic science in contrast to the aristocrats' dominance of science in Europe (Hinsley 1981:152). "Baconian science" was the label preferred by the Americans, signifying the collection and classification of data with the expectation that general laws would be perceived once enough data had been amassed and classified.

The Archaeology and Prehistoric Annals of Scotland was archaeology in the Baconian mode, contrasting to the dilettante antiquarianism, drawing on classical texts, described by Walter Scott in his 1816 novel *The Antiquary*. Wilson (1851:xi) acknowledged Scott as the originator of the modern approach to historical studies, based not on received texts but on direct apperception of the remains of the past. This approach was quintessentially democratic, open to any walker or collector, whereas the antiquarian approach presupposed elite education in the classics. The "Baconian method" was particularly useful in Scotland and America because, being beyond the boundaries of the classical empires, they have no descriptive texts, only relics. Wilson's emphasis on geology as the model and framework for archaeology sanctioned the study of such relics, absent the texts so critical to the learned antiquarians, and the popularity of field geology aligned archaeology with that accessible avocation.

Paleontologists' "comparative method" elucidating the significance of discoveries of fossils by identifying apparently related, or at least similar, contemporary exemplars was extended to archaeological relics through premising contemporary "primitive races" to be survivals from earlier epochs. It was the explanatory power of artifacts and societal customs observed in contemporary non-Western societies that drew the attention of John Lubbock, his father-in-law, General Pitt-Rivers, and Lewis Henry Morgan. Morgan explained, "However little we may be interested in the American Indians personally, their experience touches us more nearly, as an exemplification of the experience of our own ancestors . . . in the Lower Status of barbarism" (1985/1877: 148–149). Indians and fellow primitives, "vanishing races," slid into remote antiquity through this equivalence with the commentators' most ancient antecedents. Plains nations' desperate final wars against overwhelming odds and their degradation following the 1880s extermination of the bison herds seemed to warrant the appellation "savage" (Billington 1985:134–144) and reinforced European philosophers' schema of progress from nomadic hunters to the European modern Age of Commerce.

Here it is illuminating to emphasize the differences between Wilson's *Prehistoric Man* of 1876 and his *Britannica* article published soon afterward. The latter avoids applying the European universal four-stage schema to American antiquities. Taking the artifacts, architecture, and economic practices seriously, many American indigenes could be classified in the Neolithic and Bronze Ages, rather than simply as savages. Wilson (1878a/1900:339–340) states clearly that while Preconquest Lake Superior copper working was not, strictly speaking, metallurgy but rather the hammering of a malleable "stone," the Latin American civilizations were fully within a Bronze Age. No less than any of his compatriots (Prucha 1986:108–109), Wilson accepted the impossibility of indigenous nations retaining their territories and ways of life, but his humane principles tempered that view by recognizing the considerable degree of civilized development manifested by many Indian nations. In the beginning, all the world might have been like portions of America (indeed, the Ojibwa of Lake Superior), but not all America remained in savagery. Unfortunately, this nuanced view ran counter to the easy dichotomization promulgated by Manifest Destiny ideologues such as John Wesley Powell (Kehoe 1998:90; Kennedy 1994:239; Vincent 1990:35, 39).

Controversies over alleged Paleolithic remains in America, best known in the case of the Trenton gravels excavated by Charles C. Abbott with encouragement, in the 1870s, from Frederic Putnam of Harvard, illustrate both the use of the comparative method and its attendant ambiguities when applied to cultural products. Abbott's typology argument was countered by William H. Holmes and Cyrus Thomas, both affiliated with the Smithsonian's Bureau of American Ethnology, on the grounds that the crude artifacts were Holocene quarry blanks and rejects, simple products of Preconquest modern Indians (Trigger 1989:120–127). This argument Wilson reversed when he suggested that "the ruder implements of the [glacial] drift" in Europe might be quarry blanks from ancient humans as intelligent and skilled as modern Indians.

Lubbock's classic criterion for "Neolithic"—polished stone tools—should have called for the application of that term to American prehistory, since beautiful polished bannerstones were widely known among collectors of American antiquities. However, the term's implication of an agricultural stage gave pause to evolutionists like Morgan and Powell convinced that between themselves and American Indians there exists a "difference so profound that few civilized men ever comprehend the mental workings of the uncivilized man, while it is doubtful whether any uncivilized man ever comprehends the mentation of his cultured brother" (Powell 1896:xxiii–xxiv).

Indigenous agricultural methods may be misperceived when fields are called "garden beds" and their cultivation "horticulture," the usual terms for Midwestern prehistoric agriculture (Keegan 1987, esp. Riley 1987:296, 301; cf. Gallagher and Arzigian 1994). Perhaps it is inherent in a Eurocentric model that non-European configurations be marginalized. In spite of his liberal political views, Wilson never questioned the touted superiority of the northern European "race": he respected American indigenes far more than did most of his contemporaries, yet still, like them he was a Procrustes compressing and lopping the possible full import of observations incompatible with the Lockean fiction that "In the beginning, all the World was America."

Wilson's Model as an Alternative History

From an end-of-the-twentieth-century standpoint, Wilson's Eurocentric schema for prehistory is racist and imperialist. Its asserted universality assigned non-Europeans' narratives of their pasts to the realm of myth, their tellers "peoples without history" (Hegel's dictate, Klein 1997:7). The pernicious effect of the nineteenth-century comparative method endures, as Stone and MacKenzie (1990:2) note citing a study of English schoolchildren's interpretation of photographs of Third World families: "schoolgirls in Colombo went home to sharpen their flint spears while watching black and white television. . . . There were no shops and when asked where one woman got her sari from, one group of children claimed it came from 'inside an animal' killed, usually with their bare hands." The persistence of such conflation of geographical remoteness with temporal remoteness is hardly surprising, given that Lovejoy and Boas so copiously demonstrated its antiquity in Western thought (Lovejoy and Boas 1935:8, discussing "chronological" and "cultural" primitivism).

In the 1850s, would English schoolchildren so readily have presumed that distant families live in a Stone Age? When Wilson was formulating his model of prehistory, an antediluvian Stone Age was still debatable. On the one hand, Enlightenment universal histories postulated such a savage origin for humanity, and Thomsen's exhibition of a three-age archaeological classification was a generation old; on the other hand, the notion of a primordial or pre-Babel golden age was not yet relegated to myth. When it came to archaeological objects, many antiquarians readily assumed that those not obviously classical were products of Picts, Druids, pagan Slavs, and so forth—Walter Scott's *Antiquary* mistakes a modern ditch for Antonius's camp, but it never crosses his mind that the feature might be ages older than the Romans. Not until 1859 did leading British researchers agree that the association of flint artifacts and extinct fauna evidenced a geologically ancient human past (Trigger 1989:93–94; Warren 1998).

The three- or four-age prehistory that Wilson and Lubbock advocated was for its time an alternative history as politically radical as any postcolonial alternative histories today (see Schmidt and Patterson 1995 for an outline of contemporary alternative archaeological histories). William Whewell, the Cambridge don who dominated philosophy of science in mid-nineteenth-century Britain, had insisted that the "palaeontological sciences ... probably never will be able to demonstrate, what was the primitive state of things from which the progressive course of the world took its first departure ... not only invisible, but unimaginable" (quoted in Chambers 1845:127). Wilson, Lubbock, Charles Lyell, and their liberal fellows challenged that received wisdom, narrating a history of humankind that, as Wilson said, linked geology and history and by so doing positioned human history in the sciences, to be validated by material discoveries instead of debated according to one's theological or political leanings.

Hindsight shows us the naïveté with which Wilson and other prehistorians objectified human history through their series of preserved artifacts, rather slowly reinforced by actual excavation sequences. Captivated by the excitement of the machines of the Industrial Age (Lewis Henry Morgan [1985/1877:553] said the "railway train in motion ... may be called the triumph of civilization"), these scientists dared to promote a wholly secular history. In his presidential address to the British Association for the Advancement of Science in 1874, John Tyndall threw down the gauntlet: "The impregnable position of science may be described in a few words. We claim, and we shall wrest, from theology the entire domain of cosmological theory" (1970/1874:474–475).

What in the mid-Victorian era was a battle between theology and an upstart science, stereotyped in the legendary debate between Bishop Wilberforce and Thomas Huxley, was only a skirmish in the millennia-long controversies over human history and its significance. George Boas (1948) set out the variety of positions espoused by early and medieval Christian writers, some believing that Scripture recounts history, others considering much of the Bible to be allegory, some bemoaning man's fall from grace, others convinced that the New Testament must be the foundation of a doctrine of progress. Meek (1976) explicated the arguments developed by Enlightenment philosophies within the variegated continuum traceable from earliest classical writers. The four-stage universal history presented by Wilson and by Lubbock was anything but new, yet it was—especially because it was not new, but heir to millennia of heated disputation—politically charged. Progress as an innate quality of the human condition was by no means a truism in the 1850s, hence the passion in Wilson's argument for it.

Racism was a by-product of the mid-nineteenth-century paradigm for prehistoric archaeology. Especially with Wilson's (and Chambers's) view of variety-production rather than Spencerian survival of the fittest, many non-Western peoples had progressed, if not so far as the British. Wilson's mid-nineteenth-century comparisons of peoples were very different from Locke's seventeenth-century legalistic spin-doctoring to legitimate his patrons' capitalist enterprises in America (Williams 1990). Wilson had assiduously examined hundreds of human crania in collections, scientifically documenting their variety and the cradling practices affecting skull shapes, to conclude that crania demonstrate a number of races even in North America and no consistent inferiority in any race. His data supported both monogenesis and his hypothesis, shared with Chambers, that environmental factors plus intersocietal connections largely explained differences in human societies. Such a liberal and strongly empirical position nevertheless assessed non-Western societies as less developed than the European leaders in the Age of Commerce, and condoned their dispossession and domination of indigenes.

The Eurocentric schema of prehistory purveyed by Daniel Wilson accommodated American antiquities. Wilson clearly placed Latin American civilizations in the Bronze Age, and North American Mound Builders close to it—in a Chalcolithic Age, if that term had been invented. It was not Wilson's kinder, gentler Eurocentrism but the ideological dichotomy preached by Lubbock (1865:472), Morgan, and Powell that flattened America's past into savagery (Kroeber 1952:151).

Conclusion

Wilson's *Prehistoric Man* vivifies our common humanity with our indigenous predecessors, making our continent's aboriginal remains worthy of study in their own right. Morgan and his admirer John Wesley Powell were committed to legitimating the Anglo takeover of America, Manifest Destiny, as Lubbock and Pitt-Rivers were entangled in English imperialism. Their coldly scientific publications fit the canon. Although his article "Archaeology" in the ninth *Britannica* consolidated the standard presentation of prehistoric archaeology on the European model, Wilson did not formulate the conventions established in twentieth-century American archaeology; what he did spread, among an earlier generation of college students and avocational archaeologists, was a global perspective illuminating the fundamental meaning of monogenesis. That was right for Joseph Henry's era of democratic science.

Like Smithson's money, Professor Wilson's presentation of prehistoric archaeology was a European product carried across the Atlantic to promote an American science compatible with its European model. Demonstrating the broad usefulness of the Thomsen-Worsaae strategy for investigating prehistory by incorporating it in his 1851 *Archaeology and Prehistoric Annals of Scotland*, Wilson created a second breakthrough, for English speakers, through the global reach of the 1862 *Prehistoric Man*. Its final, 1876 edition organized a wealth of firsthand observations of American aborigines, artifacts, skeletons, and sites, and tested through these data several current debates on racial types and cultural development. Its highly literary style enhanced its authoritative weight, complemented by the prestige carried by the *Encyclopaedia Britannica* setting of Wilson's magisterial article. The article, commonly available in libraries, and the 2,000 copies sold of the 1876 *Prehistoric Man* positioned Wilson's geology-derived model of prehistoric archaeology and his favorable view of American antiquities in the purlieu of the American bourgeoisie. Of course the article and book were Eurocentric—the overarching framework of nineteenth-century anthropology was the already-established universal history of mankind progressing from savagery to the European Age of Commerce. Wilson's work came to be eclipsed, first by Lubbock's blatantly racist contribution to that other well-established genre boasting John Locke's brilliant treatises, and then later by the turn-of-the-century movement toward explicitly archaeological studies. Pitt-Rivers and Flinders Petrie subordinated the comparative method to seriation, both stratigraphic and typological (Trigger 1989:196–202), and Wilson's work became obsolete. In their time, 1860s to 1880s, Wilson's research in collections, his books, and his encyclopedia article fit well into American bourgeois culture and were well received. He did not initiate a Eurocentric worldview—in fact, he liberalized it through his pronouncement that some aboriginal American nations had achieved a Bronze Age—but he accepted and reprised the idea that the European course of development was paradigmatic for humankind.

7

Maine Shell Midden Archaeology (1860–1910) and the Influence of Adolphe von Morlot

Bruce J. Bourque

Introduction

The archaeological study of shell middens, which has occupied so much of my professional career, was not a particularly popular pursuit of North American archaeology during the twentieth century. Indeed, a survey of commonly used introductory texts will find no shell middens used as illustrations nor many references to shell middens in the text. This absence was not always the case, however. As we shall see, shell middens played an important role in the foundation of North American archaeology. Indeed, during the 1860s and 1870s, shell middens were the medium for transferring newly developed ideas about how to study human antiquity from Europe to North America, and more specifically, from European shell middens to North American ones. Thus, though archaeology largely turned its back on shell middens during the early twentieth century, their legacy lives on in the field methods employed by the discipline as a whole. The points of transfer from Europe to North America were the two well-known pioneering archaeological communities of the Peabody Museum at Harvard University and governmental institutions in Washington, D.C., primarily the Smithsonian Institution. Here, I will trace the course of that transfer with emphasis upon Maine, where it first became evident and was put into large-scale practice, and upon a community of scholars at Harvard. However, I will also address other geographic regions and other scholars, leaving undecided to what extent these others were influenced by or were influencing the Harvard group.

The Emergence of American Shell Midden Archaeology at Harvard

In October 1846, the renowned Swiss naturalist Louis Agassiz arrived in Boston and so impressed its scientific community that a year later he was offered, and accepted, the newly created title "Professor of Geology and Zoology" at Harvard's Lawrence Scientific School (Lurie 1960:123-140). In 1856 he was appointed director of the newly created Museum of Comparative Zoology at Harvard College, which he immediately set out to make an institutional reality. The museum's first faculty consisted of college president James Walker, Dr. Jacob Bigelow, Professor Oliver Wendell Holmes, and Professor Jeffries Wyman. Among its first cadre of student assistants were two who are relevant to the story related here: Edwin Sylvester Morse and Frederic Ward Putnam, both of whom had been with Agassiz at the Lawrence Scientific School (Lurie 1960:227-228, 240; Mark 1980:15). As had been the case with Agassiz's colleagues in Europe, many at Harvard, particularly his students, felt overshadowed by the great naturalist, a sentiment encouraged by Agassiz's "refusal to let his students publish, as their own, work they had done in the Museum" (Mark 1980:228). They were also troubled by Agassiz's overbearing personality and his adherence to special creationism in the face of increasingly popular Darwinian thought (Lurie 1960:267, 314; Mark 1980:16). As a result, most of the first group of students at the Museum of Comparative Zoology left in 1864. Nevertheless, the opportunities provided by Agassiz's museum-building enterprise allowed Wyman, Morse, and Putnam to do pioneering work in archaeological method and theory, much of it relevant to Maine shell middens. Then, on October 8, 1866, Massachusetts native George Peabody, a London-based banker and philanthropist, founded the museum named for him at Harvard University (Brew 1966a:1-2). Its first curator was Jeffries Wyman, who was promoted to director two years later (Belmont and Williams 1965; Willey and Sabloff 1993:49).

As these institutions were being founded at Harvard, prehistoric archaeology was emerging in Europe as a discipline distinct from the study of classical antiquity. Chief among its founders were John Lubbock and Henry Christy in England, Edouard Lartet in France, Japetus Steenstrup in Denmark, and Adolphe von Morlot in Switzerland (Van Riper 1993:220-221). The archaeology of these pioneers had a distinctly geological character which allowed them to conceive for the first time the possibility of reconstructing human behavior of great antiquity.

A physician by training, Wyman was excited by Morlot's account of Steenstrup's excavations in Danish shell middens, or *kjoekkenmoeddings*, published in translation in the 1861 *Annual Report of the Smithsonian Institution*, and by the museum's recent acquisition of the Clement collection of artifacts from Swiss Lake Dwellers (Brew 1966a:7). Willey and Sabloff (1993:49) have pointed out that it was very likely Morlot's 1861 article that motivated Wyman to begin research on shell middens. However, it appears that Wyman and his Harvard colleagues had also read an important later work by Morlot also published in the Smithsonian annual reports, his 1863 discussion of the Swiss Lake Dwellers entitled "An Introductory Lecture to the Study of High Antiquity."

The influence of Morlot's 1863 lecture upon Wyman appears to have been profound. Morlot's lecture contains what appears to be the earliest explicit reference to archaeology as the handmaiden of geology to reach an American audience: "We [as archaeologists] stand here precisely in the same position as the geologist who reconstructs the history of our planet. We shall therefore, borrow his method, since our mode of proceeding must necessarily present a strong analogy with his" (1863:304). Morlot gives a sense that recognizing this similarity between the two pursuits—geology and archaeology—will allow the younger to quickly and confidently shed its antiquarianism and to establish itself as a scientific discipline:

> It might seem, from what has been said, that in forming collections of antiquities, and in studying them rationally, the outlines of the science would have been soon traced, and its fundamental principles, which are always simple, readily arrived at. It is long since the collection of antiquities was commenced, but they were considered, as were at first fossils and other objects of natural history, as mere curiosities.... Again, when their meaning was sought, sterile and interminable controversies were carried on, as is always the case at the dawn of a new science, so apt is human reason to lose its way. (1863:305)

Morlot proceeded to discuss the usefulness of ethnology as a source of analogies and of the "distinctive stamp upon ... art and history ... called STYLE" (1863:306). Moreover, he goes on to tell us that "it is not enough that when making field researches we accumulate antiquities merely for the purpose of forming a collection of them. It is of the greatest interest to observe the ASSOCIATION of the objects, in order to decide which are of the same date, just as it is important to assort together the fossils found in the same stratum" (1863:307). He then addresses the issue of provenience:

> The question of special POSITION (*gisement* in French, *laderung* in German) in which objects are found, so important to geology, is not less so when we consider the traces of the human past. The peculiar position of antiquities in the various places where they are met with has often special signification. Thus, to return to the [Hallstatt] graves, their interior, carefully examined, will often reveal the funeral customs and may furnish us with notions respecting the religious ideas of the time. (1863:308)

Finally, he moves on to the matters of stratigraphy and relative versus absolute chronology:

> The question of SUPERPOSITION is connected with the preceding [special position]. It plays here as essential a part as in geology, which it furnishes with the chronological succession of the different strata, since, evidently, an overlying bed must be more recent than the one beneath it.... There are... on terra firma, cases of superposition of deposits containing human relics. They are of great value, for they establish more surely than could be done in any other manner the chronological succession of the different ages. In fact, every distinction between ages should invariably rest upon some direct observation of superposition. (1863:308)

Although Morlot cautions that "mere superposition, notwithstanding its value, can only furnish notions of *relative* chronology, expressed like those of geology, which knows of no absolute dates in numbers of years or of centuries," he concludes his methodological discussion with an attempt to show that, under special conditions of regular rates of alluvial or colluvial deposition, "dates of ABSOLUTE CHRONOLOGY are to be obtained" (1863:309).

In sum, we see in Morlot (1863) the clear outlining of all the principles of methodology familiar to the field archaeologist. Whether Morlot deserves credit as the first to make this geological connection to the study of human antiquity is not at issue here. The point is that, as we shall see below, Morlot was very likely the source of these ideas for Harvard's early archaeologists.

After Morlot's publications, Wyman immediately set about exploring shell midden sites along the northeast Atlantic coast and St. Johns River in Florida (Wyman 1868a, 1868b, 1868c). Willey and Sabloff (1993:49) characterize Wyman's Florida work as more important than his work on New England shell middens, and this may be so. Nevertheless, there are interesting outcomes of the New England research that have yet to be carefully considered.

The first is Wyman's association with Edward Sylvester Morse (Spiess 1985:104-107; Wayman 1942). Morse, a native of Portland, Maine, was initially interested in the potential of Maine shell middens as sources of natural scientific specimens. But Morse's interest in shell middens soon infected Wyman to undertake excavations in several such sites in Maine and Massachusetts. In 1868 Wyman collaborated with Morse in excavating one site at Crouch's Cove in Casco Bay, Maine (Wyman 1868a:565), and also made the first visit for the Peabody Museum to the huge shell heaps at Damariscotta (Wyman 1869:17). In this work, Wyman reveals Morlot's influence by referring to them as *kjoekkenmoeddings* and by commenting upon their stratification. Although there is no indication that Wyman actually conducted his excavations stratigraphically, he did observe that "there was a difference in time in which these layers were deposited, [which] is further indicated by the fact, that, in two of the heaps, a stratum of earth is interposed between the earlier and later deposits, as if the locality had been abandoned as a camping place, and then after a prolonged absence of the natives had been reoccupied" (1868a:571), and "In a few places there is an appearance of stratification covered by an alternation of shells and earth, as if the deposition of shells had been from time to time interrupted, and a vegetable mould had covered the surface" (1869:18).

Wyman's analytical focus extended beyond Morse's attention to mollusk species to include vertebrates. He paid close attention as well to stone, bone, and ceramic artifacts, which he compared to those of several other archaeological and ethnographic cultures, from Europe to the North American Arctic. The source of this inspiration, both in its attention to bone and to analogies from other locales, is, again, likely to be Morlot's discussion (1861:295-304) of similar contents found in the Danish *kjoekkenmoeddings*. The most important of Morlot's influences, however, can be seen in Wyman's (1866a:578-579) inferences regarding the prehistoric cultures responsible for depositing these middens, which are couched in a direct historical approach informed by historical accounts of the region's Indians. These observations apparently prepared Wyman, in his (1875) posthumously published magnum opus "Fresh-Water Shell Mounds of the St. Johns River, Florida," to recognize that the fresh-water shell middens of the St. Johns River also were stratified, and were therefore likely to be the products of human activity, instead of some natural process (Willey and Sabloff 1993:49). Moreover, in several places Wyman noted the absence of pottery in some mounds and its presence only on the top strata of others, inferring from these data a period of antiquity when the occupants had not yet learned to make it (1875:12, 22, 27, 33, 41, 47, 53).

But while Wyman moved on to Florida, Morse's interests began to shift from mollusks to the implications of shell heaps for the great age of human occupation in the region (Morse 1868; Spiess 1985:106). His interests continued to shift in the direction of archaeology after he was hired by Putnam, then the director of the new Peabody Museum in Salem, which was housed in the old East India Marine Hall of the Essex Institute of Salem (Lurie 1960:317; Spiess 1985:105; Wayman 1940). Salem was the port that initiated America's East India trade, and the Essex Institute's extensive Asian collections stimulated Morse in a new direction, Japan, where his exploration of Jomon shell middens earned him great respect by the Japanese, as well as the title "Father of Japanese Archaeology" (Imamura 1996:39-40; Morse 1879). Morse's (1879) monograph on the Omori shell mounds is modeled precisely upon Wyman's (1875) St. Johns River monograph.

The third member of this first generation of Agassiz protégés to have an impact on Maine archaeology was Putnam, who, disgruntled with Agassiz, had convinced George Peabody to found the new Peabody Museum in Salem as an institute for the study of Darwinism and to appoint him—Putnam—as its first director. However, Putnam returned to Harvard upon Wyman's death in 1874 to take on the directorship of that institution's Peabody Museum. Morse became director of the Salem institution in 1880 (Spiess 1985:106).

Putnam's interest in shell middens stems from his attendance at a meeting of the American Association for the Advancement of Science in Montreal, during which he made a brief excavation at a shell midden, noting its bone and shell contents (Mark 1980:16; Putnam 1891:2). His interest in Maine also seems to have originated prior to his return to Harvard, and it is known that he had accompanied Wyman and Morse in excavating shell middens in Ipswich, Massachusetts, and Portland, Maine, sometime prior to 1868 (Wyman 1868a:565, 568). As his personal research interests lay in Ohio and in the study of America's earliest peoples, however, Putnam later hired local operatives to conduct excavations on the Peabody's behalf.

The first, in 1880, was the amateur naturalist and fur trader Manly Hardy of Brewer (Spiess 1985:107), who conducted excavations in Maine shell middens but never published the results. Much more fruitful were the efforts of Abram Tarr Gamage (1838–1913), a postman from Newcastle (Alvin Gamage, personal communication 1997). Putnam first met with Gamage and conducted some test soundings of small shell mounds with him in September 1882.[1] He placed Gamage under contract in May 1886 to institute the collecting of archaeological materials while mining (for use in chicken feed) of the huge "whaleback" oyster shell midden in the neighboring town of Damariscotta (Sanger and Sanger 1986:67). The most remarkable aspect of Gamage's work was that it was organized to recover artifacts and faunal remains according to stratigraphic principles, organizing the excavation into ten-foot squares and one-foot arbitrary levels (Sanger and Sanger 1986:67).

Gamage, however, was not the first of Putnam's associates to conduct major excavations in the Damariscotta shell heaps, for he had been preceded by two women, as described in the local newspaper, the *Lincoln County News*, on September 11, 1885:

> Miss Studley, of the Peabody Museum, at Cambridge, Mass., and Miss Brooks of the Academy of Science at Salem, assisted by Mssrs. W. J. Knowlton and A. J. Phelps, are exploring the Damariscotta shell heaps and have made several excursions to the Bremen shell heaps. A scientific friend informs me that the shell heaps on the Damariscotta River, are the largest, the oldest and most interesting of these ancient monuments to be found in the world. They commemorate a period of unwritten history common to all nations, and are deserving of much thought and study.

Cordelia A. Studley was a medical and research assistant at the Peabody Museum and a student of Putnam's (see chapter 10). Her companion was one of two women, sisters, who were then employed by the Peabody Academy of Science in Salem, Massachusetts. It appears that the results of their work reinforced Putnam's interest in the potentials of this site, and perhaps in its imminent fate.

There is no room here to rehearse the long list of contenders for the honor of having been the first to introduce stratigraphic excavation to American archaeology. Names such as Thomas Jefferson, Ephraim Squier, Edwin Davis, and Montroville Dickeson come to mind for the early nineteenth century. However, it is fairly clear that these pioneers did not actually excavate stratigraphically, but merely imposed a stratigraphic reconstruction upon their artifact samples ex post facto. For the early twentieth century, Manuel Gamio, Alfred Kidder, Nels Nelson and Max Uhle are often mentioned (Willey and Sabloff 1993:82, 97–108). Yet it is in the accounts available for Gamage's work that we can see for the first time the rudiments of a stratigraphic excavation technique. Obviously, one must suspect the influence here of Gamage's employer, Putnam, and this seems the more likely given his then controversial views regarding the great antiquity of human occupation of the New World (Willey and Sabloff 1993:52).

Further evidence of Putnam's probable influence on Gamage comes from a lecture Putnam delivered to the University Archaeological Society at Johns Hopkins University on December 16, 1885, just before Gamage began work on the Damariscotta shell heap. In the lecture, Putnam described what must be referred to as "the Putnam museum method" in some communications in the Peabody Museum archives (Stephen Williams, personal communication 1997). An abstract of his lecture, prepared by another party (Anonymous), provides details:

> He ... gave an account of the explorations of mounds, burial places, and village sites in the Ohio valley [sic] which had been conducted, with the assistance of Dr. C. L. Metz, under his personal direction....
>
> He then described the methods which should be followed in explorations, in order that everything found, from a chip of stone to an elaborate piece of carving [to] seeds, nuts, corn cobs and bones of animals ... shall show their associations and tell their story as a whole.
>
> With these should be preserved all human remains, from fragments of bones to perfect skeletons.... All of these objects should be studied comparatively; their association should never be overlooked, and individually and collectively, they should be compared with similar groups of objects from near and remote places....
>
> Trenching and slicing, he said, could be used to express in general terms the method followed in field work. For instance, in exploring a mound a trench is first dug at the base of the mound. A slight vertical wall is made thereby showing the contact of the edge of the mound with the earth upon which it rests.... This wall is the first section of the exploration, and its outline should be drawn or photographed and its measurements noted. For the latter purpose it is best to stretch two strings over the mound, one north and south and the other east and west, and to take all

measurements from those. After this first section is made, the work is carried on by slicing, or cutting down about a foot at a time, always keeping a vertical wall in front, the whole width of the mound. Each slice thus made is a section, and whenever the slightest change in the structure is noticed or any object found, that section should be drawn or photographed, and measured as at first, and the exact position noted of any object, ash bed, or change in the character of the structure of the mound. (1886: 90–91)

The similarities between Putnam's method and Gamage's fieldwork are unmistakable.

Another aspect of Putnam's work that bears directly upon Maine archaeology was his hiring, in 1892, of Charles C. Willoughby, an artist and amateur archaeologist then living in Augusta, Maine. Willoughby immediately set out to undertake excavations at a Moorehead phase or "Red Paint" cemetery in Orland. Impressed by Willoughby's execution of the project, Putnam (1898b:387) asked him to build a model of the excavation titled "Methods of Archaeological Research by the Peabody Museum" for Harvard University's exhibit at the World's Columbian Exposition in Chicago in 1893. In 1894, Willoughby returned to Maine to excavate another Moorehead phase cemetery in Ellsworth, and in 1898 he published an impeccable monograph on the two excavations. Willoughby's previous work in Maine had been of the ordinary antiquarian kind and, although beautifully illustrated in Willoughby's book, it showed none of the analytical flare apparent in his work for Putnam. Again a puzzle, but this time we have slightly more visible evidence of Putnam's tutelary influence, for he (1898b:387) noted that "the work was ... admirable carried out in accordance with the Museum [i.e., Putnam's] methods."

Willoughby stayed on at the Peabody Museum, becoming its director upon Putnam's death in 1915. As Spiess (1985:111) has pointed out, Willoughby's lasting contribution to Maine prehistory is his recognition of diachronic changes in the region's cultures. Once again, one senses the influence of Putnam, who believed in the great antiquity of humans in the New World. Although Willoughby's tripartite division of Maine prehistory into pre-Algonquian (Moorehead phase/Red Paint), early Algonquian, and later Algonquian has been extended, the units themselves remain embedded today in the regional culture historical sequence. Willoughby retired as museum director in 1928 (Brew 1966a:5), and as emeritus director he finished his work on his monumental *Antiquities of the New England Indian*, after, as he put it, having "finished Mr. Putnam's museum."

Morlot's Influence in Washington and Elsewhere

Morlot influenced more researchers than Harvard's first archaeological generation into undertaking investigations of North America's shell middens, and brief reports on sites from other parts of the continent soon began to appear in the Smithsonian's annual reports. The first, by Charles Rau (1865), reported on oyster shell middens at Raritan Bay, New Jersey, in 1863 and 1864. Rau (1865:371) acknowledged Morlot's influence in all but name, reiterating the criteria for establishing the cultural origins of the Danish *kjoekkenmoeddings* to an absence of interbedded strata of sediment "which always characterizes marine deposits" and to the artifacts and other evidence of human activity found within them. Influenced by Darwin's inference from shell middens in Tierra del Fuego that the Fuegians lived "chiefly from shellfish" (Darwin 1848, cited in Rau 1865:374), Rau concluded that the same must have been true of the prehistoric inhabitants of Raritan Bay, even though he acknowledged that "the broken bones of animals are occasionally met with" (1865:371).

Also in 1863, members of the Nova Scotia Institute of Natural History excavated at two shell heaps on Mahone Bay, Nova Scotia (Trigger 1986:xiii–xiv). Reports on this work commented in more detail than did Rau upon the faunal contents of these middens, and noted that the presence in one midden of a locally extinct species, the oyster *Crasostrea virginianica*, might indicate considerable antiquity (Gossip 1864; Jones 1864).

Rau was followed in the Smithsonian annual reports by Paul Schumacher (1874), who, at the request of the Smithsonian Institution, inspected middens along the Pacific Northwest coast between Crescent City and the Rogue River. Schumacher's comments on the structure of these middens suggest that the stratification of shell middens had become generally accepted, but they more subtly pointed out a feature of Northwest coast middens that modern-day archaeologists (see, e.g., Stein 1992) still struggle with: "These remains are in layers, which become more and more indistinct as their age and depth increase, until the whole is reduced to a dark and ash-like earth, in which stone implements alone remain distinguishable as evidence of a prehistoric population" (1874:355). Schumacher's report is also noteworthy for observations on stratigraphy, for its extensive discussion of tool functions using ethnographic analogies, and especially for metrics it provided on skulls of individuals buried within the mound.

Also in this early series of Smithsonian Institution reports is that by Daniel Brinton (1867). It begins with a brief recapitulation of Rau's conclusions regarding the artificial nature of the New Jersey middens, but goes on to point out (1867:371) that a similar conclusion regarding "many of these deposits"—(New Jersey or more generally?)—had been reached much earlier by Vanuxem (1843). Brinton's (1867:357) main contribution to the discussion was to note that many shell mounds of coastal Florida were artificially constructed and that one at Crystal River, for example, had the form of a "truncated cone" and was "evidently altogether different from the mere refuse heaps referred to elsewhere." However, he (1867:357-358) also commented upon the freshwater clam middens he had observed along the Tennessee River and its tributaries during the Civil War.

The Smithsonian's annual report for 1871 included a very brief statement by the Reverend James Fowler (1872:389) regarding the absence of shell middens along the Northumberland Strait in New Brunswick. Its minor contribution was his assertion that "Their absence may be accounted for by the fact that the whole coast is very low, and, being composed of the soft sandstone shale of the carboniferous formation, is constantly wearing away by the action of the waves." Thus, while Brinton had noted that part of the Crystal River mound had been washed away in a recent storm, Fowler was contending that shell middens could be completely destroyed by coastal bank-face erosion. His observation would later be confirmed for the rest of the maritime provinces coastline as well as the New England coast, where lower rates of erosion have so far achieved only the partial destruction of the coastal middens (Bourque 1995:29, 243-244).

The next—and in many ways the most impressive—in this Washington-based group of researchers was William Healey Dall, who published (1877b) the results of an extensive survey of Aleutian shell middens. In the same volume, he is the author of two other pioneering studies, one (1877a) on the distribution and nomenclature of native place-names and the other (1877c) on the origins of the "Innuit," a topic upon which he also touched in his shell midden paper. Dall undertook his shell midden work during a hydrographic and geographical reconnaissance of the Aleutian Islands under the auspices of the United States Coast Survey. Excavations were made at enforced intervals of leisure, "occasioned by the party which would not permit the ordinary surveying operations of the party to be carried on" (Dall 1877b:41).

Dall was unusual among all these early researchers in actually excavating shell middens, and he was alone among them in suggesting that the differing contents of the middens reflected differing cultural patterns. Moreover, he was also alone in suggesting that some of the middens might have accumulated over a very long span of time, long enough to include both the replacement of some initial primitive, urchin-eating population by an Inuit one and the subsequent change of Inuit culture through "gradual progression" from a fishing to a hunting culture. Finally, he made extensive use of ethnographic analogy, concluding that regional variants in prehistoric Inuit culture had been "modified by the peculiar surroundings, which brought out local characteristics not common to the other branches of the same race" (1877b: 91)—in other words, cultural adaptation. To Dall, such adaptation had transformed the early "low Innuit" culture into the Aleuts, and he cites linguistic differences between living Inuits and Aleuts to bolster his conclusion (1877a:49).

As Dall's official responsibilities did not include archaeological research, his decision to do so bears further examination. Ultimately, this trail leads back to Harvard, which the Boston-born Dall attended but did not graduate from. He briefly worked under Agassiz at the Museum of Comparative Zoology, probably during the early 1860s (Glenn 1991:138–139). Moreover, Dall studied medicine while at Harvard, which suggests that he would have been associated with Wyman, although we currently have no direct evidence for such an association. One final publication by Dall deserves mention: in the 1885 edition of *Pre-Historic America*, a widely read publication written by J. F. A. du Poguet, Marquis de Nadaillac (originally published in French in 1883), Dall added significantly to the work, particularly to chapter 2 (pp. 46–79), titled "The Kitchen-Middens and the Caves," and to appendixes listing faunal species encountered in shell middens in coastal New England and Iowa (Nadaillac 1885:535–536; Stephen Williams, personal communication 1999).

Finally, there is the work of S. T. Walker (1880) on the Tampa Bay middens briefly mentioned by Brinton (1867:357). In the above group of shell mound researchers, only Dall and Walker actually excavated in a shell mound, although Walker admitted that "owing to their great dimensions, and the extreme difficulty of opening them with the limited means at my command, I was very little wiser than when I began" (1880:415–416). Perhaps because Walker was somehow "connected" to the United States Fish Commission, he was interested in the midden's contents, and upon examining them he concluded that even these large mounds were "simply the *débris*, the fragments, of former feasts" (1880:416). Although he is not explicit on this point, Walker seems to be criticizing Brinton's (1867:356) view that such sites were "the debris of villages of an icthyophagous population," suggesting instead (1880: 416) a more broadly based protein diet, including "shark, drum-fish, crabs &c., [as well as] deer, birds, &c." Walker also went beyond Brinton to speculate on how the shape and volume of shell mounds evolved over time, even providing a stratigraphic section (1880:414, Plate 1), albeit a confused and ex post facto one reflecting little true understanding of midden stratification.

One wonders to what extent the shell-midden archaeologists of Harvard were communicating with those who worked for, or published through, Washington-based institutions during the 1860s and 1870s. The Washington-based reports, while inspired by the same Morlot publications that influenced Wyman and Morse, seem to follow an internal dynamic of their own, and yet one suspects, particularly in Dall's writings, that the conversation between the Harvard and Washington-based communities was in fact more frequent than we might be led to believe by the as yet poorly developed conventions for citing earlier literature then in use. In any event, the Smithsonian's interest in *kjoekkenmoeddings* and artificial shell mounds was short-lived, essentially ending with Walker's 1880 report. At Harvard, however, such interests persisted into the twentieth century, as we shall see below.

The Second Generation

Harvard's training of students in anthropology and archaeology hit its stride under Putnam's directorship. It is not surprising, then, that Maine remained among the research venues for some of his students. Not all pursued archaeological research there, however. Jesse Walter Fewkes (Ph.D., Natural History, 1877), for example, pioneered the use of wax-cylinder technology to record Indian songs among the Passamaquoddy of Calais, on the New Brunswick border, in 1889 (Fewkes 1890).

One who did briefly pursue Maine archaeology was a young Bostonian named Oric Bates (Harvard class of 1905). Bates conducted extensive surveys of shell middens along the New England coast, from Cape Cod to New Brunswick, concentrating upon Maine. The surveys were apparently made between his graduation in 1905 and 1911 in the company of, and apparently from a yacht owned by, his father, Arlo, a native of East Machias and professor of English at the Massachusetts Institute of Technology (American Council of Learned Societies 1980:57). Arlo's notes accompany an extensive manuscript report on this work coauthored by Oric and Herbert E. Winlock (Harvard class of 1906) and the well-cataloged collection at the Peabody. Together they constitute a remarkable record of most of the important coastal sites in central Maine, and they have been of considerable help in my own work in Penobscot Bay (Bates 1911; Bates and Winlock 1912; Bourque 1992:80–103, 1995:13–18). Individual site descriptions are accompanied by photographs and stratigraphic descriptions. Artifacts recovered by their test excavations are listed in detail on a site-by-site-basis and then described on a typological basis, including the projectile points! (However, stratigraphic associations of artifacts recovered by their test excavations were apparently not recorded.) Like Morse and Wyman before them, the Bateses made inferences about this material on the basis of early historic records.

Soon after completing his Maine coast survey, Bates shifted his attention to Africa. An obituary published by his friend Archibald Coolidge (1918) provides a brief sketch of his few remaining years. Upon graduating, he took charge of the Egyptian department at the Boston Museum of Fine Arts and soon thereafter joined the Harvard University–Boston Museum of Fine Arts Egyptian Expedition. In 1909 he excavated in Tripoli and then in the Libyan desert, and published a book on the eastern Libyans in 1914. He was appointed curator of African Archaeology and Ethnology at the Peabody Museum in 1914, and in 1917 he founded the journal *Harvard African Studies*. Before his untimely death in 1918, Bates authored numerous books and articles, some of which were published posthumously (Bates 1914, 1915, 1917a, 1917b, 1918, 1927; Bates and Dunham 1918; Bates and Hooton 1918; Ruppel, Bates, and Roeder 1930).

At the outbreak of war in 1917, Bates left his wife and two small children to volunteer for military service where, only a few weeks later, he died in the great influenza epidemic of 1918. With his death ended an era of cutting-edge advances in Maine archaeological method and theory that were made by Harvard archaeologists and anthropologists but which resounded with echoes of innovations in Europe, brought home by Harvard scholars like Bates. But that era was not ended by the mere passing of one archaeologist. Rather, the change was heralded by the emergence of American anthropology onto the world stage. This can be seen clearly in Bates's prescient comments upon the future course of American anthropology, which appeared in 1917, shortly before his death:

Doubtless future Scientists will appreciate, even more deeply than can we of today, the value of the immense collections of American material bequeathed them from our times. But unless those broadening influences already at work among us shall have spent their force in vain, future scholars will reasonably complain that, in the days when opportunities were still very great, the narrow outlook of the nineteenth and twentieth centuries forever cramped and limited in America the study of primitive mankind ... that, at an hour when it was yet possible to make great collections in Asia and Africa, American interest in those fields was but fitful and sporadic.... Our present indifference, we may be sure, will not appear easily excusable to those scholars whose task it will be to grapple with the Negro problem in a far acuter form than it now presents, or who set themselves to analyze the essential characteristics of those peoples of the Far East with whom the expansion of American commerce is daily bringing us into closer contact. (1917b:479)

Epilogue: The Ghost of Morlot

As we have seen, Adolphe von Morlot was responsible for bringing from Europe to an American audience important, even foundational, new ideas about prehistoric humanity and how it could be studied using the tools of geology. And we have seen how those ideas began to take root, often in the context of shell midden research, in both of the founding institutions of American archaeology: Harvard's Peabody Museum and the Smithsonian Institution. However, more recent literature from both sides of the Atlantic has hardly recognized Morlot's existence, let alone his contribution. It seems appropriate in concluding this chapter to ask why this is so. After all, Morlot was well respected as a geologist in Europe, his thoughts upon the study of prehistoric archaeology could not have been published in a more prestigious and well-distributed medium than the annual reports of the Smithsonian Institution, and his articles there are models of scientific exposition.

The answer for America, I think, can be traced to the decline of interest in eastern North American archaeology at both the Smithsonian Institution and Harvard University at the end of the nineteenth century. At Harvard, Oric Bates's (1917b) admonition to his colleagues to extend their interests overseas while opportunity permitted marked a sharp decline in that institution's involvement in North America. Thus, by the time the "Chicago method" was developed by Fay-Cooper Cole on the basis of Putnam's "Peabody Museum method" (see chapter

11), Morlot's contribution had been transformed into an American idiom that left its founder without the credit he deserves.

But why is it that our European colleagues have not reminded us of our intellectual indebtedness to this important scientific pioneer? An approach to the answer to this question came to me when I asked an old friend, Paleolithic archaeologist Harvey Bricker, this very question. His response stopped me in my tracks: "Who is Morlot?" Bricker then went on to relate to me the succession of authority in European archaeology that followed the pioneering efforts of Edouard Lartet, who died in 1871, just as Morlot's ideas were taking root in America (Sackett 1991:114). In these events we can find important clues about Morlot's relative anonymity even among archaeologists working in his native land.

During the 1860s, Lartet, an eminent paleontologist, aided by his associate, the London banker and able amateur archaeologist Henry Christy, brilliantly synthesized the culture-historical framework of the European Upper Paleolithic that is still in use there (Sackett 1991:114). With the passing of these two pioneers, the reins of authority passed to Lartet's protégé, Gabriel de Mortillet. With this transition, however, came profound changes in approach. While the Lartet/Christy approach had emphasized geochronology based upon a paleontological understanding of faunal assemblages found in successively younger sites, de Mortillet shifted the focus to technology. As a result, according to Sackett, "Logic, in the form of simple-minded notions of technological evolution, had usurped stratigraphy as the basis of temporal ordering" (1991:115).

Another factor indirectly related to Morlot's obscurity pertains to the decline, after 1859, of unilineal cultural evolution as the controlling paradigm of ethnology, and with it the naive use of ethnographic analogy championed by Lartet and later by Morlot (Sackett 1991:116). Although de Mortillet's technologically based approach fell out of favor when Henri Breuil demonstrated its inadequacies, Breuil had also moved the discussion beyond Lartet. Thus Morlot, whose debt to Lartet seems obviously strong, was apparently forgotten.

On the other hand, it might be argued that Morlot's role in European archaeology was merely to extend the application of geological principles beyond the Paleolithic to more recent, fully modern prehistoric cultures. It will be interesting to learn more about this obscure figure, however his story comes out. It is difficult to avoid the conclusion that, whether a pioneer in his homeland or not, his influence on the development of American archaeology was profound.

8

Frances Eliza Babbitt and the Growth of Professionalism of Women in Archaeology

Hilary Lynn Chester

Introduction

Few women were involved in nineteenth-century American archaeology, and even fewer are now remembered. It is clear from comparisons with other natural and social sciences, such as sociocultural anthropology, that women were participating much more successfully in these disciplines. A combination of social factors and the nature of the field of American archaeology at that time limited women's participation and contributions. There were, however, notable exceptions: Frances Eliza Babbitt was one such.

American archaeology was considered a field-based natural science until the early twentieth century. In contrast to sociocultural anthropology, women's participation was greatly limited by this characterization of the field. Anthropology, including archaeology, went through dramatic and turbulent changes in the early twentieth century: it went from a field-based natural science to an academic-based discipline.

Contemporary claims—found primarily in the archaeological literature focusing on gender—that women's contributions are underappreciated (Levine 1991, 1994a; Parezo and Bender 1994) are well founded. The majority of the histories or biographical sketches of early American women archaeologists have two features in common: they have been written in the past 25 years, and they cover women working in the field from the 1920s to the present (e.g., see Bishop 1991; Bohrer 1979; Claassen 1992; Comber 1993; Cordell 1993; Fox 1993; Fox 1976; Frisbie 1974; Levine 1994a; Parezo and Bender 1994; Preucel and Chesson 1994; Schroeder 1979; Shears et al. 1989; Stanford and Day 1992; Sullivan 1984; Thompson 1991; White et al. 1994; Williams 1981).

Consistently, women in the earliest periods in American archaeology —the formative era of the 1870s to the 1920s—remain virtually invisible. It is clear that some characteristics of the field led to the exclusion of women, with some notable exceptions.

Despite the discouraging odds, some extraordinary women did venture into the field of archaeology in America in the nineteenth century. Frances Eliza Babbitt, a schoolteacher in Minnesota, participated briefly in the American Paleolithic debate. Babbitt was an amateur collector of prehistoric stone tools, and she became very involved with a series of quartz materials from Little Falls, Minnesota. She was in contact with many of the major players in the debates, and her finds were used repeatedly both to support and ultimately debunk the presence of Ice Age men in America. Babbitt's findings were presented in papers at the annual meetings of the American Association for the Advancement of Science (AAAS) in 1883 and 1884, and in journals such as *Science* and the *American Naturalist*.

Women were present in the other sciences of the time (e.g., see Aisenberg and Harrington 1988; Bonta 1991; James et al. 1971; Kass-Simon and Farnes 1990; Kohlstedt 1978; Rossiter 1982; Rowbotham 1973). Women were active participants in museum-sponsored lectures and in the meetings and lectures offered by scientific organizations, which were common in the second half of the nineteenth century (Bonta 1991; Croly 1898). Scientific and naturalist societies and organizations often had lectures that were available to the public, although membership in the societies was generally limited to men. In some fields, the women who were attracted formed their own auxiliary societies and clubs (Bonta 1991).

Women participated in the nineteenth-century discipline of sociocultural anthropology, conducting fieldwork like their male colleagues, but their participation in anthropology meetings was limited. Initially women were excluded from the Anthropological Society of Washington. Hence in June 1885, ten women in Washington, D.C., created a forum in which they could discuss research questions relevant to the field, establishing the Women's Anthropological Society of America, which operated until 1899 (Stocking 1960:2). In a general report by the recording secretary, Anita Newcomb McGee (Mrs. William J.) (1889b: 241), the group was described as being primarily concerned with the presentation of work done by the participants, and as a result, "no discussion has ever been given to the origin, antiquity, or primitive condition of man." While the women active in the society were aware of the current research problems and debates within archaeology at that time, such as the antiquity and origins of humans, they were not participants in those aspects of the discipline; that is, women were not undertaking fieldwork in those specializations.

Abroad, women were, in very small numbers, making significant contributions to archaeological discoveries in the late nineteenth and early twentieth centuries, particularly in classical studies. Harriet Boyd Hawes and Edith Hall both did extensive work on Crete beginning in the early twentieth century (Bolger 1994). Art history and classics were both accessible disciplines for educated women to pursue because they fit in with Victorian notions of appropriate interests for women (Cogan 1989).

The field of archaeology must be examined with the aim of understanding how the climate changed for women from the late nineteenth to early twentieth century. If the professional climate since the 1920s can be described as chilly, the earlier period should be described as glacial (Parezo and Bender 1994). The early 1920s can be characterized as a period of growth for women in American archaeology. Women were present in the field, in academic settings, and in museums, holding positions of varying status and prestige, from research assistants to university instructors. Women were finally participating in archaeology in the early twentieth century as they had been engaged in other fields of science in the nineteenth century. It would appear, then, that a change must have occurred within the discipline itself rather than in the larger realm of science in America.

Significant changes in Americanist archaeology at the turn of the century have been noted and examined previously (Meltzer 1983, 1985, 1991; Trigger 1989; Willey and Sabloff 1993). The professionalization of the field and the shifting emphasis toward academia have been identified as some of the major developments that were taking place (Darnell 1970), yet none of these changes have been explored in terms of their effect on women and their place in the field. Not only were women's traditional roles changing, but the characteristics and requisites of professional archaeologists were also being altered.

Frances Eliza Babbitt

Frances (Franc) Eliza Babbitt (1824–1891), a schoolteacher from Cold Water, Michigan, arrived in Little Falls, Minnesota, in 1878 (Brower 1902). The previous year, state geologist Newton Winchell had completed his geological and natural historical survey of Minnesota. In this report, Winchell noted the presence of glacial deposits along the Mississippi River that contained many quartz stone artifacts, as well as similar implements found intermittently on the surface. This area was very close to the town of Little Falls, in Morrison County, and the implements described by Winchell became known as the Little Falls "quartzes." Initially, Winchell's report did not generate much interest. It was not until Babbitt published reports on these materials in the *Proceedings* of the AAAS and the *American Naturalist* that the Little Falls quartzes became one of the more controversial and often-cited examples of an American Paleolithic industry.

Frances Babbitt was described by Nathan Richardson, a judge and local historian, as a geology and archaeology enthusiast (Brower 1902:42; *Little Falls Daily Transcript*, Minnesota Historical Society Library Archives, St. Paul). Almost immediately after arriving in Little Falls, she appears to have begun to explore the east side of the Mississippi River and the glacial deposits described by Winchell. In 1879, while "examining the river bank in quest of wrought quartzes" (Babbitt 1884a:597), she discovered an area containing many thousands of quartz implements on the surface. The area was a washout, further deepened by use as a wagon track. This "notch," as she later referred to it, exposed a stratum containing many sharp fragments of quartz, in many sizes. The deposit was 15 feet below the ground surface in an ancient terrace plain.

The nearest natural source of quartz was over an eighth of a mile away (Babbitt 1884a:598), and this, along with the variety of sizes of fragments present, suggested to Babbitt that the quartzes had been artificially transported to that location. As the location was in a natural drainage, as well as being only a very narrow strip of sand on the edge of the river, and distant from the source, Babbitt doubted that the artifacts were the remains of recent "aboriginal artificers." The crude level of workmanship also pointed to very great age of the artifacts: they were "distinctly paleolithic in general tone" (1884a:600). Those quartzes from the notch were then classified along with the Paleolithic implements reported by Winchell in his survey of Morrison County.

Like many other amateur naturalists and scientists at that time, Babbitt corresponded with several well-known authorities on the Paleolithic, sending not only descriptions of her finds but samples as well. Among her contacts were Newton Winchell; Frederic W. Putnam of the Peabody Museum at Harvard; Warren Upham, assistant to Winchell (who would later become the secretary of the Minnesota Historical Society); Charles Abbott, who discovered the alleged Paleolithic tools in the Trenton gravels; Henry W. Haynes of the Boston Society of

Natural History; Charles Rau, curator of the Department of Antiquities at the U.S. National Museum; and Otis Mason, curator of the Division of Ethnology at the Smithsonian Institution. Putnam and Mason were both strong advocates of amateur participation and local societies in anthropology and archaeology (Dexter 1978; Hinsley 1981:87; Mark 1980). Because of Babbitt's amateur status, it was very important to have her finds examined and verified by recognized authorities in the field. And they were—she received confirmation from Putnam that the specimens were indeed made by humans. This prompted her first presentation on the collection to the Department of American History at the Minnesota Historical Society in St. Paul, in February 1880 (Brower 1902). Her presentation was published in the two local papers, the *St. Paul Pioneer Press* and the *Little Falls Transcript*. Despite her age—nearly 60 at the time of her first discoveries—Babbitt had become a significant contributor to the American Paleolithic debate of the period.

Upham and Winchell concurred that the deposit in which the specimens were found was from the last Ice Age event (Upham 1902a, 1902b; Winchell 1902). The stratum immediately below was a glacial floodplain created by the retreat of an earlier ice sheet. The plain area would have been subjected to flooding as the existing glaciers to the north melted (Babbitt 1883). The site had been covered gently by a flood, leaving the remains relatively undisturbed. Babbitt identified distinct clusters of artifacts in this stratum. Each cluster contained a mixture of nearly perfect specimens, as well as many chips, refuse, and broken tools. Babbitt speculated that this was a work site at which "glacial man" (her term) made his stone tools.

Abbott and Upham both noted affinities between the Little Falls quartzes and the Trenton gravel assemblage (Mason 1883:370), alleged Paleolithic tools found by Abbott in glacial gravel beds along the Delaware River. Haynes noted the crudeness of the tools when compared to historically known and Neolithic specimens from New England, thus supporting the Little Falls quartzes' greater antiquity.

In 1883, Babbitt, with assistance from Upham, prepared a paper on the Little Falls quartzes for the annual meeting of the AAAS. Despite the fact that the meeting was held in Minneapolis, Babbitt apparently was not present and her paper was read by a "Mr. Upton" (Mason 1883:369; this is likely a misprint for "Upham"). The paper was subsequently published in the *Proceedings* of the AAAS (Babbitt 1883). In it, Babbitt described the artifact-bearing deposit as a thin stratum 15 feet below the ground surface. Because Winchell had already identified the level as being glacial in age, Babbitt's main focus was on demonstrating that the quartzes were from that deposit were undisturbed and were made by humans.

According to Otis Mason (1883:370), the presentation of the paper at the meeting generated an "animated discussion." Among the supporters was Putnam himself, who considered the discovery very important and the paper of great value (Mason 1883:370). On the other hand, Rev. S. D. Peet, founder of the *American Antiquarian,* voiced the opinion that the entire paper was without foundation, arguing that the quartzes were not even artifacts (Mason 1883:371).

The following year, the AAAS meeting was held in Philadelphia. The Little Falls quartz materials were on exhibit at the meetings to permit direct examination. In addition, Babbitt also wrote a description of each artifact, including its physical dimensions and possible function, and these were subsequently published in the *Proceedings* of the AAAS of that year (Babbitt 1885). Comparisons between the Little Falls implements and Paleolithic artifacts from Europe were made in order to emphasize the affinities between the European and American Paleolithics (Babbitt 1883). Babbitt shared many of the same beliefs regarding the American Paleolithic as its other more prominent supporters. The proponents of the American Paleolithic were greatly influenced by the Paleolithic in Europe; the "dispute over the length of time humans had inhabited North America had its roots in the discovery in Europe in the late 1850's that human antiquity reached back into the Pleistocene" (Meltzer 1991:15).

That same year, Babbitt published an article in the *American Naturalist* on the quartzes and the presence of "glacial man" in Minnesota (1884a). A portion of Upham's paper "Early Man in Minnesota," which described the geological context of the find, was included in her article, and her description of the quartz materials were included in his later published paper (Upham 1894). In both the AAAS and the *American Naturalist* papers, Babbitt (1883, 1884a, 1890) emphasized the unquestionable geological evidence as supported by Upham. In turn, Upham supported her finds at Little Falls in a letter to Putnam, at the Peabody Museum, in 1886: "I have entire confidence that the specimens found at Little Falls by Miss Babbitt are of the same archaeological and geological significance as the much more abundant specimens donated to your museum by Dr. Abbott."[1]

Despite the obvious cooperative efforts between Upham and Babbitt, no mention of Babbitt's work is found in Upham's unpublished papers (Minnesota Historical Society Library Archives, St. Paul). While Upham's records are incomplete until 1885, which is after the bulk of their writings on the Little Falls quartzes, this does not seem to be the reason. Babbitt's name was never listed in his records of correspondences sent, although they contained both personal and professional entries. Additionally, there was no mention of her death in his diary. Upham did include her in the Minnesota Biographies, published by the Minnesota Historical Society, though she lived in Minnesota for only a few years (Upham and Dunlop 1912). It is strange and unfortunate that she did not appear to make a more lasting impression on Upham, who appears to have been her most constant collaborator.

Babbitt's relationship with Frederic W. Putnam, however, is evident in the letters she wrote to him, which are preserved in the Peabody Museum. In one letter, she proposes to pass Putnam's name along to Winchell, the curator at the State Museum in Minneapolis, so that the two could communicate regarding the curation of her collection.[2] Her letters, though formal, include her thoughts and speculations on her findings and plans for further investigation. She is both enthusiastic and meticulous. Eager to have her finds presented to the field and to be used as corroborating evidence of Paleolithic man in the New World, she was clearly aware of the significance of her finds in the debate, and took this responsibility seriously and excitedly.

The American Paleolithic Debate

The opponents of the theory of an American Paleolithic were centered in the Bureau of Ethnology, later Bureau of American Ethnology (BAE), in Washington, D.C. The BAE scientists worked with both living Native Americans and the archaeological remains, unlike many of the Paleolithic hypothesis supporters, who worked exclusively with artifacts. "Theirs was a uniformitarian archaeology, which began with the known material remains of historic tribes and traced them backward" (Meltzer 1991:18). The existence of separate Paleolithic populations was clearly at odds with their linear theory of evolutionary progress.

William H. Holmes of the BAE was one of the strongest, most active anti–New World Paleolithic archaeologists. The opponents, and most vocally Holmes, felt that the burden of proof rested with the proponents. It was their burden to produce unquestionable evidence of the existence of people living in America during the Pleistocene because they "assume to introduce to the world cultures, peoples, and conditions not within levels of ordinary experience" (Holmes 1893b:519).

The evidence provided by the proponents, including Babbitt, was simply not acceptable to their opponents. The crudeness of the supposed Paleolithic artifacts was explained by Holmes as being rejects or accidents of stone tool manufacturing. Studies of contemporary and historic quarry sites revealed that, in fact, rejects and refuse of manufacturing did resemble the crude, supposed paleoliths (Brinton 1894:249). Discoveries at a contemporary quarry site outside Washington, D.C., the Piney Branch Quarry, by Holmes in 1890 demonstrated clearly the importance of an artifact's geological context, since the unfinished or rejected artifacts resembled the European paleoliths (Meltzer 1991:16). The Little Falls quartzes, when examined by Holmes, were among the paleoliths to be dismissed as quarry rejects: "The quartz objects from Minnesota, usually known as the Babbitt finds, of which much has been said and written, prove on careful examination to be modern workshop refuse settled into the talus of the glacial terrace" (Holmes 1892b:296).

In addition to questioning the validity of the artifacts, Holmes also questioned the accuracy of the geological assessments of the contexts. He felt strongly that "until students of the great questions of chronology and culture acquire a thorough scientific knowledge of geology as well as all early phases of human art the discussion in which they indulge can be of little value" (Holmes 1893b:51). Not only were the artifacts and their contexts subject to criticism, but even more inflammatory, much of Holmes's and the BAE's criticisms of the notion of an American Paleolithic were accompanied by criticisms of the proponents themselves, exacerbating the debate.

Unlike the Paleolithic supporters, the BAE was not influenced by European archaeology. The BAE archaeologists were a motley assortment of natural scientists, coming from a wide variety of fields. Few of them were college educated, and those who held degrees were commonly from other disciplines, such as geology and botany. These BAE employees valued their field experience over formal training or familiarity with the literature. Holmes considered himself and the other Washington-based workers professionals, and he was very critical of both the part-time enthusiasts working in the field and the "armchair" archaeologists, the synthesizers who did little or no actual fieldwork.

The "aping of European science" (Meltzer 1991:26) and the lack of real field experience were both seen as serious shortcomings of the non-BAE archaeologists. Holmes, in many of his papers published in journals such as *Science*, openly criticized the amateur element, blaming them for creating the controversy: "The fact is the field has up to this time been occupied mainly by amateurs who have not mastered the necessary fundamental branches of science. The work done is mainly their work, the literature produced is mainly their literature, and the world has received its impressions from this" (Holmes 1893b:29–30). Clearly, Holmes was attacking not only the true amateurs and enthusiasts, such as Babbitt, but also people such as Putnam and Winchell. This is due in part to the direct competition for sites between the BAE and other private institutions, such as the Peabody Museum, as well as with the local scientific societies, such as the Minnesota State Geological Society (Meltzer 1991:27).

The Paleolithic debate continued to rage, primarily in the pages of *Science*, through the early 1890s. Babbitt had died by then, and she was not present to hear the criticisms of her work or its vigorous defense by proponents of an American Paleolithic. Holmes's criticisms of the Little Falls site were countered by, among others, Haynes (1893a, 1893b), Upham (1894), and Wright (1892a, 1892b, 1893). Charles Abbott (1892a, 1892b) wrote many letters, often scathing and satirical, defending his work and the work of people like him against Holmes's attacks on amateurs. The crusade against the American Paleolithic eventually presented such a hostile atmosphere that few people continued to work on the subject (Meltzer 1991:24, citing A. V. Kidder).

Social Context

Babbitt's foray into the Paleolithic debate was atypical for women in the field of archaeology, but it was somewhat more in keeping with the role of women in other science fields. Women were participating in the other sciences in America during the nineteenth century, although they were usually on the periphery (Kohlstedt 1978). Women in science around the mid-1800s were usually untrained amateurs, working primarily independently. The natural sciences, particularly botany, ornithology, and entomology, were taken up by women enthusiasts (Bonta 1991). The Victorian era was one that valued the beauty of nature, as seen in the popularity of the existential poets and popular naturalists at that time: Wordsworth, Thoreau, and Muir. Bird watching, nature walks, and sketching were all acceptable feminine pastimes that could easily be adapted to scientific queries. Many women collected insects and small plant and floral specimens and maintained herbaria (Kohlstedt 1978:84). The study of botany was considered very much an extension of a woman's domestic duties, which also included gardening.

"Most of the prominent women naturalists entered the field in the late nineteenth and early twentieth centuries at the same time that the men had already begun to specialize, hence the women naturalists . . .

depended on the male specialists for help" (Bonta 1991:15). These relationships with male scientists were not typically partnerships; botanists such as Asa Gray and William Darlington maintained correspondences with women, who would send them specimens (Kohlstedt 1978:84). Obviously, the men gained by their protégées' assistance, and some, like Charles Darwin and John James Audubon, acknowledged their contributions (Bonta 1991:xiii). Many of the women naturalists were also teachers, soliciting up-to-date scientific material for their classes (Kohlstedt 1978:86-7; Talbot 1910).

Many prominent men in science encouraged women to teach. Amos Eaton, an instructor of natural sciences and a popular lyceum lecturer in the early 1800s, wanted more sciences taught in schools overall, and he encouraged the women he taught and corresponded with to teach the natural sciences rather than do research (Kohlstedt 1978:87). Women were increasingly teaching in the more advanced levels, particularly at women's secondary schools and seminaries. At this early stage, though, women were primarily teaching science to enrich their students, without intending to launch their own scientific careers.

Women continued to be encouraged to teach in the latter half of the century as well. Louis Agassiz, a geologist and professor at Harvard in the 1860s and 1870s, supported women as assistants to scientists, who could then take their experience and training and teach others (Kohlstedt 1978:90). By the late 1880s, teaching other women and children was no longer the only scientific position women could attain. Women were holding positions as laboratory assistants, even as supervisors over other assistants, usually in academic settings, as mentioned earlier. The alternative to these jobs was individual study, with dependence on public lectures and correspondence with male scientists.

The Lyceum and lecture series, popular in the early half of the century, attracted many women. These lectures enabled women to participate as amateurs and enthusiasts, for their own personal enlightenment and enrichment, which was a socially acceptable pastime (Benton 1913; Blair 1980). Scientific and social clubs often formed as a result of these lectures; for example, the Jamaica Women's Club of New York was so formed to study botany and horticulture (Croly 1898:882). The clubs in which women were allowed to participate, as well as clubs made up exclusively of women, were generally only local organizations and not in direct contact with the larger, more professional scientific organizations (Rossiter 1982:75).

The AAAS, the most prestigious interdisciplinary national organization, was one of the first scientific societies to allow women to attend its meetings, as early as the 1850s, and permitted women to present and publish papers in the 1860s. It appears from an examination of the table of contents of the *Proceedings* of the AAAS that women were presenting and publishing papers in all of the fields in small numbers, which steadily increased between 1870 and 1885.

In many respects, Babbitt is typical of the kind of women actively participating in science in the late nineteenth century. She was a schoolteacher and conducted her fieldwork in her spare time; she communicated with experts in the fields she was pursuing, yet worked independently and locally; she was active in local scientific and historical societies, even submitting articles to their publications. Babbitt spent time at a local Ojibwa Indian reservation, perhaps teaching or providing other social service.[3]

Yet Babbitt's choice of fieldwork, the position of prominence that her finds held, and the significance of her publications are not typical. Archaeology, a field-based natural science at that time, was not in keeping with Victorian notions of femininity. Babbitt would hike along the banks of the Little Falls River in all seasons, collecting stone tools, including club heads weighing several pounds. She wrote to Putnam that she investigated one particular locale after a period of prolonged cold and an especially heavy snowfall in order to examine the effects of runoff on the frozen ground, and the subsequent effects on the archaeological deposits.[4]

The Professionalization of Anthropology

The changes in American anthropology incorporated many of the same issues and dilemmas that were taking place in the Paleolithic debate, particularly issues of professionalism, training, and conflicts between the government bureaus and the private institutions. Regarding the latter, a dramatic shift in the locus of influence—from the Washington-based bureaus to the universities—occurred. The increase in the number of academic departments and the subsequent increase in academically trained anthropologists had a tremendous effect on the discipline's structure and community, its goals and methodologies, and, most importantly for this study, practitioners (Hinsley 1981; Meltzer 1985; Stocking 1960). Most anthropologists in the nineteenth century were amateurs, with only loose affiliations with localized scientific societies. The criticisms that Holmes had leveled at his rivals, like Babbitt, in the field (i.e., their unprofessional, amateur status) were the same ones that were turned around and aimed at the BAE in the early part of the twentieth century as newly created university departments began creating a new group of "professional archaeologists."

There was a general trend toward professionalization in all of the sciences in America in the late nineteenth century (Kohlstedt 1978; Rossiter 1982). This professionalization of the scientific fields had begun in other physical sciences beginning around 1870, but the natural history fields remained open to amateurs well into the early twentieth century (Goldstein 1994:591–592). In fact, some historians who focus on the history of sciences do not distinguish between amateurs and professionals in the nineteenth century, arguing that this dichotomy did not exist until the twentieth century. Others, while maintaining the distinction between amateur and professional, emphasize the significant contributions that were made by amateurs, both to the general body of knowledge of a field and to the actual shaping of the field (Goldstein 1994:591–592). What is generally agreed upon, though, is the decline of the amateur's significance in the various fields by 1900 due to the growing importance of education and training.

The amateurs and (what were at that time considered) professionals may have belonged to the same community, but it was "not without hierarchy" (Goldstein 1994:594). Even in the early twentieth century, amateurs continued to be active in science, but there was a much more pronounced division between them and their educated colleagues. In some fields the amateurs and professionals drifted apart, forming separate circles and societies; in other fields the two maintained contact, but the amateurs were subordinated and their activities directed by the professionals (Goldstein 1994:597).

The founding of the American Anthropological Association (AAA), the first national organization devoted exclusively to anthropological topics, is frequently seen as a turning point in this process for anthropology. Its founding involved a "lengthy and occasionally quite bitter controversy over the character and the aims of the Association," and was "part of a much broader process . . . the professionalization of American anthropology" (Stocking 1960:1).

Two of the main players in the affair were Franz Boas of Columbia University and William J. McGee, the acting chief of the BAE. Both Boas and McGee wanted a national-level organization devoted to anthropological pursuits, but the similarities end there. Boas desired an exclusive organization, one that would admit only anthropologists of high quality, or which at the very least would include an elite group of fellows (Stocking 1960:2). Many of the other scientific societies had such exclusive positions in their organizations, individuals who were given extra privileges and had more influence in decision making. McGee, on the other hand, favored a more inclusive organization, one that would encourage and serve to unite local societies. He wanted to unify the research problems and exert control over the local societies through the AAA, despite the fact that this meant including the very local societies Holmes claimed were ruining the field. McGee's personal background, lack of formal education, and association with the Anthropological Society of Washington, an eclectic organization with many amateur members and active participants, may have made him more sympathetic to the amateurs. Boas resisted an inclusive organization, which he thought would dilute good research work (Stocking 1960:9). He wanted to ensure that the new professional, academically trained anthropologists would take and retain control.

Social Anthropology: The Welcoming Science

Social anthropology has been referred to as the welcoming science because of its apparent openness toward women (Parezo 1993a; Parezo and Bender 1994). Early ethnological fieldwork in America took place mainly among the Native American tribes. Much of the work was funded by the Bureau of Ethnology (later renamed the BAE), but other work was also funded by the U.S. Geological Survey, several universities, and private sponsors. As in many of the other natural sciences at the turn of the century, very little formal education or training was expected of the researchers. Otis Mason (1888b:5) remarked in an address to the Anthropological Society of Washington in 1888 that "Every man, woman, and child that has sense and patience to observe, and that can honestly record the thing observed . . . may be an anthropologist."

The lack of necessary training opened the field of anthropology to anyone with the interest and financial support. Women were not merely tolerated in the field, but actually considered by some as a necessity, as a true asset. Ethnographic fieldwork involved spending long periods of time closely interacting with people in order to better understand their society. It was believed that women had better rapport with the subjects because they were natural communicators (Parezo 1993a:4). Women's natural tendencies to be patient and nurturing, from experience or predisposition to caring for children, were qualities they could draw on in the field. Other Victorian qualities of women were also seen as assets: their meticulous attention to detail and their unassertive personalities. Women were not threatening to the people they studied.

Women were perceived not only as having better listening and empathizing skills, but it was recognized that they had access to facets of the society closed to men. Perhaps women's biggest perceived contribution was their ability to study women and children, thus providing a more well-rounded picture of the society under examination. Women were seen as enriching the field by other anthropologists, particularly Franz Boas, who sought deep understandings of individual cultures (Lurie 1966:33).

This complementarity between male and female researchers was especially productive among married couples, of which there were many. In these collaborative teams the wife was brought in to anthropology through her husband. These women have been called "anthropologists by marriage" (Lurie 1966:34), although this term undervalues the significance of the contributions made by the wives by insinuating that the women were tagging along and not working with any volition of their own.

Women did not strictly confine themselves to "female data," that is, studies of women and children and the domestic domains of society. Most of the early women anthropologists, such as Matilda Coxe Stevenson, Erminnie Smith, and Alice Fletcher, did write on more general, universal research questions. Stevenson, for example, "quickly went beyond the sexually restricted interests that Powell and Baird had carved out for her," also doing research on religion, economics, language, medicine, and many other topics, working closely with both men and women as informants (Parezo 1993b:41).

The fact that research topics had become gendered not only limited the types of work women were encouraged or even allowed to do, but also generated asymmetrical values on the different research subjects (Parezo 1993a:5). Questions that required quantitative analysis were tackled by men, while women continued to study the more descriptive questions. Men were also more often looking at the political and social issues, which were viewed as more important and generally more influential on the rest of society (Lurie 1966:79). This gender separation between the subjects studied may not have been due to gender divisions within the societies studied so much as to the Victorian notions of gender. "Men were unwittingly reluctant to deal with matters in the field that were beneath their notice at home" (Lurie 1966:78).

It may have been those very Victorian notions, ironically, that attracted women to anthropology in the first place. Middle- and upper-class women were expected to involve themselves with problems of social welfare and religion. Some of the early women anthropologists were also involved in welfare and reform movements, not only from genuine compassion, but also from a mandate for community responsibility that had been implanted at an early age (McGreevy 1993:299). Alice Fletcher began her anthropological career as an advocate of Native American reform. She was very much responsible for securing land rights for the Omaha tribe that she worked with through the Omaha Act of 1882 (Lurie 1966:49). Babbitt, like Fletcher, had contact with Native Americans living on reservations, and she wrote articles based on observations made while working with the tribes (Babbitt 1881, 1884b, 1884c, 1886/1911, 1888).

Women were drawn to social anthropology, and for the most part they were able to go to the field and conduct research, needing no more special training than their male counterparts. Once in the field, though, women experienced discrimination in their positions in the field, in the limits on their professional advancements, and in the recognition from their peers. As was common in other sciences in the late nineteenth century, women were much more frequently the gatherers of data, while men were the analysts and interpreters. The Victorian ideal qualities of womanhood were not conducive to becoming a scientist. Scientists needed to be rigorous, competitive, dispassionate, objective, and rational, while women at that time were encouraged, even taught, to be passive, sensitive, compassionate, and delicate. These qualities made them especially good at gathering data, but less inclined to formulate interpretations and defend them among their peers. As anthropology struggled at the turn of the century to become a rigorous science, there was little room for feminine compassion and empathy. As a result, women were rarely project directors, professors, or analysts, but rather assistants and fieldworkers (Parezo 1993a:5).

Frederic W. Putnam encouraged and maintained many correspondences with women interested in anthropology and archaeology, including Babbitt. Putnam was a member of the National Institute, an association for the promotion of higher education for women (Dexter 1978:5). Several women were employed at the Peabody Museum, and Alice Fletcher, Erminnie Smith, and Zelia Nuttall were Putnam's most professionally recognized students. The extraordinary success of Smith, Fletcher, and, to a slightly lesser degree, Nuttall in the AAAS has been tentatively attributed to Putnam's position as general secretary of the AAAS (Rossiter 1982:80). Fletcher received the first fellowship ever awarded to a woman at Harvard as a result of his sponsorship (Dexter 1978; Mark 1980:67). In 1893, Putnam wrote to a Mrs. Henderson: "Several of my best students are women, who have become widely known by their thorough and important works and publications; and this I consider as high an honor as could be accorded to me" (Dexter 1978:5).

Putnam also encouraged and maintained many correspondences with amateur enthusiasts interested in archaeology and anthropology. Many of these correspondences were with women, such as Babbitt. Putnam did not draw distinctions between amateurs and professionals, but rather welcomed and encouraged everyone (Mark 1980:53).

It appears that anthropology, and the sociocultural field in particular, was not as receptive to women as generally portrayed. There were several very influential and successful women whose contributions were recognized and remembered within and beyond the field. These women are often remembered and either credited or criticized by the contributions made by their mentors, or by how closely they followed a mentor's guidance. This is very true of the women who were supported by Boas, who are often remembered as students of Boas rather than as individual scholars (Parezo 1993a:13). They are not credited with having their own thoughts, but merely with acting on or reacting against their mentors. Additionally, and perhaps more damaging, the most prolific women were considered exceptional to the point of being atypical, rather than representative of women's capabilities.

"Although women were actually welcomed into anthropology because of an erroneous notion that they could and would be the only ones to obtain necessary information, the miscalculation worked to the advantage of women as individuals. They did not have to dissipate their energies in fighting for their rights but could apply them toward earning the esteem of their colleagues" (Lurie 1966:80). Compared to the status and roles available to women in other sciences, sociocultural anthropology was neither better nor worse than many of the lab-based sciences. Women were researchers, data gatherers, instructors, and assistants; some women were able to publish independently too and design their own research projects and fieldwork. All this was in contrast to archaeology during the same period.

Archaeology: The Less Welcoming Science

Similar niches did not occur in the field of archaeology until the early decades of the twentieth century. This was due mainly to archaeologists' notions of what fieldwork entailed and what qualities archaeologists should possess. "In the twentieth century U.S. popular myth, women are viewed as being highly observant, intuitive, patient, good listeners, and good at learning languages. These are all qualities that are deemed valuable to ethnographers. Archaeologists, on the contrary, are supposed to be mechanical, technically oriented, physically strong and commanding" (Cordell 1993:203). Most male archaeologists simply believed that the field conditions were too rigorous and demanding for women; perhaps many women also believed this of themselves. Additionally, many archaeologists believed that women's family responsibilities, particularly bearing and raising children, would interfere with their fieldwork, and with their careers in general (Wormington 1981:v). Victorian notions of appropriate conditions and behaviors of women certainly did not fit with the contemporary perceptions of archaeologists' activities.

The early women archaeologists were all exceptional women; they did not fit the Victorian mold of femininity, which no doubt contributed to their attraction to and success in archaeology. Mentors were integral in the success of women in archaeology, although the relationships between male archaeologists and their female protégées are not as commonly discussed as they are in sociocultural anthropology. A. V. Kidder, Byron Cummings, and Edgar Hewett supported a number of women in archaeology, though they are not as often remembered for this as Boas or Putnam have been. Hewett, though giving more jobs to women and helping more in their placement in the Southwest than anyone else, was not known to be a feminist. Hewett was a fair man, but he may have hired women because they could be paid less (Cordell 1993:220).

Kidder was the first male archaeologist to offer a field school for women, in which three women conducted an excavation in 1929 through the University of New Mexico. Frances Watkins, Isabel Kelly, and Eva Horner spent the summer excavating the Tecolote site, near Las Vegas, New Mexico. Women often had a difficult time because, unlike men, they could not get positions as volunteers, which was a common way to enter the field, as most projects did not have or allow mixed-sex crews (Cordell 1993:205). Once they were given or made the opportunity, they were happily engaged. Watkins (1930:13) describes their experience as "the first time, I believe, in the history of Southwestern archaeology—an expedition led and directed by women, with no men in the party, was sent out into the field," further noting (1931: 178) that "field work is the most interesting, although not the most important, phase of archaeology, and I may as well admit we all enjoy it the most." Watkins discusses archaeology as a profession especially suited for women, differentiating between the old style of archaeology, in which only a "strong right arm and willing mind" are needed (Watkins 1931:174), with the archaeology they were practicing. She believed that women were well adapted to the new methods, which required an education in theory and science, as well as field training (Watkins 1931:177).

Conclusion

Between the late nineteenth century and the early twentieth century, general perceptions of femininity, women's work, and appropriate activities for women changed relatively little. Very few women were active in archaeology in the nineteenth century, and fewer did their research in the United States. The twentieth century witnessed a dramatic increase in the number of women participating and making significant, long-lasting contributions, even shaping the field. What conditions allowed, even encouraged, this change?

The mid–nineteenth century was a period of tremendous growth in the popularity of science in the United States. Lectures and Lyceum series were common in both large cities and small towns. Lecturers would travel across the country, speaking as well as collecting and gathering both information and specimens. Science was not limited to the rich or well educated; the natural sciences were especially accessible. Individuals could explore, collect, and make observations; the only real requisites were enthusiasm and interest. There were also being formed at this time large institutions, which served as clearinghouses, sending out their own researchers, but also soliciting data from amateurs. These institutions, in return, often published material on new discoveries and ideas.

Many communities had their own local societies, in which various topics were discussed and research results were compared and shared. These local clubs and societies provided a forum for amateurs to share their interests and also served to mediate with the larger scientific organizations and institutions. The individualized and amateur-oriented qualities of science in the mid–nineteenth century made sciences fairly accessible to women, particularly those fields that complemented their household responsibilities.

The popularity of science contributed to the development of science departments in colleges and universities. As sciences moved into academia in the late nineteenth century, the amateur societies remained popular; people continued to correspond and contribute to professional scientists. However, amateur contributions had less of an impact on the fields themselves. Research performed within academic settings was more highly valued and more influential in driving the scientific disciplines.

Beginning in the 1870s, women had increasing access to higher education, which in turn led to other opportunities. In the sciences, women were gradually able to take classes and be involved in research. The sciences that required large amounts of data gathering and repeated experiments, such as astronomy and chemistry, brought many women into the laboratories.

Armed with their experience, some women were able to work their way up in the field, ultimately making their own contributions. As the number of women increased in the universities and colleges, so did the number of women in higher positions, such as senior researchers, instructors, and even professors. Gaining these footholds in the universities was crucial in attracting and training new women in the fields. Mentors, it has been demonstrated, have had a tremendous effect on the numbers and successes of women in the sciences and in academia in general.

Other factors, such as the social obligations and expectations placed on women in the nineteenth century, also affected the degree to which they participated in sciences, as well as which sciences. The Victorian model of womanhood placed many constraints on women's activities and behavior, limiting their education, topics of study, and certainly many of their outdoor and public activities, which were deemed too strenuous or unladylike. The converse is also true, since the notions of women's work and responsibilities also encouraged many activities. The reform movement, in which many social, economic, and moral problems in society were identified and attempts made at solving them, stemmed from Victorian ideals.

Women were the watchdogs of morality, religion, and the welfare of those unable to care for themselves. While a woman's primary responsibility was to her own family, making improvements in society in general was seen as an extension of this duty because it involved making a better society for her family. Through the reform movement, many women became interested in, among other things, the welfare of Native Americans. Several women entered the field of anthropology as ethnologists through their involvement with and concern for Native Americans.

Women were able to create and fill niches in the field of sociocultural anthropology while maintaining most of their feminine qualities. The notion that women were more compassionate and empathetic, better listeners, and more patient than men led to the belief by some anthropologists that women were ideally suited for ethnographic work. Museum work and work with material culture were also perceived to be suitable for women, given their attention to detail and appreciation of beauty, and their organizational skills. These beliefs, accurate or not, enabled women to enter the field of sociocultural anthropology and to engage in fieldwork in the nineteenth and early twentieth centuries.

At the early stages of the discipline, academic training was limited, and rare among anthropologists, though women attained the advanced degrees as departments developed. Women were relatively successful when the field was open to untrained individuals, and they were increasingly successful as the discipline became more professional. Like the other sciences in which women frequently worked, such as chemistry, astronomy, botany, and zoology, women in social anthropology were primarily the assistants—the field or lab workers. This is contrasted with archaeology, in which there were no acceptable roles for women in the early days, before the discipline became professionalized. Anthropological training or education was not necessary in nineteenth-century archaeology; archaeology was very much a natural science as opposed to a social science. Most of the early practitioners were trained or had experience in other natural sciences, predominantly geology, but also zoology, anatomy, and even botany. Field experience was much more highly valued than formal training. It was precisely this type of experience that women had the most difficulty attaining.

The rugged outdoor fieldwork necessary in archaeology was not socially acceptable for women; in fact, many people believed that women were physically incapable of enduring such work conditions. Interestingly, most male archaeologists were also supporters of these beliefs and were resistant to letting even willing women into the field. Married couples who engaged in geology and archaeology together are the earliest exceptions. Even in these examples, though, the women were not considered peers or colleagues by other archaeologists.

Only when archaeology became an academic science, in which training and background education were valued, were women able to enter the field in numbers. For women, these changes meant clear-cut requisites to be an archaeologist: education and field training. By the early twentieth century, women were able to get advanced degrees in anthropology and archaeology, although it was still very difficult. Despite the hardships and financial and social pressures these women endured, their perseverance paid off. The opportunities to go into the field, such as the Tecolote field school, were increasing, as was their support by male peers. Once women had proven themselves in the classroom and the field, they were able to make respected and lasting contributions.

In this context, Frances Eliza Babbitt was clearly an exceptional woman. So little is known of her that it is difficult to speculate about her motivations, her methods, or her perceptions of the field of archaeology in the nineteenth century and her position in it. As an unmarried schoolteacher, Babbitt was typical of the women entering science fields in the 1800s, but her choice of fields and the extent of her impact on the field are not typical. That she published papers in both local and national scientific societies demonstrates an exceptional degree of determination. At the time of her research and publications and beyond her death, her work was referred to, criticized, and defended by the participants in the Paleolithic debate. Her work was never criticized because she was a woman, but merely because of her amateur status—something her male colleagues were accused of equally. Her supporters took her work seriously, even using her findings in their own interpretations.

The trend in archaeology, in which women entered the field initially with background training, differs from women's patterns in other sciences, including sociocultural anthropology. Without the existence of niches for amateurs that were also appropriate for women, there were few opportunities for women to enter the field until the field itself changed. Frances Babbitt provides an example of what one woman could accomplish despite the conditions. However, her case also demonstrates the difficulties women had as amateurs in a field that had no place for them.

9

Henry Chapman Mercer
Archaeologist and Cultural Historian

David L. Browman

Introduction

Henry Chapman Mercer (1856–1930) was one of the pioneers in the development of archaeological excavation technique. He employed and published explicit stratigraphic excavation techniques in 1895 in Mexico in his search for Paleoindians some two decades before the work of Manuel Gamio and Franz Boas, and he appears also to have conducted stratigraphic excavations in Pennsylvania during the same period. The intellectual roots of Mercer's technique seem to come from French paleontology via Marcellin Boule and Albert Gaudry, and most likely can be traced back via the French connection to the work of William Pengelly at Brixham Cave in England (Browman 1997). Mercer's methodology, however, seems to have had little impact on North American archaeologists, probably because in 1897 he quit conducting archaeological excavations and began a new career studying and preserving the remains of eighteenth- and nineteenth-century American material culture (he also became a superb tile maker). His lack of methodological impact upon prehistoric archaeology is similar to the situations involving William B. Nickerson, George H. Pepper, and Frank Russell, three other American archaeologists who seem to have been conducting stratigraphic excavations in the 1890s, but whose methods also seem not to have been transferred into the active repertoire of American archaeology of that period.

For historical archaeologists, Mercer's main contributions relate to his work after 1897, up to his death in 1930. Mercer became interested in the rapidly disappearing evidence of American arts and crafts, particularly eighteenth- and nineteenth-century American tools, and he made it his business to attempt—both by re-creation of method in the case of tiles and pottery, as well as simply collecting type specimens—to preserve the early American technical heritage. Thus the second part of this chapter briefly summarizes some of his contributions in this latter area. However, because the principal thrust of this volume is upon prehistoric archaeology, my major focus is on the first part of Mercer's career, as a prehistoric archaeologist.

The argument developed for the first part is as follows: (1) that Mercer's fortuitous involvement with the Lenape stone, and his attempt to validate it, led him to an interest in demonstrating the existence of paleolithic[1] occupations in the Americas; (2) that this interest resulted in his taking advantage of a later opportunity to link up with the University of Pennsylvania, where he was influenced by Charles Abbott and Edward Cope; (3) that his attempt to evaluate Abbott's claims for the antiquity of artifacts in the Trenton gravels, in conjunction with intellectual directions under the mentorship of Cope, resulted in his contact with French paleontologists and archaeologists, from whom he seems to have learned the methodological tools that he subsequently employed to address the question of Terminal Pleistocene occupation in the Americas; (4) that he thus employed the techniques learned in France in testing dozens of American caves between 1893 and 1896, in the search for possible Paleolithic tools, in some cases explicitly employing stratigraphic excavation techniques; and (5) that with the loss of direct association with Abbott, due to Abbott's resignation from the museum, and with Cope, due to Cope's death, coupled with Mercer's failure to identify any Paleolithic remains in his cave research, Mercer shifted his focus to experimental replication and museology by 1897. Mercer's departure from the circle of active excavators may explain why his early stratigraphic excavation methods, two decades before the work of Gamio, Kidder, and Nelson, apparently went unnoticed by the nascent discipline of American archaeology.

Part I: The Prehistoric Archaeology Years and the Influence of European Paleontology and Prehistory

Mercer's Contributions to Prehistoric Studies

Henry Chapman Mercer's roots and career are very much tethered to Doylestown in Bucks County, Pennsylvania. Born in Doylestown on June 24, 1856, Mercer later attended the same preparatory schools as his uncles and father, a family tradition (Mercer 1926:633). After entering Harvard in 1875, in his junior and senior years he developed an interest in art history, taking classes from Charles Eliot Norton and joining the Art Club (Dyke 1996:6-7). Williams (1991:121) suggests that Mercer may have done some work with Frederic Ward Putnam at this time. The history work he did in his junior year may have involved some reading on early American history with Justin Winsor, the college librarian at Harvard (Reed 1987:10), as Mercer later in his career conducted correspondence with Winsor and utilized some of the plates in Winsor's eight-volume history for designs for his ceramic tile work in his later career (Reed 1987:125).

After his graduation from Harvard in 1879, Mercer, as had his cousins, initially read law with the firm of his uncle, Peter McCall, a former mayor of Philadelphia (Dyke 1996:7; Reed 1987:10). His uncle died in 1881, so Mercer finished his training with the firm of Fraley and Hollingsworth for the rest of that year. As soon as he was certified to practice law in November 1881, being admitted to the Court of Common Pleas in Philadelphia, he left for Europe with his Harvard classmate Arthur Astor Carey, the same Carey who (we will see later) was instrumental in getting Mercer involved in the American Arts and Crafts movement (Reed 1987:10). Thus most sources suggest that it is highly doubtful that Mercer actually practiced law after he was admitted to the Philadelphia Bar Association.

Mercer's interest in historical concerns grew at this same time. In 1880 he helped to found the Bucks County Historical Society, and he maintained his association with this group throughout his life, later becoming one of its principal patrons as well as its president from 1911 until his death in 1930 (Mason 1956:154, 161). In late 1881 he began a series of trips to Europe and the Near East, trips that included floating the Danube and the Nile and visiting all the tourist spots in England, Germany, France, Italy, Turkey, and Egypt (Freeman 1996:64). On those trips "he sketched, photographed, collected all sorts of objects, [and] investigated historic sites"; "art work and historical researches continued to play important roles" (Dyke 1996:7, 9). Thus his exposure in his Harvard College training to the work of Norton in art and art history seems to have been a formative factor in his life.

The Lenape stone case is the first good evidence of Mercer's involvement in American archaeological concerns. Today, experts agree that this stone gorget, with its incised design showing a fight between a mammoth and a group of Indians on one side, is a forgery. It was reported by its "finder," Bernard Z. Hansell, to have been plowed out of a field on his farm near Doylestown in 1872. The Lenape stone then passed into the hands of 18-year-old Henry D. Paxson (later one of the directors of the Bucks County Historical Society), who had begun collecting local Indian artifacts in 1876, at the age of 12. In 1881, Hansell agreed to sell the first half to Paxson; later that same year, Hansell sold the second half to Squire Albert S. Paxson (Henry's father) in order to pay his taxes (Sandford 1965:1, 45, 49). The Lenape stone first came to Mercer's attention in 1882, when Henry Paxson loaned it to Captain John S. Bailey, a local antiquarian, who gave a talk on the stone at the Bucks County Historical Society (Fackenthal 1930:4; Mercer 1885:2, 61–68; Wilson 1899:321).

The Lenape stone became a significant component of Mercer's research and contributions in the next dozen years. Through his interest in assessing the authenticity of the stone, Mercer became involved in investigating the possibility of the association of humans with late Pleistocene fauna in the New World. Captain Bailey also brought the Lenape stone to the attention of Professor Henry Carvill Lewis—a member of the Second Geological Survey of Pennsylvania, and of the Academy of Natural Sciences in Philadelphia. Professor Lewis was a good friend of Charles Conrad Abbott's (Kraft 1993:5, 1996:1), who the decade before had begun championing the possibility of the great antiquity of the artifacts from the Delaware River Trenton gravels. Lewis and Abbott would later form part of an important conduit for Mercer's association with the Academy of Natural Sciences in 1889 and with the University of Pennsylvania in 1891.

Even from the first discussions of the Lenape stone, Mercer apparently was one of only a few individuals convinced of its authenticity. He spent considerable time studying and describing the stone, trying to link the 20 pictographs on it to a condensed version of the presumed migration myth of the Delaware (or Lenape) Indians, the Walam Olum myth as detailed in Constantine Rafinesque's (1783–1840) writings (Williams 1991:118; see also chap. 3). In 1885 he published *The Lenape Stone; or, the Indian and the Mammoth*, in which he laid out his arguments for its genuineness. It is a mark of Mercer's meticulous methodology, later also seen in his cave excavation reports, that he considered the possibility of fraud in this analysis, and that he not only sought, but published, a series of professional opinions on the stone, most of which were in opposition to his own position. In his introduction to the volume, Mercer acknowledged that no scientific observer was present at its discovery; that the stone had been cleaned several times since and thus many of the tests of the era were rendered impossible; and that particularly in the Philadelphia area there had been several fraudulent artifacts produced by counterfeiters "within the last few years" (Mercer 1885:iii).

Mercer devotes the last third of this monograph to the reports of outside observers such as Professor Lewis, Professor Daniel C. Brinton, and other individuals whose opinions he quotes virtually verbatim (1885:61–93). These period experts were essentially in concert in making a series of observations that cast doubt on the Lenape stone. Among the reasons they most frequently advanced to argue that the Lenape stone was a forgery were (1) the similarity (to the point of near identity) of the incised mammoth design on the Lenape gorget to the mammoth design on an artifact found in France in 1864; (2) the fact that some of the incised lines failed to meet across the break in the stone; (3) the freshness and lack of patination of the incised lines; and (4) the fact that the incised lines seemed to have been made by a steel tool.

Even among the local Buck County residents, Mercer was apparently in a minority in believing in the Lenape stone's authenticity. Within two years of Captain Bailey's first public description of the stone, the local weekly Doylestown paper, *The Intelligencer*, referred to the stone as a "forgery" in its August 9, 1884, edition, and it repeated the charge of "counterfeiting" two weeks later on August 23, 1884 (Kraft 1996:2). In the September 6 issue, a letter from Brinton indicates that he had first been shown the stone by Professor Lewis, and found it to be a modern fraud (Mercer 1885:68–69). Even Charles Abbott, who was so convinced of the genuine antiquity of the Trenton gravel materials, considered the Lenape stone a forgery (Kraft 1996:2).

Mercer, however, remained persuaded of its authenticity, and he paid for the publication of his monograph in 1885 to make the case for its genuineness. He continued to argue for its importance during his employment at the University of Pennsylvania (Mercer 1897g:177), and even later, in a 1907 talk to the Bucks County Historical Society, he still championed its authenticity (Mercer 1907:493). Some evidence suggests that he never recanted this view, as in 1919 he searched for and located Rafinesque's unmarked grave and put a marker on it. And later, in 1924, Mercer was active in getting Rafinesque's remains transferred to a crypt at Transylvania College in Lexington, Kentucky, where Rafinesque had taught, and had written part of the Walam Olum (Williams 1991:115, 121). It was, of course, Rafinesque's Lenape migration myth that Mercer had believed the gorget to represent.

While the Lenape gorget is usually the archaeological reference most American prehistoric archaeologists have heard of, if they have heard of Mercer's work at all, it is Mercer's subsequent work at the University of Pennsylvania from 1891 to 1897, where he dedicated himself to exploring caves, searching for possible supporting evidence of late Pleistocene occurrences of humans in North America, that is of particular importance to the argument here. During the course of this work, Mercer conducted and published some of the first explicitly stratigraphic excavations in North America, at least two decades before Manuel Gamio, Alfred Kidder, and Nels Nelson (Browman and Givens 1996). As indicated above, Mercer's association with the University of Pennsylvania may well have derived from his contacts with Abbott, Brinton, and Lewis. He appears to have been invited to work at the university by Abbott, who had just been hired as the curator of the Department of Archaeology and Paleontology, a department newly created at the university in 1889 (Madeira 1964:19). Mercer returned home from one of his several European trips in October 1889 to find an invitation from William Pepper, president of the university, to join the newly organized Archaeological Association of the University of Pennsylvania; he accepted the invitation and joined early in 1890 (Reed 1987:10). The following year, Mercer was appointed one of ten "managers" of the Department of Archaeology and Paleontology of the Museum of Science and Art, later known as the University Museum (Dyke 1996:11; Reed 1987:14), joining individuals such as Charles Abbott, Daniel Brinton, Edward Cope, Stewart Culin, and Sara Stevenson.

Mercer's early work for the museum was primarily directed toward evaluating the antiquity of purported Pleistocene artifacts from the Delaware River valley, perhaps not surprising in view of the fact that Dr. Charles Abbott had helped to recruit him (see discussion of Abbott below), and that another well-known museum colleague, Professor Daniel Brinton, also seemed interested in having the Trenton materials authenticated (Brinton 1887:291). Mercer spent considerable time inspecting the site of Abbott's find, doing his own excavations and conducting his own surface surveys in the vicinity, where he located some prehistoric quarries (see Mercer papers 1892 to 1897). As a result of these investigations, Mercer came to agree with Professor William Holmes that the Trenton gravel argillites were nothing more than quarry blanks and thus not the late Pleistocene tools Abbott (1872, 1873, 1876) believed them to be.

Mercer arrived at this conclusion in his standard meticulous fashion, evaluating the evidence from his own investigations of known modern North American aboriginal quarry material (Mercer 1892), from his examinations of Neolithic and Paleolithic quarries in Europe (Mercer 1893, 1894i, 1895a), and from his own careful excavations of local quarries in the Delaware River region (Mercer 1894b, 1894d, 1894g, 1894h, 1897c, 1897h). Mercer (1898) employed great care while conducting excavations as part of a blue-ribbon panel of specialists who participated in test examinations of the Trenton site in 1897 (involving, according to the report at the American Association for the Advancement of Science, the following archaeological and geological experts: Charles C. Abbott, Harrison Allen, Stewart Culin, Arthur Hollick, William H. Holmes, George N. Knapp, Henry B. Kummel, William Libbey, John C. Smock, Rollin D. Salisbury, Ernest Volk, Thomas Wilson, and George Frederick Wright—a sort of precursor to the Folsom situation of 1927). In the field tests he helped excavate, Mercer may have employed artificial one-foot stratigraphic units, but he clearly recorded every artifact in situ, in three-dimensional coordinates, such that Leslie Spier was later able to employ Mercer's materials in his own studies of the Trenton argillites, crediting Mercer with providing "the first precise account of the argillite culture" (Spier 1918:177). Mercer's conclusion, based on his own excavation data, his previous experience with quarries, and the geological interpretations of Kummel (1898:350), was that the Trenton gravel argillites were quarry materials, clearly Holocene in nature (Mercer 1894b:85, 1895a:383, 1898:380).

The critical events resulting in Mercer's methodological innovation of conducting stratigraphic excavation in the Americas appear to have occurred in 1891 and 1892. In 1891, in the course of his work with evaluating the Trenton materials, he met the French scholars Marcellin Boule and Albert Gaudry, who, while attending a scientific conference in Washington, D.C., had arranged a visit to inspect the Trenton gravel sites (Mercer 1893:37). In 1892, at the invitation of Gaudry and Boule, Mercer traveled to France, where he reviewed the French sites and methodology (see discussion below on Boule and Gaudry as well). Mercer subsequently kept a lively correspondence with Boule (until Mercer shifted careers in 1897), sending him information on American sites and cave explorations (see, e.g., Boule 1893, 1894a, 1894b, 1896, 1900) and receiving in return information about the latest work in the Upper Paleolithic in France (see Mercer's monthly columns in the *American Naturalist* for the years 1894 to 1897).

Mercer was in Europe from the late fall of 1892 through mid-spring of 1893 as an honorary member of the U.S. Archaeological Commission to the Columbian Historical Exposition at Madrid, commemorating the Fourth Century of the Discovery of America, to collect specimens for the Department of Archaeology and Paleontology of the University of Pennsylvania, and also to attend the International Congress of

Anthropology in 1893 (Mason 1956:155; Mercer 1893, 1894a, 1895a, 1897c). In part he owed his invitation to one of his colleagues in the department, Stewart Culin, who was secretary of the Archaeological Commission delegation (Reed 1987:170). Mercer had prepared an exhibition of a cache of 117 argillite blades that he had found at Ridge's Island along the Delaware River the previous year as part of his demonstration of the recent origin of the Trenton materials, for which he was awarded a bronze medal at this exposition (Dyke 1996:11; Reed 1987:14).

While in Europe for this exposition, Mercer also visited the excavations at Abbeville, Amiens, Chelles, Menchecourt, Saint-Acheul, and other sites in France, San Isidro in Spain, and Caddington in England, and examined the collections of Boucher de Perthes and d'Ault du Mesnil from the Somme River valley. He saw as well the English specimens in the British Museum, including those excavated by Pengelly from Brixham Cave in Torquay. He purchased specimens from the workmen at Abbeville and Chelles but noted that he did so with extreme care, as forgeries by quarry workmen were very common (Mercer 1897c:11). He was most pleased with actually finding a Paleolithic tool in situ at San Isidro, near Madrid (Mercer 1897c:16).

Mercer was awarded a "Diplôme d'Anthropologie" in Paris in 1893 (Dyke 1996:11), but it is unclear whether this was solely honorific or from some kind of training with Boule, de Mortillet, and Gaudry. He came back from his trip convinced that cave exploration was the solution to his quest for Pleistocene associations of humans, noting, "Excavation is what we need, and identification of specimens with fixed geological horizons. Evidently we must make haste slowly" (Mercer 1894a:68). After viewing the European prehistoric tools, he was even more convinced that the Trenton gravel specimens were nothing more than quarry workshop preforms (Mercer 1893:970), and he returned to the United States persuaded that the proper place to find evidence of late Pleistocene human occupations would be in caves, not open-air sites. Having observed such evidence in the ongoing work he had visited with Boule, Gaudry, and other European archaeologists, as well as through reading reports for other cave finds in Asia and Africa, he argued that "in the subterranean floor deposits of the New World, therefore, we may suppose that the problematic existence of Pleistocene man might be soonest and easiest demonstrated" (Mercer 1896c:30).

Mercer's quest for evidence of the New World Paleolithic, he noted, "had occupied my thoughts since 1890" (Mercer 1896b:12). Between 1893 and 1896 he conducted test excavations at more than three dozen caves in North America. Several of the caves in the Pennsylvania area he found very badly disturbed, particularly from the excavations for saltpeter by gunpowder makers for the Revolutionary War, the War of 1812, and the Civil War (Mercer 1897a:41). Mercer's most important archaeological excavation work occurred after Abbott resigned, and Mercer was named to replace him in 1894 as Curator of American and Prehistoric Archaeology at the museum. As noted in the discussion of the Lenape gorget, Mercer had a style of dispassionate and meticulous description of his fieldwork and finds. One of his contemporaries, and a mentor, paleontologist Edward Cope, noted with approval that Mercer's excavations were conducted "with great care, . . . saving all the fragments met with, carefully classified as to position" (Cope 1895:597), something unusual for the day; and later, when Mercer shifted his passion to historic material culture, this meticulous record keeping remained one of his hallmarks, such that it was noted that he kept "detailed records of his work, including expense accounts down to the price of a cup of coffee" (Snyder 1985:3).

Mercer's implementation of stratigraphic excavation is of particular interest. His first explicit use of stratigraphic excavation may date to 1894, after he assumed the museum curatorship, at one or more of the sites in Pennsylvania. There is indirect evidence that he employed one-foot levels to excavate the jasper quarry site at Lehigh Hills in 1894 (Mercer 1894b:87). Mercer conducted excavations at the Port Kennedy bone cave in Pennsylvania in 1894, 1895, and 1896 (Mercer 1895b, 1899a), but it is only in the final report for the expedition that he discusses his excavation technique. The excavation at Port Kennedy employed artificial stratigraphic units reminiscent of the procedure William Pengelly had employed at Brixham Cave in England. Mercer excavated the site in one-foot vertical levels, with each excavation unit being three feet square and one foot in depth, and indicated that this procedure was employed for each of the three seasons (Mercer 1899a:271–272). Such care in his excavation technique allowed him to define an earlier, preceramic level underlying a ceramic level at an excavation at Lower Black Eddy, along the Delaware River (Mercer 1894g:304, 1897c:78, 1898:377). According to Williams (1991:120), Mercer may have been among the first American investigators to make this observation.

The most explicit description of Mercer's methodology is contained in his report of his series of cave excavations in 1895 in the Yucatán of Mexico. Mercer became involved in excavations in the Yucatán through the help of John White Corwith of Chicago. Corwith had become interested in Mercer's attempt to find paleolithic relics at Port Kennedy, first visiting in November 1894, and thus decided to fund a major expedition to search for paleolithic activities south of the border (Mercer 1895b, 1896b:13). Mercer had by 1894 plumbed several dozen caves in the eastern United States, but because he had failed to find the hoped-for evidence of paleolithic occupations, he thought he might have better luck in Mexico or South America. Mercer initially considered working in the Lagoa Santa area of Brazil, or in various caves in Peru (Mercer 1896b:13). However, Professor Angelo Heilprin, a colleague of his in the Academy of Natural Sciences of Philadelphia, informed Mercer that there were many large, dry caves in the Yucatán, so it was agreed that the Corwith-funded expedition would go to explore these caves for evidence of Pleistocene human occupations.

Mercer indicated that his excavation strategy in the Yucatecan caves was by "culture layers" (Mercer 1896b:12). He described his method as "working horizontally into them and picking out specimens from their matrices with the trowel," and removing the contents of each horizontal layer before proceeding into the next (Mercer 1896b:27, 109). In many of the caves he employed artificial six-inch vertical levels, in others one-foot levels, but he coordinated these excavation units into cultural layers in his descriptions, and in his illustrations he carefully identified the materials excavated in situ from each layer of that cave.

Why do we know so little about Mercer's stratigraphic excavation? One could argue that his career change in 1897 removed him from the mainstream of American archaeology so that he did not connect with the group of individuals involved in developing the discipline. After all, he was active in conducting archaeological excavations only between 1891 and 1897, so there would only have been a limited period of contact with other professionals in the field. As was typical for the time, the bulk of his work, whether papers or notes, only provides information on the results, not the method employed. Because most of his publications between 1894 and 1897 did not describe his method, it would have been difficult for other practitioners to appreciate the methodological innovations he had developed and employed. The place of publication may also have limited access; many of his contributions were published in limited-circulation University of Pennsylvania sources, such as the Papers of the Department of American and Prehistoric Archaeology or the Series in Philology, Literature and Archaeology. He published only one paper in the *American Anthropologist* (Mercer 1894b); otherwise, only short notes on the results—not method—of his excavation work appeared in the *American Naturalist*,

The Archaeologist and in the annual proceedings of the American Philosophical Society and the American Association for the Advancement of Science (where he had been elected a Fellow in 1893) between 1892 and 1898.

Although the excavation profile published in Mercer's paper in the *American Anthropologist* (1894b:87) illustrated one-foot stratigraphic excavation units, the text does not explain his methodology, and even the most interested reader would not have understood his technique. Thus, it appears that unless an archaeologist had visited Mercer at Pennsylvania between 1894 and 1896 (the years when we can clearly demonstrate that he was doing explicit stratigraphic excavation) or had access to the few limited-circulation reports in which he discussed his methods, Mercer's stratigraphic excavation technique would pass unknown. The single best opportunity Mercer would have had to demonstrate and possibly pass on his method was in the blue-ribbon panel examination of the Trenton gravels argillite culture in 1897—but if he indeed did employ the method, its importance became lost in the passion of the participants arguing whether or not the tools were evidence of "glacial man."

Additionally, as Williams (1991:120) suggests, it may simply be because of Mercer's earlier association with the Lenape stone, which was discounted as a fraud by most of the archaeologists of the day, that little heed was paid to his methodological contributions. Most recently, a reviewer of a draft of this chapter suggested that homophobia may have been another possible contributing cause, observing that Mercer "was an 'odd' fellow to his Harvard classmates, and a somewhat solitary homosexual" (name withheld, personal communication, February 26, 1998).

THE AMERICAN COLLEAGUES

Edward Drinker Cope, Ph.D. (1840–1897)

Edward Drinker Cope of Pennsylvania and Othniel Charles Marsh of Yale were competitors and antagonists in early American paleontology. Both had independent funding and sought to outbid each other to secure the most important fossils for their institutions. Cope was initially a student, then instructor, at the Academy of Natural Sciences in Philadelphia, and later as Professor, in 1889, with the University of Pennsylvania. In 1873 he convinced Ferdinand V. Hayden to open the *Paleontological Bulletin* as a venue for him, as well as other colleagues, to publish and secure quick credit for the discovery of new fossils

(Conaway 1995:106), but the reorganization of the U.S. Geological Survey in 1878 left Clarence King—a Marsh ally—in control of publication, and Cope lost his publication outlet (Rainger 1991:18). In 1879, with King's backing, Marsh secured the position that he and Cope had been vying for with the U.S. Geological Survey, which resulted in Marsh being, in effect, in control of paleontological publication through the *American Journal of Science* (Rainger 1991:17). Hence Cope sought to secure his own publication outlet, and in 1877 he purchased the *American Naturalist*. The last issue of that year (vol. 11, no. 12, p. 758) announced the ownership change, and henceforth Cope is listed as the copyright holder until his death in 1897.

The *American Naturalist* has a linkage to important archaeological figures in the nineteenth century. Frederic Putnam was its coeditor from its founding through the last issue of 1875, when he resigned because of his recent appointment at Harvard University's Peabody Museum. Mercer (as we note below) provided an important contact point for the exchange of archaeological information for several years through his position as associate editor with Cope. Mercer's replacement in 1897 was Frank Russell. (Russell was the first American archaeologist for whom I have found documentation that he provided classroom instruction in archaeological excavation methodology in a course taught at Harvard in 1900–1901 [see Chapter 11]. As early as 1885, Putnam had offered private tutorials on how to conduct explicitly stratigraphic excavation, but these were not officially a part of the Harvard College curriculum.) However, from the beginning, publication expenses of the *American Naturalist* resulted in a major financial strain on Cope, primarily because of the "bone wars" being waged between himself and Marsh. This resulted in a circular that was issued by 13 prominent previous supporters of the journal, including Alexander Agassiz, James D. Dana, Asa Gray, Othniel Marsh, and John S. Newberry, in which they withdrew intellectual support for the journal (Wallace 1999:175). By the early 1880s Cope could no longer afford to purchase specimens from collectors and had to abandon fieldwork, although he did encourage continued exploration by his associates at the University of Pennsylvania.

Cope was one of Mercer's principal mentors at the University of Pennsylvania. In 1889, when the Department of Archaeology and Paleontology (the forerunner of the current University Museum) was formed, Cope was included as the paleontologist, being supported by his faculty salary from his appointment to the university earlier that year. Cope had a long-term interest in archaeology, presenting papers on archaeological discoveries he made in New Mexico in 1874 (Cope 1876, 1879) and in Nebraska in 1876 (Wallace 1999:129), but he was particularly interested in finding evidence of humans in association with Pleistocene fauna, in part because this was a "hot topic" being discussed by his paleontological colleagues in Europe. Between 1868 and 1871 he had explored a series of caves, finding paleontological specimens but no human evidence (Cope 1895:596). He was instrumental in getting Mercer involved in the early 1890s in continuing these cave excavations (Madeira 1964:20–21; Osborn 1931:155); thus it is his influence, along with that of Boule and Gaudry, that got Mercer involved in cave archaeology as the proper locale to search for the evidence of humans at the end of the last Ice Age.

Cope may have been the principal means by which Mercer met Albert Gaudry, for Cope had met Gaudry in Paris in 1878, and between 1878 and 1890 he relied upon Gaudry for support in his conflicts with Marsh (Osborn 1931:244–251, 402). Cope and Dr. Lewis Woolman secured Mercer's election to membership in the Academy of Natural Sciences of Philadelphia in 1893, and Cope also is credited, in part, with Mercer's election as a Fellow of the American Association for the Advancement of Science in 1893 (Reed 1987:xvi). Cope, as editor and owner, was responsible for naming Mercer to a position on the *American Naturalist* as well. In 1894 Mercer took over the monthly section in the *American Naturalist* entitled "Archaeology and Ethnology" from Thomas Wilson of the Smithsonian. Mercer wrote this column for three years, until 1897, when, upon Cope's death, a new editor for the *American Naturalist* was selected and the ensuing editorial realignment resulted in Mercer losing his assistant editorship to Frank Russell.

Cope was convinced that "the existence of Paleolithic man in North America" would be found, contemporary with *Equus* and *Mylodon* fauna (Cope 1895:599). He supported Abbott's Trenton work, writing that "the attempt of Mr. W. H. Holmes to discredit these alleged discoveries does not appear to me to be successful" (Cope 1895:595) (although in this he later was proved wrong). He expected Mercer to ultimately find the definitive evidence, noting that in 1893 Mercer had embarked on a program of excavating caves in the Kanawha, Ohio, and Tennessee River drainages, and reporting with hope in 1894 that "from the results of Mercer's labors so far, it looks as though there may have been two sets of cave deposits of different ages" (Osborn 1931:156). Cope did the analysis of all the faunal remains from these excavations for Mercer, which ultimately included caves in Illinois, Indiana, Kentucky, Pennsylvania, Virginia, West Virginia, Tennessee, and even one in southern Texas, as well as open-air sites in Maine, New Jersey, and Pennsylvania.

Charles Conrad Abbott, M.D. (1843–1919)

Abbott had received his M.D. from the University of Pennsylvania in 1865. He began his excavations in the Trenton gravels of New Jersey as early as 1867 and had begun sending information about his project to Frederic Ward Putnam while Putnam was still at the museum in Salem (Abbott 1872, 1873; Hinsley 1985:61). Abbott and Putnam had known each other a decade earlier, when both shared an interest in collecting ichthyological specimens.[2] Later, in 1875, Putnam recruited Abbott to be one of his growing group of part-time collectors for Harvard University's Peabody Museum (Putnam 1898c), an association that lasted until Putnam retired in 1909. Putnam sponsored Abbott for a museum curatorship at the University of Pennsylvania in 1889 (Hinsley 1985:65), and when the Department of Archaeology and Paleontology was organized there in 1891, Abbott was the only full-time salaried employee, as the curator of American Collections. Edward Cope, curator of Paleontology, and Herman Hilprecht, curator of Babylonian Collections, were supported by their faculty salaries from other academic departments at the University of Pennsylvania, and Sara Stevenson, curator of Egyptian Collections, was a volunteer (Madeira 1964:20). Abbott resigned from the department in 1893 after a conflict of opinion with Daniel Brinton, Stewart Culin, and the overseeing board over whether the direction of the museum ought to be to secure objects for display or to engage in research. Shortly thereafter, Brinton fell victim to the same forces, withdrawing from the museum in 1894 (Darnell 1970:82–83; Hinsley 1985:66; Madeira 1964:20; Winegrad 1993:21). Mercer, who had been working for the museum under Abbott's direction, was named to replace Abbott as curator of American Collections in 1894, a position he held until he resigned in 1897 (Mason 1956:155).

Among Mercer's first tasks for the university under Abbott's supervision was the search for the source of stone for the alleged Ice Age tools that Abbott had championed near Trenton. Abbott became increasingly convinced that his finds from the Delaware gravels near Trenton represented examples of paleolithic tools similar to those being reported in Europe. None of the reputed Trenton paleolithic tools had been found in situ by Abbott, Boyd Dawkins, Haynes, Putnam, or the other experts who had visited the Trenton gravel sites. After having found genuine Paleolithic specimens from San Isidro, Chemin de Post, and León, Mercer was particularly keen to find a similar object in place at Trenton. Abbott clearly was one of the influential individuals in this period of Mercer's career. Mercer made a number of trips to the Trenton site, where he conducted his own explorations. He also conducted additional regional surveys in which he located probable quarries.

Early in his work at the University of Pennsylvania, Mercer decided that he wanted in situ context, no doubt due to the kinds of criticisms directed at the Lenape gorget. To this end, he believed that such a context was most likely to occur in caves (as had been suggested to him by Boule as well as Cope) rather than in redeposited river gravels. The loss of two of his mentors—Abbott from the museum in 1894 and from personal friendship in 1896 over conflicts on the Trenton gravels artifacts, and Cope by death in 1897—seems likely as one of the contributing factors in Mercer's decision to resign his curator position in 1897 and shift his research to his newly discovered interest in historic material culture.

THE FRENCH COLLEAGUES

Albert Gaudry (1827–1908)

Albert Gaudry and Marcellin Boule came to visit the Trenton site while participating in the International Congress of Geology in Washington, D.C., in 1891. They were initially taken out to the site by Charles Abbott and Thomas Wilson, but Mercer mentions that they later accompanied him to revisit the locale. The visit and tentative acceptance by Boule and Gaudry of the Trenton materials put a stamp of approval on the site for the Europeans (Obermaier 1924:93). Subsequently, as a member of the U.S. Commission to the Madrid Exposition of 1892 and 1893, Mercer visited Boule and Gaudry in France and collected tools from Abbeville, Saint-Acheul, Chelles, and other locales (Mercer 1893). It is from Gaudry's and Boule's influence, I believe, that Mercer derived his ideas about excavation technique, as he spent several months touring various European archaeological sites recommended by Boule, Cope, and Gaudry before returning to Pennsylvania, where he not only took over the curation of the Trenton materials (because Abbott had resigned) but also began his own research seeking "Paleolithic" American Indians.

Gaudry had been the principal French scholar who had worked in 1859 with Evans, Lyell, Prestwich, and others when they had come to assess Boucher de Perthes claims. Evans, Lyell, and Prestwich were all fresh from William Pengelly's Torquay work, and they imparted to

Gaudry the empirical basis (i.e., stratigraphic excavation) for the British certainty that humans and extinct fauna had coexisted. Gaudry and Lyell went together in June 1859 to visit the Amiens sites, after Prestwich and Falconer had reported on the evidence.

Just beginning his career as a paleontologist, Gaudry decided to put in some excavations of his own as well. He extracted nine hand axes, along with teeth from an extinct ox, from a depth of 14 feet, in the same level at which nearby he also recovered rhinoceros, elephant, and hippopotamus bones (Boule and Vallois 1957/1921:15; Gaudry 1859:466; Grayson 1983:191). Gaudry then presented his findings on September 26 and October 3, 1859, to the Académie des Sciences in Paris, published in the proceedings for October 1859, which signaled the official recognition by the French learned world of the same event occurring simultaneously in England, the abandonment of the age-old denial of the antiquity of humans (Prestwich 1859:634, 1860:254; Schnapp 1996:314).

The English paleontological establishment (Evans, Falconer, Lyell, Prestwich, etc.) cites Gaudry, and Gaudry and de Mortillet cite the English (Pengelly, Prestwich, Evans, etc.); thus it is clear that the French were well aware of the breakthrough in excavation methodology that had occurred in England at Pengelly's work at Brixham Cave. Later, about 1882, Gaudry was part of the team teaching Prince Albert I of Monaco prehistoric archaeological technique. Prince Albert studied paleontology with Gaudry, prehistoric archaeology with Gabriel de Mortillet, and physical anthropology with Léonce Manouvrier. Prince Albert I came away from this training speaking of having learned an important new technique: stratigraphic excavation (Villeneuve 1906:31).

Pierre Marcellin Boule (1861–1942)

Marcellin Boule did his doctoral training in Paleolithic studies with Gaudry in 1886 and 1887 (Richard 1999b:263). As noted above, Boule and Gaudry traveled together in 1891 to the Trenton gravel site to inspect its reputed Paleolithic assemblages, where they met Mercer. When Mercer returned to Europe in 1892 and 1893, Boule spent considerable time with him. Boule had only a few years before written a summary essay on the evidence for Upper Paleolithic humans, mentioning the Trenton gravels as the principal contender for a site of that antiquity in North America (Boule 1888:656). Thus Boule, having just written on the subject, was quite interested in inspecting the Trenton site firsthand. He and Gaudry came away convinced of the reality of the tools, and they assumed that the associations were the same as in Europe. Boule (1893:37) published arguments in support of Abbott's interpretation, and opposed to Holmes's explanation. Among other significant research, Boule (1905), through the use of experimental archaeology, was a pioneer in demonstrating the methods by which eoliths could be produced without any human intervention.

Boule was much more directly involved in excavation work than Gaudry; the two collaborated primarily on a series of paleontological studies. However, Boule and Émile Cartailhac published jointly on a series of archaeological excavations. Later, with the help of Cartailhac and Cartailhac's student Abbé Henri Edouard Breuil, Boule persuaded Prince Albert I of Monaco to fund the Institut de Paléontologie Humaine (Gruber 1970). Prince Albert then hired Boule as director and Hugo Obermaier and Abbé Breuil as professors of this institute. As I have pointed out elsewhere (Browman and Givens 1996:83), Obermaier and Breuil provided Nels Nelson with his first training in stratigraphic excavation in 1913. Boule helped to found *L'Anthropologie* and was its coeditor from 1893 until 1930; he also started another publications series, the *Annales de Paléontologie*, in 1906 (Richard 1999b:263-264). Boule and Mercer seem to have kept up an active correspondence until perhaps 1897, for Mercer published notes and news sent by Boule in his column in the *American Naturalist* from 1894 to 1897, and Boule similarly published reference to Mercer's work in *L'Anthropologie* from 1894 to 1900.

Louis Laurent Marie Gabriel de Mortillet (1821-1898)

Gabriel de Mortillet is less a principal in the matter of Mercer than a critical component of the developing French context. His initial work in archaeology had been in Italy and Switzerland between 1853 and 1864, while in exile. De Mortillet was very interested in material culture, and in 1864 he founded the journal *Matériaux pour l'Histoire Positive et Philosophique de l'Homme*; his interest in material culture led to revolutionizing the periodization of prehistoric European cultures. He was the first individual to suggest employing a type site, and defining the culture with respect to the attributes of the artifacts from the type site and type unit, rather than utilizing a major faunal type to define human cultural phases, as had been done up to that point (Richard 1999a:98). He first proposed this idea in 1867, and he had the sequence mainly worked out (cultures such as Aurignacian, Mousterian, Perigordian, Solutrean, etc.) when he proposed it at the International Conference of Archaeology and Prehistoric Archaeology at Brussels in 1872. The complete sequence was in place by 1883 (de Mortillet 1883:151; Schnapp 1996:322; Van Riper 1993:195).

In 1868, at the request of Jeffries Wyman, de Mortillet sold a collection of 3,000 examples of tools from Abbeville, Amiens, Saint-Acheul, and other French Paleolithic sites to the Peabody Museum, two years after the museum's founding (Brew 1966b:42). These items had previously been part of de Mortillet's "Paris Exposition" in 1867 for the Second International Congress of Archaeology and Prehistory, and they had been published in *Matériaux pour l'Histoire Positive et Philosophique de l'Homme* (Daniel 1968:62).[3] This was the largest of three collections that Wyman had purchased to solve one of the needs that the Peabody Museum had noted when founded, that is, "the gathering of means for making direct comparison between the implements of the stone age of the old world and the new" (Wyman 1869:11). Charles Abbott studied these materials after he became one of Putnam's field volunteers, and he thought he saw similarities with his Trenton gravel assemblage. Abbott wrote de Mortillet concerning his finds in the Trenton gravels, and based on the illustrations Abbott had mailed to him, de Mortillet sent a letter in 1879 to Abbott supporting the Trenton site as paleolithic, a letter Abbott published in 1881 (Kraft 1993:4).

De Mortillet was the key member in the training in 1882–1883 of the excavation team of Prince Albert I of Monaco, resulting in the explicit decision by Prince Albert to pursue stratigraphic excavations, and thus the subsequent linkages with Boule, Obermaier, and Breuil to Mercer and Nelson, as noted above. In 1876, at the École d'Anthropologie, where de Mortillet held the chair in prehistoric archaeology from its founding in 1876 to his death in 1898, he taught the first courses ever in archaeology in France; initially independent, this school was later integrated into a unit then called the École de Louvre, which became part of the Sorbonne. From 1876 to 1880 he was in charge of teaching the "détermination des débris humains au moyen de l'archéologie" in the school. From 1880 to 1883 the focus turned specifically toward prehistoric archaeology, with specific trips to the quaternary beds at Chelles, Saint-Acheul, Amiens, Abbeville, Montières, Menchecourt, and other Paleolithic locales. According to MacCurdy (1899:912), de Mortillet had "trained a majority of all who are now teaching" anthropology and archaeology in the 1890s in France. His successor, Louis-Joseph Capitan, is said to have taught the first explicit methodological course on excavation in 1899, "Exposé détaillé des méthodes générales à mettre en oeuvre pour l'étude de la préhistoire: stratigraphie" (L'École d'Anthropologie de Paris 1907:51–53). De Mortillet and the Ecole, along with Boule and Gaudry, form a definitive part of the context of French prehistory in the 1880s and 1890s that Mercer came in contact with in his European studies. Their students appear to be materially involved in the creation of the first edition, in 1906, of the *Manuel de Recherchés Préhistoriques*, a 332-page manual that dealt with, among other things, the methods for excavating sites, advocating the excavation of each archaeological stratum separately, the establishment of trench units of .70 meters in width and .20 meters in height to excavate thicker deposits, and the utilization of control points to locate all artifacts horizontally and vertically as recovered.

Geoffroy d'Ault du Mesnil

Mercer notes that "geologist" Geoffroy d'Ault du Mesnil showed him the locales of Saint-Acheul and Abbeville in the Somme River valley during his 1892–1893 trip (Mercer 1893:964). Here was another individual to investigate as one of the possible sources who may have acquainted Mercer with the idea of stratigraphic excavation. But who was d'Ault du Mesnil? Most standard sources of the period do not mention him, the exception being the recent summary of Coye (1997). From what I can glean, he seems to have started out as a wealthy collector who, because of his interest in prehistory, became self-taught in geology. His first professional listing is in 1884, as a member of the Association Française pour l'Avancement des Sciences, where he lists himself as a "geologist," and as conservator and administrator of the "Musées à Abbeville." The recurrent use of "museums" seems to imply that he had charge of the Boucher des Perthes museum in Abbeville as well as his own. His association with these museums continued until 1904, when he retired and moved to Paris.

The collections of Abbevillian and Acheulian tools in d'Ault du Mesnil's museum apparently rivaled that of Boucher de Perthes, for in 1883, when de Mortillet showed Prince Albert I of Monaco the kinds of tools he should look for at the Grimaldi caverns, they visited the collections of both Boucher de Perthes and d'Ault du Mesnil (Villeneuve 1906:31). In 1883 the students of L'École d'Anthropologie de Paris also made a special trip to inspect the collections in the Boucher de Perthes and d'Ault de Mesnil museums (L'École d'Anthropologie de Paris 1907:53).

D'Ault du Mesnil conducted his own excavations, but apparently primarily to work out the depositional geology of these materials and other alleged early sites such as Thenay (d'Ault du Mesnil 1885, 1886;

d'Ault du Mesnil et al. 1885). De Mortillet (1891:250) and Wilson (1899:315) indicate that d'Ault du Mesnil produced the first geological study detailing the correlation of stone artifacts with geological strata at Abbeville and Saint-Acheul. This work was presented first at the Limoges session of the Association Française pour l'Avancement des Sciences in 1890 (d'Ault du Mesnil 1891; de Mortillet 1891:250). It was not published in those proceedings, however, but appeared later in the *Revue Mensuelle de l'École d'Anthropologie* (d'Ault du Mesnil 1896). Abbé Breuil indicated that part of his interest in prehistoric archaeology developed when d'Ault du Mesnil, who was one of his relatives, showed Breuil around the sites of Saint-Acheul and Abbeville in 1894 (Straus 1994:190). Later, d'Ault du Mesnil seems to have become interested in the Neolithic stone assemblages (Salmon et al. 1898) and also in the local menhirs and megalithic cultures. He served as the vice-president and president of the Commission for Megalithic Monuments from 1898 to the 1900s, and also one term as the president of the Société d'Anthropologie of Paris (L'École d'Anthropologie de Paris 1907:iv; Revue Mensuelle de l'École d'Anthropologie 8:411, 1898).

Because it was after visiting with de Mortillet in 1883, and also seeing d'Ault du Mesnil's collections, that Prince Albert wrote back to his excavation supervisor that they had been excavating wrong, that there was a new method, involving excavation by strata (Villeneuve 1906:31-32), at first it appeared that d'Ault du Mesnil may have been a possible source for the ideas of actual excavation by archaeological stratigraphic levels, but subsequently it proved to be de Mortillet who had passed on this technique to Prince Albert. Indeed, if it is fair to intuit method from family connections, d'Ault du Mesnil's lateral nephew, Comté Robert du Mesnil du Buisson, who worked in Near Eastern archaeology for many years, suggested that proper excavation was via massive trenches, even employing steam shovels (Bade 1934:8; Du Mesnil du Buisson 1934, 1968), clearly not the fine-scale stratigraphic excavation methodology sought in this chapter. Hence, while d'Ault du Mesnil now can be identified as a significant figure in French Paleolithic archaeology in the 1880s and 1890s, his importance was not in terms of developing excavation procedures.

Part II: The American Arts and Crafts Years

While in the Yucatán in 1897, Mercer evinced an interest in a new area—ethnographic and historic material culture. Based on field observations during the Corwith expedition in Mexico, he published a short piece on Yucatecan potters and their technology (Mercer 1897j). His subsequent researches took him two directions: collecting various tools of eighteenth- and nineteenth-century American pioneers, and developing handcrafted pottery and ceramic tile industries.

Several factors seem likely to have contributed to this career change. Mercer had spent nearly six arduous years fruitlessly searching for Pleistocene evidence of humans in the Americas, and he had exhausted the research design he had come back from France so enthusiastic about beginning after his training with Boule and Gaudry. His principal cave-archeology mentor, Edward Cope, had died, and as a result Mercer had lost his position as associate editor of the *American Naturalist*. His analysis of the Trenton gravel artifacts, with his determination of the artifacts there as quarry blanks and preforms instead of Upper Paleolithic hand axes, had alienated his former ally, Charles Abbott. Stewart Culin, who controlled the laboratory space at the university's museum, had gotten into a fight with Mercer over the large amount of space Mercer was using for his lithic collections and, in a pique, had him thrown out of the labs (Reed 1987:16). As a result, Mercer resigned his position at the university in 1897 and returned to his hometown of Doylestown, where he began working out of the Bucks County Historical Society.

Mercer immediately started collecting obsolete utensils and tools from his neighbors. He argued that American hand tools were rapidly disappearing, with more change, he said, in the last 2 or 3 generations than had taken place in any 15 or 20 generations previously (Wertime 1978:45). Mercer turned quickly to his new interests, opened an exhibit of 761 objects entitled "The Tools of the Nation Maker" at the Bucks County Historical Society in 1897, and published his initial collection in an annotated catalog (Mercer 1897k), which was revised as additional items were acquired. This exhibit was very space-consuming, and he soon was forced to move the collections from the Bucks County Historical Society to his own house. Over the next three decades he built up one of the finest collections of Colonial and early Federal artifacts of its kind (Freeman 1996:62). These include a multitude of items, such as apple-butter makers and anvils, baskets and buggies, copper pots and china plates, covered wagons and carpentry tools, door hardware and decorated iron stove plates, and so on (Mercer 1897i, 1897j, 1899b, 1923, 1929).

Mercer later built a museum structure to hold his collections, a structure he transferred to the Bucks County Historical Society at his death, along with an endowment to support the facility, which is now known as the Mercer Museum. At the time of its dedication in 1916, this museum had 14,428 historic implements, in addition to a library of 8,000 volumes. At the time of Mercer's death in 1930, the museum had 24,800 historic objects; by 1945 it boasted a collection of 25,668 specimens and a library of more than 45,000 volumes; and by the mid-1980s the historic tool collection had more than 30,000 specimens according to one source, or as many as 50,000 according to a second source (Dyke 1996:26; Freeman 1996:62; Mann 1945:24; Reed 1987:6; Snyder 1985:3). In addition to the historic tools and the library, this museum also housed Mercer's private collection of 10,000 prehistoric archaeological artifacts from Bucks County and the surrounding region, including the Lenape stone, in the North Tower of the museum (Lessey et al. 1958:12; Mann 1945:34).

After his conflict with the Bucks County Historical Society in 1897 over space for his historic tool collections, Mercer turned to developing his ideas regarding pottery and tiles (Reed 1987:17, 18, 30, 176 n. 15). He initially focused on pottery, but soon his emphasis shifted to tiles; "abandoning an attempt to revive the craft of pottery in Bucks County, he became hell-bent to rank as a first-class manufacturer of Arts and Crafts hand-crafted tiles, and he succeeded" (Freeman 1996:62), becoming one of the leaders of the turn-of-the-century Arts and Crafts Movement (Mondragon 1998). The Society for Arts and Crafts had been founded in Boston in 1897 by two of Mercer's classmates, Arthur Astor Carey and John Templeman Coolidge, and one of his professors, Charles Eliot Norton, among others; Norton was the first president, and Carey was elected to succeed Norton (Reed 1987:29). Norton had been Mercer's professor for his junior and senior years at Harvard, Carey and Coolidge had been members with Mercer in the Art Club, and Carey had been the individual with whom Mercer toured Europe right after he had finished his law training. Thus it is not surprising to see Mercer almost immediately involved in the Society for Arts and Crafts; he was elected as a "Craftsman" member in 1900 and promoted to a "Master" in 1902 (Dyke 1996:16–18).

In 1900, Mercer patented his own technique for applying slips, underglazes, and clear overglazes to relief tiles (Driscoll 1996:258), with other patents for further developments in subsequent years. He also became involved in some early architectural experimentation with ferroconcrete construction. When he built his 66-room estate, Fonthill, which was finished in 1912, he employed poured reinforced concrete techniques and decorated it with a series of the tiles that he had developed in his Moravian Pottery and Tile Works, which he had established in 1899 and renovated in 1912 (Dyke 1996:19; Harlow 1933:540).

Mercer was awarded the Grand Prize in the St. Louis World's Fair of 1904 for his tiles; the prestigious medal from the Boston Society of Arts and Crafts in 1913; and the gold craftsmanship medal by the American Association of Architects in 1921 for his use of tiles and concrete (Coolidge 1930:444; Reed 1987:79). For his work with both historic tools and the Arts and Crafts tiles, he received an honorary degree from Franklin and Marshall in 1916 and from Lehigh University in 1929 (Dyke 1996; Reed 1987). The majority of his over 200 publications were related to this second phase of his life; 47 of these papers were published through the Bucks County Historical Society (Fackenthal 1930).

Concluding Remarks

Mercer's archaeological ideas may have their intellectual roots in Pengelly's work in Torquay. Mercer's European connection thus seems to be first from Pengelly and his associates to Gaudry and de Mortillet. From Boule, de Mortillet, and Gaudry the method was passed on to some Americans, such as Henry Chapman Mercer. But Mercer does not seem to have trained any students in this excavation technique. Thus it is the second generation of French students, such as Obermaier and Breuil, that seems to be most influential in ultimately transferring the method to the next generation of North American archaeologists, that is, to Nels Nelson and his peers. In this sense, then, I do not see any evidence that Mercer learned his techniques from any American colleagues, such as Frederic Ward Putnam and his students, who independently also were practicing explicit stratigraphic excavation technique. (Because of Mercer's extensive connections with Harvard, Putnam remains a possible source, but archival research so far has turned up no evidence to support any direct influence.) The best available documentation indicates that Mercer was exposed to the idea through his European contacts, particularly in his associations with Boule and Gaudry. Mercer employed his European-derived techniques in at least two sets of cave excavations in Pennsylvania in 1894, and also in both Pennsylvania and Mexico in 1895. The shift in his career direction in 1897, one that led him out of both active field excavation and prehistoric archaeology, no doubt in large part explains why he had little impact on the development of archaeological methods among his contemporaries.

For historical archaeologists, the period of Mercer's life from 1897 to 1930 is of particular significance, especially in terms of his collections and publications. Mercer's books are required reference materials in my historical archaeology class, as they are for the classes of many of my colleagues. Mercer has his greatest recognition in the field of fine arts; as Reed (1987:xxi) notes, Mercer transformed the art of ceramic tile manufacture in America between 1900 and 1930, with his work becoming one of the most distinctive products of the American Arts and Crafts Movement. The bulk of this chapter thus deals not with that for which Mercer is best known, but rather with the nineteenth-century context of intellectual development of a significant archaeological methodology. For the investigation of the evolution and spread of this intellectual concept (i.e., excavation actually employing explicitly a priori defined and controlled vertical and horizontal stratigraphic units, rather than just armchair, post facto stratigraphic interpretation), it is the brief period of his life from 1891 through 1897 that is of most import for the history of prehistoric archaeological methodology.

10

Frederic Ward Putnam

Contributions to the Development of
Archaeological Institutions and
Encouragement of Women Practitioners

David L. Browman

Introduction

One common thread that seemed to recur in the group discussions of the papers presented at the Second Willey Symposium was the underappreciated importance of Frederic Ward Putnam (1839–1915) of Harvard University's Peabody Museum. Either Putnam or the influence of his work at the Peabody Museum seems to be a significant part of the papers (which now comprise the chapters of the second part of this volume) by Bruce Bourque, Harvey Bricker, and Hilary Chester, as well as mine, and his importance is mentioned by some of the other contributors as well. Curtis Hinsley (1999:144) recently characterized Putnam's interaction with individuals during the early period of his tenure at the Peabody Museum as "his correspondence school in archaeology that functioned simultaneously as a collecting arm for the Peabody Museum." Putnam's interactions with Frances Babbitt, Albert Tarr Gamage, and William Baker Nickerson, discussed in the various chapters, are excellent examples of this "correspondence school."

I had read the biographical studies of Putnam by Ralph Dexter, Curtis Hinsley, and Joan Mark, as well as Gordon Willey and Jeremy Sabloff's synthesis of the historical development of Americanist archaeology, so I had some appreciation of Putnam's work. Initially I had shied away from digging deeper into his contributions, in part because his official bibliography contained over 400 items. The review of that body of work seemed to be a massive undertaking best left to someone who could devote several years of his or her scholarly life.

However, as I began to write the introduction to this volume, I found that to understand the development of late-nineteenth-century Americanist archaeology, there were some contributions of Putnam of such importance in establishing the intellectual context that they needed to be addressed. As I worked on elaborating this context, the argument became so massive that ultimately it was separated into this new chapter. Moreover, in the process of doing this research I stumbled across a very important linkage between Putnam's "Peabody Museum method" and Fay-Cooper Cole's "Chicago method," one that seems previously to be unappreciated, which came about through Putnam's "correspondence school" strategy. Originally another section of the introduction, that research also developed into such a long piece that it became a second separate chapter (see chapter 11).

The minimalistic historical context for Putnam might (1) start with the reasons for his recruitment into science and then archaeology through the influence of people such as Henry Wheatland, Louis Agassiz, and Jeffries Wyman; (2) deal with his institution building, both in terms of national learned societies such as the American Association for the Advancement of Sciences as well as museums and anthropology departments in New York, Cambridge, and Berkeley; and (3) include some additional commentary on the development of his methods and techniques. In addition, (4) an important component of the recruitment of individuals into archaeology by Putnam might be termed his "equal opportunity" approach, as he was responsible for assisting and encouraging many women in archaeology. The "correspondence" approach thus must be broadened to incorporate the contributions of these individuals as well.

Henry Wheatland, and Putnam's Recruitment

Henry Wheatland (1812–1893) was a key mentor in Putnam's life, not only in terms of his recruitment into science and archaeology but also in terms of continuing guidance and support, such as through the Board of Trustees of the Peabody Museum of Harvard University, to which Wheatland was first appointed in 1867 and for which he served as secretary from 1873 until his death in 1893 (Brew 1966b:1). Wheatland, a graduate of Harvard in 1832, was one of several founders of the Essex County Natural History Society in 1834, and he served as its secretary from 1835 until it merged with the Essex Historical Society in 1848 to become the Essex Institute (Brooks 1893:4). He then served as secretary and treasurer of the Essex Institute from 1848 to 1868 and as its president from 1868 to 1893. The American Association for the Advancement of Sciences (AAAS) was a learned society upon which

Putnam left a lasting imprint; it appears that Wheatland, who was one of its founding members in 1848, and advanced to a Fellow in 1874 ("Fellow" was a category only instituted at that time [Bruce 1987:79]), was an important factor in Putnam's selection as permanent secretary of the AAAS in 1873 and his tenure in that position for 25 years.

In a retrospective in a volume honoring Wheatland, Putnam (1893:61) indicated that Wheatland had been his mentor at Essex when he was entering his teens, that "he was my father in science, and to him, with the consent of my parents, am I indebted for my instruction under Agassiz, Wyman and Gray. It was he who answered Agassiz's letter that took me to Cambridge when a boy of sixteen," and "together we worked for the development of the [Essex] Institute" during the next quarter century.

According to Goodell (1893:11), "It was while Agassiz was preparing his chapter on embryology in the first monograph of his *Contributions to the Natural History of the United States*, that, having occasion to study the unique collections of turtles then in our cabinets, he was so struck with the intelligence of the young curator to whom he was referred by Dr. Wheatland that he invited him to join his staff at Cambridge." Recently papers have been added to the archives at the Peabody Museum that confirm this scenario in Putnam's own words. In a letter written on February 14, 1860, Putnam reported that he started his teenage years working in a local bookstore, but in January 1856 he began to study natural history at the Essex Institute:

> Professor Agassiz made a visit there for the purpose of seeing our turtles, and as I was the only one there I had to show him about all I could and in fact began to like him very much before Dr. Wheatland came.... A few days after I concluded to accept his invitation to go to Cambridge and see his Museum.... In the meanwhile Dr. Wheatland had written to him and it was arranged that I was to go and see him, and if the visit was satisfactory I should make arrangements to study with him.... He said if I would come and study with him for a term, he would see what I could do and agreed with Dr. Wheatland to take me without charging me the usual fee for tuition.[1]

Putnam further commented in that letter that he was not quite 16 when he first went and that in January 1857, at the age of 17, he was made a private assistant to Professor Agassiz with a salary of $200 per year and with a rent-free room at the museum. Other sources suggest that the first meeting between Putnam and Agassiz may have been in 1855 (Mark 1980:15; Tozzer 1936:125).

Putnam and the Lawrence Scientific School Faculty

Putnam entered the Lawrence Scientific School at Harvard when he went to study under Jean Louis Rodolphe Agassiz (1807-1873). Until 1871, the Lawrence Scientific School (1847-1906) was the only place at Harvard University with advanced instruction in physical and natural sciences (Hughes 1930:413). In fact, it had been established specifically to attract Agassiz. Agassiz had come to Boston to give lectures in the Lowell Institute, whose first curator for three years beginning in 1840 had been Jeffries Wyman (Smith 1898:18), and had enormous success. James Lowell wanted to keep Agassiz as a speaker, so he arranged with his friend Abbott Lawrence to put up money for the Lawrence Scientific School to ensure that Agassiz would come in 1847. Professor Eben Norton Horsford (the father of Cornelia Horsford, discussed later in this chapter) was named to chair this school (Agassiz 1930:400; Bruce 1987:163; Smith 1898:39, 41; Weeks 1966:51-52; Williams 1991:206-210).

Putnam thus entered the Lawrence Scientific School in 1856, was appointed assistant to Agassiz in 1857, and studied there with Agassiz, Wyman, and Asa Gray until 1864 (Anonymous 1915a, 1915b; Dexter 1966a:152). The Lawrence Scientific School had no meaningful entrance exam, no courses common to all students, and no special knowledge required other than the study done under one professor; the minimum residence for the B.S. was one year, although most students took two or three years (Bruce 1987:328). Agassiz employed 19 assistants (Agassiz 1930:402) while Putnam was at the Lawrence Scientific School (1856 to 1864), most of whom went on to become significant and noted contributors to science. Individuals named as collaborators (and thus presumably these 19 assistants) included Alexander Agassiz, Joel A. Allen, Thomas Barnard, Albert S. Bickmore, Henry J. Clark, Josiah P. Cook, Caleb Cooke, Alpheus Hyatt, William James, Theodore Lyman, John McCrady, Edward S. Morse, John M. Ordway, Alpheus S. Packard, Jr., Frederic W. Putnam, Samuel H. Scudder, Nathaniel S. Shaler, William Stimpson, and Addison E. Verrill (Agassiz 1930:402; Davis and Daly 1930:311; Dexter 1965:27; Lurie 1960:240, 317; Mark 1930:378; Tozzer 1936:126).[2]

Science was learned as part of an apprentice-style system at that time. With Agassiz's establishment of the Museum of Comparative Zoology (MCZ) in 1859, Putnam had hopes of rapid advancement to a professorship. He wrote his family on October 21, 1859, that he, John M. Ordway, and Nathan Shaler had helped Agassiz prepare a report to the Harvard College Corporation and Board of Trustees on the development of the MCZ on the previous day:

> I shall get my appointment soon from the Museum, as an assistant, and that will be quite a step toward a professorship. In the plan which we gave in last night it was stated that three professorships would be needed as soon as possible in the Museum, one as a professor of embryology, which [Henry J.] Clark will have; one as professor of invertebrates, which will not be filled until [John M.] Ordway is old enough to take it; and the other professor of vertebrates, which I suppose will come to me, in fact Professor [Agassiz] has told me that that is his idea about the matter.[3]

For me, this letter sheds light on an enigma noted by virtually all commentators on Putnam's career, namely, that he received his B.S. only in a post facto granting decades after he had left the program, and that the lack of degrees seemed to have significantly affected acceptance by Putnam's colleagues at Harvard, first for his appointment as director of the Peabody Museum, and later in his delayed appointment as Peabody Professor of Anthropology. This letter indicates to me a euphoric Putnam, a student who believed he was on a fast track to getting a professorship, such that one can understand that he might easily presume that degrees were superfluous certificates because his mentor, Agassiz, had seemingly guaranteed him a professorship.

Time drew on longer and longer. As noted, the typical B.S. degree might take as little as one year, and Harvard was seen as particularly rigorous in requiring an additional two years for a Ph.D., while many other institutions at the time were granting Ph.D. degrees with only an additional year of study (Haskins 1930:451; Mark 1980:52). The student assistants became increasingly restive. The proverbial "straw that broke the camel's back" was a new set of regulations issued by Agassiz for the students at the MCZ, formalized on November 19, 1863. Rules 4 and 5 prohibited the assistants or students from having private collections and from working for any other institution (Lurie 1960:317). Most (if not all) of the students had taken additional positions during their apprenticeship with Agassiz. Agassiz complained that they had not consulted him about taking these jobs, and that they were pressuring him to be allowed to publish papers, when he did not think they were ready. These new regulations, apparently viewed by all of the students as oppressive, resulted in what Dexter (1965, 1966a) called the "Salem Secession," and in late 1863 and the first months of 1864 almost all of Agassiz's students left (Dexter 1965:37; Lurie 1960:240, 316).

The Salem Years: *American Naturalist* and the AAAS

Why the "Salem Secession"? Wheatland had hired Putnam to work in Salem at the Essex Institute while he was also working with Agassiz, and several of Putnam's colleagues—including Cooke, Hyatt, Morse, Packard, Shaler, Stimpson, and Verrill—found temporary positions working under the sponsorship of the institute when they left the MCZ (Davis and Daly 1930:312; Dexter 1965:27, 37; Lurie 1960:317; Mark 1980:19; Wyman 1868a:568). Putnam was named first a curator, then director of the Essex Institute from 1864 to 1870, and when the Museum of the Peabody Academy of Sciences of Salem was formed out of a merger of the museums of the Essex Institute and the East India Marine Society, through an endowment from George Peabody in 1867 and 1868, Putnam became the director of that museum from 1869 to 1873 (Dixon 1935:277; Tozzer 1936:126). Putnam also continued his association with the Essex Institute, serving as its vice-president from 1871 to 1894 (Anonymous 1915a, 1915b).

The formation of the Museum of the Peabody Academy of Science of Salem was the result of Putnam's active collaboration with several of his Agassiz classmates who had left the MCZ with him—Hyatt, Morse, Packard, and Verrill (Dexter 1965:27, 37; Mark 1980:19). It was at this same time, in 1868, that Hyatt, Morse, Packard, and Putnam founded the *American Naturalist*. According to its masthead, the journal was edited for the first two years by all four, but from 1870 to 1875 it was coedited by just two of the founders—Putnam and Packard. Once Putnam took over the job at the Peabody Museum in 1875, the editorship was more than he could easily handle. The journal was sold to Edward D. Cope in 1877, with editorship shared for the first few years between Cope and Packard, then taken over by Cope (see discussion of Cope in chapter 9 of this volume). In addition to founding the journal, Putnam also established a printing office, known as "The Salem Press," where many scientific reports were published (Morse 1915:4). Putnam's colleagues published in both of these venues.

It is during the Salem period that we can see Putnam's developing archaeological interests. For example, his first publication in archaeology, "On the Indian Grave on Winter's Island, Salem, 1865," (Putnam 1866) was based on work carried out under the aegis of the museum in Salem (Tozzer 1936:140). And as noted below, it is during this period that Putnam, Cooke, and Morse, working out of the Salem museum, assisted Jeffries Wyman in the excavation of various shell mounds near Eagle Hill, Ipswich, in 1867 (Wyman 1868a:568). From 1868 to 1876, when he began publishing his work in the Peabody Museum organs, Putnam published 32 additional papers on archaeological investigations (Tozzer 1936:140–144), mainly in the *American Naturalist*, the *Proceedings of the Essex Institute, Salem*, and the *Proceedings of the Boston Society of Natural History* (of which he was a member, as well as having been a curator from 1859 to 1868).

The Salem "interlude" also saw the establishment of the long-term linkage between Putnam and the AAAS. Agassiz had been one of three "founders" of the AAAS from the old Association of American Geologists and Naturalists in 1848, along with Benjamin Peirce (also a Harvard professor) and Henry Rogers (Bruce 1987:254). Another of the important people in Putnam's training, Jeffries Wyman, had been named the first permanent secretary of the AAAS in 1848 (Murowchick 1990:56). Putnam had joined the AAAS in 1856, at Agassiz's suggestion. The first AAAS meeting that Putnam attended was the 1857 session in Montreal, and it was here that we have the first recorded indication of Putnam's later interest in archaeology, as during these meetings he reports (F. W. Putnam 1899:1) visiting a shell heap at Mount Royal on the outskirts of Montreal (now Mount Royale Park; see Dexter 1985:135) and observing some artifacts mixed in with the shell deposits. By 1869 the rift between Agassiz and the students who had resigned from his program had healed. Thus with the support of Agassiz, Wyman, and Wheatland, among several others, Putnam was elected permanent secretary of the AAAS in 1872. In 1873 he began serving in this position, which he held until 1898, when he was elected president of the AAAS for the 1898–1899 term (Anonymous 1915a; Tozzer 1936:131).

The Influences of Jeffries Wyman and Asa Gray

Jeffries Wyman was the second of the three professors who had trained Putnam during his MCZ days. Because he was the first curator of the Peabody Museum (from 1866 to 1874), and because he seems to have supervised some of the first excavations by Putnam, Wyman is a critical figure to consider in seeking the roots of Putnam's archaeological ideas. Although the definitive answer of how much influence Wyman had on the methods that Putnam later developed remains to be written, Wyman provides a connection between Putnam and the European methods, particularly as popularized in America by Adolphe von Morlot.

Wyman's interest in archaeology apparently began as early as 1846, when he started a correspondence with Ephraim Squier on mounds. Wyman conducted his first shell mound excavations in 1852 (Murowchick 1990:57) and subsequently was involved in a major expedition to Argentina, Chile, and Peru, collecting artifacts in 1858 and 1859. In the 1860s he continued excavations on shell mounds in Massachusetts and Maine and began work on shell mounds in Florida, with his most important work conducted on the Florida mounds in the late 1860s and 1870s (Murowchick 1990:57–59).

The question of what kind of influence Wyman had on Putnam remains open. In part this is because we do not yet have a good handle on the precise techniques employed by Wyman. He was apparently very much influenced by the discussion of the European methods worked out by the French, as popularized in two English translations of papers by Morlot in the 1861 and 1863 Smithsonian Institution volumes, making specific reference to Morlot's papers in various of his publications in 1867 and later (Murowchick 1990:59; see also chapter 7 in this volume for Morlot's influence). We know that Wyman employed particular care in his excavations: he made careful notes on the context from which artifacts derived; he observed and recorded changes in strata as they correlated with artifact category, noting that in some mounds pottery occurred only in upper layers, with lower zones lacking pottery; his description and analysis of ceramic technology and decoration was not matched until the twentieth century; and he made such careful zooarchaeological investigations that he was able to support an argument for possible human cannibalism on the Florida mounds based on the correlation between the treatment of some human bones excavated displaying the same patterns found on butchered and boiled deer bones (Gifford 1978:61; Murowchick 1990: 60–61; Williams 1991:68; Wyman 1874).

Wyman had several opportunities to pass his method on to Putnam via actual field demonstrations. In addition to the other relationships the two had at Harvard, Putnam worked with Wyman on field excavations in Maine and Massachusetts in 1867 (Wyman 1868a), and the two kept in active contact until Wyman's death in 1874. For the present time, we could suggest that Wyman became enthusiastic about more rigorous methods after reading the European experts such as Morlot and from his contacts with individuals such as de Mortillet in purchasing European Paleolithic[4] collections for the Peabody Museum, and that he passed these concerns about more rigorous methods on to his former student and later colleague, Putnam, particularly in the 1867 excavation project.

Asa Gray was the third of Putnam's instructors during the MCZ days. He not only is a linkage to Putnam's training in this fashion, but also through later direct involvement with the Peabody Museum. Gray served as interim director of the Peabody Museum for a year between Wyman's death in 1874 and Putnam's appointment in 1875. In addition, Gray subsequently served on the Board of Trustees of the museum, and he and Wheatland were the principal supporters of the push in 1885 to name Putnam as professor as well as curator of the museum, an appointment that was delayed until 1887 because of the opposition of Alexander Agassiz (Loius Agassiz's son), who was apparently still angry because of Putnam's involvement as one of the "ringleaders" of the "Salem Secession" of 1863-1864 (Dixon 1930:210; Dorsey 1896:79; Hinsley 1992:132).

Developing Patterns: 1875 to 1900

The works of Dexter, Hinsley, and Mark, as well as the necrologies by Dixon, Peabody, Tozzer, and others, deal in much greater detail than we need with the events from 1875 to 1900. However, for the purposes of setting up the context for this chapter, I want to touch briefly upon two areas—Putnam's teaching methods and his contributions to developing anthropological institutions.

Putnam had been trained in an informal, apprentice, or mentor type of internship system by Wheatland at the Essex Institute, and later by Agassiz, Wyman, and Gray at the Lawrence Scientific School. This is the pedagogical system he employed when he began working at the Peabody Museum. Because he was initially not on the faculty, his teaching at first was in terms of a series of public lectures he gave at places like the Lowell Institute of Boston and the "Harvard Annex" (later Radcliffe). By 1886 he had developed a brochure advertising 38 lectures on American archaeology (see Table 10.1).

One could argue that it was because of the lack of official students as well as the need to develop the Peabody Museum collections that Putnam began an extensive correspondence with avocational archaeologists around the country; that he invited them to visit with him

Table 10.1 Summary of the list of 38 lectures on American Archaeology, listed by Putnam in 1886.

"The first fifteen lectures are planned to give in a continuous course a review of the prehistoric peoples of America."
1. Chipped Stone [included a review of early man in America]
2. Flaked, Polished and Pecked Stones
3. Fire, Potsherds [included a discussion on origins of pottery]
4. Types of Pottery [Atlantic coast; Ohio, Cumberland, and, Mississippi Valleys]
5. Pottery continued [Pueblo Region; Mexico; Central America]
6. Pottery concluded [Peru; Lake Titicaca; Brazil]
7. Wood, Bone, Antler, Horn, Shell, Fabrics
8. The Metals
9. Village sites
10. Burial Places [Little Miami, Cumberland, and Central Mississippi Valleys]
11. Mounds and Earth Works
12. Mounds connected with Ceremonies
13. Fortifications
14. Architecture
15. Types of Man in America

"The following course of ten lectures, prepared especially for the Boston 'Teachers Course,' will be given elsewhere if desired."
16. First Period of the Stone Age. Early Man in America. Second Period of the Stone Age
17. Fire and Cooking; Potsherds
18. Types of Pottery
19. Wood, bone, antler, horn, shell, stone, fibres
20. Copper, Silver, Gold, Iron, Bronze
21. Village-sites, Burial-places, Burial-mounds
22. Altar-mounds and Religious-works
23. Fortifications and Architecture
24. Diverse peoples in America; review of the evidence
25. Origin of the Americans; Routes of migration

"The following lectures have been delivered at the Museum in Cambridge, and, in part, at the Lowell Institute, Boston, at the Peabody Institute Baltimore, and in other places."
26. A General sketch of American Archaeology. Preglacial Man in America
27. The Shellheaps and the story they tell
28. American Caves and their contents
29. The Mounds and their contents
30. The Stone-grave people of the Cumberland valley
31. Ancient Earthworks and Fortified Towns
32. The Altar-mounds of the Ohio valley and the Religious Rites of their Builders
33. The Ancient Arts of the North American Peoples

34. The Pueblos and Cliff-houses of Utah, Arizona, Colorado and New Mexico
35. The Archaeology of Mexico and Central America
36. The Archaeology of South America
37. Ancient Peruvian Art
38. The proper methods of Exploration

---

in Cambridge; that he wrote them letters of instructions on how to properly secure specimens; that in some cases (e.g., Nickerson) he sent them on excavations; and that he arranged for the Peabody Museum to obtain their collections—all of which constituted what Hinsley (1999:144), as previously noted, has termed Putnam's "correspondence school" of archaeology. Putnam's first formal students in American archaeology were not to be found until after his appointment as professor in 1887, and even then not until three years later, in 1890, when a curriculum had been approved. These first students included two graduate students, George A. Dorsey and John G. Owens, and three undergraduate students, Marshall H. Saville, Frank H. Gerrodette, and Allan Cook (Dexter 1980:188). The works of Dorsey, Owens, and Saville are well known to students of the history of the period. With respect to the other two undergraduate students, I found that Gerrodette (1866-1951) did a senior paper on the historic distribution of tribes in Mesoamerica (Gerrodette 1892) and conducted some limited excavation work in Pennsylvania (Swauger 1940), but went on to read law at Harvard, leaving archaeology (Harvard University Archives, HUG 300). I was unable to find any record of further scholarly work by Cook, except for a short season of excavations of a burial site in Maine. Cook enlisted in the Spanish-American war and served in Cuba and the Philippines. After the war he hoped to help make ethnological collections for the Peabody Museum in the Philippines, but died there in March 1990.

Putnam arranged the growing archaeological collections in the museum by geographical area rather than by industry or evolution, a scheme he had learned from Agassiz and the MCZ staff (Dorsey 1896:92; Mark 1980:19); the Smithsonian, in contrast, arranged collections by presumed evolutionary and technological sequence regardless of area of origin (Mark 1980:22). This difference was the root of one of the arguments that came to dominate Boasian discussions of the early twentieth century (and one should note that Boas was trained in museum work by Putnam).

The differences in approach between the Smithsonian and Putnam in terms of organizing collections were reflected in differences in collecting methods as well. Hinsley (1999:147) notes that Putnam increasingly began referring to "thorough" and "systematic" methods in the period from 1885 to 1887, indicating a developing rigor of methodology. As noted in chapter 11 in this volume, it appears that Putnam had taken on the role of championing a new, stratigraphic recovery technique at least by 1885. Putnam's associates became sensitive to this methodological zeal; thus Charles L. Metz (in a letter to Putnam on January 20, 1884) referred to "Smithsonian methods" when denigrating simple grave robbing as contrasted to his recovery work, and (in a letter to Putnam on November 6, 1886) referred to a report of collectors dynamiting a mound as opening it "*à la* Smithsonian" (Dexter 1982:28).

Much of the reconstruction of Putnam's methods in this chapter and the next has been handicapped because Putnam's publications deal primarily with descriptive work, rarely mentioning method except between 1885 and 1887. From very early on in his work at the Peabody, this was a pattern, one that seems to have been driven perhaps more by a lack of time than of interest. For example, in a letter to Metz of May 12, 1883, Putnam writes: "I've been so driven with lecturing and writing and raising money (which comes hard just now) that I can't get time to look or study the specimens that come in from all parts as I would like to. I have never been driven so before" (Dexter 1982:26). Dexter (1982:28) suggests that this also was in part because Putnam always hesitated to create publicity of any kind until the fieldwork was completed so as to avoid looting of a site.

The limited role in formal training of students by Putnam, even in the 1890s and 1900s, may be in part due to the time commitment involved in his contributions to institutional development. As noted above, he played a major role in starting the *American Naturalist*, through his position as Permanent Secretary of the AAAS (in helping to appoint the editors and tailoring the journal *Science*), and through the publications of the Peabody Museum and the Essex Institute. Along with Charles Eliot Norton, Putnam was one of the handful of individuals who sent the circular letter proposing a "Society for Archaeological Research" in the spring of 1879; after more than 100 positive responses, this resulted in the founding meeting, on May 10, 1879, of the Archaeological Institute of America (AIA) (Turner 1999:278). Inter-city rivalry may have been in part involved in the founding of the AIA, for at the same time in the spring of 1879 that the Boston archaeologists were forming the AIA, the archaeologists in Washington, D.C., were involved in founding the Anthropological Society of Washington (ASW). Later Putnam was instrumental as one of the founders of the American Anthropological Association (AAA), as well as other, smaller anthropological interest groups. His influence in the founding of the AAA may be underappreciated, for as Flack (1975:126) has pointed out, Putnam was president of the AAAS in 1898, when representatives of the AAAS met with the ASW and agreed that the AAAS would pay off the debts for the *American Anthropologist* (old series) and would also provide the mechanism for continuing the journal (new series) as long as the ASW ceded control to a new group being formed under the aegis of Section H (Anthropology) of the AAAS, a new group that ultimately became the AAA.

Equally important with respect to the reasons for Putnam's limited role in training in this period, the beginning of formal classes in anthropology in 1890 also coincided with his intensive work in developing other anthropological research institutions. In early 1890 he suggested to the director of the proposed 1893 World's Columbian Exposition in Chicago that there should be a major anthropological display at this exposition. Once that proposal was accepted, Putnam spent a major portion of his time between 1891 and 1894 devoted to that exposition in his position as chief of Department M, Department of Archaeology and Ethnology. In addition to hiring individuals such as Boas, he appointed 75 to 100 of his students and associates from his Peabody Museum connections as staff members during the period from 1891 to 1894 (Dexter 1966a:153, 1966c:315). The collections remaining from the exposition after it closed, and also some of the staff, became the basis for the anthropology department for what today is the Field Museum in Chicago.

Almost immediately after resigning from the Columbian Exposition in 1894, Putnam became involved in developing the anthropology department at the American Museum of Natural History in New York, with a joint appointment from 1894 until he resigned in 1903; also, in 1901 he began talks with the University of California–Berkeley, resulting in his joint appointment there in developing the department and museum from 1903 to his retirement in 1909; and still further, he found time to advise the Academy of Natural Sciences of Philadelphia on developing anthropological expertise (Dexter 1996a, 1996b, 1996c; Tozzer 1936; Wissler 1915). Between 1875 and 1900 he was also directing excavations in 37 different states, Mesoamerica, and South America, as well as developing the Peabody Museum, so it is not surprising that we do not have an unencumbered picture of Putnam's ideas on archaeological method and technique, but need to extract it piecemeal.

Women in Late-Nineteenth-Century American Archaeology

Although, as Irwin-Williams (1990:6) notes, standard histories of American archaeology (e.g., Daniel or Willey and Sabloff) fail to mention a single contribution by a woman archaeologist prior to 1915, a number of women were involved in archaeological endeavors prior to that date. Levine (1994b:24), in defining her "first generation" of women in archaeology, all of whom contributed to the field prior to 1900, sees this as part of the "persistent myth" that women did not contribute to archaeology until quite recently.

In chapter 9 in this volume, Chester refers to the pioneering work done by Frances E. Babbitt and mentions the support Babbitt received from Putnam. As noted below in the discussion of specific individuals, Putnam was instrumental in recruiting a number of women into archaeological activities. Many of the women I mention interfaced with Putnam, who provided them moral and financial support and encouraged them in several other ways. For example, in his position as Permanent Secretary of the AAAS from 1873 to 1898, Putnam seems to have been very active in recruiting women to membership in the association, as can be seen in part by the list of 25 individuals in Table 10.2. During Putnam's tenure, Erminnie A. Smith was the first woman to serve as an officer (Secretary) of Section H, in 1885, but other women discussed below served in official capacity in the anthropology section up until 1900 as members of the Section H nominating committee or section committee, as Councillor, and even as President (Alice C. Fletcher): Matilda C. Stevenson (1892, 1894, 1898), Anita Newcomb McGee (1892, 1894, 1897), Mary L. D. Putnam (1892), and Alice C. Fletcher (1895, 1896, 1897, 1898, 1900). In addition, in 1887 and 1888, Alice Fletcher and Matilda Stevenson served as representatives of the general AAAS in lobbying Congress for the first antiquities protection bill.

Moreover, Putnam engaged in some of the first formal teaching of women students in archaeology. The second wife and widow of his mentor Louis Agassiz, Elizabeth Cabot Cary Agassiz (1822–1907), helped to found "The School for the Collegiate Instruction of Women" at Harvard in 1879, and became its president. Although the establishment of this women-only school, linked with Harvard, was first advertised in February 1879, apparently the official name was not agreed

Table 10.2 List of the date of enrollment as a member and election to Fellow status of women in AAAS from 1876 to 1901.*

	Member	Fellow
Frances E. (Franc) Babbitt	1883	1887
Fanny D. Bergen		
Virginia K. Bowers		
Alice Eastwood	1901	1901
Alice C. Fletcher	1879	1883
Christine Ladd Franklin	1898	1899
Mary Tileston Hemenway		
Fanny Hitchcock	1886	
Cornelia Horsford	1894	1897
Ada M. King	1890	
Anita Newcomb McGee	1888	1892
Jeannette Robinson Murphy		
Zelia M. Nuttall	1886	1887
Lucy E. Peabody	1901	
Alice E. Putnam	1908	
Elizabeth D. Putnam	1896	
Mary L. D. Putnam	1901**	
Erminnie A. Smith	1876	
Jennie/Jane Smith	1879	
Matilda C. Stevenson	1892	1893
Sara Y. Stevenson	1884	1895
Cordelia A. Studley		
Laura O. Talbott	1887	
Mary Copley Thaw	1892	
Harriet Newell Wardle	1898	1911

*These women delivered papers and served as officers at annual meetings in the anthropology section of the AAAS between 1876 (the date of establishment of a permanent section for anthropology) and 1901. All but one year of this period was under Putnam's tenure. Not all of the women who delivered papers became members or Fellows.

**Mary Putnam had been a member of the AAAS Section H-Anthropology nominating committee in 1893; it is not clear why she was not officially listed as a member until 1901.

upon until April 25, 1882 (Paton 1919:201, 206). Partly as a consequence, the school acquired the colloquial name of the "Harvard Annex." Putnam gave occasional lectures in this school. The earliest such record that I have so far located is for January 19, 1882, with a diary entry as follows: "Lectured before ladies of the Annex. 'Comparisons of American Pottery.' 2-3 o'clock. 17 present also 4 other ladies not of Annex. Altogether, lecture and preparing for it took 4 hours."[5] This women's school changed its name in 1893 to Radcliffe College, with Elizabeth Agassiz continuing to serve as its president (Paton 1919:243).

In 1893, Putnam wrote to a Mrs. Henderson: "Several of my best students are women, who have become widely known by their thorough and important works and publications; and this I consider as high an honor as could be accorded to me" (Dexter 1978:5). As Rossiter notes (1982:80), "Putnam's influence and importance appear all the greater when one compares the women's performance in Section H of the AAAS with their reception by the all-male Anthropological Society of Washington in 1885"—the group that rejected Matilda Stevenson's application for membership in that year based on her sex, and which only in 1899 finally admitted 49 women transfer applicants from the Women's Anthropological Society (Lurie 1966:38).

According to Rossiter (1982:80), Alice Fletcher, Erminnie Smith, and Zelia Nuttall were Putnam's most professionally recognized students, and "the incredible success of Smith, Fletcher, and to a slightly lesser degree Nuttall" in presenting papers at the annual meetings of the AAAS, and subsequently getting them published, was due in large part to Putnam's position as permanent secretary of that group and his support of their work. In 1877, Putnam was instrumental in getting a separate permanent section (later Section H) for anthropology established at the AAAS. My scan of the list of papers presented (as elaborated below; also see others in Table 10.2) indicates that more than two dozen women delivered papers from the time of its establishment through 1900.

According to Levine (1994b:24), the "first generation" of women in archaeology in North America prior to 1900 included four individuals —Alice Fletcher, Mary Hemenway, Zelia Nuttall, and Matilda Coxe Stevenson—although later Levine (1994b:25) refers in passing to Alice Le Plongeon. A similar listing set forth 30 years earlier by Lurie (1966:31) included Alice Fletcher, Zelia Nuttall, Matilda Stevenson, and Erminnie Smith. Hinsley (1992:132) mentions several additional women involved in archaeological studies who could be added to this "first generation" list: Frances E. Mead, Alice E. Putnam, Jennie Smith, Sara Yorke Stevenson, and Cordelia Studley. In addition, women such as Frances E. Babbitt, Alice Eastwood, Mary Parke Foster, Phoebe Apperson Hearst, Fanny Hitchcock, Cornelia Horsford, Margaret Whitehead Magill, Elizabeth Duncan Putnam, Mary Louisa Duncan Putnam, Mary Copley Thaw, Harriet Newell Wardle, Jeannette Williams, and Julia J. Wirt, though not mentioned in the compilations of Hinsley, Levine, and Lurie, should also be candidates for the "first generation." While these women were involved in a wide range of work, below is a brief summary of some of their more important activities relating to North American archaeology from 1877 to 1900. Most of these women were nominated for membership in the AAAS, and of the 18 who were nominated, half of them were also advanced to Fellow status in the association (see Table 10.2).

More or less in alphabetical order, I provide a brief summary of some of the relevant activities of this "first generation" of women archaeologists. They fall in two broad categories: those women actually doing fieldwork or analyses in archaeology, and a smaller but equally important group of women who provided explicit financial support to women doing archaeology.

Women Conducting Archaeological Research

Frances Eliza Babbitt (1824–1891), who often signed herself as "Franc" (discussed in chapter 8), was one of the early women Fellows of the AAAS (see Table 10.2). She presented four papers on her work to Section H in the few years before her death. A quick scan of the sources of the time indicates that she was in contact with many of the individuals involved in Americanist archaeology and that her work was widely known. Babbitt contributed sets of the Little Falls quartzes to Putnam and the Peabody Museum as well as to Charles Abbott, Henry Haynes, Otis Mason, and Charles Rau (Babbitt 1883:390, 1890:334; Brew 1996b:37). Thomas Wilson (1890a:630, 1890b:701) contacted her to secure examples of the Little Falls paleoliths for the U.S. National Museum. Putnam (1888:421–424) and Starr (1892:293) referred to Abbott's Trenton gravels and Babbitt's Little Falls quartzes as the two most important American Paleolithic sites. William H. Holmes (1892a: 280–281) made a special trip in 1892 to view the site and assess the materials. Thus it is clear that these better-known American archaeologists of the period were well acquainted with her papers and research.

Alice Cunningham Fletcher (1838–1923) began a correspondence with Putnam in 1878 while seeking information for her lecture series on American Indians. She first came to the Peabody Museum as a student in 1880, working on the Omaha and Nez Percé, and was appointed in 1882 as "Assistant in American Ethnology" (Dorsey 1896:89; Hinsley 1992:132). For this reason, she is often referred to as the first Peabody Museum ethnologist, although she was much involved in archaeology as well. She began her career "studying the archaeological remains in the Ohio and Mississippi valleys" (Fletcher, in Willard and Livermore 1897, 1:293). In 1878 she began presenting a series of four "Lectures on Ancient America" in New York, Boston, and other East Coast cities. She illustrated these lectures ("The Ancients—Here and Elsewhere"; "The Lost Peoples of America"; "Ceremonies of the Moundbuilders"; "Antiquities of Coast and Cave") with hand-drawn pictures of artifacts and sites (Mark 1988:32). Fletcher may have met Frances Babbitt in November 1879 when she presented her lectures in Minneapolis—Fletcher had traveled to Ohio, Illinois, Wisconsin, and Minnesota in 1879, giving an expanded series of 11 lectures on these archaeological topics (Mark 1980:63, 1988:32), and we know that Babbitt was actively involved in archaeological researches at the time. Under Putnam's aegis, Fletcher also participated in the excavation of shell mounds in Maine, Massachusetts, and Florida beginning in 1878, and in 1886 and 1887 she helped Putnam lobby to save the Serpent Mound in Ohio (Levine 1994b:25; Mark 1980:63; Temkin 1988:95; Wilkins 1971:630).

At Putnam's suggestion, Fletcher joined the fledgling Archaeological Institute of America in 1879. She was a major influence in the AIA's direction of research after 1899, when the organization became involved in establishing research in the American Southwest, and was a key player in helping to found the School of American Archaeology in 1908-1909 (Hinsley 1992:133; Mark 1980:80-84, 1988:319-323). She was also one of the original members and officers of the Women's Anthropological Society of America, where she gave several papers and established archaeology as one of six subsections (McGee 1889b:240-241; Mendenhall 1893:7). She was the first holder of the Mary Copley Thaw Fellowship in American Archaeology and Ethnology, established in 1890, and the first woman to hold any fellowship at Harvard, thanks to the strong support of Putnam (Dexter 1980:188; Dorsey 1896:89; Mark 1980:67).

Fletcher was a prolific contributor on the archaeological scene of the time. She was a consistent contributor to the annual reports of the Peabody Museum from 1884 on (Hough 1923:257). She and Erminnie Smith authored 11 out of 14 papers by women published in the *Proceedings* of the AAAS in the 1880s, and 10 out of 16 printed "by title only" (Rossiter 1982:80). My own research indicates that she alone was responsible for 16 of the papers in anthropology between 1877 and 1900. Much of Fletcher's work in the 1880s (as well as that of Erminnie

Smith) was financed by the Bureau of Ethnology (later called the Bureau of American Ethnology) (Rossiter 1982:63). Fletcher was the chairman or "Secretary" of Section H, Anthropology, in the AAAS in 1896–1897, and she also served on other committee positions for the association. When Section H became involved in the founding of the new version of the *American Anthropologist* at the turn of the century, Fletcher was named to the 10-member editorial board in order to make the journal more representative of the entire field. For the 1893 International Congress of Americanists, held in conjunction with the 1893 Columbian Exposition, five women gave papers, including Fletcher and Sara Y. Stevenson, both Putnam's protégées, and Fletcher was a member of the planning committee (Rossiter 1982:98). In addition, Putnam appointed Fletcher, Zelia Nuttall, Matilda Coxe Stevenson, and Sara Y. Stevenson as four of the five women judges for the Jury of Awards for Ethnology in the Columbian Exposition in Chicago. Later, she and Zelia Nuttall were on the advisory committee that oversaw the establishment of the museum and anthropology department at the University of California–Berkeley (Dexter 1966b:315). Although the focus here is contributions prior to 1900, it should be remembered that Fletcher became a very significant player in the AIA and served as President of the AAA in 1904 and of the American Folklore Society in 1905 (Chauvenet 1983:42, 54; Mark 1988:290, 320, 332).

Alice Dixon Le Plongeon (1851–1910), the wife of Augustus Le Plongeon (1826–1908), became involved in a series of early excavation projects in the Mayan area between 1873 and 1884. She had gone to the Yucatán fresh from being married in London in 1873, and she spent the next two decades working with her husband excavating at places such as Chichén Itzá and Uxmal. In materials she supplied to a listing of famous nineteenth-century American women, she noted that "The work among the ruins was laborious, not only in the matter of exploring and excavating, but in making hundreds of photographs, in surveying and making molds, by which the old palaces of Yucatan can be built in any part of the world" (Le Plongeon, in Willard and Livermore 1897, 2:459).

Le Plongeon is not listed as giving papers at the International Congress of Americanists, or Section H of the AAAS, the two major places for Americanist archaeologists to communicate, but she did publish a series of papers in her own right on the Maya (Le Plongeon 1879, 1885, 1886, 1887, 1896, 1897). Desmond and Messenger (1988:104) indicate that she tried to present a paper at the 1887 meetings of the AAAS, but Daniel Brinton, who did not like the work of her husband, effectively prevented the paper from being accepted. Le Plongeon is listed as one of the three important Americanist women archaeologists in a short note about Zelia Nuttall in the *Scientific American* (Anonymous 1895a:83). But because her husband had some "bizarre theories" about the Maya and because her work was linked with his, "she was all but forgotten" by World War I (Desmond 1989:141), even though "on her own she made significant contributions to the understanding of the social history and living conditions of the Maya," and she and her husband "made a worthwhile contribution to American archaeology with their photographic documentation, descriptions, and drawings," including the first cross-section drawings of an archaeological excavation in the Maya area (Desmond and Messenger 1988:130, 95).

Zelia Maria Magdalena Nuttall (1858-1933) was born in San Francisco but raised in Europe, where she studied at Bedford College, London, before returning to San Francisco (Sarah Demb, personal communication, May 2000). She met Alphonse Louis Pinart (1852-1911) in 1878, when he made a trip to California, and they were married in 1880 (Parmenter 1966:22). Pinart, in addition to his ethnological and linguistic interests, also collected archaeological specimens along the Pacific Coast from Alaska to Peru in the 1870s and 1880s (Darnell 1998:41; Parmenter 1966; Tozzer 1933:475). The marriage was short-lived. Parmenter (1966:24-25, 27) indicates that within a year of being married, Pinart was took off on a long voyage, such that for several months he was unaware of the birth of their only child in April 1882. In addition, Parmenter (1966:1) notes that while Pinart had been wealthy as a young man, by 1883 he had run through all of his inherited wealth as well as Nuttall's money. They were effectively separated by the end of 1881, but Nuttall did not receive a formalized deed of separation from him until 1884, and the divorce was not granted until 1888.

Thus between 1880 and 1888 she was referred to as Mrs. Nuttall-Pinart, and her first works in archaeology were published under that name. This may have contributed to the suggestion made by several scholars that Pinart had a substantial influence upon Nuttall. However, other than a short trip they took together to the Spanish West Indies during 1880 and 1881, she was not in the field with Pinart. Rather, it appears that while she may have been introduced to the general idea of anthropology by Pinart, her archaeological contributions derive from her own work. In 1884-1885, Nuttall went to Mexico, her mother's birthplace (Chinas 1999:559), for five months with her mother, younger brother, sister, and daughter. During this time she worked for the National Museum and collected terra-cotta heads from Teotihuacán, the analyses of which she wrote up for her first publication in 1886. She was appointed as an unpaid "Special Assistant in Mexican Archaeology" at the Peabody Museum in 1886, a position she held for 47 years (Chinas 1999:559; Dorsey 1896:90). Putnam tried to get her to accept the more intensively involved position of "Curator of Central American Archaeology," but she declined (Dorsey 1896:90; Parmenter 1971:640). During part of her tenure at the Peabody Museum, she, like Fletcher, also was a Thaw Fellow.

Nuttall had her first paper published in the *American Journal of Archaeology* in 1886 and was made a Fellow of the AAAS in 1887—one of the handful of women initially so honored (see Table 10.2 for the list of women Fellows in anthropology). She, along with Alice Fletcher, Matilda Stevenson, and Sara Stevenson, served as four out of the five women judges for the 1893 World's Columbian Exposition, again in large part due to Putnam's position with the 1893 event (Rossiter 1982:98). She and Fletcher worked together on a variety of projects, and both were part of the lobby for increased studies in Americanist projects at the AIA. While much of her later work is perhaps more ethnographic in nature, she was involved in archaeology as well even later, conducting excavations in Coyoacán and being involved in the early training of Manuel Gamio (Chinas 1999:560).

Erminnie Adelle Platt Smith (1836–1886) was a cousin of Putnam's and another of his protégées (Jayanti 1988:328; Lurie 1971a:312). She was elected to membership in the AAAS in 1876, was the first woman doing anthropology to be published in the journal *Science,* and was perhaps the first woman to conduct scientific anthropological fieldwork (Lurie 1966:32, 41). As noted above, in the 1880s, she and Alice Fletcher published 11 out of the 14 papers published in the *Proceedings* of the AAAS, 10 out of 16 papers "by title only," and she was the third woman from all scientific fields to be published in the *Proceedings* (Rossiter 1982:80). In my own survey of papers presented in Section H of the AAAS between 1877 and 1900, I found a total of 17 papers listed for Erminnie Smith, the most for any woman anthropologist. In 1885, with her election to Secretary of Section H, she became the first woman to hold any office in the AAAS.

Much of Smith's research in the 1880s (and also that of Alice Fletcher) was financed by the Bureau of Ethnology (Rossiter 1982:63). Smith was also one of the original members of the Women's Anthropological Society of America, along with colleagues such as Fletcher and Matilda Stevenson (McGee 1889b:240). In 1887 and 1888, Fletcher and Matilda Stevenson served as representatives of both the Women's Anthropological Society of America and the American Association for the Advancement of Science to lobby for a bill in Congress to have Mesa Verde and ruins on the Pajarito Plateau declared a national park (Fletcher and Stevenson 1889; Parezo 1993b:60). Although they were unsuccessful, they thus established the groundwork for the successful effort, partly funded by Mary Hemenway, to preserve Casa Grande, and also for the later Antiquity Act of 1906.

Matilda Coxe Evans Stevenson (1850-1915), sometimes referred to as Tilly, was mainly involved in ethnographic studies, but she also carried out surface collections of prehistoric ceramics from the cliff dwellings in New Mexico and Arizona in the 1880s and 1890s. In 1872 she married James Stevenson (1840-1888), a member of the U.S. Geological Survey of the Territories, and began exploring and collecting with him in Colorado, Idaho, Wyoming, and Utah between 1872 and 1878. In 1879 the Survey moved to Arizona and New Mexico, and for the next two decades she collected archaeological specimens as well as ethnographic materials (Holmes 1916:553; Levine 1994b:25; Lurie 1971b:373; National Cyclopaedia 1929, 20:54; Parezo 1993b:40). The results of some of her early surface collection work is contained in her 1883 article (Stevenson 1883). Her written contributions are much greater than bibliographic scans would suggest, as the convention of the time was that for a husband-and-wife team, only the husband's name was usually listed; thus Spencer Baird in 1882 noted that the contributions for his agency listed as "James Stevenson" were actually the work of both James and Matilda (Parezo 1999:730).

Although Tilly Stevenson was associated with the Bureau of Ethnology (later the Bureau of American Ethnology) for much of the last two decades of the nineteenth century, she is best known for being the founder of the Women's Anthropological Society of America in June 1885 and for chairing its biweekly meetings (Levine 1994b:25; Holmes 1916:55; McGee 1889a:17, 1889b:240). The Women's Anthropological Society started with 11 members, but it rapidly grew to 56 individuals (Rossiter 1982:83). A number of women interested in archaeology met with this group, including not only Fletcher, Hearst, Nuttall, and another of the group's original ten cofounders, Sarah Scull (who wrote on Greek archaeology), but also the women from families of prominent men with North American archaeological interests, such as Caroline Healey Wells Dall, Mary Porter Tileston Hemenway, Anita Newcomb McGee, and Emma Dean Powell (Croly 1898:341-343; Moldow 1987:90, 149, 152, 155; Rossiter 1982:83). With the growth of the group, the membership was divided into specialized sections: archaeology, child life, ethnology, folklore, psychology, and sociology (Flack 1975:128).

Tilly Stevenson was elected a Fellow of the AAAS in 1893. From her archaeological site surveys in the Southwest she developed an interest in protecting ruins from looting, and in 1887 and 1888 she joined with Alice Fletcher to represent the Women's Anthropological Society of America and the AAAS in lobbying for legislation to try to create a park including Mesa Verde and the Pajarito Plateau (Parezo 1993b:42). She served, at Putnam's invitation, along with Alice Fletcher, Zelia Nuttall, and Sara Y. Stevenson on the panel of five women composing the Jury of Awards for Ethnology in the Columbian Exposition in Chicago in 1893 (Rossiter 1982:98). In a letter written to a colleague (quoted in Parezo 1993b:42), she argued that "archaeology and ethnology must be worked together in order to secure results of real scientific value."

Yet another Stevenson, Sara Yorke Stevenson (1847–1921), sometimes referred to as Mrs. Cornelius Stevenson, was a founding member of the Archaeological Association of the University of Pennsylvania in 1889, which evolved into the current University Museum (Winegrad 1993:21). The position of curator of Egyptian collections was established in 1889 with the creation of the Department of Archaeology and Paleontology, and Sara Stevenson became the unsalaried curator of the Egyptian and Mediterranean Section from 1890 though 1905. Through her advocacy, the Egyptian, Mediterranean, and Babylonian sections of the museum, which were under her guidance in the early 1890s, thrived; for example, in 1893, $8,000.00 was spent for collections in her area, while Stewart Culin, who was in charge of the American and Prehistoric Sections, received authorization for only $331.20 for additions to those collections (Conn 1998:93). She served as the secretary of the committee to establish the Free Museum of Science and Arts, and in 1895, with the opening of the University Museum, she replaced Culin as Secretary of the board for the Department of Archaeology and Palaeontology, a position she held until being elected president in 1904 (Meyerson and Winegrad 1978:126). Culin had wanted to emphasize research, while Stevenson had wanted to emphasize display and education in the new museum (Darnell 1970:83, 1988:59; Madeira 1964:20; Meyerson and Winegrad 1978:126). She was the first woman to receive an honorary degree (Sc.D.) from the University of Pennsylvania, in 1894 (Meyerson and Winegrad 1978:117), and the only woman trustee of the Philadelphia Commercial Museum, from 1894 to 1901 (Conn 1998:104).

Sara Stevenson was also in charge of ethnographic exhibits at the World's Columbian Exposition in 1893 (at the invitation of Putnam), and she served, along with Alice Fletcher, Matilda Stevenson, and Zelia Nuttall, on the exposition's Jury of Awards for Ethnology (Rossiter 1982:98). A special act of Congress was necessary to permit women to serve on the Jury of Awards for Ethnology in 1893, after which Stevenson was promptly elected vice-president of the jury (Meyerson and Winegrad 1978:126). She continued to receive strong support from Putnam for her endeavors at Pennsylvania until she resigned from her position in 1905. Sara Stevenson did much of the fund-raising for the new museum at the University of Pennsylvania in 1897 (Cheyney 1940:351), was elected to both the AAAS and the American Philosophical Association, and also gave several papers at various International Congress of Americanists meetings (Meyerson and Winegrad 1978:127). Although many of her archaeological interests were outside North America, in her capacity as fund-raiser and museum board officer she was instrumental in securing funds for part of the North American archaeology that the University of Pennsylvania museum conducted during the 1890s. In addition, as with most of the women mentioned here, it is of note that the sources consulted all indicate the strong support she received from Putnam.

Cordelia A. Studley (1855–1887) was a medical student who seems to have first been recruited to work on the osteological collections from the excavations of Edward Palmer in Coahuila, Mexico, which the Peabody Museum acquired. She was appointed "Assistant," Somatology, at the Peabody Museum in 1882, and thus became the museum's first physical anthropologist (Brew 1966b:30). She continued working in this position through 1886, when, according to Putnam (1887:569), "she felt the necessity of obtaining an addition to her income" and left to take a higher-paying job. Her paper (Studley 1884) on the Coahuila materials is one of the earliest such studies on Mexico. She also presented an analysis of some of the burial remains recovered from the Turner mound group and other mounds from Madisonville, Little Miami Valley, Ohio, excavations by Putnam and Metz, at the AAAS by Putnam's invitation (Anonymous 1884:344; Studley 1885). Bourque (chapter 7 of this volume) refers to a report that Cordelia Studley was a co–leader of an excavation season of shell mounds in Maine in 1885 and that she also conducted excavations in Massachusetts during her tenure. Studley was another woman student recruited and encouraged by Putnam; her untimely death in 1887 terminated what was developing into a stellar career.

Mary Parke Foster, Cornelia Horsford, Harriet Newell Wardle, and Julia Wirt show up in my initial survey of publications as individuals with archaeological interests who presented only one paper prior to 1901, and who thus are representatives of a larger group of women of unknown number with only transitory visibility in nineteenth-century archaeology. For example, one of the sources searched was the list of presentations at the annual meetings of the AAAS. For the 25-year period covering 1876 to 1901, from the beginning of a separate subsection for anthropology (later Section H) until the turn of the century, I identified 65 papers presented by women: 18 by Alice Fletcher, 17 by Erminnie Smith, 5 by Zelia Nuttall, 4 each by Franc Babbitt, Anita McGee, and Laura Osborne Talbott, 3 by Virginia K. Bowers, 2 by Matilda Stevenson, and 1 each by Fannie D. Bergen, Christine Ladd Franklin, Fanny (Mrs. Romyn) Hitchcock, Cornelia Horsford, Ada M. King, Jeannette Robinson Murphy, Cordelia Studley, and Harriet Newell Wardle.

Of this AAAS list, only two of these papers are on North American archaeology by individuals not already discussed: Cornelia Horsford and Harriet Newell Wardle. Cornelia Horsford (1861–[?]) gave her first presentation on the evidence for Vikings in Massachusetts at the forty-seventh meeting of the AAAS in 1898, a topic on which she subsequently published several papers after 1900. She had taken over the investigation of the possibility of Vikings in New England from her father, Eben Norton Horsford (1818–1893), who had taught at the Lawrence Scientific School, and like her father, she conducted some archaeological excavations to investigate this idea (Williams 1991:206–209).

The second individual, Harriet Newell Wardle (1875–1964), gave her first paper at the forty-ninth AAAS meeting in 1900 (Wardle 1901:317–318). She later wrote a series of articles on eastern archaeological sites such as Moundville and Indian Knoll and artifacts such as spindle whorls, textiles, and baskets (Wardle 1903, 1906, 1912, 1919, 1920). She had started out in 1899 working for the Academy of Natural Sciences in Philadelphia, where she later became the curator of the Clarence B. Moore collections (Mason 1965:1513), but in 1929, when the academy phased out anthropology, she shifted to the University Museum at the University of Pennsylvania, where she remained for the rest of her career, until 1948. Wardle was one of a group of women very active in the discipline, but often in the background. For example, she, Fletcher, Hearst, and Nuttall, along with Sarah A. Scull (an expert in Greek mythology at Pennsylvania), Elizabeth Mead Hyde (who worked for the

U.S. National Museum), and Lucy E. Peabody (from Denver), were all members of the Anthropological Society of Washington, members of Section H of the AAAS, and founding members of the AAA (as determined from the membership rosters for these organizations in 1902). Wardle also was on the executive committee of the AAA during the Boas censure of 1919 (Pinsky 1992:181).

We need also to consider women such as Alice Eastwood, Mary Parke Foster and Julia J. Wirt, who appear in the literature reporting on archaeological materials, but for whom we have little other information relevant to their contributions to archaeology. Alice Eastwood (1859–1953) was a distinguished pioneering botanist, who began her work in Colorado and Utah. During the period of 1889 to 1895, she made several visits to the Wetherill ranch, "Alamo," and in 1892 and 1895 she made special plant collecting trips with (Benjamin) Alfred Wetherill. According to the biographies of Wetherill (Fletcher 1977) and Eastwood (Wilson 1955), Alice Eastwood searched for rare plants above the cliff dwelling ruins, while Alfred and Richard Wetherill dug about in the ruins, gathering relics for the Denver Museum and for the 1893 Columbian exposition. She identified plants utilized in the prehistoric textiles, baskets, and matting recovered by the Wetherills (Eastwood 1893:375–376; Fletcher 1977:167–169), making her one of the first archaeological "paleoethnobotanists." She knew the region's archaeology well enough that she was credited by Nordenskiold with providing him with the necessary letter of introduction to the Wetherills when he came to America in 1891 to investigate ruins in the Southwest (Steen 1979:20). Reyman (1999:214) has recently suggested that in addition to identifying plant products from the ruins, that Eastwood also actually participated in the excavations with the Wetherills.

Mary Parke Foster was a founding member and a vice-president of the Women's Anthropological Society of America between 1885 and 1889 (Croly 1898:341; Women's Anthropological Society of America 1889:13). According to Anita McGee, during this period, out of 47 presentations by members, there were only two papers on archaeology, one of which, "The Ancient Ruins of Mexico," was presented by Foster. Mary Foster's work was based on seven years' residence in Mexico, during which period "some expeditions . . . were made, and certain ruins explored for the first time by a foreign lady" (McGee 1889a:21, 1889b:241–242).

As a corresponding member of the Davenport Academy of Natural Sciences, Julia J. Wirt reported on her part in the 1876 excavations of a mound near Utah Lake, Utah (Wirt 1878). There were no doubt many other individuals like Alice Eastwood, Mary Foster and Julia Wirt who contributed to the growth of North American archaeology, those who are referred to in limited instances and then disappear from the printed archeological record.

Women Supporting Women in Archaeology

Phoebe Apperson Hearst (1842–1919) was a philanthropist who made important contributions to archaeology. William Pepper of the University of Pennsylvania got her interested in archaeology in the 1880s. She became a collaborator of both Pepper and Sara Y. Stevenson, helping to purchase collections for their new museum and to fund archaeological projects in Florida, Mexico, Italy, and Egypt for the period of roughly 1890 to 1898 (Darnell 1970:81; Snead 1999:257–258; Wilson 1971:172). Hearst was also a patron of the Women's National Science Club during its existence from 1891 to 1899 (Rossiter 1982:59). With the death of William Pepper, and after a disagreement with Sara Stevenson on her work for the museum, Hearst returned her interests to her home area of California. She had funded a joint University of Pennsylvania–University of California at Berkeley expedition to Egypt in 1898, but from 1899 until 1904 it was to become a Berkeley-only project (Kuklick 1996:102). She funded the research of a number of Americanist archaeologists, including Max Uhle's work in both Peru and California, Frank Cushing's work in the Florida Keys, Zelia Nuttall's work in Europe and Mexico, and some of Alice Fletcher's projects, and also provided a major grant to Putnam to look for the ancient peoples of America during his California years (Mark 1988:281, 286). Hearst is probably best known in most anthropological circles for the agreement she made with Frederic Putnam in 1901 to head an anthropological initiative at the University of California–Berkeley, which resulted in the founding of the museum and department, Putnam's direction of the department from 1901 to 1909, and much of funding for its first decade of existence, including archaeological excavation projects by Nels Nelson and Max Uhle.

Mary Porter Tileston Hemenway (1820–1894) was another philanthropist who explicitly supported the work of women in archaeology. In 1840 she married Edward Augustus Holyoke Hemenway (1803–1876), a Boston merchant and Harvard College graduate who also had been a philanthropist (McChesney 1991:282). Just as Hearst had done after the death of her husband, Mary Tileston Hemenway made a number of grants to Americanist archaeology and also to Harvard; her collection of archaeology books is an important segment of period resources in the current Tozzer Library. Because of her many contributions to Americanist studies, Hemenway was made an honorary member of the Women's Anthropological Society of America, which was founded in June 1885.

Mary Hemenway was responsible for funding the Hemenway Southwestern Archaeological Expedition of 1886-1894, which not only supported the fieldwork of Frank Hamilton Cushing and others, but, more importantly, paid for a handsomely illustrated, five-volume publication series of the results, the *Journal of American Ethnology and Archaeology*, which came out between 1891 and 1908 (Keller 1971:181; Tileston 1927:60-61). She employed a number of women on her own staff and stipulated that her archaeological grant funds should be for both women and men (Levine 1994b:24).

One of the women so involved was Jeanette Webster Williams, a "gifted archaeologist" (Crane 1894:709) who was in charge of the Hemenway Archaeological Collection of Prehistoric Antiquities. She helped display the finds of the Hemenway expedition in Madrid in 1892 (Williams 1895), and had just completed a chapter on Tusayan Orange Ware of northeastern Arizona for the *Journal of American Ethnology and Archaeology* in 1894 when she died of pneumonia, just a few months before Mary Hemenway died (Crane 1894:709; Levine 1999:143).

Another woman involved in the Hemenway Southwestern Archaeological Expedition was Margaret Whitehead Magill (1863-1935), later married to Frederick Webb Hodge. She was the sister of Emily Tennison Magill, who had married Frank Cushing in 1882. She accompanied the Cushings on their 1882 and 1886 expeditions, and she again accompanied them on the 1888-1889 Hemenway expedition, where she met Frederick Hodge. Hodge had joined the expedition, at John W. Powell's direction, to serve as Cushing's secretary and assistant in archaeology, and subsequently he and Margaret Magill married in 1891 (Lonergan 1999:910). Margaret Magill did a "superb" series of drawings of Zuni pots and designs, and because she enjoyed the work, occasionally she and her sister's husband (Frank Cushing) went exploring the Zuni area for archaeological sites and archaeological and ethnological artifacts (Mark 1980:103, 106, 107, 129).

In addition to her Southwest expedition, Mary Hemenway was also a principal lobbying and financial support for 1890 bill that established the Casa Grande National Monument outside Tucson (Mark 1988:143), which helped to set the stage for the later Antiquity Act of 1906. As well, she utilized part of her inherited estate to establish one of the major fellowships in American archaeology and ethnology at the Peabody Museum in 1890 (the first Hemenway Fellowship went to John G. Owens for his work in Mesoamerica in 1892), and she worked closely with Frederic W. Putnam on a number of issues (Dorsey 1896:97). Also, because she was active in working with Elizabeth Cabot Cary Agassiz in support of the women students of "The School for the Collegiate Instruction of Women," which became Radcliffe College in 1893, the women's gym on the Radcliffe campus has been named for her.

Mary Sibbet Copley Thaw (1842-1929) is yet another philanthropist who contributed to the growth of archaeology and to women in archaeology. Thaw was the second wife (in 1867) of William Thaw, who had been an important stockholder in both rail lines and steamship lines (Buck 1936:297; Marquis 1966:1225). Like Mary Hemenway, she used part of her inherited estate upon her husband's death to fund archaeological research, establishing one of the major fellowships in American archaeology and ethnology at the Peabody Museum in 1890. The first Thaw Fellowship was awarded to Alice Fletcher in 1891, and later Zelia Nuttall was also partly supported by a Thaw Fellowship (Dixon 1930:211). The importance of this fellowship at the time might in part be judged by the reception held in 1891 in Washington, D.C., upon the announcement of Alice C. Fletcher as the first awardee: over 800 people came to honor the first Thaw Fellow (Mark 1980:73).

Anita Newcomb McGee (1864-1940) married William J. McGee in 1888 and accompanied him on archaeological field trips (Dearing 1971:464). But more importantly for the argument developed here, she was a significant early woman M.D. in the late nineteenth century, and was also very active in the organizing aspects for women in anthropology, serving as the secretary for the Women's Archaeological Society of America after joining in 1888 (McGee 1889a, 1889b). She was elected to membership in the AAAS in 1888, and to Fellow in 1892; she presented several papers at annual meetings of the AAAS, was a member of several committees, and served as Secretary of Section H in 1897-1898, succeeding Alice Fletcher, and replacing Harlan I. Smith, who had resigned.[6] During her tenure as head of Section H, she contributed one very explicit archaeological paper, the summary of the discussion of the Trenton gravel "glacial man" special session at the AAAS (McGee 1897).

Hinsley (1992:132) lists Putnam's assistants—Alice E. Putnam, Jennie Smith, and Frances H. Mead—among his nineteenth-century women working in archaeology. He considered these three as candidates because of the material assistance they provided Frederic Putnam in running his archaeological operations.

Alice Putnam was one of three children (Eben, Alice Edmands, and Ethel Appleton Fiske) Frederic Putnam had with his first wife, Adelaide Martha Edmands, whom he married in 1863 and who died in 1879 (Anonymous 1915a, 1915b; Tozzer 1936:125). Frederic Putnam involved his family, both his second wife and his children, in his work to some extent. For example, three days after he married his second wife, Esther Orme Clarke, in Chicago in 1882, they left for an archaeological excavation project in Ohio with Charles L. Metz (Dexter 1982:25). Putnam's archival papers include references to his son, Eben, going with him as a boy on some of his father's field investigations. However, the child involved most in Putnam's archaeological work was not his son, but his daughter Alice, who was first hired as an assistant in the museum in 1886 and worked many years thereafter in an official capacity (Hinsley 1992:132, 1999:148). Alice also worked many additional years in an unofficial capacity: the Putnam Papers at Harvard University's Peabody Museum contain a number of letters from Alice to her father in which she discusses archaeological issues and communications with various of her father's colleagues from professional scientific meetings she attended for him. She served as her father's eyes and ears at these meetings once his health began to fail.[7]

Jennie (Jane) Smith first began working for Frederic Putnam in 1875 (Hinsley 1999:144). Elected a member of the AAAS at the twenty-ninth meeting in 1879, she remained a member through Putnam's tenure as Secretary (1873–1897) and President (1898–1899). She thus seems to have been in large part Putnam's assistant in conducting his activities for the AAAS, although she also was involved in the operations at the Peabody Museum. She was listed as "Miss Jennie Smith" in the AAAS annual membership lists from 1879 to 1891, but from 1892 until she dropped her membership in 1899 she is listed as "Miss Jane Smith."

Frances Harvey Teobert Mead (1847–ca.1915) was a museum assistant who served as Putnam's secretary from 1889, being hired just before Putnam's involvement with the World's Columbian Exposition in Chicago, until her retirement with his death in 1915. She wrote detailed reports of exhibits at the exposition for various states (Mead 1894); at Putnam's urging (in part in his position as an associate editor of the journal), she wrote a review of the Peabody Museum's displays for *Records of the Past* (Mead 1905), which includes a very interesting glimpse of what the museum looked like a century ago; she provided the first detailed bibliography of Putnam's work for the well-known anniversary volume (Mead 1909); and she collected historic and environmental notes on Conejos Canyon area of Colorado, where she took her vacations for more than 40 years, materials that have been edited and published (Mead 1984).

One of the most important aspects of the work of Francis Mead, Alice Putnam, and Jennie Smith, for this volume, was their work as Putnam's assistants. For example, many of the routine communications from Putnam to Nickerson referred to in chapter 11 of this volume, such as those acknowledging receipt of artifacts sent to the Peabody Museum, asking questions about schedule, and the like, were written by Francis Mead (or earlier, Jennie Smith); Putnam would simply pen a short instruction on top of a letter received indicating how Mead or Smith was to respond. The contributions of these three women to archaeology may be buried in the anonymity of these positions, but without their assistance Putnam could not have functioned so smoothly in his job.

A number of women were instrumental in securing ethnographic and archaeological collections for the Peabody Museum; two of the more important not yet mentioned are Sophia Bradford Ripley Thayer and Harriet Arnot Maxwell Converse. Sophia Thayer (1833–[?]) had married the well-known jurist James Bradley Thayer (1831–1902) on April 24, 1861 (Williston 1936:405). Among other issues, Thayer worked on Indian law in the Dakotas and was instrumental in the passage of the Dawes Bill of 1887, and it may be in these venues that Sophia Thayer became involved in securing artifacts. In addition, Sophia Thayer was a cousin of Ralph Waldo Emerson, whose house the Thayers frequently visited. Because Mary Hemenway was also a good friend of Emerson's (McChesney 1999:543), no doubt Sophia Thayer was further encouraged by knowledge of Mary Hemenway's work in archaeology.

Harriet Arnot Maxwell Converse (1836–1903) started out penning poetry, but after 1881 her interest shifted to writing on the myths and legends of the New York Iroquois. Both her grandfather and father had been adopted into the Seneca tribe, and her husband, who had lived with the Indians in the West, where he had become a skilled bowsman, was also adopted into the Seneca (Fenichell 1985:189; Fenton 1971:375; Hardy 1993:99). Their New York City house became a center for visiting Indians. In 1884, Harriet Converse herself was formally adopted into the Seneca, and in 1891 she became the first white woman to be named a chief of the Six Nations, confirmed by the tribe in 1892 (Converse, in Willard and Livermore 1897, 1:201; Fenichell 1971:375;

Hardy 1993:100; Romeyn 1999:360). She collected and wrote up ethnographic information on the Iroquois, but these reports are viewed today as rather amateurish and sentimental (Fenichell 1985:190; Fenton 1971:375). Most important for our theme, however, she began purchasing and donating both archaeological and ethnographic artifacts in the 1890s, items which she contributed (and sold) not only to the Peabody Museum, but also to the American Museum of Natural History and the Museum of the American Indian (Fenichell 1985:189; Fenton 1971:376; Hardy 1993:101). It was in connection both with her ethnographic activities and her acquisition and donation of archaeological materials that she had correspondence with Putnam.

Two other women included in Table 10.2, Mary Louisa Duncan Putnam (1832-1903) (Mrs. Charles E. Putnam) and Elizabeth Duncan Putnam (1867-[?]), were both associated with the Davenport Academy of Natural Sciences in Iowa, an academy that was active in archaeological explorations. In some ways, this Putnam family is part of what we might call a mini-dynasty of individuals interested in archaeology. They were in fact distant relatives of Frederic W. Putnam (W. C. Putnam 1899:4). Mary Louisa Duncan Putnam, her husband Charles Edwin Putnam, and all of their children—Benjamin Risley Putnam, Charles Morgan Putnam, Edward Kirby Putnam, Elizabeth Duncan Putnam, George Rockwell Putnam, Henry St. Clair Putnam, John C. Putnam, Joseph Duncan Putnam, and William Clement Putnam—became life members of the academy (E. D. Putnam 1920:177).[8] During the quarter century of our interest, three members of the family served as president of the academy—Mary Louisa in 1879-1880 and again from 1900 to 1903, Joseph Duncan in 1881-1882, and Charles E. Putnam from 1885 to 1887; Edward K. later filled the same position in 1907 and later.

The earliest members of the family to become members seem to have been Mary Louisa and her son Joseph Duncan (1855-1881), who joined the academy in 1869. Mary L. D. Duncan was the first woman member of the academy, as well as its first woman president in 1879 (Starr 1897:87). Joseph Duncan had a lifetime interest in entomology, but he was interested in archaeology as well, and he and his mother are listed as contributors of lithic artifacts to the academy in the first volume of the *Proceedings of the Davenport Academy of Natural Sciences* (1876:221). Joseph Duncan helped to establish the *Proceedings* series, and after his death Mary Louisa served as the president of the publication committee for the next 20 years, with the *Proceedings* published in large part during most of this period from a bequest from the will of Charles E. Putnam (1825-1887), who is perhaps better known for his involvement with the Davenport tablets (Hodge 1903a:174; E. D. Putnam 1907:xv, xxiv; Rossiter 1982:84). Mary provided the academy with publication funds and leadership for many years, in part to commemorate the archaeological interests of both her husband and her eldest son (Joseph Duncan), but also because she herself had an active interest in archaeological questions. She avidly attended meetings of Section H of the AAAS as well as the International Congress of Americanists (Starr 1903:633), and in 1893 she served as a member of the Membership Committee of Section H, although she herself was not officially nominated as a member of the AAAS until 1901. Many of her children also became involved in Section H. In addition to her sons Joseph Duncan, Edward, George, and Henry, her daughter Elizabeth Duncan Putnam also became a member, in 1896 (see Table 10.2). Elizabeth Putnam later also served as the Secretary of the Davenport Academy of Natural Sciences, and thus, like her mother, became involved in the support of the academy's archaeological activities.

Many of the women involved in Americanist archaeology from 1875 to 1900, briefly discussed above, were either directly or indirectly recruited by the activities of Frederic W. Putnam. Their number may be a surprise to many readers, as for the most part, histories of Americanist archaeology have overlooked their participation.

11

Origins of Stratigraphic Excavation in North America

The Peabody Museum Method and the Chicago Method

David L. Browman

Introduction

A number of recent sources have suggested that the "Chicago method" of artificial stratigraphic units revolutionized mound excavation in the United States in the 1930s and 1940s, and they have credited its origin to Fay-Cooper Cole. However, evidence suggests that this method of mound excavation was first developed by Frederic Ward Putnam at the Peabody Museum half a century earlier. Putnam's techniques, sometimes referred to as the "Peabody Museum method" in the literature of the 1890s and 1900s, were learned by an avocational archaeologist, William Baker Nickerson, who had studied at the Peabody Museum with Putnam, in 1885 and 1886. While Putnam was instrumental in passing on this method of stratigraphic excavation to several other archaeological researchers, it is through Nickerson that the method appears to have been transferred to Cole.

During the first season of the University of Chicago archaeological program in 1926, the field crew fortuitously secured unpublished copies of excavation reports by Nickerson that detailed work conducted by the Peabody Museum method. The excavation method described in Nickerson's work was adopted by the Chicago crews, and it formed the basis of a technique, practiced in later projects, that became known as the Chicago method.

Where Putnam derived his original method is not yet clear. Summaries of the first stratigraphic excavation in Europe in 1859 were available in U.S. publications by 1862, if not earlier. Putnam began archaeological excavations as early as 1865 (Putnam 1866), nine years before he took over the Peabody Museum position, and he collaborated with

Origins of Stratigraphic Excavation / 243

Jeffries Wyman on shell mound excavations in 1867 (Wyman 1868a: 565, 568, 581, 584). Putnam's interest in archaeology stems from a few years earlier, when, during attendance at meetings in Montreal in August 1857, he took a field trip and collected materials from a shell heap at Mount Royal, Montreal (Putnam 1899:1). Putnam's original method may have been derived from his interpretation of European reports from 1859 and later, combined with his own field experiences. At this point, more research is needed to surmise the precise linkages involved in the development of Putnam's methods.

Mid-Nineteenth-Century Information on Stratigraphic Excavation Techniques

In 1858, William Pengelly employed a pioneering method of excavating by archaeological stratigraphy at Brixham Cave to provide the first accepted evidence of contemporaneity of humans and extinct fauna. The French quickly picked up this method that same year, and Gabriel de Mortillet used it in an excavation then, which helped to verify the findings of Jacques Boucher de Perthes (Browman 1997). (Note that a specific distinction is being made here between actual explicit excavation of archaeological sites by strata and post facto interpretation of archaeological deposits using stratigraphy, which seems to have been done first perhaps 160 years earlier than Pengelly, by Olof Rudbeck in 1697.)

It is evident from scanning many publications from this period that most American archaeologists were reading some of this material and had accepted the general idea that stratigraphic excavation might be the appropriate technique to employ in cave excavation. Thus, to this extent it can be argued that Pengelly's work provided the model and impetus for early controlled excavation in cave archaeology in the United States. But whether these period archaeologists would agree that this same stratigraphic excavation technique could or should be employed in mound excavation—the other frequent excavation type-site of the nineteenth century—was not at all clear. The idea of applying stratigraphic excavation principles to mound sites and to associated habitation sites seems to have taken much longer to disperse into the archaeological mind-set.

The Smithsonian Institution published "instructions" on excavation methodology from 1862 onward in order to provide collectors with guidance in securing materials for the Smithsonian Institution and the U.S. National Museum collections. These widely circulated directives seem to be the likely vehicle for passing on some of the particulars about European techniques. In the earliest published directive, George Gibbs (1862:395, 1867/1863:6) suggested that an excavator of a burial mound or shell midden should note if it "exhibited any marks of stratification," with any artifacts recovered noted as to "the depth at which they were discovered." That is, for mounds and habitation sites he recommended the use of post facto stratigraphic *interpretation*, but he did not suggest using stratigraphic units as an actual excavation technique. For cave excavations, however, the technique suggested was different. Based on the experience of recent excavation projects in England (particularly at Brixham), Gibbs (1862:395–396) suggested that for caves, "the superficial earth should be carefully removed over a considerable space and results, if any, being kept separate and marked accordingly.... underlying materials should then be cautiously removed and sorted over, each layer being kept by itself.... every fragment of bone or other evidence of animal life should thus be preserved and marked with order of its succession in depth."

The method that Pengelly had evolved, beginning with his work in Brixham Cave in 1858 and later elaborated in the work at Kent Cavern, appears to be that advocated by Gibbs. This method involved laying out a grid system of one-foot by three-foot horizontal units, and a vertical control by means of a combination of natural strata and arbitrary one-foot levels, continuing the excavation to four feet beneath the sterile floor, which allowed Pengelly to produce a catalog in which he entered the find number and the three-dimensional position of every bone and every artifact (Pengelly 1897:75; Prestwich 1874:476–477, 482; Warren and Rose 1994:4, 11, 32). Up until 1858, "the standard method of scientific excavation was to sink vertical shafts through the deposits being studied," with archaeologists excavating barrows by digging single shafts in the middle of each, and geologists and paleontologists excavating caves using multiple vertical shafts in different parts of the cave to determine where the richest deposits of fossils were, and then simple extracting these latter in one unit (Van Riper 1993:87).

A decade after Gibbs's directive, a revised version from Joseph Henry (1878:4) proposed that the proper way to excavate a mound was "by sinking a shaft from the centre of the apex, or by cutting a ditch on a level with the ground," essentially reverting to the pre-Pengelly methods. However, Charles Rau (1883:481), in subsequent directives, returned to Gibbs's suggestions of two decades earlier, writing that a cave deposit "should be entirely removed in sections, its stratification (if there is any) carefully noted, and the relative position of each discovered artifact noted." Government museum archaeologists, beginning with Gibbs, thus suggested the use of careful stratigraphic control in excavation of cave deposits, but they were less certain of the utility of this method for mound projects. However, a scan of the literature of the period indicates that their admonitions regarding the need for stratigraphic control and for detailed inventories with respect to provenience were noted more in the breach than in execution for the next half-century.

Frederic Ward Putnam and the Peabody Museum Method

Frederic Ward Putnam (1839–1913) directed students and researchers in American archaeology for nearly four decades. In the materials so far accessed, I find that Putnam was less than explicit in detailing his methods in his written reports. Thus we must seek additional clues regarding his research methodology from commentaries by students and colleagues. This search is made more difficult because "Putnam gave few formal courses of instruction. Following Agassiz's example, he much preferred to have his students meet him in the laboratory for informal instruction" (Tozzer 1936:130). Until the early 1890s, Putnam gave instruction only occasionally, as dictated by an individual's need or request. In part this was because of the paradigm for anthropology at the time, which, according to Stocking, was "an anthropology oriented toward public lecturing and the display of artifacts collected by the lecturer," that is, "a kind of Lyceum type of anthropology or Chautauqua anthropology" (Stocking and Montague 1979:5, 16). Thus, as discussed below, Putnam's first commentaries on archaeological techniques are disclosed in precisely this kind of public lecture format, and it is only a good deal later that formal, extended classroom instruction was initiated.

While Putnam had been Curator of the Peabody Museum since 1875, and had been appointed Professor of Anthropology in 1887, he thus had only a few informal students until the Division of American Archaeology and Ethnology was established in December 1890 (Dixon 1930:210–211; Willoughby 1923:501). An early brochure described the program in its first year as follows: "A course of special training in archaeology and technology, requiring three years for its completion, will be given by Prof. Putnam. It will be carried on by work in the laboratory and museum, lectures, field-work, and exploration, and in the third year some special research. The ability to use French and Spanish will be necessary. For this course a knowledge of elementary chemistry, geology, botany, zoology, drawing, and surveying is required, and courses in ancient history, ancient arts, and classical archaeology are recommended as useful" (Starr 1892:291).

Hence Putnam began regular instruction in his labs only in 1890, with five students; this number had increased to eight by 1894. However, Putnam did not teach an official university course in American archaeology and ethnology until 1896-1897, when the Peabody Museum was finally integrated with the university, at which point the program had increased to six graduate and ten undergraduate students (Dorsey 1894:372; Willoughby 1923:501). According to Dixon (1930: 211), the first regular course in anthropology at Harvard was given by Dorsey, who had just received his Ph.D. in 1894, and served as Assistant Instructor in 1895-1896, but left in 1896 after having received the appointment to the Field Museum job in Chicago. Putnam did some teaching in 1895-1896 and 1896-1897, and by 1898 he was assisted by his next two Ph.D. students—Frank Russell (Ph.D. 1898) and Roland B. Dixon (Ph.D. 1900) (MacCurdy 1899:914; Williams 1969). The first reference I have found to a class at Harvard focusing on explicit discussion of fieldwork methods is in 1902, when Putnam is listed as teaching a "Special course in American Archaeology and Ethnology, including museum, laboratory, and field work" (MacCurdy 1902a:214).

Putnam, however, had developed a rigorous excavation method at least by the early 1880s. A short news item in *Science* (Anonymous 1883:581) reported that "Mr. F. W. Putnam, of the Peabody Museum, Cambridge, announces his readiness to give lectures on American archaeology, based upon the course delivered last year before the Lowell Institute." By 1885, Putnam was offering a series of 38 public lectures, derived in part from the Lowell Institute course materials, which he gave for fees to help support the museum's work (see chapter 10, Figure 10.1). Of particular importance in the argument here is "Lecture No. 38," which was listed in the advertising brochure (Putnam 1886a:6) as "The Proper Methods of Exploration." Lecture No. 38 appears to be the same lecture described as being "On the Methods of Archaeological Research in America," which Putnam gave at Johns Hopkins University on December 15, 1885. The anonymous correspondent summarizing Putnam's lecture reported:

Trenching and slicing, he said, could be used to express in general terms the method followed in field work. For instance, in exploring a mound, a trench is first dug at the base of the mound. . . . The wall is the first section of the exploration, and its outline

should be drawn or photographed and its measurements noted....
After this first section is made, the work is carried on by slicing;
or cutting down about a foot at a time, always keeping a vertical
wall in front, the whole width of the mound. Each slice thus made
is a section, and whenever the slightest change in the structure
is noticed or any object found, that section should be drawn or
photographed, and measured as at first, and the exact position
noted of any object, ash bed, or change in the character of the
structure of the mound. (Putnam 1886b:91; reprinted in Williams
1973:1–4)

Putnam no doubt was employing this method in his 1884 excavations of Marriott Mound No. 1. Regrettably, while it is clear from reading his report that he employed great care in excavation—for example, giving each artifact a separate catalog number (Mitra 1933)—the report does not detail excavation strategies (Metz and Putnam 1886). More of the methodology is reported in a short note on the annual meeting of the American Association for the Advancement of Science (AAAS) of 1884. The correspondent, in commenting on Putnam's presentation of the work he and Metz conducted at the Turner mound group at Madisonville, Ohio, reported: "The very careful manner in which the exploration had been carried out—the earth taken away and examined shovelful by shovelful—was shown, and the results of the work enumerated and illustrated by diagrams and photographs in great number" (Anonymous 1884:344).

In his 1887 report on work at the Schmitz Mound in the Little Miami River valley, Putnam briefly reported employing the excavation method he had described in his 1885 lecture, noting that "the work of exploration was begun by digging a straight trench down to the clay hard-pan across one edge of the mound and another on the opposite side. The mound was then cut down in slices, throwing the earth behind and always keeping a vertical wall in front" (Putnam 1887/1973:237).

Putnam seems to have taken on the mission of zealously spreading his new views on proper excavation technique. For example, the correspondent reporting on the anthropology papers given at the 1885 meetings of the AAAS noted that "Mr. F. W. Putnam gave some very practical and detailed directions as to the proper exploration of mounds, pleading earnestly for thorough work in all explorations; and illustrated its value by several examples from his own recent investigations" (Anonymous 1885:234). In a later report in 1888, Putnam noted that "our methods of thorough exploration have set an example which others are following, so that American archaeology can no longer be regarded as consisting of indiscriminate collection of relics of the past" (cited in Barnhart 1999:4).

Hinsley suggests that Putnam developed his method from his work on the Ohio Hopewell mounds. "It was here, encamped in the river valleys of southern Ohio in the humid summer months of the early 1880s, with his family, [Dr. Charles] Metz and [Charles F.] Low, that Putnam spent the happiest and most productive days of his anthropological career. Here, too, in conjunction with the Madisonville doctor, Putnam established his reputation as the first systematic archaeologist in North America, the man who would train the next generation" (Hinsley 1992:130). Although the Ohio work clearly allowed Putnam to fine-tune his techniques, the roots of what becomes known as the Peabody Museum method actually began prior to his Ohio mound explorations—started, perhaps, as early as 1857 with his first documented archaeological collecting on a shell mound, developed by trial and error during his first serious excavations begun as early as 1865 in Maine and Massachusetts, and clearly elaborated in his series of lectures on methodology in the early 1880s.

Additional information on Putnam's excavation methodology can be gleaned from his colleagues' description of his procedures, and also in the reported excavation techniques employed by individuals he trained, such as Roland B. Dixon, Charles Peabody, George Pepper, Frank Russell, Charles Willoughby, and others tied to the Peabody Museum at Harvard. In one of the earliest outside reviews of Putnam's new method, his colleague Otis Tufton Mason (1838–1908) reported that for mounds, the "Putnam method has been to take the structure entirely down, on the theory that the tumuli are not concentric series of conical shells with a core, but a series of horizontal layers" (1885:755), and that in Putnam's procedure, "every ounce of earth passed backward through a screen or sieve" (1888a:525).

Charles Clark Willoughby (1857–1943) was trained by Putnam and Metz at the Ohio projects (Hooton and Willoughby 1920:7; Willoughby and Hooton 1922:7, 11, 14). Willoughby, like Putnam, was rather mute in his writings about his specific excavation methods. In his early excavations of mounds in Maine, Willoughby employed the grid method advocated by Putnam, referring to use of a 10-foot grid at Orland and a 12.5-foot grid at Bucksport in 1892 (Willoughby 1898:402, 415), with a bit more detail on his report of the 1894 excavations at Ellsworth, where he noted that the "ground to be explored [was] taken off into

Origins of Stratigraphic Excavation / 249

sections ten feet square ... [with] workmen throwing the earth behind them as they advanced, keeping a perpendicular wall of gravel in front," employing this method to locate the artifacts and features found with respect to east-west/north-south measurements from the grid, and their depth below surface (Willoughby 1898:390).

While the verbal description in Willoughby's text was somewhat scant, thanks to the need for exhibits for the 1893 World's Colombian Exposition in Chicago, we do know that Willoughby was employing precisely Putnam's method. As Putnam remarked in his editorial note introducing Willoughby's report (Putnam 1898b:387), "the work was so admirably carried out in accordance with the Museum methods, that it was decided to use the material from the Orland site to illustrate the 'Methods of Archaeological Research by the Peabody Museum'" which was at the exposition. Thus, in addition to displaying copies of specimens, photographs, sketches, and field notes, a plaster model was constructed for the exhibit, which included scale stakes set on the 10-foot square grid system, details of stratigraphic working faces, and the like (see illustration in Putnam 1898b:388, and Frontispiece herein). The fair-goer in 1893 would have found the exhibit referred to in the exposition's official catalog as follows: "Peabody Museum—see also Harvard University exhibit in Department of Liberal Arts for illustration of the museum methods of exploration" (Putnam, in Williams 1973:179). After the fair, the exhibit was transferred to the Peabody Museum, where, as a "special exhibit of the state of Maine ... [i]t has been so arranged that it furnishes a good example of the method of exploration established by the Museum. Models, photographs, and drawings supplement the series of specimens in the case" (Mead 1905:72).

Frank Russell's (1868-1903) early educational training took place at the University of Iowa, where he received a B.S. in 1892, specializing in zoological collections from the Canadian Northwest. Between 1892 and 1894 he continued research in the Arctic North on a University of Iowa expedition, and based on this work he was awarded an M.S. from Iowa in 1895 (Hodge 1903b:738). He subsequently enrolled at Harvard, where he received a second B.A. in anthropology in 1896, an M.A. in 1897, and a Ph.D. in 1898 (Marquis 1966:1068). His dissertation work was on Eskimo remains from Labrador, continuing his Canadian research ties.

Shortly after Russell enrolled in 1896, George Dorsey, who had been appointed to teach in 1894, resigned his position at Harvard to take a position at the new Field Museum in Chicago. Russell, upon receiving his B.A., was recruited by Putnam to fill in for Dorsey, and was appointed Instructor of Anthropology in 1897 (Dixon 1930:211; Hodge 1903b:738; Putnam in Nutting 1903:4), one of three faculty, along with Putnam and Roland B. Dixon (Putnam 1898a/1973). During this period Russell also served as Vice-President of Section H (Anthropology) for the AAAS (Hodge 1903b:738). Russell continued postgraduate research in the Subarctic until he contracted tuberculosis. He took a medical leave of absence from the faculty at Harvard in 1901, when he went to the American Southwest and worked with Pima and Papago Indians under a contract with the Bureau of American Ethnology, hoping that the climate would effect a cure of his disease (Hodge 1903b:738). He felt recovered enough to return to Cambridge in the fall of 1902 to resume his teaching, but suffered a relapse; he took another leave from his teaching duties in March 1903, and died at Chloride, near Kingman, Arizona, in November 1903.

Russell, in his Harvard "*Anth 4*. Prehistoric Archaeology—European Ethnology" course lecture of November 5, 1902, dealt with the proper methodology for cave investigations.[1] The anonymous student taking notes (Russell 1902) wrote down that Russell stated that proper excavation procedure in caves required one to "divide the cave into blocks one foot deep and three feet square." Thus Russell was instructing his students to employ the same kind of excavation methodology that Pengelly and others had been using in Europe in terms of stratigraphic control in cave excavation, and very similar to the surface plan of the method that Putnam was instructing his students to use in mound excavation. These 1902 lecture notes are important because they are the first classroom example in an American university where we can clearly document explicit stratigraphic excavation techniques being taught. Putnam had passed on such methods by personal letter and by example, and through what Stocking has called the "Chautauqua or Lyceum method" (Stocking and Montague 1979:16) of public lectures, but the idea of full-term class lectures was a new and different approach which took Putnam longer to develop, and they do not seem formalized in the 1890s. Russell had no archaeological training prior to arriving at Harvard, and Putnam was Russell's principal instructor, so it is most likely that Russell learned this technique from Putnam, and Russell thus may have presented the first *formal* classroom instruction at Harvard detailing Putnam's archaeological methods.

Roland B. Dixon (1875–1934) and John R. Swanton (1873–1958), both trained by Putnam in the 1890s, are better known in anthropology for nonarchaeological contributions. But Drooker (1997:117) reports that it was not until their excavations in 1897 (along with the later excava-

Origins of Stratigraphic Excavation / 251

tions by Raymond Merwin, also of the Peabody Museum) that adequate archaeology was done at Madisonville. She states that the methods employed by the Peabody Museum crews in 1897 and later provided for the first modern, well-provenienced artifact recovery, tied in by grid system and depth.

George H. Pepper (1873–1924) received training from Putnam, 1895–1896, prior to beginning the excavation of Pueblo Bonito from 1896 to 1900. Jonathan E. Reyman has long argued that Pepper was conducting controlled, stratigraphic excavations at Pueblo Bonito at this time "in at least some of the rooms" (Reyman 1998:16). The fact that the unpublished notes on his work at the American Museum of Natural History include substantial information on his excavation procedures, indicating exceedingly careful recording of artifact context in three dimensions, provides solid support for this argument. Regrettably, in his published papers Pepper made little mention of his methodology.

Charles Peabody (1867–1939) was trained by Putnam, receiving his Harvard Ph.D. in philology in 1893 (Williams 1998:2). In his 1901–1902 excavations in Mississippi (where he was assisted by William C. Farabee, who had just received his M.A. in anthropology from Harvard in 1900), Peabody reported setting up a grid system dividing the mound into five-foot squares, indicating that "the system of excavation was that practiced by the Peabody Museum" (Peabody 1904:28). Within this five-foot grid system, the method was "that of making successive cuttings down to the level of the surrounding ground, and thus, by throwing the soil from each new cutting into that preceding, making possible a thorough examination of the distance excavated, yet leaving the ground more or less in its original condition. At each five feet, description of the wall of soil in front of the excavators were taken" (Peabody 1904:23).

Peabody also employed a metric version of this technique, not only in his later work in Europe, but also in the United States. For example, in a cave excavation in Missouri he employed a one-meter grid system, using letters and numbers on opposite axes, and excavated across the site in vertical sections, keeping running vertical profiles, as had been suggested by Putnam (Peabody and Moorehead 1904:13). And in a mound excavation in North Carolina he employed a two-meter grid, also making cross-section profiles at each two meters (Peabody 1910: 427–428).

Although Warren K. Moorehead worked with Charles Peabody, and with other Harvard students trained in the Peabody Museum method as early as 1892, when he participated in Peabody Museum expeditions to the C. M. Hopewell mound site in Ross County, Ohio, and also to the San Juan River pueblos in New Mexico (Byers 1939:287), Moorehead did not employ this strategy on his own until about 1919 or 1920, and then only occasionally. Moorehead (1910:366), in fact, took a rather skeptical view of such excavation rigor, arguing that "if some of our students would, for a few years, lay aside cameras, ground-plans, tapeline," and instead study collections and typologies, "much more progress would ensue."

The Peabody Museum method was employed by other excavators trained at the Peabody Museum at this time. For example, George F. Will and Herbert J. Spinden (1906) utilized the Putnam vertical slicing method on a five-foot grid system in their 1905 Peabody Museum excavation project on the Plains. Putnam's last student may have been Fred H. Sterns, who first began receiving support from Putnam in 1909. Sterns reported using standard Peabody Museum excavation technique in his 1912 Ph.D. research of a grid of three-foot squares, making running cross-sectional diagrams and plat maps, cataloging materials by provenience, and in some places employing a soil auger to determine the limits of features (Gradwohl 1978:191).

After nearly two decades of experience following his first excavations of shell mounds in 1865 and 1867, Putnam had clearly developed a rigorous technique for excavating artificial mounds, a method he was explicitly lecturing students on employing by at least as early as 1885. This method involved setting up a grid system with right-angle axes, dividing the mound into five-foot sections, and then vertically slicing the face of the mound at perhaps one-foot intervals, and making profiles at every five-foot section (or more often if features were found). It is this method that Charles Peabody called the "Peabody Museum method." It is also this method that the amateur archaeologist William B. Nickerson learned from Putnam in the 1880s, a method that, as we will see below, was taken directly from Nickerson's notes by the first University of Chicago field program in 1926, and which was subsequently adopted by Fay-Cooper Cole and his students, to become recast as the "Chicago method."

William Baker Nickerson: Pioneer Midwestern Archaeologist

Nickerson, an extremely interesting avocational archaeologist who learned his excavation techniques from Frederic Ward Putnam, seems to have been indirectly responsible for passing these techniques on to the first University of Chicago archaeological field party. Nickerson was born in approximately 1860 and died in the spring of 1926 in Kidder, Iowa. He supported himself most of his life through work as a railroad signal tower and telegraph operator.

The earliest communication found in the archives between Nickerson and Putnam is a letter of July 14, 1884.[2] In that letter, Nickerson approached Putnam for funds to continue a mound survey he had been conducting in the Fox River valley near Elgin, Illinois. Putnam sent his assistant, John Cone Kimball, to visit Nickerson in September or October 1884; a letter from Kimball to Nickerson on November 28, 1884, indicates that Putnam was very interested in Kimball's report of his visit to Nickerson's mound excavations and wanted to receive a full written report. Subsequently, in 1885, the railroad transferred Nickerson back east, where he seems to have been stationed alternatively at a railroad station in Millbury, Massachusetts, and another at Meriden, Connecticut. He continued to send archaeological specimens to the Peabody Museum, now from archaeological surveys in Massachusetts and Connecticut, according to his correspondence, and arranged visits with Putnam at the museum in April 1885 and in later months.

Putnam seems to have recruited Nickerson in their meeting in 1885 as a "student assistant." In his annual report for 1885, Putnam wrote (1886c:494) that "for about a year Mr. W. B. Nickerson has been engaged as a volunteer assistant in field work for the Museum. In March, 1885, he partly explored a group of burial mounds in the Fox River valley, near Elgin, Illinois . . . afterwards he was associated with the work in Ohio."

Copies of letters from May 1885 indicate that Putnam was working on setting up a meeting between Nickerson and Dr. Charles Metz, who was conducting mound excavations in Ohio for the Peabody Museum. Nickerson did make the trip to Ohio, working at the Turpin site with Metz in 1885. According to Penelope B. Drooker (personal communication, April 14, 1999), Nickerson was the first person working on the Ohio mounds to notice and map rows of postholes, based on references in Metz's papers at the Cincinnati Historical Society. In a letter of June 15, 1886,[3] Putnam sent Nickerson some mementos of the Turpin work, remarking, "By this mail I send you two photographs which will remind you of your Ohio trip."

On the masthead of the 1886 annual report, W. B. Nickerson is listed as a student assistant hired in 1885. But this association did not last long. Putnam (1887:568) wrote that "it is with regret that I am called upon to state that two of our former collaborators have been obliged for pecuniary causes to seek other fields of labor, and the loss of their assistance is one of the reasons that has led me to suggest the possibility of the foundation of a form of scholarships. . . . The first called from us was Mr. Nickerson, a young man, who during the time he was associated with us in our work of special explorations in the field, evinced an aptitude for archaeological research, which I greatly regret could not have been further encouraged by providing a small salary for his support." Thus it seems evident not only that Nickerson received direct instruction from Putnam at the Peabody Museum in 1885 and in 1886, but that Putnam also had arranged for Nickerson to secure additional experience in hands-on mound excavation in Ohio under the direction of Metz.

Later in 1887, the railroad moved Nickerson to the Cascade Junction Station in Forsyth, Michigan, where he continued work in mound exploration in his spare time. Putnam arranged for Nickerson to join Metz again at the excavations at Marietta Mounds in the summer of 1887, but Nickerson had to withdraw owing to work obligations. Nickerson wrote in a letter the following spring (March 28, 1888) that he had received Putnam's instructions on excavations, which indicated that it was necessary to go three to five feet below the last cultural layer to make sure sterile soil has been reached, and he thanked Putnam for his invitation of March 24 to work with Putnam in Ohio that summer.[4] While nothing in the later correspondence of that year refers to this trip, it seems likely that Nickerson may have gone to work with Putnam in Ohio, because in a letter of reference of June 12, 1893, Putnam wrote to the University of Wisconsin geologist (and later university president) Charles R. Van Hise (1857–1918) that Nickerson had worked for him in Ohio 15 years earlier, that Nickerson had also worked with him in Cambridge, and that Nickerson subsequently had conducted artifact collections in Michigan for the Peabody Museum.[5]

Subsequent correspondence includes several letters from Putnam to Nickerson acknowledging receipt of the collections he made for the museum in his work in Michigan and Illinois. Later, in a letter of reference to Edward K. Putnam (1868–1939) of the Davenport Academy of Natural Science on July 5, 1901, Frederic Putnam wrote that Nickerson was "one of my students a number of years ago" and further noted that he "has done some first rate work in archaeological exploration for this museum [Peabody]. Every summer I have sent him a sum of money that he might explore a mound during his vacation" (quoted in Herold 1971:27).

Nickerson tried for years to secure work as an archaeologist. In addition to requesting Frederic Putnam's support in 1893 for the Wisconsin job with Van Hise, Nickerson also had written Putnam that year about the possibility of working for him at the World's Columbian Exposition in Chicago. Putnam's secretary, Frances. H. Mead, replied on April 12, 1893, that Putnam "fears there will be no positions available that you would care to fill, and there are only a few under his control and these are mostly filled by young men who did volunteer work for the department during the past two seasons. The salaries attached to these positions are very small, if any, not exceeding $30 a month, which will not cover living expenses in Chicago at this time."[6]

Nickerson continued to hope to find full-time archaeological employment. He asked Putnam in 1896 whether Director Frederick Skiff (1851–1921) of the Field Museum in Chicago might need assistance in doing archaeological excavations. In 1900 he noted that he had contacted Dr. George A. Dorsey (1868–1931) of the Field Museum to see if any positions were available; he contacted Dorsey again later that year, and at the same time he wrote Putnam to see if Putnam might find Nickerson a curatorship at the new anthropology department and museum at Berkeley. In the fall of 1900, Nickerson wrote to Dr. Frederick Starr at the University of Chicago about the possibility of a position doing archaeological work, and he later reported to Putnam that Starr replied that he expected to begin to conduct some excavations "soon," leading Nickerson to hope that he might be hired.

In spite of the lack of full-time archaeological employment, Nickerson persisted for years conducting excavations in his vacation periods. The railroad had moved Nickerson to Polo, Ogle County, Illinois, in late 1893, and in early 1894 moved him to the Portage Curve Station, near Galena, in Jo Daviess County, where he spent much of the next decade. In a letter that year, he invited Putnam, when Putnam took "his annual trip," to stay a few days in Galena, and recalled having first worked with Putnam 10 years earlier. In a letter to Putnam on April 3, 1895, Nickerson detailed his preparations for excavation of mounds in the Galena area, checking to make sure that he understood the Peabody Museum procedures properly: "As I understand it, a mound should be taken down in the inverse of the order of its creation, when necessary, in order to understand the structure; trenching of course to find the strata and to obtain an occasional plan section. The Ohio experience gave me an insight into the use of the compass in locating and subsequent charting that is simply invaluable."[7] In an October 29, 1895, letter[8] he continued his description of this methodology, referring to using a grid system with right-angle axes, dividing the mound into five-foot sections, and subdividing each five-foot section into four blocks of 15 inches each (horizontal and vertical measurements). During this Galena/Portage Station period, Nickerson made extensive maps of many mounds, conducted a series of excavations with funds from the Peabody Museum, sent several collections so recovered back to Cambridge (as indicated by his cover letters sent with the collections, and acknowledgments from the museum in correspondence files), and also began to write up an extensive summary of his work and findings in Jo Daviess County.

In 1906, Nickerson sent Putnam a revised draft of his Jo Daviess County manuscript. Although Putnam sent it back, with a notation on the margin that it was not of a style appropriate for the Peabody Museum memoir series, Nickerson continued to work on the manuscript, sending back later drafts (as indicated by cover letters in the correspondence), with the last one apparently sent in 1913 (Nickerson 1913a). Nickerson was quite proud of having learned his methods under Putnam's tutelage. Although the methods were implicit in earlier letters, such as simple reference to employing the "slice" method in various excavation projects, he was much more explicit in the letter of October 29, 1895, discussing his excavations at Galena, Illinois. In this letter, and also in the Jo Daviess draft report, he outlined the methodology he had learned from Putnam as follows: utilizing sections of five-foot width, defined by intersecting right-angle grid systems; subdividing each vertical face of each section into four "blocks" of 15 inches on a side, for closer excavation and profiling control, as necessary; and numbering his collections in a daily running catalog, which recorded finds by grid units, sections, blocks, and depths.

This marks a time when Nickerson apparently came to increasingly think of himself as an archaeologist. He published a series of articles summarizing his work in Illinois in the journal *Glimpses of the Past* between 1908 and 1912. Nickerson mentioned in a letter to Putnam in 1911 that he had moved from Illinois across the river to Epsworth, Iowa, where he had briefly done excavation work for Davenport Academy in the fall of 1908, a position he had finally obtained after first having applied to do the work with the academy in 1901 (Herold 1971:iii). In addition to the 1908 season, Nickerson also conducted subsequent excavations in Iowa in 1921 (Nickerson 1921).

Between 1912 and 1915, under agreements with Harlan I. Smith, Nickerson conducted fieldwork in southwestern Manitoba for the Geological Survey of Canada (Capes 1963; Dyck 1998:120–122; Nickerson 1913b, 1914a, 1914b). Although he had originally expected to do considerably more work in Manitoba, the outbreak of war in Europe severely reduced the amount of archaeological work being done under the Anthropological Division of the Geological Survey of Canada. From 1914 to 1916 the number of contract researchers fell from 6 to 2 and then to 1, the annual field parties from 11 to 3, and expenditures from $8,000 to $650 (Richling 1998:107). When money for continuing his work in Canada was interrupted, Nickerson returned to fieldwork in Illinois and Iowa, continuing excavations and survey in 1913 and 1921 (Nickerson 1921), and in 1913 and 1916 he was hired to conduct archaeological surveys in Minnesota by the Minnesota Historical Society (Nickerson 1988).

Thus we see that Nickerson had nearly a 40-year career in midwestern American archaeology, from at least as early as 1884 through 1921 (or later). He consulted with Putnam at the Peabody Museum intensively between 1885 and 1887, just when Putnam was actively beginning to advocate what became known as the Peabody Museum method. However, it was the accidental rediscovery in 1926 of Nickerson's work (which included a detailed description of his implementation of the Peabody Museum method) by two University of Chicago graduate students (Paul Martin and John Blackburn) that resulted in his most lasting contribution.

Fay-Cooper Cole and the Chicago Method

Based on the association of Fay-Cooper Cole (1881–1962) with the Chicago method, he was listed by Frederick Eggan as "one of the founders of modern archaeology" (1962a:412) and "one of the architects of modern archaeology in the eastern United States" (1962b:643). Cole had done some postgraduate work at the University of Chicago after graduating from Northwestern in 1903, but in 1906 George Dorsey offered him a job at the Field Museum (Cole 1952:162; Eggan 1962a:412; Griffin 1952:dedication), where he took part in an expedition to the Philippines to study the Tinguian between 1906 and 1908, and returned to serve as a curator for Southeast Asia at the museum (Jennings 1962:574). The Field Museum then permitted him to pursue some additional graduate work with Franz Boas at Columbia, where he received his Ph.D. in 1915, with an emphasis in folklore, which he had published in the Field Museum journal *Fieldiana* that year (Cole 1915a, 1915b).

Cole joined the University of Chicago faculty in the sociology department in 1924 to replace Frederick Starr, who had just retired, and further to develop an anthropology program. Cole had had considerable success in tapping the Laura Spelman Rockefeller Memorial funds for support of his developing program, but in 1926, when Edward Sapir and Cole requested money to develop an archaeology program, they were turned down. The Cole-Sapir request was then channeled to the University of Chicago's Committee on Local Community Research, and approval was granted on May 31, 1926, to initiate archaeological fieldwork. Cole moved quickly to establish the program, purchasing and outfitting a field vehicle and sending two graduate students, Paul S. Martin and John Blackburn, out to Jo Daviess County by June 27, 1926 (Bennett 1947:iii; Martin and Blackburn 1926), to begin part of the systematic survey of Illinois, as suggested by the Committee on State Archaeological Surveys of the National Research Council (Cole 1927:314).

Paul S. Martin (1899–1974) was the graduate student director of the first University of Chicago field excavations in Jo Daviess County in 1926, and he was Cole's first student in archaeology to receive his Ph.D., in 1929. Martin's initial fieldwork in 1925 had been for the Milwaukee Public Museum on Wisconsin mounds (Longacre 1976:90). As the individual with the most experience (one season), he was thus put in charge of the first Chicago archaeological field season (Martin and Blackburn 1926). Martin and Blackburn were sent into the field with very little background. One week after they arrived in Galena, Martin noted that he had written Cole to find out about the Smithsonian Institution work that the local people told them about; and a few days later he noted the need to find out about some Bureau of American Ethnology reports on the area that the local informants had apprised them of, which he and Blackburn had not previously heard or known of (Martin and Blackburn 1926, field notes of July 3 and 7, 1926).[9]

It was only after they had been in the field for a month that Martin and Blackburn learned about the extensive work of William Baker Nickerson, who had just died that spring, and sought out his widow. She turned over to Martin and Blackburn all of Nickerson's daily notes, sketches, maps, photos, and plans, as well as a copy of the 1913 manuscript on Jo Daviess County. In his evaluation of Nickerson's materials and methods, Martin wrote:

> A cursory examination of his notes, plans and final report were enough to convince us that he was a *most* careful worker—almost too careful—and very scientific. His method of digging mounds

was modern as was all his work.... I shall recommend to Dr. Cole the publishing *in toto* his final report, because the Peabody has known of it for 29 years[10] and have never published or mentioned his work, although done for them, and the work was of a most important type and is a real chapter in the sadly needed book of mound information. This work must be published. (Martin and Blackburn 1926, field notes, August 11)

Following the field survey of two months, an additional month of excavation was planned in 1926. Martin (1927:57–58) wrote:

In September all the students that were available were brought up to Galena and set to work to do actual excavating. Before work was started, however, there was held a general meeting to decide by what methods the mounds should be dug. Undercutting was tried and found to be undesirable in that region where burials and artifacts may be situated at any level. Trenching was also given a trial but used only when time began to get short. The best method for the excavation of conical mounds appeared to be the removal of dirt in horizontal and vertical squares—staked out beforehand by means of a transit. A clean "face" or wall from the floor upward was maintained as work progressed into the mound—so that the workers could see at any time banding or stratification that might appear—or signs that assured the finding of burials or artifacts.

This last method is just what Martin and Blackburn had learned about six weeks earlier from Nickerson's notes.

A review of the field notes by the entire Chicago crew (Paul Martin, John Blackburn, Wilton Krogman, and Robert Redfield) indicates that they initially began operations using a team of horses and a scraper, undercutting the mound faces, only stopping to clean the face and take post facto stratification measurements when rains prevented further work (Martin et al. 1926, field notes for September 2, 3, 4, and 7, 1926). The field notes are somewhat terse, so it is not apparent how soon they began employing Nickerson's method, but it is clear from Martin's (1927) evaluation of this first field season that the earlier methods of trenching—using a horse-drawn dredge and undercutting the mounds, which Martin had employed in 1925 in Wisconsin—proved unsatisfactory and soon gave way to use of Nickerson's superior methodology.

In spite of Martin's recommendations to Cole, nothing was done about publishing Nickerson's manuscript until the early 1940s. At that time, Cole charged John W. Bennett with writing up the 1926 and 1927 field seasons of the University of Chicago project. In the process of preparing to do this, Bennett found Martin's reference to Nickerson's work and sought it out in the files. After reading Nickerson's 1913 Jo Daviess manuscript, he decided to include a good portion of this report in his summary document as well (Bennett 1942, 1947). Bennett noted that "Nickerson not only displayed extreme technical sophistication, but had a breadth of viewpoint conspicuously lacking in his day," and "With few qualifications, we can say that Nickerson's techniques and interpretive balance were as mature and sophisticated as those of the finest dirt archaeology of today. We also feel that in general his system of notebook recording in the field (tremendously detailed and pictorial), profile and ground plan drawing, and grid-and-level coordination were considerably in advance of anything of his period" (1942:122, 124).

It was, in fact, Putnam's Peabody Museum methodology that Nickerson employed, and as noted above, a strong argument can be made that Martin and his colleagues from that first season in 1926 brought the method back to Cole, who wholeheartedly adopted it as the method for future projects. Bennett (1998:293) explicitly states that Nickerson "developed all the same techniques Cole and Deuel called the 'Chicago Method': located the loci for all finds with a transit, measured profiles and ground plans, and so on." Among Nickerson's contributions, Bennett (1942:123) further noted the following:

(1) He used a datum plane for recording all artifacts and locating features on his profile drawings. He called it a "zero base line";

(2) He used a five-foot grid system, staking out his mounds and excavating his "blocks" by levels measured from the datum plane. Two main axes divided the dig into "sections," each of which had its own numbered "blocks";

(3) He recorded all his finds on coordinated ground plans and five-foot profile drawings, with detailed symbol keys. His profiles and ground plans appear in alignment on single large sheets, so that they can be read with a minimum of reference to the text;

(4) He used a mattock exclusively for vertical excavation, carefully smoothing his profiles, and planing his floors with a sharpened shovel; and

(5) He relocated all his excavations with stakes marking the trench limits, and burying these stakes when he restored the mound.

These new methods, tested at the end of the first season in 1926, were again employed during the second University of Chicago summer field season in 1927—by Martin and Krogman in Jo Daviess County, and possibly also by George Langford at the Fisher Mounds. In a brief note on this second season, Cole (1929a:344) referred to use of a new method where ground plans now "were made every five feet" so that all artifacts could be accurately located. These techniques were the beginning of what later Cole termed the Chicago method.

The graduate students involved in these first few seasons of the University of Chicago field schools were basically responsible for establishing the field procedures, as Cole had no previous training in archaeology, and administrative duties kept him back on the university campus. When Cole wrote up "recent trends" in anthropology for the American Philosophy Society in 1929 (Cole 1929b), he detailed changes in linguistics, physical anthropology, and ethnology but was not yet conversant enough to comment upon similar trends in archaeology. Jesse Jennings, who was involved in class work and field projects at Chicago from 1929 to 1933, noted that during his time there was only one class in archaeology, "Old World Prehistory," and that "archaeology was learned in the field and library" (Jennings 1994:57). Although Jennings does not name the instructor for the prehistory class, James Griffin (1976:6) says he took his first archaeology course in European archaeology in 1931–1932 under Harry Hoijer. As Stocking (1979:27) notes, Cole's personal role or contribution to these early field schools was not pedagogic or methodological, but mainly organizational and administrative.

Cole's earliest complete discussion of what becomes called the Chicago method is in the 11-page *Guide Leaflet for Amateur Archaeologists* (National Research Council 1930). In 1929–1930, Cole was named chairman of the Division of Anthropology and Psychology of the National Research Council. As chairman, he was in charge of the Midwest Archaeological Conference held in St. Louis in May 1929, and was responsible for preparing the resulting *Guide Leaflet* (Guthe 1967:435). In this leaflet, Cole wrote that the proper excavation of mounds was by establishment of right-angle-based grid lines, dividing the mound into five-foot squares. Excavations in these units should then be carried forward "much as you would cut a loaf of bread" (National Research Council 1930:9). Cole further described the method in subsequent Committee on State Archaeological Surveys sessions, where he indicated that the proper method to excavate a mound was to stake it out in five-foot squares, with a trench carried forward into the mound itself by cutting thin strips from top to bottom for the distance of a foot or more (National Research Council 1932:76).

The method Cole recommended was in fact the old Putnam/Peabody Museum "slice" method that Nickerson had utilized and which Martin and Krogman had copied from Nickerson. By 1930, with the beginning of excavations in Fulton County, the University of Chicago graduate student supervisors had modified the procedure, shifting to 6-inch levels (and 6-inch by 6-inch control blocks) in the 5-foot by 5-foot units, instead of 15-inch levels (and 15-inch by 15-inch blocks), for greater stratigraphic control (Cole and Deuel 1937:7, 25, 271). This standardized "6-inch levels in 5-foot squares" method was carried on in other later Chicago projects, such as Kincaid (Cole et al. 1951:32), and it is the method that Cole and other members of the Division of Social Science of the National Research Council advocated in 1939 as proper procedure (Guthe 1939:529).

Thorne Deuel was Cole's field director for the projects in the 1930s and 1940s. Hence a logical line of investigation would be to ascertain Deuel's importance in this question of method. A review of Deuel's background and work (to be published elsewhere) indicates that his contribution was primarily in his meticulous and rigorous (some writers have used the term "regimented" in the light of his military association) implementation of this excavation strategy for all University of Chicago projects that he supervised.

That Cole was unaware that the method his graduate students were utilizing in the field was really Putnam's Peabody Museum method seems evident from a number of lines of evidence. In spite of his boyhood fascination with the romance of archaeology, he began his tenure at Chicago with no previous experience in archaeology or in archaeological excavation. In addition, Cole, for perhaps the first decade of his field school operations, appears not to have known the earlier literature of regional archaeological explorations. Thus, as noted above, Cole sent his first crew into the field with no knowledge of even the most basic previous work in the area, as evidenced by Martin's comments in his field notebook. Cole's lack of familiarity with Midwest archaeology during the first decade of Chicago fieldwork was also observed and commented upon by contemporary archaeologists—with remarks, for example, such as those of Moorehead (1937:375), who, in his review of Cole and Deuel's (1937) *Rediscovering Illinois*, reported that "Dr. Cole has given very little credit to previous explorers in the Illinois field."

The idea that this was a "new" method invented at Chicago seems to have developed rather early in the literature, and over time it has grown to mythic proportions. Thus, for example, Gordon Willey, in his M.A. thesis on the methods of archaeological excavation, observed (1936:47): "Dr. Cole of the University of Chicago has worked out a well-organized grid system.... He sets two base zero lines.... Five foot squares are then located with reference to these lines." Or as Griffin reported (1976:6): "The Chicago field program was assisted by the development of an excavating and recording methodology developed over a period of time from a variety of sources, and issued by the National Research Council Committee on State Archaeological Surveys Reprint and Circular Series No. 93. This 'Guide Leaflet for Amateur Archaeologists' had a wide distribution." Griffin (1985:268) later observed: "The University of Chicago field schools of the late 1920s and 1930s were of vital importance in improving field techniques, particularly for the large relief labor programs of the 1930s." Fagette (1996:11, 41) commented that under Cole's leadership, "what became known as the Chicago field method emerged," and indicated that Griffin credited James Ford and his influence in Works Progress Administration projects for disseminating what "became the standard approach for southeastern archaeology in this time period." Binford gives Cole far more credit than anyone else as primary developer (Sabloff 1998:11), stating that Cole "was basically said to be the man who started 'modern archaeology.' ... Almost all of the people who later ran the WPA projects were trained by Cole in the '20s. So Cole's techniques became the standard for good archaeology during the WPA [era].... Almost all of in a sense putting American archaeology on a methodological footing was started by Fay-Cooper Cole."

The folklore thus has developed in American archaeology that Cole invented this method, but as argued above, the evidence indicates that Cole was rather more the disseminator than the inventor. Cole had a significant impact in part through his administrative abilities, his charismatic prominence, and his service in several national-level archaeological groups. Stocking's (1979:17) evaluation of Cole's work at Chicago is that while he was "a genial, self-effacing man of no great intellectual pretensions, Cole was an able lecturer and a remarkably effective organizer and administrator." Thus while the Chicago method was basically the old Peabody Museum method reprised, Cole was very successful in serving as a charismatic spokesman for popularizing the technique, so much so that many archaeologists have been misled into believing that he developed the original idea.

Summary Remarks

One of the strands of development of modern archaeological excavation technique begins with William Pengelly's 1858–1859 stratigraphic excavation work in caves, a technique that seems subsequently to have been taken up by French archaeologists working in caves and to have later spread to the United States (Browman and Givens 1996; see also chapter 9 of this volume). At this point it is not clear where Putnam secured his ideas on excavating mounds, as he also came to the job with no previous formal training in archaeology, although he had been conducting amateur excavations with Jeffries Wyman and others as early as 1865 (see also chapter 10 in this volume). But by at least as early as 1885, he had developed a mound excavation strategy, herein called the Peabody Museum method, which through the vehicle of Nickerson's work was subsequently refurbished as the Chicago method in the 1930s and 1940s. The techniques employed by modern North American archaeologists in explicit stratigraphic *excavation* rather than stratigraphic *interpretation* (stratigraphic *interpretation* was done by Olof Rudbeck in 1697, at least 160 years earlier than Pengelly's stratigraphic *excavation*) appear to have their origins in a series of developments with their roots in procedures that evolved between 1859 and 1885.

12

George Grant MacCurdy
An American Pioneer of Palaeoanthropology

Harvey M. Bricker

Introduction

George Grant MacCurdy was one of the principal interpreters to American anthropologists of European research in palaeoanthropology during the first third of the twentieth century. He was born in Warrensburg, Missouri, on April 17, 1863, and was killed in a traffic accident in New Jersey on November 15, 1947. The details of MacCurdy's life are well recounted in two obituaries published in the anthropological literature (Hencken 1948; McCown 1948), to both of which are appended bibliographies of MacCurdy's published work. The focus of this chapter is more limited. A century ago, MacCurdy was one of those relatively few individuals who were constructing anthropology as a professional and academic discipline in the United States—he was, for example, one of the founders of the American Anthropological Association in 1902. My task in this chapter is to examine how MacCurdy was shaped by European scholarship and how, in turn, he served to transmit European techniques and research results to the generation of U.S. archaeologists and anthropologists that came of age professionally between the two world wars.

The Harvard Years

When George MacCurdy (originally McCurdy; he later changed the spelling of his surname to please his distant relative and benefactress, Evelyn MacCurdy Salisbury [MacCurdy 1946:26]) entered Harvard College in 1891, at the age of 28, he had already been trained as a public school teacher at the Missouri State Normal School in Warrensburg and had taught at various schools in rural Missouri throughout the 1880s (1946:4-5). He spent three years at Harvard, two as an undergraduate (A.B., 1893) and one as a graduate student (A.M., 1894). The education and training he received at Harvard were not inappropriate to his eventual career as a palaeoanthropologist and archaeologist, but they were aimed in a quite different direction. He majored in geology and biology at Harvard College; as a graduate student, he wrote two master's theses, one in geology (on the Eocene of Virginia and Maryland) and one in zoology (on an aspect of fish morphology) (1946: 16, 23).

In the summer of 1892, before his senior year in college, MacCurdy did a field school course in geology in upstate New York and New England, followed by a brief course in biology at the recently established Woods Hole Biological Station in Massachusetts (MacCurdy 1946:17-18). In 1894, immediately after receiving his master's degree, he spent part of the summer as a research assistant to Alexander Agassiz at the latter's private marine laboratory in Newport, Rhode Island. This assistantship was a reward given annually to the two top graduate students in zoology at Harvard, of whom MacCurdy had been one in 1893-1894 (1946:20-24). Also in 1894, MacCurdy was introduced by his benefactors, the Salisburys (discussed below), to the eminent Yale palaeontologist, Othniel C. Marsh, who would play a crucial role in determining MacCurdy's future career (1946:21). It was the case, therefore, that when MacCurdy finished the American phase of his education he was a well-trained and well-connected specialist in natural history (zoology and geology), not at all in prehistory or human origins.

Although MacCurdy must have had some contact with archaeologists and the discipline of archaeology during his Harvard years, there is very little evidence of this.[1] According to his own account, he took courses in geology and biology, of course, and in English composition, French, and German, but there is no mention of archaeology (1946:16). He had met Frederic Ward Putnam, Director of the Peabody Museum, socially; he noted in his autobiography (1946:18) that Putnam "loves to talk of his profession ... and almost persuades me to enter his field of research." This seems little more than a polite turn of phrase, however; there is no evidence that MacCurdy contemplated archaeology as a profession while he was a college student. Several years later, when MacCurdy *was* beginning to consider palaeoanthropology as a career, he reflected with some chagrin that his previous training in archaeology was "almost negligible" (1946:31).

When MacCurdy did his year of graduate work in 1893-1894, he took a job as one of the Harvard College proctors in order to defray some of his living expenses. That fall, apparently as a routine matter, a listing of the names of Harvard's proctors was published in a Boston newspaper. This list was seen by a woman in Connecticut, a Mrs. Evelyn MacCurdy Salisbury, the wife of a retired Professor of Arabic and Sanskrit at Yale, Edward Elbridge Salisbury. Mrs. Salisbury wrote to MacCurdy (or McCurdy, as it was then) in November 1893 with a series of questions about his family history. The Salisburys were serious, well-published genealogists, and Mrs. Salisbury concluded, once she had received the answers to her questions, that young George, the Harvard graduate student, was her third cousin once removed (MacCurdy 1946:21). From the establishment of this previously unknown kinship there resulted a series of circumstances and events that determined the course of the rest of MacCurdy's life. He was taken into the lives of the (childless) Salisburys like a son, and their home in Old Lyme, Connecticut, became his home from the time he left graduate school in 1894 until his death in 1947 (1946:147). In the summer of 1894 the Salisburys offered to fund a year in Europe for MacCurdy "for travel and general improvement" and to have the opportunity of meeting European scientists. With the acceptance of this invitation began the final stage of MacCurdy's formal training and the start of what was to be his professional career.

The Influence of European Scholarship

George Grant MacCurdy made the first of his many trips to Europe in September 1894 at the age of 31, supposedly for a stay of one year. One of the major purposes of the trip was to meet European scientists working in his fields, geology and zoology. In accord with the custom of the time, MacCurdy carried with him a number of letters of introduction from American educators and scientists that were intended to facilitate his cordial reception by European notables. Some of the most valuable were from the Yale palaeontologist, Othniel Marsh, to various of his European colleagues. For example, while in Paris during the winter of 1894–1895, MacCurdy used Marsh's introductions at the Muséum d'Histoire Naturelle to meet the palaeontologists Marcellin Boule and Albert Gaudry (MacCurdy 1946:38). Gaudry would become MacCurdy's teacher at the École d'Anthropologie two years later, as discussed below.

Discussions with scholars like Boule and Gaudry and visits to European natural history museums must have made human palaeontology and the archaeology of the Pleistocene increasingly salient to Mac-Curdy. In a February 1895 letter to MacCurdy, Professor Salisbury recounted a conversation he had had with Professor Marsh about the recent discovery of the skeletal material of *Pithecanthropus erectus* in Java. It was about this time, said MacCurdy in his autobiography (1946:38), that "for the first time my attention is called to fossil man, to the study of which I am later to devote my life." Later that spring, Salisbury sent MacCurdy a copy of the translation made by Marsh of Eugène Dubois's preliminary article on *Pithecanthropus erectus* (1946:39). By this time, MacCurdy was interested enough in palaeoanthropology to write to the Professor of Anthropology at Oxford, E. B. Tylor, seeking career advice. Tylor's reply, although encouraging, was apparently not specific enough to impel MacCurdy to action (1946:48).

MacCurdy made his career decision a few months later, in September 1895, while attending an International Zoological Congress in Leiden, Netherlands. He had attended other scientific meetings during his year in Europe, but this one had a special attraction—his Yale mentor, Professor Marsh, had come to Europe to participate in the congress. The scientific highlight of the meetings for MacCurdy was a paper on *Pithecanthropus* by Dubois, who had just returned from Java. As part of his presentation, Dubois exhibited the actual fossil specimens he had found at Trinil (MacCurdy 1946:50). This experience seems to have tipped the balance for MacCurdy in favor of a career in palaeoanthropology. He wrote in his autobiography (1946:51): "The more I ponder over the 'Missing Link,' the more I am inclined to turn especially to the study of fossil man and his culture. Since my previous studies in the fields of geology and zoology make a suitable foundation for this prospective new field, the present may turn out to be a turning point in my career." Professor Marsh approved, as did Professor Salisbury. More to the point, perhaps, Salisbury offered to pay for one more year in Europe so that MacCurdy could study prehistoric archaeology at a European university. MacCurdy chose Munich as the place to study, moved there, and made arrangements with the University of Munich's physical anthropologist, Professor Johannes Ranke, to begin formal study when the university began its fall session. However, back in New Haven, Professor Marsh had decided that the best place for MacCurdy to study would be the University of Vienna and had sent word to this effect through Professor Salisbury. So it was, after a quick move from Munich to Vienna in the fall of 1895, that MacCurdy started his European university training in the Austro-Hungarian capital (1946:51–52).

It appears, from some brief mentions in MacCurdy's autobiography (1946:53, 56), that he took four courses during his first semester at the University of Vienna in the fall of 1895. He took a course in prehistoric archaeology from Dr. Moriz Hoernes (1852-1917), who became MacCurdy's principal adviser during his year at Vienna. Hoernes was then a curator at the Naturhistorischen Hofmuseum and a lecturer at the university, at which he was named Professor in 1899. By the time MacCurdy studied with him, Hoernes had published a general text on prehistory (*Die Urgeschichte des Menschen*, 1892) and had been doing archaeological field research for more than a decade in Bosnia-Herzogovina (Meyers Lexikon 1927, 6:4-5). A second course was taken from Emil Zuckerkandl (1849-1910), then Professor of Anatomy. A comparative anatomist, Zuckerkandl specialized in the human skull and its pathologies (Meyers Lexikon 1927, 12:1876). MacCurdy (1946:53) said that he benefited from "special use of his laboratory and its anthropological material, especially crania." About MacCurdy's other two courses, I know nothing except who offered them. Matthus Much (1832-1909) was a prehistorian whose published works deal with the Neolithic and later prehistory of Austria and with prehistoric art. Philipp Paulitschke (1854-1899) was a geographer and ethnographer who had traveled widely in Africa and had published a two-volume work on his specialty (*Ethnographie Nordostafrikas*, 1893-1896); he held a *Dozent* position at the university (Meyers Lexikon 1927, 9:478).

During MacCurdy's second semester at the University of Vienna, in the spring of 1896, he took another archaeology course from Dr. Hoernes, one in vertebrate paleontology from a Professor Waagen, and one in general ethnology from Dr. Michael Haberlandt, a young lecturer in ethnology who later (1910) became Professor at the university and Director (1912) of the Museum für Volkskunde (MacCurdy 1946:56; Meyers Lexikon 1927, 5:882-883). In addition to these formal courses, MacCurdy (1946:56) mentions having attended occasional lectures by Eduard Suess, a physical anthropologist specializing in human racial variation, and Professor Otto Benndorf, a classical archaeologist. By the end of the academic year 1895-1896, Professor Salisbury had offered MacCurdy the financial support for a second year of European university study. Following the advice of Dr. Hoernes, the École d'Anthropologie in Paris was the institution chosen for this further training (1946:61). After a summer of touristic travel in Austria-Hungary and Switzerland, MacCurdy moved from Vienna to Paris in the fall of 1896.

For one wishing training in what is today called palaeoanthropology, Paris was the best place to get this training at the end of the nineteenth century, and if MacCurdy had received his initial advice from an American prehistorian who knew something about Europe (e.g., Henry Mercer) rather than from an American palaeontologist (Othniel Marsh), he would almost certainly have gone there in the first place. For more than two decades, since its founding by Paul Broca, the École d'Anthropologie had supported advanced research and instruction in human palaeontology and Palaeolithic archaeology. When MacCurdy entered the school in 1896, its faculty included great pioneers of the field like Gabriel de Mortillet (who was, however, at the very end of his career, dying in 1898) and Albert Gaudry, as discussed further below. On the other hand, seen in hindsight, it is true that throughout the 1880s and 1890s palaeoanthropology in France was in a deep trough between two waves (Sackett 1981, 1991:113-116; Smith 1966:13-15). The glory days of Edouard Lartet's founding formulations were long gone, and the later efforts of Gabriel de Mortillet had had the negative effect of moving Palaeolithic archaeology off of its palaeontological and stratigraphic foundations. The "Aurignacian battle," as a result of which the edifice was reseated on its foundations by Henri Breuil, was still almost a decade away (Sackett 1981:86–87). Also, although some major sites of Upper Palaeolithic parietal art had already been discovered—for example, Altamira in 1879 and La Mouthe in 1895—recognition of the true antiquity of such art by the leaders of the field would not occur until the new century (Breuil 1952:15-16). Despite these unfavorable historical reflections, Paris was still the best place for MacCurdy to be in 1896, and the course of his career shows that he took full advantage of the opportunities Paris offered.

MacCurdy's autobiography provides very little specific information about his year at the École d'Anthropologie. We know that he went to the school five days a week and that he spent a fair amount of time in the physical anthropology laboratory of Professor Manouvrier measuring the skulls of modern criminals (MacCurdy 1946:65, 67). Beyond that there is little more than the names of the faculty members from whom he took courses or whose lectures he attended. Professor Gabriel de Mortillet (1821–1898) held the chair of "prehistoric anthropology" (Palaeolithic archaeology) that had been created for him when the school was founded (Minvielle 1972:274–275). His son, Professor Adrien de Mortillet (1853–1931), had been since 1889 the first holder of a chair of "ethnology" (Minvielle 1972:275), but his activities at the school had to do primarily with prehistoric ethnology—that is, prehistoric archaeology. The most eminent scholar on the faculty of the École d'Anthropologie at the time of MacCurdy's study there was Professor Albert Gaudry (1827–1908), who, as a young paleontologist, had gone to Amiens with Charles Lyell in June 1859 to confirm the favorable assessment of Boucher de Perthes's claims made a few months earlier by Joseph Prestwich and Hugh Falconer (1972:15; see also chapter 9 in this volume).[2] Much later, in 1895 (the year before MacCurdy's study in Paris), Gaudry had played a less noble role in the history of Palaeolithic archaeology, attacking as erroneous the claimed Pleistocene antiquity of the parietal art reported by Émile Rivière from the cave of La Mouthe in Les Eyzies (Minvielle 1972:166). Professor Léonce Manouvrier (1850–1927), in whose laboratory in the École des Hautes Études MacCurdy worked during his year in Paris, was a medical doctor and physical anthropologist who had been the assistant of Paul Broca, the founder of the École d'Anthropologie (MacCurdy 1927a). A paper on the *Pithecanthropus erectus* materials from Java that Manouvrier had written was translated into English by MacCurdy during his year of study and published the next year in the United States (MacCurdy 1897). Another eminent faculty member at the school in 1896–1897 was Dr. Louis Capitan (1854–1929), a practicing physician as well as an active prehistorian; in 1898 (after MacCurdy had left Paris), Capitan became the Professor of Prehistoric Anthropology at the École d'Anthropologie upon the death of his former teacher, Gabriel de Mortillet (Minvielle 1972:266). Three other faculty members mentioned by MacCurdy are Professor Ernest-Théodore Hamy (1842–1908), a physical anthropologist, Mexican specialist, and founding director of the Trocadéro ethnological museum (MacCurdy 1909); Alphonse Milne-Edwards (1835–1900), a zoologist who worked with fauna from Palaeolithic sites (Meyers Lexikon 1927, 8:482; Petit Larousse Illustré 1975); and Professor Georges Hervé (1855–1933), a physical anthropologist of the anthropometric school (to judge from his publications).

In the summer of 1897, having completed his year of study in Paris, MacCurdy set out on a leisurely trip to St. Petersburg, Russia, to attend the International Geological Congress scheduled for late August. For most of the trip he was traveling with Marcellin Boule and some other French palaeontologists. His route was through Belgium, Germany, Denmark, Norway, Sweden, and Finland, with numerous visits to prehistorians and museums of prehistory along the way. Post-congress excursions took MacCurdy to Moscow, Kazan, and Kiev; finally, in late September, he arrived in Berlin. Through circumstances not explained in his autobiography, a decision had been made for MacCurdy to spend one more year of study in Europe, this time at the University of Berlin (MacCurdy 1946:69–75).

About his year as a student in Berlin (1897–1898), MacCurdy says very little in his autobiography that has to do with his classes. (Perhaps this short shrift reflects a waning enthusiasm—he must have been hearing many things in the lecture halls for the third time in three years!) We know the names of four people from whom he took courses. Professor Felix von Luschan (1854–1924) was a physical anthropologist and ethnographer specializing in the study of the peoples of Africa (Meyers Lexikon 1927, 7:1361). Professor Wilhelm von Waldeyer-Hartz was a human anatomist and physical anthropologist (1927, 12:963). Professor Adolf Erman (1854–1937) was an Egyptologist who held, in addition to his university chair, the position of director of Berlin's Egyptian Museum (1927, 4:173–174). The fourth faculty member (and the only one about whom MacCurdy wrote with any warmth or enthusiasm) was the great Americanist Eduard Seler (1849–1922), the first holder, since 1889, of the new Chair of American Language, Ethnology, and Archaeology (Anonymous 1990:xvii). Seler had just returned to Berlin from a two-year research trip to Mexico and Guatemala (Seler-Sachs 1990:xix). MacCurdy took courses from him in the prehistory and ethnology of the Americas, including the study of some of the Mexican painted codices (MacCurdy 1946:76, 78).[3]

After three years in three national capitals, MacCurdy's European studies came to an end in the summer of 1898. Back in New Haven, his supporters, Salisbury and Marsh, had been successful in arranging academic employment for him when he returned. While in Berlin that summer MacCurdy received a letter from the Secretary of the Yale Corporation notifying him of his "appointment to an instructorship in prehistoric anthropology in the Graduate School" (MacCurdy 1946:81).

What, then, had been the results of the European university years? The formal training MacCurdy had received in human palaeontology and Palaeolithic archaeology was of a breadth and quality that could not be exceeded in the 1890s. Courses in ancillary fields like human skeletal biology, later European prehistory, Egyptology, and the archaeology and ethnology of Mesoamerica increased the scope of his comparative perspective. Added to his Harvard education in geology and zoology, this European training gave MacCurdy unmatched qualifications to pursue a career of research and teaching in palaeoanthropology. Surely no other scholar of his generation in the United States was better prepared for such a career. The other major result of Mac-

Curdy's years in Europe was the network of professional contacts he had begun to construct. Building on the letters of introduction he had taken with him when he started his "grand tour" year in the fall of 1894, he had, by the time he left Europe in 1898, made the personal acquaintance of most of the leading scholars of his field in France, Germany, Austria-Hungary, and—to a lesser extent—the United Kingdom. These contacts, nourished and extended through the years, would be essential to the success of his later career, particularly the field activities of the American School of Prehistoric Research.

MacCurdy returned to New Haven in September 1898, at the age of 35, to take up his instructorship at Yale, working under Marsh's direction (MacCurdy 1946:84). As he began his instructorship, he started work on a Ph.D. dissertation dealing with the controversial subject of "eoliths" in Europe: Were chipped lithic objects of late Tertiary and early Quaternary age truly the products of human workmanship that defined an Eolithic stage preceding the Palaeolithic stage represented by the Abbevillian and later tool-making traditions? Based on this study (MacCurdy 1905), which reached conclusions totally unacceptable nearly a century later(!), he received a Ph.D. from Yale in 1905. Thus began the career of an American palaeoanthropologist whose professional formation in that discipline had been almost entirely European.

An American Broker of Palaeoanthropology

The remainder of this chapter is concerned with examining the ways in which European scholarship may have influenced American anthropology and archaeology as a result of George Grant MacCurdy's training and subsequent activities in Europe. I believe that this involves looking at three different roles played by MacCurdy during his career: first, the organization man; second, the author of *Human Origins*; and third, the principal founder and director of the American School of Prehistoric Research.

THE ORGANIZATION MAN

No sooner had MacCurdy returned from Europe than he became very active in anthropology at the national level. "The national level" in the late 1890s meant primarily Section H (Anthropology) of the American Association for the Advancement of Science (AAAS) (neither the American Anthropological Association nor the Society for American Archaeology having yet been founded).[4] Anthropology had been represented in the AAAS almost since its founding in 1847, and it had been recognized with its own section since 1882 (MacCurdy 1902b:532; Mitra 1933:202-203). MacCurdy gave what appears to be his first paper to Section H at its August 1899 meeting in Columbus, Ohio. The paper, entitled "Extent of Instruction in Anthropology in Europe and the United States," obviously drew on his intimate knowledge of the European academic milieu. He immediately became active in AAAS committee work, and he served as Secretary of Section H for several years at the beginning of the century (McCown 1948:519). In a short paper commenting on the twentieth anniversary of the establishment of Section H, MacCurdy reviewed the content of the communications presented to it compared with those presented to its British, French, and German counterparts during the same period of the late nineteenth century. The results of the comparison showed clearly, he argued, that "American anthropologists have been working in relatively greater isolation than have European anthropologists," and he expressed the hope that in the next 20 years American anthropology would develop "an enlarged horizon," producing work that would become "less and less local and fragmentary" (1902b:534). MacCurdy was elected Chairman of Section H and AAAS Vice-President for 1905-1906. His vice-presidential address, published in *Science* in 1907, was a long and detailed didactic review of European prehistory from the "Eolithic" to the painted caves of the Magdalenian.

Because MacCurdy was so active in the affairs of Section H, it is not surprising that he was one of the founders of the American Anthropological Association (AAA) in 1902. The AAAS anthropologists had their winter meeting in Chicago in 1901, and MacCurdy was there as Section H Secretary. At the Chicago meeting, a committee of 10 persons made final plans to found an "American Anthropological Association" at the next national convention of the AAAS, to be held in Pittsburgh in June 1902. The Chicago organizing committee had as its members Franz Boas, Stewart Culin, Roland B. Dixon, George A. Dorsey, Livingston Farrand, J. Walter Fewkes, George G. MacCurdy, William J. McGee, Frank Russell, and Frederick Starr. These 10 plus about 30 other Section H members formally founded the American Anthropological Association in Pittsburgh on June 30, 1902 (MacCurdy 1946:97-97A; Mitra 1933:204).[5] It is worth noting here the very broad base and intellectual diversity of the AAA at its beginning, a diversity of which palaeoanthropology was an integral if small part. MacCurdy went on to serve as Secretary of the AAA from 1903 to 1916; later, after more than a decade out of office, he was the association's president for the calendar year 1931 (McCown 1948:516).

In addition to carrying out his duties for the national organizations (short published reports of the annual meetings of the AAA and of Section H of the AAAS), MacCurdy used the pages of their journals for publishing short reports and book reviews written by him concerning European developments in palaeoanthropology. Between the beginning of the century and 1917, when he resigned as AAA Secretary, there were 13 such contributions in *Science* and 20 in the *American Anthropologist*. The books he reviewed during these years included works of his former teachers (de Mortillet and Hoernes) and numerous others. Because the books had been written originally in German (five examples), French (four), Spanish (one), and Danish (one), English-language reviews must have been regarded as helpful by many American anthropologists. MacCurdy, who knew virtually everyone working in Europe and read all the relevant European literature, worked hard at keeping American anthropologists informed. He stated this intention, which seems obvious in the hindsight of history, very explicitly in the last paragraph of his 1905 paper in the *American Anthropologist* on "The Eolithic Problem": "If in the writing of this paper even one of several results is accomplished, I shall feel justified in the attempt, and well repaid for the labor expended. While introducing to Americans certain European authorities, it may also serve the role of interpreter, and lead to a better understanding and appreciation of what is being done on the other side of the Atlantic" (1905:470).

THE AUTHOR OF *HUMAN ORIGINS*

The second aspect of MacCurdy's influence on American anthropology was his authorship of an encyclopedic text, *Human Origins*, in 1924. That he would eventually write such an ambitious work is not surprising, because by the time of World War I his reputation as an expert on palaeoanthropology was well established in the United States. For some years he had been writing general review articles for scholarly audiences (e.g., MacCurdy 1910), more popular audiences (e.g., MacCurdy 1912), and general encyclopedias (MacCurdy 1916). One measure of his expert status was the invitation he received in 1916 to be part of a panel convened by the State Geologist of Florida, E. H. Sellards, to investigate the claim of Pleistocene antiquity for human bones, nonhuman faunal material, and artifacts that had recently been found at Vero, Florida. The other members of the panel were geologists T. W. Vaughn, O. P. Hay, and R. T. Chamberlain, and the physical anthropologist from the U.S. National Museum, Aleš Hrdlička. The panel of experts reported separately, and MacCurdy's verdict was a politely phrased rejection of the claimed Pleistocene antiquity: "in the face of the irreconcilable differences between the combination of anthropological phenomena on the one hand and palaeontological on the other, ... to say one is assured of the accuracy of the conclusion that the human remains and artifacts from Vero are of the Pleistocene period is to base one's conclusion on a forced correlation" (MacCurdy 1917:261). It would be, one may recall, another decade before the Pleistocene age of an archaeological site in the United States would be confirmed at Folsom, New Mexico (Figgins 1927).[6]

When MacCurdy finally wrote a general synthesis of his field, it was *Human Origins: A Manual of Prehistory*, a two-volume, 950-page compendium of Old World prehistory and human palaeontology from the early Palaeolithic through the Celtic Iron Age. His coverage of Europe was based to a large extent on his personal knowledge of the sites and collections. In the decade preceding World War I, MacCurdy had spent several summers in Europe touring Palaeolithic sites as they were being excavated. He made the switch from observer to participant in 1912 when he dug for a while with Hugo Obermaier at El Castillo in Spain and, later that summer, started his own excavations at the Middle and Upper Palaeolithic Grotte de la Combe, near Les Eyzies in southwestern France (MacCurdy 1914). The research for the book was interrupted by World War I. MacCurdy wrote in his autobiography (1946:138): "One of my regular lecture courses at Yale is called 'Human Origins,' and I have been storing up data for a book which will bear the same title. . . . Now in August, 1914, war on a colossal scale has begun in Europe. The hope of an early return to Europe to gather more data for my prospective book now seems dim indeed. My attention is turned to other things." The book project was taken up again after the war. He did much of the writing in Paris during the fall and winter of 1921–1922 during a sabbatical leave from Yale, and the book was published in 1924.

MacCurdy's *Human Origins* was not merely a narrative condensation of prehistoric sequences. A 118-page appendix contained a catalog of Palaeolithic sites in Europe. For each site, the information given included its location, its excavation history, the primary bibliographic references, and a summary of the stratigraphic sequence. MacCurdy's explanation of why he had included these 118 pages is of interest to historians looking at the adoption of the stratigraphic method by American archaeologists. He said in the book's preface (MacCurdy 1924, 1:viii–ix):

> The adoption by prehistorians of the stratigraphic method as a guiding principle has placed prehistoric research on a scientific basis and given a new and sustained impetus to archeologic endeavor. It is in recognition of the importance of this method that the author has devoted a long appendix to culture sequence as revealed by practically all the known Paleolithic stations. This feature is the result of a long period of painstaking labor, including the checking up of the data by a personal visit to a majority of the sites listed.... This portion of the book is unique, and the author hopes it may be as useful to his readers as it has been to him in the preparation of the rest of the work.

A briefer (40-page) catalog of Palaeolithic art provided summary information on European sites at which parietal or mobiliary art had been found. A 136-page chapter with its own bibliography constituted a copiously illustrated site-by-site catalog of human palaeontological sites, from Trinil to Olduvai to Paviland. For many American anthropologists in the period between the wars, MacCurdy's *Human Origins* would have been the richest source of information available on palaeoanthropology, a field for which the primary literature was inaccessible to many.

THE DIRECTOR OF THE AMERICAN SCHOOL OF PREHISTORIC RESEARCH

What may well have been the most important way in which George Grant MacCurdy transmitted elements of European palaeoanthropology to American anthropology was through the activities of his creation, the American School of Prehistoric Research (ASPR), particularly its summer field schools at European archaeological sites and museums. The context for this organization was established gradually, over a period of decades, before its actual founding. What the School eventually became had its roots not only in MacCurdy's formal European training (1895 through 1898) but also in four extended trips he made to Europe between 1900 and 1912 (MacCurdy 1946:98–134). On these trips (through England, Scotland, France, Belgium, Switzerland, Germany, Denmark, Italy, and Austria-Hungary) he attended professional meetings, visited museums and archaeological sites, and—above all—

strengthened and widened his network of European colleagues. During two of the trips (the summers of 1908 and 1912), his traveling companion for part of the time was Charles Peabody, who was to be a cofounder of the ASPR, the source of its first year's operating funds, and its field director in 1922 (1946:108, 118, 151, 157). On the summer trip in 1900, MacCurdy met for the first time the Abbé Henri Breuil (1946:87), who helped and supported MacCurdy in various ways throughout the latter's career, including serving as the ASPR's field director in 1937. The first meeting with Denis Peyrony occurred during the summer trip in 1903 (1946:99); it was Peyrony who, a few years later, gave MacCurdy his first opportunity to direct the excavation of a Palaeolithic site. His first acquaintance of Dr. Léon Henri-Martin (1864-1936), at whose instigation the ASPR was founded, was made on the 1912 trip (1946:120).

Of these four pre–World War I trips, the latest, in 1912, was the most important in shaping the rest of MacCurdy's career. After having spent a short time as a guest excavator at El Castillo, a long-term project at Puente Viesgo, Spain, sponsored by the Institut de Paléontologie Humaine in Paris and directed by Hugo Obermaier (like MacCurdy, a former student of Hoernes at Vienna), he recorded his conviction that "The prehistorian learns much by seeing excavations in actual operation" (MacCurdy 1946:122). This view, that students should visit sites under excavation and, if at all possible, dig there briefly themselves, was to become a guiding operating principle of the ASPR. After his time at El Castillo, MacCurdy traveled north to the Dordogne region of France, where Peyrony arranged for him to lease and excavate a small rockshelter, the Grotte de la Combe, south of Les Eyzies. The shelter, which contained a sequence of occupations running from Denticulate Mousterian through Mousterian of Acheulian Tradition and Chatelperronian to early Aurignacian (MacCurdy 1914; Movius 1995:248), was completely emptied by MacCurdy and his workmen in just a few weeks. During this period, he was a witness to an important palaeoanthropological discovery, as he recounted in his autobiography (1946:131): "Capitan and Peyrony are digging at La Ferrassie; so I take a day off to dig there with them by invitation. And it is a lucky day; for Capitan and Peyrony discover two human skeletons of the Neandertal type (Mousterian age)." The Neanderthal skeletons in question turned out to be three, not two—La Ferrassie 3 in one grave pit and La Ferrassie 4 and 4bis in a second grave pit (Heim 1984:250). That these were true Neanderthal burials, with the human remains placed in deliberately excavated pits, was formally documented by a committee of experts.[7]

This crucial summer of 1912 ended with a trip to Geneva in September, in the company of Marcellin Boule and Henri Breuil, to attend the International Congress of Anthropology and Prehistoric Archaeology[8] (MacCurdy 1946:132–134).

The impetus toward further European fieldwork that must have resulted from the very successful 1912 trip was derailed by World War I. MacCurdy was in New Haven when the war began in August 1914, and during the war years he occupied himself with other matters, including research in American archaeology that is not the concern of this chapter. However, less than six months after the 1918 armistice, threads were coming together that would return MacCurdy to Europe as the director of a new organization for training Americans in palaeoanthropology, the American School of Prehistoric Research.

The impetus for the creation of what eventually became the ASPR came from the French physician and palaeoanthropologist Dr. Léon Henri-Martin, and it started in the context of American relief work in war-ravaged France. MacCurdy recounted the relevant circumstances in his autobiography (1946:150):

> My old friend, Dr. Charles Peabody, now doing post-war work for a Franco-American Committee writes from Paris on March 12, 1919, inviting me to spend the summer in France. . . . On May 3, another letter comes from Peabody, enclosing one from Dr. Henri Martin, whose epoch-making discoveries at La Quina (Charente) are now well known. The latter suggests that a school of prehistoric studies, somewhat after the plan of our American Schools of classical studies in Athens, Rome and Jerusalem, might be established in France. This to me is not a new idea, for ever since my student days in Europe, I have been hoping to see a prehistoric link formed that would bind the New World to the Old World.

Henri-Martin's suggestion, strongly supported by Peabody, was implemented by him and MacCurdy. In January 1920 a committee of the AAA was appointed by President Clark Wissler to act with a similar committee of the American Institute of Archaeology to look into the feasibility of founding an American School of Prehistoric Studies in Europe (the original name of the ASPR). The AAA committee members were MacCurdy, Charles Peabody, and Aleš Hrdlička. The formal founding of the School occurred in February 1921; MacCurdy was named its director, and the first summer field school was held that summer, primarily at Dr. Henri-Martin's site of La Quina. Peabody supplied the operating budget of that first field school (MacCurdy 1922, 1946:151–156). The School was incorporated in 1926 under its new name, the American School of Prehistoric Research (Hall 1927).

The scale of operations for the first summer field school was modest. MacCurdy's report (1922:146) speaks of "a small group of American students," and the autobiography (1946:151) names Alonzo W. Pond, then a student at Beloit College in Wisconsin, as the school's scholarship holder during that first summer. A few additional details about the field school are included in an interview with Pond near the end of his long life. The interview was conducted on July 28, 1985, by Michael Tarabulski, a student at Beloit College between 1978 and 1982, who kindly made available to me a tape of the relevant passage and other very useful unpublished information about Pond.[9] The information provided by Tarabulski makes it clear that there were only two students in 1921, Pond and a woman referred to by nickname as "K" Crockett (almost certainly the Adele Crockett included in the compiled list of field school participants in all field seasons published by Brew [1966b:55–56]).

Pond's recollections of MacCurdy were quite cordial, and he had a high respect for his professional competence.[10] The professional contacts Pond had made in 1921 with the leading figures of French Palaeolithic archaeology stood him in very good stead just a few years later when he was employed by the Logan Museum of Beloit College to acquire for it what soon became very significant Palaeolithic artifact collections (White 1992).

Over the next decade and a half, until 1938, 15 more summer field schools were held in Europe—primarily in France, Spain, and Czechoslovakia. The scale of the operation increased in the second and subsequent years, usually with about seven or eight students (Table 12.1). With two exceptions (1922 and 1923, when he was busy finishing *Human Origins* and other matters), MacCurdy himself was the field director of the summer programs until 1931, when—at age 68—he allowed this task to devolve upon others, primarily former students of the field school. Separate field projects were cosponsored by the School in southwest Asia, most importantly the work in the Mount Carmel caves directed by Dorothy Garrod. During this time, a minimum of 116 students went through the field school, gaining firsthand familiarity with European prehistoric sites and collections and with the prehistorians who were working there.

How this worked in practice may be illustrated with reference to the 1930 summer session, which began in Paris on July 1 and ended

Table 12.1. ASPR Summer Field Schools

Year	Director	Students	Excavations
1921	George Grant MacCurdy	2	France
1922	Charles Peabody	ca. 7	France
1923	Aleš Hrdlička	ca. 7	
1924	George Grant MacCurdy	8–12	France
1925	George Grant MacCurdy	ca. 8	France
1926	George Grant MacCurdy	7	France, Czechoslovakia
1927	George Grant MacCurdy	ca. 11	France
1928	George Grant MacCurdy	6 or more	France
1929	George Grant MacCurdy	10 or more	France
1930	George Grant MacCurdy	12	France, Spain, Czechoslovakia
1931	Charlotte D. Gower	7	France, Czechoslovakia
1932	Vladimir J. Fewkes	8	Yugoslavia
1933	Vladimir J. Fewkes	3	Czechoslovakia, Yugoslavia
1934	Vladimir J. Fewkes	5	Czechoslovakia
1937	Henri Breuil and H. Kelley	6	France
1938	Vladimir J. Fewkes	4	Czechoslovakia

Source: Data compiled from annual reports of the ASPR director and the directors of the summer field schools for the summers of 1921 through 1938 from Fewkes 1934, 1935, 1939; Hrdlička 1923; Kelley 1938; MacCurdy 1922, 1925, 1926, 1927b, 1928, 1929, 1930, 1931a, 1932, 1933, 1934, 1935, 1938, 1939; Peabody 1923.

in Prague on September 3. In addition to longer stays in France and Czechoslovakia, MacCurdy and the students traveled in Spain, Switzerland, and Germany (MacCurdy 1931a). The students got excavation experience at three sites: (1) the Abri des Merveilles (Sergeac, Dordogne, France), a rockshelter containing Mousterian and Noaillian occupations (MacCurdy 1931b; Movius 1995:302–303) that had been leased by MacCurdy and excavated by ASPR students every summer since 1924; (2) the Middle and Upper Palaeolithic cave site of El Pendo near Santander, Spain, where the ASPR students joined the excavations of Jesus Carballo (1931); and (3) the Neolithic site of Homolka in Czechoslovakia. In addition to these sites, the students visited about 50 other sites and many museums and private collections. As part of some of these visits, the students heard lectures by 15 different European prehistorians (MacCurdy 1931a). This program was typical of the summer field sessions. In later years, after MacCurdy's work at the

Table 12.2. ASPR Field School Students in the Summer of 1930

L. Cabot Briggs (Harvard)
Jeanne Ernst (Mount Holyoke)
John P. Gillin (Wisconsin)
Robert Greenlee (Northwestern)
Robert H. Merrill (Michigan)
John Z. Miller (Lehigh)
Panchanan Mitra (Calcutta)
Theodore D. McCown (Berkeley)
Cornelius B. Osgood (Chicago)
Froehlich G. Rainey (Chicago)
Lucille Serrem (Columbia)
Sol Tax (Wisconsin)

Source: MacCurdy 1931a:3

Abri des Merveilles had finished, the students received excavation experience for shorter periods at a series of other sites.[11]

Almost all the regular, full-time students in the ASPR summer field schools were young men and women from U.S. colleges and universities. A list of the students in the 1930 summer field school (Table 12.2) serves as an example. Unfortunately, no complete list of these students can now be compiled. A partial list I constructed from published sources and MacCurdy's autobiography overlaps heavily with a similar list compiled by the Director of Harvard's Peabody Museum, J. O. Brew (1966b:55–56), on the occasion of the museum's centennial. Both my list and Brew's contain a few names not on the other one. Combining the information (and excluding from Brew's list excavation supervisors and MacCurdy family members who were not students), it is seen (Table 12.3) that the ASPR had a minimum of 79 students; other information (Table 12.1) suggests that 20 or so students remain unaccounted for. Of the 79 known ASPR students, 29 (37 percent) were women. This is a notable observation for the 1920s and 1930s, but I do not find it surprising. It corresponds to what I saw for myself when I entered the world of European Palaeolithic archaeology in the early 1960s—a world in which women were then and had been for two generations among the leaders of the field.

MacCurdy repeatedly emphasized the explicit function of the ASPR as a European training ground for American academicians who were themselves to be responsible for producing future generations of American anthropologists. In his report on the sixth summer field school,

Table 12.3. Students in the ASPR Summer Field Schools

Robert McCormick Adams	A. Andrews Hrubec
F. W. Aldrich	Elizabeth B. Jackson
Curtice M. C. Aldridge	Oleh Kandyba
Harriet M. Allyn	William H. Kelley
Emily S. Bayless	Henry M. Kendall
Virginia Beggs	Frederica de Laguna
Ethel Boissevain	Homer D. Little
Lloyd Cabot Briggs	Derwood W. Lockard
Edwin C. Broome Jr.	Malcom Lloyd
James B. Bullitt	Ursula McConnel
Frank Carney	Theodore D. McCown
(Mrs. Frank) Carney	Robert H. Merrill
Herdman F. Cleland	John Z. Miller
Adele Crockett	Panchanan Mitra
Agnes C. L. Donohugh	Dwight W. Morrow Jr.
Anthony Eastman	Hallam L. Movius Jr.
Robert W. Ehrich	Eduardo Noguera
Jeanne Ernst	Cornelius B. Osgood
H. R. Fairclough	Stephen Phillips
Frances E. Felin	Alonzo Ponds
Vladimir J. Fewkes	Froehlich G. Rainey
C. Daryll Forde	E. B. Renaud
Robert A. Franks Jr.	Frederick L. W. Richardson
Anne H. Fuller	Helen H. Roberts
James Harvey Gaul	J. Townsend Russell Jr.
John P. Gillin	Ruth Sears
Bernard Charles Glueck Jr.	Lucille Serrem
Hetty Goldman	Sol Tax
Eugene A. Golomshtok	Edna Thuner
Charlotte D. Gower	Emily Wadsworth
Josephine G. Graton	Laurence P. Walker
Robert F. Greenlee	Grant T. Wickwire
Martha Hackett	Malcolm Willey
A. Irving Hallowell	George D. Williams
Frances M. Hammond	H. V. Williams
Harriet Hammond	Vesta Wood
Frank C. Hibben	George Woodbury
(Mrs. Frank C.) Hibben	Eugene C. Worman Jr.
George Sumner Hill	
Bruce Howe	
Gertrude Howe	

Source: Data compiled from Brew 1966:55–56 and from the sources listed in Table 12.1.

that of 1926, MacCurdy (1927b:16) reported that "Former students of the School are at present making use of their training in prehistory as holders of positions, teaching and curatorial, in seventeen institutions." The ASPR, as an institution for in-field training of American anthropologists in palaeoanthropology, did not survive World War II and the Cold War. In a larger sense, however, MacCurdy's goals for the School were amply realized, and his success was recognized by the profession at the time of his death. In a necrological "appreciation" of MacCurdy published in England, the American physical anthropologist Earnest Hooton (1950:188) wrote a line that seems, half a century later, to have been an accurate prophecy: "The American School of Prehistoric Research is Dr. MacCurdy's monument and should perpetuate his memory, not necessarily in name or in details of present organization, but in its continuing contributions to our knowledge of ancient man and in its raising up of new generations of prehistorians and of amateurs of the study of man."

Conclusion

George Grant MacCurdy deserves recognition as an American pioneer of palaeoanthropology because he was doing it, teaching it, and training others to do and teach it in the formative years of academic anthropology in the United States. His active contributions to scholarly and professional societies and the publication of his encyclopedic textbook helped to assure the inclusion of the study of both the cultural and biological aspects of human origins as an integral part of anthropology during those formative years. Because so much of the early-twentieth-century scholarship in palaeoanthropology originated in Europe, MacCurdy acted as an American broker of European scholarship in this field, a role that his extensive European training equipped him to do very well.

MacCurdy's principal impact on American anthropology came through the activities of the American School of Prehistoric Research, which gave American archaeologists, ethnologists, and physical anthropologists firsthand field experience with palaeoanthropology in Europe and southwest Asia. Although most of the School's original students have passed from the scene, some of its "grandstudents" and "great-grandstudents" are today active American practitioners of palaeoanthropology. One such grandstudent, John Yellen, is the founder and president of the Paleoanthropology Society, an organization of archaeologists and biological anthropologists from all over the world who meet annually in the United States to present and review recent developments in palaeoanthropology. Earnest Hooton's view of MacCurdy's contribution was a prescient one.

Acknowledgments

I am grateful to David L. Browman and Stephen Williams for having invited me to participate in the March 1998 Society for American Archeology History of Archeology Committee (SAA-HOAC) symposium on "Historical Views of American Archaeology's Connections to Europe before World War I." I would never have undertaken such an assignment but for Dave Browman's persuasiveness, and I could not possibly have completed it without the steady stream of critical research materials sent to me by Steve Williams during the months preceding the Seattle symposium. I am deeply indebted to Sarah R. Demb, Museum Archivist of the Peabody Museum of Archaeology and Ethnology at Harvard University, for her help in supplying needed archival material and in granting access to George Grant MacCurdy's unpublished autobiography, the original copy of which is curated at the Peabody Museum. I am, finally, very grateful to Michael Tarabulski for having made some very useful unpublished material available to me, including portions of his recorded interview with the late Alonzo Pond, a student in the first of MacCurdy's summer field schools in France.

Notes

Introduction

1. Although often thought of as a rare book, thus suggesting why it is not cited more often, the facts are that a recent computer search shows that more than 50 "hard" copies are in libraries from California to the East Coast, and that it is available on microfilm as well.

Chapter 1

1. One of the joys of researching a new topic is the act of discovery, and so it was with my own finding of this new term (the Strait of Anian) for the well-known Bering Strait connection between Asia and the Americas. It is not a new term by any means, as I will set forth in the following pages, but this is its first use in American archaeological literature as far as I know. However, it should be noted that the Strait of Anian has been discussed extensively by American historians and other cartographic scholars for more than a century.

2. I have been greatly aided in my "Anian" search by the most helpful research of Dr. Greg Finnegan, Research Librarian at the Tozzer Library, Harvard University. There are even some poems that have been written on this subject! I am also indebted to Laura Holt, Librarian at the Laboratory of Anthropology of the Museum of New Mexico, Santa Fe, for much help in getting access to many important volumes, especially via interlibrary loan.

Chapter 2

1. The title of this chapter is taken from a sentence in Jefferson's 1784 *Notes on the State of Virginia*, Query XI, although there is also a 1549 English poem about the New World with the phrase "or whens they cam" (Hud-

dleston 1967:110) and a very similar phrase in the work of John Bartram (1751/ 1798:74–75) as well. I could not have pursued this topic as effectively as I did without the great aid of two seldom-used but not ancient volumes—Panchanan Mitra's 1930 Yale Ph.D. dissertation, published in Calcutta in 1933, and Lee Huddleston's 1966 University of Texas Ph.D. dissertation, published in Austin in 1967. Their thorough and extensive scholarship was very enlightening and a joy to use.

2. The suggestion that the Tartars (aka Tatars) were the source of the Indian occupation of the New World has a long published history starting ca. 1600. The connection via the area of the Strait of Anian is equally old because the word "Anian" equaled what we now term the "Bering Strait." Some early-seventeenth-century maps had the word "Tartars" (referring to the people) stretched across northeast Siberia, tied to the Mongol hordes from the Gobi region of Mongolia.

3. Wherever "origins" is employed in this chapter, it is to be understood as the particular origins theory of the individual being discussed.

4. I will be using the term "Transatlantean" to refer to those peoples thought to have been early settlers in the New World who came from the Old World via the Atlantic Ocean. I have come to the use of this terminology in concert with my colleague Terry Barnhart as a result of discussions we had on this subject in 1993. "Transatlantean" is meant to include all such groups touched on in my 1991 book *Fantastic Archaeology*, although it was not used therein. For the period covered in this paper, it would include the Carthaginians, the Lost Tribes of Israel, Spanish, Romans, etc. As very few early sources gave much strength to "Transpacific" voyagers, I will not use it much in this chapter. The Chinese were most often cited. Just to touch all bases, a few scholars felt that an overland route from northern Europe via Iceland and Greenland might have been used, but I will include those in my "Transatlantean" category just to simplify the terminology.

5. The entire Brerewood quotation in Barton's volume runs to some 45 lines. Barton's comment (1798:iv) is that Brerewood "is a man of much learning but his book ... is written in an extremely obscure and painful style." Although I have not read anything of Brerewood's but this long quote, I agree that his prose is very difficult.

6. While such concern pro or contra Tartarian origin seems of little importance today, these very pages of Kalm's volume have added some unfortunate paragraphs to some important writings about a century later. When John Reinhold Forster published Kalm's volume in London in 1771, he added some footnotes. So what? Well, it just so happens that Kalm had footnotes too; the only way to tell who wrote which is to look at the very end of each footnote for a tiny little "f." Kalm's footnotes have no initial at all. At least in my 1972 reprint edition, no mention of this information is there. Indeed, the only way I now know what to look for was that the very careful scholar Panchanan Mitra pointed this out in his 1933 volume *A History of American Archaeology*.

Mitra, in discussing Kalm's work, quotes from Samuel Haven's well-known 1856 volume *The Archaeology of the United States*. Haven (1856:20) says that Kalm felt that the Tartarian inscription mentioned above was tied to the followers of Kublai Khan. What Mitra correctly points out is that that reference to the "Khan" is in *Forster's* footnote, not something written by Kalm. It does show a pattern of thought in the 1750s, as Haven states, but not by Kalm.

7. Queries about the veracity of Carver's book began very soon. In 1789 the Connecticut-based scholar Noah Webster published in the July issues of his magazine *The American Museum* the following: "I have several times heard and read doubts being suggested, whether Carver made the extensive tour he has described; or whether his book be not compiled from those of Charlevoix, Hennepin, &c." Webster and other naysayers were wrong about the trip narrative, but I feel correct about part of the rest of the book. Carver did make quite careful notes on the Indians, and even some drawings. However, the earlier French explorers did as well.

8. Timothy Severin, as far as I know, is the most recent scholar to publish a further discussion of Carver. He provides a good background on his early life and had access, via microfilm from the British Museum, to Carver's original manuscript. He confirms the extent of Carver's trip to the Sioux, for example. Another interesting tidbit (Severin 1967:197) is that while Carver was in London trying to get his book published in 1773, he suggested to a group of "gentlemen" that he might cross Russia and look for Indian origins on his way to North America. I have discussed this above. Severin is quite supportive of Carver in general, but then he suggests that "ghostwriters" were the source for many of other wild additions in the text, which is a reasonable notion but unprovable. I also feel that Severin (1967:198) did not understand the real value of the origins chapter; he even confuses Adair's 10 reasons for deriving the Indians from the Lost Tribes as being a notion held by Carver. It certainly was not.

9. One of my most interesting discoveries about Barton was the existence of an obituary statement written in Philadelphia, in 1816, by his first cousin William Paul Crillon Barton (1786–1856). This Barton was also a medical doctor who filled the professorship in botany that was vacated by Benjamin Barton's death. This note, published in a rather obscure journal, *The Portfolio*, transcends any such document that I have ever read. W. P. C. Barton, in whose home the orphaned B. S. Barton lived for some years during his late teens, starts his necrology with a description of his cousin's early life and describes in great detail the wonderful quality of B. S. Barton's artistic talents in drawing, which verifies the accuracy of delineation of the botanical specimens he described. But then, when discussing Professor Barton's ascendancy to Professor Rush's position in medicine, following Rush's death, W. P. C. Barton changes his style entirely. He tells us of Barton's almost lifelong illness of "irregular gout" and describes in excruciating detail his later acute attack of "haemoptistis." First he says that Barton's reading habits were "desultory, ir-

regular, and to all appearance hasty," and next that he was "a man of uncommon genius and excellent professional talents." In his lectures on medicine, we are first told that "he was eloquent and instructive," but then that "his emphasis . . . was studied, forced, and often inappropriate. In his lectures, his diction was cacophonous and unpleasant." But we are also told: "As a parent, he was kind, tender and indulgent, to a fault." W. P. C. Barton concludes this interesting declamation: "Such, gentlemen, was the late Professor Barton! May not such a man be truly called great!" My only warning is that W. P. C. Barton's oration is a copyist's delight; with some different quotes one can make Benjamin Smith Barton either a fool or a genius.

10. I do not mean to suggest that I refuse to accept the notion that the recently discovered Kennewick man in Oregon is a legitimate problem in New World anthropology. The suggestion by some that this individual might be of a different "strain" of early Asian heritage does not bother me at all. W. W. Howells has proposed (1995) such an early form that might be ancestral to other migrants leaving Asia at this time or even earlier.

11. I want to acknowledge with thanks the help John Kelly provided in locating an obscure source on Benjamin Smith Barton, and the splendid work David Browman did in energetically tracking down biographic and bibliographic information.

Chapter 3

1. The term "Neobagun," as Daniel Brinton first recognized, is a truncation by Rafinesque of the Ojibwa word "Nah-o-bah-guh-he gun-nun," which is supplied in an Ojibwa song text in Part II of Tanner's *Narrative* (Brinton 1885:152; Tanner 1830:351–362). The words denote the "four song sticks" upon which that particular *Midewiwin* song was recorded in pictographs. Rafinesque mistakenly used the term to refer to all Ojibwa *Midewiwin* songs (and erroneously retranslated the term as "male tool"). For a discussion and examples of Rafinesque's theft of pictographic materials from Tanner's *Narrative* and their use in the Walam Olum, see Oestreicher (1995a:130, 144–146, 172–177, 184–186, 193–198).

2. The term "Linnique peoples" is Rafinesque's own name for the Algonquian-speaking tribes. It is an adaptation of the Delaware Indian self-designation Lenape, "common person," or (redundant) Lenni Lenape, "common, common people," which Rafinesque typically spelled *linni linapi*. Because Rafinesque had read the legend in Heckewelder (1819/1876:47–53) that all the Algonquian tribes were descended from the Delaware, he crafted the term "Linnique" as a designation for the entire Algonquian stock.

3. Rafinesque's Volney essay (1834a) and an appended "supplement" (1834b) were discovered in 1982 at the Royal Institute of France by historian Joan Leopold and identified a year later by Jean Rousseau.

4. To avoid confusion, I have followed the standard spelling "Walam Olum."

5. The Lenape or Delaware Indians are a people of the Algonquian language family who once inhabited what is now lower New York State, all of New Jersey, eastern Pennsylvania, and the northern part of the state of Delaware. The term "Delaware" first came into use in 1610 when Delaware Bay was named after Sir Thomas West, Lord de la Warr, the first governor of Jamestown. By the mid-eighteenth century the term "Delaware Indian" had come to refer not only to the native people of the lower Delaware River region but to migrants from the upper Delaware and Hudson Valleys. By the mid-nineteenth century, following a series of tragic removals, most Delaware had resettled in parts of southern Ontario, Wisconsin, and Oklahoma.

6. John Witthoft, Ives Goddard, and James Rementer expressed their suspicion and disbelief in the Walam Olum because of the similarity of words with those in the Moravian sources or the absence of grammatical structure in the text. James B. Griffin (1955) argued that the time frame in the Walam Olum contradicts recent data provided by radiocarbon dating and that the entire document is suspect, while William Hunter and more recently Stephen Williams (1991) have criticized Rafinesque's character and noted that the Walam Olum suspiciously resembles the thesis of history in Rafinesque's *Annals of Kentucky* (1824). Herbert C. Kraft has argued that the description of the peopling of the Northeast in the Walam Olum is not borne out in the archaeological record and that the pictographs used in the Walam Olum bear no resemblance to any petroglyphs of the Lenape or other Indians of the Northeast (1986:7). And W. W. Newcomb, observing that the social structure of the Delaware did not harmonize with that depicted in the Walam Olum, argued that it was a recent, albeit authentic, Delaware Indian document (1955/1974).

7. Neither the circumstances nor the individuals from whom the Walam Olum was supposedly obtained were ever clearly explained by Rafinesque. According to his brief and ambiguous account, he received the tablets from "the late Dr. Ward," who in turn had received them from an unspecified Lenape Indian in 1820 as payment for a medical cure (Rafinesque 1836a, 1:122, 151). Rafinesque further claimed that several years later he received from another unspecified individual a series of epic songs in the Delaware language that accompany and explain the glyphs (1836a, 1:151). In addition, an epilogue was purportedly obtained from one John Burns, about whom Rafinesque left no further information (1836a, 1:140-141).

8. Rafinesque was certainly one of the few naturalists before Charles Darwin to regard species and genera from an evolutionary point of view. "All species might have been varieties once," he wrote, "and many varieties are gradually becoming species by assuming constant and peculiar characters" (1836d, 1:6). But those crediting Rafinesque with anticipating Darwin's theory of evolution have failed to consider the enormous influence that Darwin's grand-

father, "the celebrated Dr. [Erasmus] Darwin," exerted upon the general public as well as upon Rafinesque himself. Nor have they adequately appreciated the nature of Charles Darwin's original contribution.

Some four decades before Rafinesque's discussion of evolution (and also preceding the work of Lamarck), Erasmus Darwin argued that all nature had evolved from a single original filament, and "exists in a state of perpetual improvement by laws impressed on the atoms of matter by the great CAUSE OF CAUSES" (1801, 2:240; Greene 1996:167–168). Extinction of old species was itself the result of "this gradual production of the species and genera" (Greene 1996:168). Darwin wrote treatises and poetry on the subject; Rafinesque consciously imitated Darwin's ideas and his poetry. If Rafinesque deserves credit as an early pioneer of the theory of evolution, it is in this context.

What set Charles Darwin apart from all his predecessors, including his grandfather, was that he provided an unparalleled mass of evidence for evolution and an explanation as to how it works. By demonstrating that natural selection was a means by which species evolved, Darwin removed evolutionary theory from the realm of speculation to the scientific recognition that evolution was an integral fact of nature. Ironically, Darwin cited Rafinesque as an early pioneer of evolution in the third edition of his *On the Origin of Species* (1861:7), but he seems to have been unaware of the tremendous influence exerted by his own grandfather, Erasmus Darwin, upon Rafinesque.

9. The evidence for the fraudulence of the Walam Olum has been advanced in Oestreicher (1994, 1995a, 1995b, 1996). A more extensive presentation of the evidence and a history of the hoax is currently under preparation for the *Memoirs* of the American Philosophical Society.

10. Although the story of the conquest of the Mound Builders in the Walam Olum is based mainly upon legends recorded by Heckewelder (1819/1876:47–53) and Cusick (Beauchamp 1892:10–11), it deliberately furthered a popular idea among Euro-Americans that the Mound Builders were a civilized race that had emigrated from the Old World (in this case, Atlanteans), only to be destroyed by savage hordes of American Indians.

11. As Michael J. Franklin points out in his *Sir William Jones: Selected Poetical and Prose Works* (1995), Jones in part defended Christian tradition in his published writings to avoid attack and the "incurring in his European readers the very prejudices [against Hindus and other non-Christian peoples of central and eastern Asia] he wished to allay" (Franklin 1995:350). Privately, Jones wrote to a friend in 1787: "I am no Hindu; but I hold the doctrine of the Hindus concerning a future state to be incomparably more rational, more pious, and more likely to deter men from vice, than the horrid opinions inculcated by Christians on punishments without end" (in Franklin 1995:350).

12. Sir William Jones, who first discerned the existence of an Indo-European proto-language, and brought to the debate the solid command of some dozen languages, including Sanskrit, rejected the notion that an original primitive tongue could be restored. He criticized the mistaken etymologies of Jacob Bry-

ant, Bailly, and others, which often betrayed ignorance of the languages cited (Jones 1788b/1979b:343–345; 1794a/1979c:22–23). The "language of Noah," Jones contested, was "lost irretrievably"; after a diligent search, he was unable to find even "a single word used in common by the Arabian, Indian, and Tartar families," except what had been borrowed through more recent contacts (Jones 1794b/1979d:485–489). By contrast, Jones argued, much was to be learned about the most ancient migrations through broad comparison of languages within each family, and through comparison of the various cosmologies. The sciences of comparative linguistics and mythology had begun in earnest.

13. Obtaining partial translations and summaries of ancient Chinese texts was not a problem for Rafinesque. The American Philosophical Society Library had a large collection of works on China by Jesuit missionaries and by other scholars and travelers. Rafinesque's writings list over a dozen books he perused on the subject (Rafinesque 1835:367–376; 1836a, 2:110–113). That such works were incorporated into the Walam Olum is established not only by the content of the epic but also by Rafinesque's remarks, which repeatedly sought to underscore the links between the early sections of the Walam Olum and the "Asiatic period" of Amerindian history it allegedly described (Rafinesque 1836a, 1:145–146). Further, his other discussions covering China, "Mosaic [biblical] history" in *The American Nations*, and elsewhere present parallel scenarios to the Walam Olum (Rafinesque 1832–1833:22–26; 1836a, 2:110–159).

14. Serving as a judge in British-ruled India, Sir William Jones discovered that Sanskrit and the languages of Europe had shared the same ancestral tongue. An Indo-European proto-language must have once existed, he affirmed, which spread out from the table lands of central Asia (Jones 1788b/1979b:348–349,355; 1794b/1979d:483–492). Jones held that Iran was the most likely place out of which the Indo-Europeans and other peoples had diverged following the biblical flood (1794b/1979d:487). He further classified, albeit incorrectly, the world's languages as being either "Indian" (Indo-European), "Tartar," or "Arabian." All three language families were supposedly descended from Shem, Ham, and Japhet, the three sons of Noah (1794b/1979d:479–492). Although the ancient biblical classification of mankind is no longer acceptable to contemporary Western scholarship, it is important to recall that in Jones's time, philology was an infant science and information was scarce. Scholars continued to rely upon Scripture in an effort to discern the earliest history of mankind.

15. In chapter 10 of *The American Nations*, Rafinesque liberally paraphrased (as usual, without citation) arguments raised by Georges Cuvier in the latter's famous *Essay on the Theory of the Earth* (1815). At times Rafinesque's language echoes Cuvier's with striking concordance. The evidence is presented in full in my forthcoming work on the Walam Olum (to be published by the American Philosophical Society).

16. Rafinesque's fragmentary knowledge of Hebrew was based largely upon the mistaken views of Antoine Fabre d'Olivet—a nineteenth-century gram-

marian who followed the tradition set forth by Court de Gébelin in the latter's *Monde Primitif*. Fabre d'Olivet's *The Hebraic Tongue Restored* (1815) was to become a model for Rafinesque's approach to languages in general and to Hebrew in particular (cf., for example, Rafinesque's "The Haytian Language Restored"). Fabre d'Olivet contended that the original, pristine Hebrew of Moses (which he erroneously identified as pure Egyptian) had become so corrupt that its true spiritual and historical meaning was lost to all but a few Cabalists. In short, he "restored" Moses' "true" meanings by dispensing with the traditional vowel system preserved by the Masoretes (Jewish scholars who flourished between approximately A.D. 500 and 1000), by mistakenly interpreting instead certain consonants as vowels, by truncating Hebrew words beyond recognition to their alleged "roots," by comparing unrelated but similar-sounding word fragments, and finally, by computing the alleged symbolic values of each letter in each "root"—a concept he adapted from Jewish mysticism (Fabre d'Olivet 1815/1921).

17. A large variety of spellings for this Chinese term appeared in Rafinesque's source materials. Rafinesque simply adopted Barrow's rendering.

18. Bryant believed that the term *Manes* and similar-sounding designations were ultimately derived from the name of Noah himself. Having read in Diodorus of the worship of the sacred bull *Mneuis* by the ancient Egyptians in Heliopolis (Bryant 1774-1776, 2:415), and reading also in the same source of the first lawgiver, *Mneues* (whose name sounded nearly identical to *Mneuis*), Bryant concluded that the bull was merely a symbol of the lawgiver. *Mneues*, Bryant argued (or, as he was known in Crete, King *Minos* or *Min-oas*—*Meen* to Herodotus), was a "contraction of Men-Neuas, the Lunar God Neuas, the same as Noas, or Noah" (1774-1776, 2:417-419). As for the widespread worship of the lunar deity (and the alleged connection between the very name "moon" and the similar sounding *Manes*, or Noah), Bryant contended that this was due to the new moon resembling the shape of the biblical ark. Reverence for the moon, Bryant held, was rather a commemoration of Noah and his ark, hence the frequent lunette designs in ancient art and hieroglyphs (1774-1776, 2:420-421, 442-449, etc.).

19. As Rafinesque informs us in *The American Nations:* "the Gods of one Nation might be Devils for others . . . Giants might be deemed Dwarfs by foes . . . and viceversa" (1836a, 2:205).

20. Rafinesque found abundant support for the idea of "animalization" in his source materials. In an essay concerned with the ancient books of the Hindus, Francis Wilford observed that the "first inhabitants of Sanc'ha-dwipa . . . are described by the mythologists as elephants, demons, and snakes" (1794/1979:346). Similarly, John Lawson wrote that the Indians of South Carolina sometimes employed animal names, such as "Eagle, Panther, Alligator, or some such wild Creature" (1709:195). That similar examples of tribes, clans, and individuals named after animals could be found almost universally through-

out the world encouraged Rafinesque's eighteenth- and nineteenth-century predecessors to conclude that the numerous fables and myths that unscientifically described talking animals were actually allegorical "primitive" symbols for tribes of humans, clans, or individuals.

21. Rafinesque learned of the Ojibwa culture hero Nanabush from reading McKenney's *Sketches of a Tour to the Lakes* and Tanner's *Narrative* (McKenney 1827:302-305; Tanner 1830:351ff.). Because Rafinesque believed that all the Algonquian tribes, including the Ojibwa, were descended from the Lenape, and because he did not have a Lenape name for the flood hero, he reasoned that the Lenape would have once used the same term for Noah that the Ojibwa did.

22. The controversy regarding the origin of Chinese and Egyptian writing systems and their possible connection was epitomized in the eighteenth-century dispute over the nature of the inscriptions on the "Bust of Isis," allegedly in Turin. Almost certainly fraudulent, the bust was made famous in intellectual circles by M. Needham with his contention that the "Egyptian" symbols on the bust could be identified with Chinese (Iversen 1961/1993:Plate XVII, 106-107; *Mémoires* 1776:v-x). The bust was illustrated in Rafinesque's source, *Mémoires Concernant L'Histoire, Les Sciences, Les Arts, Les Moeurs, Les Usages, &c. Des Chinois* (Missionaires de Pekin 1776). At least some of the symbols on the bust were incorporated by Rafinesque into his "Graphic Systems of America" and into the Walam Olum proper (for examples, see Oestreicher 1995a:165-166, 188-197, 206-213, 216-221, 225-226).

23. When, for example, Caleb Atwater, then laboring on the first major survey and description of the earthworks, observed in John D. Clifford's Lexington museum a vessel with three sculpted heads that had been unearthed from a mound, he wrote: "Does it not represent the three chief gods of India, Brahma, Vishnoo and Siva? Let the reader look at the plate representing this vessel, and consult the 'Asiatic Researches,' by Sir William Jones; let him also read Buchanan's 'Star in the East,' and the accounts there found of the idolatry of the Hindoos; and, unless his mind is formed differently from mine, he will see in this idol, one proof at least, that the people who raised our ancient works, were idolators; and, that some of them worshipped gods resembling the three principal deities of India. What tends to strengthen this inference, is, that nine murex shells, the same as described by Sir William Jones in 'Asiatic Researches,' and by Symmes in his 'Embassy to Ava,' have been found within twenty miles of Lexington, Kentucky, in an ancient work ... These shells, so rare in India, are highly esteemed and consecrated to their god Mahadeva, whose character is the same with the Neptune of Greece and Rome" (Atwater 1820:238-241).

24. Humboldt's work marked the dawn of a new epoch, providing the first opportunity most Europeans and Euro-Americans had ever had to see specimens of Mayan hieroglyphic writing (although they did not then recognize it as "Mayan") and alerting readers to the presence of great civilizations that had

once flourished in the Americas. "I have collected," Humboldt wrote in his introduction, "whatever relates to the origin and first progress of the arts among the natives of America" (1814, 1:1).

25. In Macpherson's *Temora*, the King of Inis-huna is listed as *Conmor*, "Mild and Tall" (Macpherson 1763:69). Accordingly, Rafinesque grafted a Lenape equivalent of this name into the Walam Olum: *Gunitakan*, translated "Long and mild." Well versed in Macpherson's epic, Rafinesque understood that if he was going to use the same Celtic name that appeared in *Temora*, he would have to render it in a Lenape manner, in accord with his sources. There is simply no reason why this word—entirely ungrammatical and inappropriate—would appear in the Walam Olum other than to mimic Macpherson.

26. Rafinesque created the name *Wallam-olum*, "Painted Record," by truncating *Wallam-* (which he claimed meant "painted") from *WALLAMåning*, "place of red PAINT," and *Olum-* from *OLUMapies*, "we [sic, read 'well'] tied, well bundled up" (Heckewelder 1834:365, 384). Rafinesque twisted the meaning of *Olum-* (in reality a meaningless truncation) to signify a bundle of written sticks or "records" and drew further associations with the Irish *Ollamh* or "bards" who kept the ancient records (1836a, 1:150–151). *Olum*, therefore, was a universal "primitive root" as integral to the Delaware language as to the Celtic.

Rafinesque's rendering of *Olum* as a "bundle" of writings or records was also based upon what he had read concerning the earliest type of writing in China, which was inscribed upon bamboo slips and tied together in bundles. That Amerindians also drew pictographs on pieces of wood or bark convinced Rafinesque that the custom of keeping bundles of record sticks was a universal one and reflected a common origin. Rafinesque's etymology also seems to have been based upon the French word *olim*, "ancient statute-book."

27. Those who have depicted Rafinesque as making original and correct observations regarding the nature of the Mayan hieroglyphs are apparently unaware of the extent to which he recycled those same observations from his source books. For the evidence, see Oestreicher (1995a:103–115, 136–138, 227–229).

28. The second letter to Champollion was also published in the *Atlantic Journal* (Rafinesque 1832–1833:40–44), and a third was scheduled to appear in a subsequent issue, but according to Rafinesque's own account: "While this [the second] letter is going to press, we hear of the death of the learned Champollion, a great loss to sciences and erudition. The three letters directed to him were written in January, February and March of this year [1832], while his career was yet unimpaired; but they were as much intended for the learned all over the world, as for himself, and therefore were printed instead of being sent. The third which is to appear in the next number, will however be inscribed to Klaproth as a substitute" (44). The publication of the third letter, however, was "postponed" by Rafinesque and never appeared in print (195).

29. This paper is dedicated to my esteemed teacher and friend, Professor

Robin Fox of Rutgers University, who helped make my study of the *Walam Olum* possible. I am indebted to Paul J. Oestreicher for his invaluable editorial assistance with this paper. My sincere thanks to David L. Browman for his careful editing and patience, and to Stephen Williams for his suggestions and help.

Chapter 4

1. Squier was elected to membership in the Societe des Antiquaries de France in ca. 1851, the Geographical Society of Paris in 1852 and 1856, the Anthropological Society of London in 1865, the Société d'Anthropologie de Paris in 1868, and the Berlin Anthropological Society in 1872. His membership certificates in European learned societies are in the Ephraim George Squier Papers, New York Historical Society.

2. Davis to John Davis, Chillicothe, February 22, 1847, Squier-Davis Papers, American Antiquarian Society, Worcester, Massachusetts.

3. Sources for this and the following two paragraphs are the following: Gliddon to Squier, Pittsburgh, March 15, and Cincinnati, April 23, 1847, Ephraim George Squier Papers, Library of Congress, Washington, D.C.; Allibone 1900:678; Burke 1848:170-174; and Gliddon 1847a, 1847b. Ephraim George Squier Papers, Library of Congress, Washington, D.C.

4. Davis to Squier, Chillicothe, June 12, 1847, Ephraim George Squier Papers, Library of Congress, Washington, D.C.)

5. Gliddon later became an agent in Squier's ill-fated Honduras Railway scheme, and he died in Panama on November 16, 1857, while working in that capacity. He was perhaps Squier's closest friend. Regrettably for scholars of Squier's career, the whereabouts of Gliddon's personal papers are unknown. If extant, the Squier letters within them would likely shed new light on Squier's closeted views on separate origins.

6. Humboldt appears to have been no less impressed with Squier's researches than Jomard and other European savants. "With Dr. Morton's Crania Americana," he is reported as saying, "the work of Mr. Squier constitutes the most valuable contribution ever made to the archaeology and ethnology of America" (quoted in Seitz 1911:12). Squier later acquired several volumes from Humboldt's library (Sabin 1876:254-260).

7. Bartlett to Squier, New York, November 13, 1846, Ephraim George Squier Papers, Library of Congress, Washington, D.C.

8. Gliddon to Squier, Philadelphia, September 21, 1847, Ephraim George Squier Papers, Library of Congress, Washington, D.C.

9. Gliddon to Squier, Charleston, November 21, 1847, Ephraim George Squier Papers, Library of Congress, Washington, D.C.

10. Gliddon to Squier, Charleston, November 21, 1847, Ephraim George Squier Papers, Library of Congress, Washington, D.C.

11. Gliddon to Squier, Bayswater, England, October 20, 1848, Ephraim George Squier Papers, Library of Congress, Washington, D.C.

12. Davis to Bartlett, Chillicothe, October 28, 1846, John Russell Bartlett Papers, John Carter Brown Library, Brown University, Providence, Rhode Island.

13. Squier to "My Dear Sir:—" [Joseph Henry], letter draft, New York, December 6, 1847, Ephraim George Squier Papers, Library of Congress, Washington, D.C. Internal evidence shows Henry to have been the intended recipient of this letter. Because this is a draft, it is possible that Squier never sent the letter, but even so it clearly indicates the direction in which his investigations were heading.

14. Henry to Squier and Davis, Washington, D.C., February 16, 1848, Ephraim George Squier Papers, Library of Congress, Washington, D.C.

15. Squier to Henry, New York, February 21, 1848, Ephraim George Squier Papers, Library of Congress, Washington, D.C.

16. Squier to Samuel George Morton, New York, September 27, 1848, Ephraim George Squier Papers, Historical Society of Pennsylvania, Philadelphia.

17. Squier to Morton, New York, December 28, 1848, Ephraim George Squier Papers, Historical Society of Pennsylvania, Philadelphia.

18. Squier 1851b. The manuscript was accepted for publication by the Smithsonian on October 20, 1849, after being reviewed by Brantz Mayer and William W. Turner of the American Ethnological Society, but did not appear in print until 1851. The year 1849 is often incorrectly cited as the date of publication. Henry also allowed Squier to republish the work with the original engravings and plates as Squier 1851c.

19. Squier announced that four additional titles in the American Archaeological Research series were either prepared or in advanced stages of completion: *The Archaeology and Ethnology of Central America, The Mexican Calendar, The Mythological System of the Ancient Mexicans,* and *The Semi-Civilized Nations of New Mexico.* He never completed those works, but he did place several articles dealing with those subjects.

20. Squier to Morton, New York, February 12, 1851, Ephraim George Squier Papers, Historical Society of Pennsylvania, Philadelphia.

21. Squier to Samuel George Morton, Providence, Rhode Island, May 4, 1851, Ephraim George Squier Papers, Historical Society of Pennsylvania, Philadelphia.

22. Squier to Samuel George Morton, New York, September 1848, Ephraim George Squier Papers, Historical Society of Pennsylvania, Philadelphia.

23. The following account is based on Squier's "Report" in the *Journal of the Anthropological Society of New-York* (1872: 16–17, 20).

24. Only fifty copies of the third volume survived the fire that destroyed the office of the Society's printer in the autumn of 1851 (American Ethnological Society. Printed Announcement, 1860. Ephraim George Squier Papers, Li-

brary of Congress, Washington, D.C.). The volume was not republished until 1909 (Boas 1943:7).

Chapter 5

1. Rau to Joseph Henry, August 10, 1865. Charles Rau papers. Smithsonian Institution, National Anthropological Archives, Washington, D.C.
2. Rau to Joseph Henry, October 26, 1863. Charles Rau papers. Smithsonian Institution, National Anthropological Archives, Washington, D.C.
3. Rau to Joseph Henry, November 5, 1863. Charles Rau papers. Smithsonian Institution, National Anthropological Archives, Washington, D.C.
4. Rau to Joseph Henry, November 29, 1867. Charles Rau papers. Smithsonian Institution, National Anthropological Archives, Washington, D.C.
5. Rau to Joseph Henry, October 26, 1863. Charles Rau papers. Smithsonian Institution, National Anthropological Archives, Washington, D.C.
6. Rau to Joseph Henry, December 27, 1867. Charles Rau papers. Smithsonian Institution, National Anthropological Archives, Washington, D.C.
7. Rau to Joseph Henry, April 10, 1868. Charles Rau papers. Smithsonian Institution, National Anthropological Archives, Washington, D.C.
8. Henry to Rau, April 11, 1868. Smithsonian Institution, Charles Rau papers, Record Unit 7070, Box 1. Washington, D.C.
9. Henry to Rau, June 6, 1868. Smithsonian Institution, Charels Rau papers, record Unit 7070, Box 1. Washington, D.C.
10. Henry to Rau, June 6, 1868. Smithsonian Institution, Charels Rau papers, record Unit 7070, Box 1. Washington, D.C.
11. Henry to Rau, November 29, 1867, and December 27, 1867. Smithsonian Institution, Charles Rau papers, Record Unit 7070, Box 1. Washington, D.C.
12. As noted by Bourque in Chapter 7, Rau also conducted additional shell midden excavations in 1864.
13. Spencer F. Baird to Rau, April 23, 1868, and Henry to Rau, May 10, 1875. Smithsonian Institution, Charles Rau papers, Record Unit 7070, Box 1. Washington, D.C.
14. Spencer F. Baird to Rau, April 23, 1868, and Henry to Rau, May 10, 1875. Smithsonian Institution, Charles Rau papers, Record Unit 7070, Box 1. Washington, D.C.

Chapter 6

1. Chambers stated, "It has pleased Providence to arrange that one species should give birth to another, until the second highest gave birth to man" (1844:234); "variations of a fundamental plan, . . . the variations being merely modifications of that plan to suit the particular conditions in which each particular animal has been designed to live" (1844:192).

2. In a letter to Lyell dated December 13, 1865, Wilson remarks: "Agassiz has a grand ethnological scheme in view—too colossal I fear to be carried out in full—but which I hope will receive some help from his present explorations. The last time I was in Boston, he took me down to a subterranean region, and opening a series of large jars he produced out of alcohol with which they were filled, the heads of Chinese, Indians, &c., thus preserved with the flesh, hair, & perfect as in life. He contemplates being able ultimately to secure a series of illustrations of leading types of man, preserving not merely the head, but the whole body. But he complained that even the New England mind was not yet sufficiently advanced to admit of his giving publicity to his scheme" (MS Lyell I, Edinburgh University Library).

3. These incorporated papers are found in the 1876 edition of *Prehistoric Man:* shells, 1:129–130; Lake Superior mining, 1:199–235; Norse, 2:82–99; sculptured boulders and cup-markings, 1:89–94; crania, 2:112–236.

Chapter 7

1. Putnam's diary, Box 1.12, Putnam Papers 999-24, Peabody Museum Archives, Harvard University. Transcribed by Eben Putnam.

Chapter 8

1. Warren Upham papers, Minnesota Historical Society Research Center, St. Paul, Minnesota.

2. Letters from Frances Babbitt to Frederic W. Putnam. Lot of 1881. Accession file 83-66, Collections Department, Peabody Museum, Harvard University.

3. Information on Frances Babbitt's teaching career can be found in the Annual Report of the Principal or Superintendent, Morrison County School District 1880–1883; Superintendent's List of Teachers, Morrison County, 1883; and Teacher's Term Reports—Morrison County School District, 1883–1884, in the Minnesota Historical Society Library Archives, St. Paul, Minnesota.

4. Letters from Frances Babbitt to Frederic W. Putnam. Lot of 1881. Accession file 83-66, Collections Department, Peabody Museum, Harvard University.

Chapter 9

1. "Paleolithic" with an uppercase "P" is used in reference to the Old World culture. "Paleolithic" with a lowercase "p" is used in reference to putative, but since dismissed, New World situations.

2. Charles C. Abbott to Frederic W. Putnam, April 26, 1860. Putnam Papers 999-24, Box 1.12, Peabody Museum Archives, Harvard University.

3. Gabriel de Mortillet to Jeffries Wyman, July 1, 1868, de Mortillet Papers, Peabody Museum Archives, Harvard University.

Chapter 10

1. Extract from a letter from Frederic W. Putnam, February 14, 1860, Box 1.7, Putnam Papers 999-24, Peabody Museum Archives, Harvard University.

2. See also Outgoing Putnam Correspondence, 1858-1876, n.d., Box 1.7, Putnam Papers 999-24, Peabody Museum Archives, Harvard University.

3. Extract from a letter from Frederic W. Putnam, October 21, 1859, Box 1.7, Putnam Papers 999-24, Peabody Museum Archives, Harvard University.

4. "Paleolithic" with an uppercase "P" is used in reference to the Old World culture. "Paleolithic" with a lowercase "p" is used in reference to putative, but since dismissed, New World situations.

5. [Eben Putnam's] transcription of Putnam diary, January 19, 1882, Box 1.12, Putnam Papers 999-24, Peabody Museum Archives, Harvard University.

6. List of Officers, Section H, Proceedings of the AAAS 46:391, 1897.

7. Alice Putnam letters to Frederic W. Putnam, 1895-1905 (4 items), Box 1.2, Putnam Papers 999-24, Peabody Museum Archives, Harvard University.

8. Life Members list in the Proceedings of the Davenport Academy of Natural Sciences 3:64, 1881, and 10:277, 1907.

Chapter 11

1. Peabody Museum Collections Department, Harvard University, de Mortillet accession file 68-13: Anth 4 Notes, October–November 1902.

2. The trajectory of Nickerson's movements, and the correspondence and the comments extracted from this correspondence, referred to here and elsewhere in this chapter, are extracted from the following archival sources:

(a) Peabody Museum Collections Department, Harvard University, Nickerson Correspondence accession files 00-26A-B, 1895-1901, Correspondence of William B. Nickerson to Frederic W. Putnam, 18 letters: July 31, 1894; September 14, September 16, October 29, 1895; May 6, July 14, 1896; July 23, September 6, October 15, 1897; February 22, August 29, September 19, 1898; February 10, 1899; January 8, April 17, June 3, November 18, 1900; March 2, 1901.

(b) Pusey Library, Harvard University Archives, UAV 677.38, Correspondence of William B. Nickerson to Frederic W. Putnam: Accession 85-30—Record 298, July 14, 1884; Record 323, March 9, 1885; Record 328, March 28, 1885; Record 324, April 25, 1885; Record 325, April 30, 1885; Record 326-327, May 18, 1885; Record 322, July 18, 1885; Accession 87-22—Record 460, September 8, 1887; Record 461, November 15, 1887; Accession 89-19—Record 504, March 19, 1888; Record 505, March 28, 1888; Accession 85-30—Record 575, September 3, 1889; Accession 96-13/42-5/00-26—Record 793, February 25, 1895; Record 794, April 3, 1895; Accession 42-5—Record 795, August 21,

1895; Accession 42-5/00-26—Record 869, February 17,1896; Accession 96-13—Record 870, May 30, 1896; Accession 00-26/42-5—Record 871, November 27, 1896; Accession 42-5—Record 904, January 3, 1897; Record 905, March 15, 1897; Record 906, November 26, 1897; Accession 00-26/42-5—Record 952, May 5, 1899; Record 953, June 2, 1899; Record 954, June 15, 1899; Record 955, July 5, 1899; Record 956, September 4, 1899; Record 963, April 14, 1900; Record 964, June 26, 1900; Accession 85-30/96-13/00-26/42-5—Record 1003, March 20, 1906; Record 1004, April 7, 1906; Accession 00-26—Record 1124, August 4, 1911; August 22, 1911.

(c) Illinois State Museum Library Rare Book Room, William B. Nickerson Records. Archaeology of Jo Daviess County, Illinois, 1895–1901: Explorations of W. B. Nickerson. Report to the Peabody Museum of American Archaeology, Harvard University, 147 pp.; Archaeology of Jo Daviess County, Illinois, 1895–1901: Explorations of W. B. Nickerson. Reporting to the Peabody Museum of American Archaeology, Harvard University—revised copy; Archaeological Field Notes, Portage, Illinois, 1897. Original draft of report rendered Prof. Putnam, covering the exploration of Mound No. 25 at Portage, 1899. Special Exploration at Portage, Mound No. 26, June 29, 1899. Explorations in Illinois and Iowa, 1913–1921, Stenographer's Notebook. Correspondence from Frederic W. Putnam (and from his assistants John C. Kimball, Frances H. Mead, and Jennie Smith, writing for Putnam) to William B. Nickerson: August 25, November 28, 1884; March 17, May 6, May 19, May 23, May 30, October 16, 1885; February 1, March 22, June 2, June 15, 1886; April 18, 1887; September 29, 1888; April 12, May 10, June 12, July 18, 1893; March 16, September 12, 1895; May 25, December 9, 1896. Correspondence from William B. Nickerson to Frederic W. Putnam, January 13, 1897; April 17, 1901. Correspondence from Frederic W. Putnam to Charles R. Van Hise, June 12, 1893. Correspondence from Charles R. Van Hise to William B. Nickerson, June 19, 1893. Correspondence from Charles E. Brown to William B. Nickerson: November 15, November 26, 1912; April 21, May 6, June 27, July 7, October 10, October 23, 1913. Correspondence from William B. Nickerson to Charles E. Brown, May 5, 1908.

3. Illinois State Museum Library Rare Book Room, William B. Nickerson Records. Correspondence from Frederic W. Putnam to William B. Nickerson, June 15, 1886.

4. Pusey Library, Harvard University Archives, UAV 677.38, Correspondence of William B. Nickerson to Frederic W. Putnam: Accession 89-19, Record 505, March 28, 1888.

5. Illinois State Museum Library Rare Book Room, William B. Nickerson Records. Correspondence from Frederic W. Putnam to Charles R. Van Hise, June 12, 1893.

6. Illinois State Museum Library Rare Book Room, William B. Nickerson Records. Correspondence from Frederic W. Putnam (from his assistant Frances H. Mead, writing for Putnam) to William B. Nickerson, April 12, 1893.

7. Pusey Library, Harvard University Archives, UAV 677.38, Correspon-

dence of William B. Nickerson to Frederic W. Putnam. Accession 96-13/42-5/00-26—Record 794, April 3, 1895.

8. Peabody Museum Collections Department, Harvard University, Nickerson Correspondence accession files 00-26A-B, 1895-1901, Correspondence of William B. Nickerson to Frederic W. Putnam, October 29, 1895.

9. Illinois State Museum Library Rare Book Room, William B. Nickerson Records. Illinois Archaeology, University of Chicago Field Expedition Notes with cross references to card index, maps and photos, also alphabetical numerical key to all photos, Summer 1926 (June 26 to August 28), Paul S. Martin and John F. Blackburn; and Journal of Mound Exploration in vicinity of Galena, Illinois, in September 1926 (August 31 to September 20, 1926), Paul S. Martin, John F. Blackburn, Wilton Krogman, and Robert Redfield.

10. Twenty-nine years is inaccurate. Subtracting 29 from 1926, the date of these fieldnotes, does not bring one to the date of either manuscript, 1899 or 1913.

Chapter 12

1. A question left unanswered by my research is whether MacCurdy's acquaintance with Charles Peabody, who became one of his closest friends and professional colleagues, dates from the Harvard years. Peabody, who had received his A.M. from Harvard in 1890, was working on his Ph.D. in "Philology" (awarded in 1893) while MacCurdy was an undergraduate. Peabody's degree probably had to do with the archaeology of classical and other Old World cultures, and he went on to serve as Instructor in European archaeology at Harvard from 1906 to 1908 (Williams 1998). It seems probable that MacCurdy met Peabody at Harvard, but the first mention in the autobiography (MacCurdy 1946:107) is for September 1906. By that time, MacCurdy was teaching at Yale and Peabody was about to begin teaching at Harvard. During the return trip to New Haven from an International Congress of Americanists meeting in Québec, MacCurdy visited Peabody at the latter's mother's summer home in the Adirondacks.

2. As recounted by Browman (see chapter 9 of this volume), Albert Gaudry and the French human paleontologist Marcellin Boule visited the Trenton gravels in New Jersey in 1891 to assess the claims of great antiquity made for a series of lithics found there. These French experts (who apparently drew the wrong conclusions!) were accompanied by the American prehistorian, Henry Chapman Mercer. Shortly thereafter, in 1892 and 1893, Mercer spent some time with Gaudry and Boule in France; according to Browman, it was probably from them that Mercer learned about techniques of stratigraphic excavation.

3. MacCurdy's interest in these codices, of which only facsimiles existed in Berlin, was sufficiently strong that, during a between-semesters visit to Rome in the spring of 1898, he sought, unsuccessfully, to obtain a permit to use the Vatican Library so that he could see some of the originals. He gives an

amusing account in his autobiography (1946:78–79) of how he sweet-talked his way into the library anyway and managed to examine the original Codex Vaticanus.

4. The only other nongovernmental organization of major scope at that time was the Anthropological Society of Washington, which had been founded in 1879 within the intellectual orbit of John Wesley Powell and the U.S. Bureau of Ethnology (Mitra 1933:203–204). This society started publication of the *American Anthropologist* (o.s.).

5. According to MacCurdy (1946:97A), the other Section H members who were founders of the American Anthropological Association were F. Baker, C. P. Barrows, Charles P. Bowditch, A. F. Chamberlain, Alice C. Fletcher, A. S. Gatchett [Albert S. Gatschet?], J. N. B. Hewitt, F. W. Hodge, William H. Holmes, W. Hough, Aleš Hrdlička, A. E. Jenks, Alfred L. Kroeber, B. Laufer, Otis T. Mason, W. Mathews, M. L. Miller, James R. Mooney, Clarence B. Moore, E. S. Morse, W. W. Newell, C. L. Owen, John Wesley Powell, Frederick W. Putnam, Marshall H. Saville, H. I. Smith, John R. Swanton, Cyrus Thomas, and E. S. Wood.

6. When, in the summer of 1927, a Folsom point was found in situ, still embedded in its matrix, and in tight association with the bones of an extinct form of bison, "immediately, all work was stopped, and telegrams were sent to leading institutions requesting that they send representatives to examine the new find" (Wormington 1957:25). (This cautious action was taken because other projectile points found at Folsom earlier in 1927 and in 1926 had not been accepted as in true association with the bison bones.) I do not know if one of those telegrams went to Yale, but if it did, MacCurdy was not available to examine Folsom as he had examined Vero. In the summer of 1927 he was directing the seventh session of his summer field school in France. The experts who "certified" Folsom were Barnum Brown, Frank H. H. Roberts, Jr., and A. V. Kidder (Wormington 1957:25).

7. It is to be regretted that MacCurdy's account (1946:131) of the discoveries at La Ferrassie in 1912 does not include exact dates. Even without them, however, it does provide some information about the committee of experts that is not given in published accounts. As I have summarized elsewhere (Bricker 1989), the excavation of the two suspected grave pits was delayed, after their initial discovery, until a group of experts could be gathered to observe the stratigraphic circumstances as the excavation was being done and provide formal testimony about the significance of the finds. According to Peyrony (1939:237), the scientific leaders of the field were invited to come to La Ferrassie, and six responded to the call—Pierre Paris, G. A. Blanc, Henri Begouën, Jean Bouyssonie, Henri Breuil, and Hugo Obermaier. What MacCurdy's cursory remarks do is to explain how five of these six (all but Pierre Paris) came to be in Dordogne at the relevant time. MacCurdy's story is that Count Henri Begouën had arrived from his home in Ariège a day or so before the discovery for the explicit purpose of seeing for the first time some of the classic Palaeolithic sites of the

Dordogne (a statement of Peyrony [1939:237] supports the notion that this was Begouën's first professional visit to the Les Eyzies area). Henri Breuil had come down from Paris, again before the discovery at La Ferrassie, in order to serve as Count Begouën's guide to the local sites. On the morning of the discovery, Breuil and Begouën were off on their tour, but, having gotten the word somehow, they showed up at La Ferrassie before the end of work that day. Jean Bouyssonie arrived from Brive that same afternoon. Hugo Obermaier, directing the Institut de Paléontologie Humaine excavation at El Castillo in Cantabria, had been summoned, presumably by telegram, but it took him until the evening of the following day to get to Les Eyzies from Puente Viesgo. Because of the need to wait for Obermaier before continuing at La Ferrassie, the experts who had arrived first were at loose ends on the day following the discovery. Breuil and Begouën continued their site tours, including a visit to MacCurdy at his Grotte de la Combe excavations. When Obermaier arrived in Les Eyzies, he was accompanied by Baron G. A. Blanc, an Italian prehistorian, who had a week or so earlier taken MacCurdy's place as guest excavator at El Castillo. It was, I think, on the morning of the next day that the work of exhuming the Neanderthal skeletons began under the watchful eyes of the experts. The official statement signed by the experts and the two excavators (Peyrony 1939: 237–238) says that the witnessing was done on August 8, 1912. If the other events happened just as quickly as possible, the initial discovery of the burials at La Ferrassie (the day MacCurdy was excavating there) would have been August 6, 1912. MacCurdy played no part in these events beyond his presence at the site on the day of the initial discovery, and his autobiography makes no mention of the fact that all these important visitors functioned as a validating committee for the Neanderthal burials. He must have been fully preoccupied with the problems of emptying the Grotte de la Combe as quickly as possible!

8. If MacCurdy heard Breuil give the oral version of his classic paper on the subdivisions of the Upper Palaeolithic (Breuil 1912), which codified the victory of Cartailhac and Breuil over the school of de Mortillet in the "Aurignacian battle," it seems to have made no impression, because he makes no mention of it in his account of the congress.

9. As he explained to me in an e-mail communication dated December 10, 1998, Michael Tarabulski, while he was a student at Beloit College in 1982, "became a friend of the then 88-year-old Alonzo Pond and collected some of his memories in letters and on tape." This project in oral history culminated in the production of a documentary film (Tarabulski and Teicher 1986) about a Logan Museum expedition to Algeria in 1930, in which Pond had an important role. More information about the photographic documentation and other archival material relevant to Pond is given by White et al. (1992).

10. The Tarabulski interview contains other indications of the modest beginnings of the ASPR summer field school program. According to Alonzo Pond, the availability of the summer scholarship was announced in letters sent to all departments of anthropology in the United States. Pond applied, and af-

ter he had been awarded the scholarship he learned that he had been the only applicant! The scholarship was small, and it did not cover the cost of travel to and from the field site in France. To supplement his meager funds, Pond found himself obliged to work as the "assistant" to a local farmer, a M Boisseau, who was paid three francs an hour to haul away the backdirt in his donkey cart (MacCurdy 1946:151). Thus Pond was both honored student and manual laborer. M Boisseau and the valiant donkey were immortalized photographically (MacCurdy 1922:62, Fig. 1c), but this pose does not include the learned assistant.

11. One of the five sites in France at which the ASPR students excavated briefly in 1937 was the Abri du Roc Saint-Cirq (Saint-Cirq-du-Bugue, Dordogne), a small Magdalenian rockshelter, where they worked under the supervision of its excavators, Homer H. and Lilia Kidder (MacCurdy 1946:230). Homer Kidder, the older brother of A. V. Kidder, had been with R. W. Pumpelly at Anau at the beginning of the century (Williams 1998). Because of the linkage suggested by Williams between the Anau project and the adoption of stratigraphic methods by American archaeologists (A. V. Kidder and others), it is of interest that the work of Homer Kidder at Saint-Cirq was later characterized by Denise de Sonneville-Bordes (1960:392) as "careful excavations" ("des fouilles soigneuses"), in contrast to the "unmethodical excavations" ("des fouilles sans méthode") of the French prehistorian who had dug there earlier. (Mme de Sonneville-Bordes was not, in my experience, given to empty praise of foreign archaeologists.) There was not much left of the Abri du Roc Saint-Cirq by the time the Kidders got to it in 1935, and their excavation records were archived, not published. They had, however, previously established a solid reputation in French Palaeolithic archaeology by the excavation and full publication of the Magdalenian site of Puy de Lacan, near Brive, Corrèze, in 1929 and 1930 (Kidder and Kidder 1932, 1936a, 1936b). Although the publications are concerned primarily with the stone tools and art objects recovered, there are clear indications in both the photos and the text that the stratigraphic method was at work here. For example, speaking of their first season's work in the talus slope in front of the rockshelter, the Kidders described the excavation of the four strata they recognized (1936a:442): "These four beds we excavated systematically in the summer of 1929, one layer at a time, working uphill."

References

Abbott, Charles Conrad
- 1872 The Stone Age in New Jersey. *American Naturalist* 6:144-160, 199-229.
- 1873 Occurrence of Implements in the River Drift at Trenton, New Jersey. *American Naturalist* 7:204-209.
- 1876 The Stone Age of New Jersey. *Smithsonian Institution Report for 1875*, 246-380. Washington, D.C.
- 1892a Palaeolithic Man in North America. *Science* (o.s.) 20(510):270-271.
- 1892b Paleolithic Man: A Last Word. *Science* (o.s.) 20(515):344-345.

Acosta, José de
- 1590 *Historia natural y moral de las Indias.* Seville: Casa Juan de Leon.

Adair, James
- 1775 *The History of the American Indians.* London: Edward and Charles Dilly.

Adams, Thomas R. (editor)
- 1992 *The History of Travels in the West and East Indies by Pietro Martire d'Anghiera, et al., 1557.* Delmar, N.Y.: Scholars' Facsimiles and Reprints.

Agassiz, George R.
- 1930 The Museum of Comparative Zoology, 1858-1928. In Samuel Eliot Morison, ed., *The Development of Harvard University since the Inauguration of President Eliot, 1869-1929*, 400-412. Cambridge: Harvard University Press.

Aisenberg, Nadya, and Mona Harrington
- 1988 *Women of Academe: Outsiders in the Sacred Grove.* Amherst: University of Massachusetts Press.

Allibone, George Austin (editor)
- 1900 *A Critical Dictionary of English Literature and British and American Authors.* Vol. 1. Philadelphia: Lippincott.

American Council of Learned Societies
  1980 *Concise Dictionary of American Biography.* 3rd ed. New York: Scribner.
Anghiera, Pietro Martire d'
  1912 *De Orbe Novo: The Eight Decades of Peter Martyr d'Anghera.* 2 vols. Trans. and ed. Francis Augustus MacNutt. New York: Putnam.
Anonymous
  1845 Preface. [probably John Russell Bartlett]. *Transactions of the American Ethnological Society* 1:iii-x.
  1848 Preface. [probably John Russell Bartlett]. *Transactions of the American Ethnological Society* 2:iii-viii.
  1853 The St. Clair County Library in Belleville. *Belleville Advocate,* March 30.
  1862 Negeremancipation in Jamaika. *New Yorker Staats-Zeitung,* June 14.
  1883 Notes and News. *Science* (o.s.) 2(38):581.
  1884 Proceedings of the Section of Anthropology. *Science* (o.s.) 5(87):342-346.
  1885 Proceedings of the Section of Anthropology. *Science* (o.s.) 6(136):230-234.
  1886 On Methods of Archaeological Research in America. *Johns Hopkins University Circulars* 5(49):89-92.
  1895a A Woman Archaeologist. *Scientific American* 73(6):83.
  1895b Anthropology in Harvard University. *Science,* n.s., 2(29):72-73.
  1915a Prof. F. W. Putnam Dies in Cambridge. *Boston Sunday Herald,* August 15.
  1915b Prof. Frederic W. Putnam. *Boston Evening Transcript,* August 16.
  1990 Publisher's Preface to the New (1960) Edition. In J. Eric S. Thompson and Francis B. Richardson, eds., *Eduard Seler: Collected Works in Mesoamerican Linguistics and Archaeology* (English translations of German papers from *Gesammelte Abhandlungen zur Amerikanischen Sprach- und Alterthumskunde,* made under the supervision of Charles P. Bowditch), 1:xvii-xviii. Reprint edition. Labyrinthos, Culver City.
Appel, Toby A.
  1992 A Scientific Career in the Age of Character: Jeffries Wyman and Natural History at Harvard. In Clark A. Elliott and Margaret W. Rossiter, eds., *Science at Harvard University: Historical Perspectives,* 96-120. Bethlehem: Lehigh University Press.
Ash, Marinell, and colleagues
  1999 *Thinking with Both Hands: Sir Daniel Wilson in the Old World and New.* Ed. Elizabeth Hulse. Toronto: University of Toronto Press.
Asiatic Researches
  1979- *Asiatic Researches Comprising History and Antiquities: The Arts,*
  1980 *Sciences, and Literature of Asia.* 24 vols. New Delhi: Cosmo Publications (originally published by The Asiatic Society [1788-1835]).

Atwater, Caleb
- 1820 Description of the Antiquities Discovered in the State of Ohio and Other Western States. *Archaeologia Americana: Transactions and Collections of the American Antiquarian Society* 1:105-267.

Babbitt, Frances (Franc) Eliza
- 1881 Red Lake Notes. *Bulletin of the Minnesota Academy of Natural Sciences* 2(3):86-101.
- 1883 Vestiges of Glacial Man in Central Minnesota. *Proceedings of the American Association for the Advancement of Science* 32:385-390.
- 1884a Vestiges of Glacial Man in Minnesota. *American Naturalist* 18(6): 594-605, 18(7):697-708.
- 1884b Indian Implements of the Northwest. *Science* (o.s.) 3(67):589-590.
- 1884c Some Implements of the Minnesota Ojibwa. *Science* (o.s.) 4(97):527-529.
- 1885 Exhibition and Description of Some Palaeolithic Quartz Implements from Central Minnesota. *Proceedings of the American Association for the Advancement of Science* 33:593-599.
- 1886/ Account of the Battle of Pokegama. Reprinted in Newton H. Winchell,
- 1911 ed., *The Aborigines of Minnesota: A Report Based on the Collections of Jacob V. Brower, and on the Field Surveys and Notes of Alfred J. Hill and Theodore H. Lewis*, 736-737. St. Paul: The Pioneer Co.
- 1888 Illustrative Notes Concerning the Minnesota Ojibwas. *Proceedings of the American Association for the Advancement of Science* 36:303-307.
- 1890 Points Concerning the Little Falls Quartzes. *Proceedings of the American Association for the Advancement of Science* 38:333-339.

Bade, William Frederic
- 1934 *A Manual of Excavation in the Near East: Methods of Digging and Recording of the Tell es-Hasbeh Expedition in Palestine.* Berkeley: University of California Press.

Barnhart, Terry A.
- 1983 A Question of Authorship: The Ephraim George Squier-Edwin Hamilton Davis Controversy. *Ohio History* 92:52-71.
- 1986a An American Menagerie: The Cabinet of Squier and Davis. *Timeline* 2(6):2-17.
- 1986b Curious Antiquity? The Grave Creek Controversy Revisited. *West Virginia History* 46(1-4):103-124.
- 1989 Of Mounds and Men: The Early Anthropological Career of Ephraim George Squier. Ph.D dissertation, Department of History, Miami University, Oxford, Ohio.
- 1996 The Iroquois as Mound Builders: Ephraim George Squier and the Archaeology of Western New York. *New York History* 77(2):125-150.
- 1999 Frederick Ward Putnam. In John A. Garrity and Mark C. Carnes, eds., *American National Biography*, 18:4-5. New York: Oxford University Press.

Barrow, John
  1806 *Travels in China, Containing Descriptions, Observations, and Comparisons, Made and Collected in the Course of a Short Residence at the Imperial Palace of Yuen-Min-Yuen, and on a Subsequent Journey through the Country from Pekin to Canton.* 2nd ed. London: T. Cadell and W. Davis.

Bartlett, John Russell
  1868 Report of Hon. John R. Bartlett. *Proceedings of the American Antiquarian Society* 49:51–79.

Barton, Benjamin Smith
  1787 *Observations on Some Parts of Natural History: To Which Is Prefixed an Account of Several Remarkable Vestiges of an Ancient Date, Which Have Been Discovered in Different Parts of North America, Part I.* London: Charles Dilly.
  1798 *New Views of the Origin of the Tribes and Nations of America.* 2nd ed. Philadelphia: John Bioren.

Barton, William Paul Crillon
  1816 A Biographical Sketch Read Pursuant to Appointment before the Philadelphia Medical Society, 16th February 1816, of their Late President Professor Barton. Reprinted in *Portfolio* 1(4):276–282. Philadelphia: n.p.

Bartram, John
  1751/ *Observations on the Inhabitants, Climate, Soils, Rivers, Productions,*
  1798 *Animals and Other Matters Worthy of Notice, by Mr. John Bartram (with a Note on Niagara Falls by Peter Kalm).* London: (a pirated volume).

Bates, Arlo
  1911 Notes. Manuscript on file, Accession No. 19-22, Peabody Museum, Harvard University, Cambridge.

Bates, Oric
  1914 *The Eastern Libyans, an Essay.* London: Macmillan.
  1915 The Name Osiris. *Journal of Egyptian Archaeology* 2:207–208.
  1917a Ancient Egyptian Fishing. *Harvard African Studies* 1:119–271.
  1917b The African Department of the Peabody Museum. *Harvard Graduate Magazine* 25(100):479–485.
  1918 Siwan Pottery. *Harvard African Studies* 2:299–304.
  1927 Excavations at Marsa Matruh. *Harvard African Studies* 8:123–197.

Bates, Oric, and Dows Dunham
  1918 Excavations at Gammai. *Harvard African Studies* 2:1–121.

Bates, Oric, and Earnest A. Hooton
  1918 On the Origin of the Double-Bladed Swords of the West Coast. *Harvard African Studies* 2:187–193.

Bates, Oric, and Herbert E. Winlock
  1912 Archaeological Material from the Maine Littoral. Manuscript at the Peabody Museum, Harvard University, Cambridge.
Beals, Ralph L.
  1957 Father Acosta on the First Peopling of the New World. *American Antiquity* 23(2):182–183.
Beauchamp, William M.
  1892 *The Iroquois Trail, or Foot-prints of the Six Nations, in Customs, Traditions, and History, in Which Are Included David Cusick's Sketches of Ancient History of the Six Nations.* Fayetteville, N.Y.: H. C. Beauchamp.
Belmont, John S., and Stephen Williams
  1965 *The Foundations of American Archaeology.* Mimeographed. Cambridge: Peabody Museum.
Bennett, John W.
  1942 W. B. Nickerson: Pioneer in Scientific Archaeology. *American Antiquity* 8(1):122–124.
  1947 *Archaeological Explorations in Jo Daviess County, Illinois: The Work of William Baker Nickerson (1895–1901) and the University of Chicago (1926–1932).* Chicago: University of Chicago Press.
  1998 *Classic Anthropology: Critical Essays, 1944–1996.* New Brunswick: Transaction Publishers.
Benton, Caroline French
  1913 *Woman's Club Work and Programs.* Boston: L. C. Page.
Bieder, Robert E.
  1986 *Science Encounters the American Indian, 1820–1880: The Early Years of American Ethnology.* Norman: University of Oklahoma Press.
Billington, Ray A.
  1985 *Land of Savagery, Land of Promise: The European Image of the American Frontier in the Nineteenth Century.* Norman: University of Oklahoma Press.
Bishop, Ronald L.
  1991 Anna O. Shepard: A Correspondence Portrait. In Ronald L. Bishop and Frederick W. Lange, eds., *The Ceramic Legacy of Anna O. Shepard,* 42–87. Boulder: University Press of Colorado.
Blair, Hugh
  1760 Preface. In James Macpherson *Fragments of Ancient Poetry, Collected in the Highlands of Scotland, and Translated from the Galic or Erse Language.* Edinburgh: G. Hamilton and J. Balfour.
Blair, Karen J.
  1980 *The Clubwomen as Feminist: True Womanhood Redefined, 1868–1914.* New York: Holmes and Meier.
Boas, Franz
  1943 The American Ethnological Society. *Science* 97(9505):7–8.

Boas, George
- 1948 *Primitivism and Related Ideas in the Middle Ages.* Baltimore: Johns Hopkins University Press.

Boewe, Charles E.
- 1994/ The Other Candidate for the 1835 Volney Prize: Constantine Samuel
- 1988 Rafinesque. In Joan Leopold and Jean Leclant, eds., *The Prix Volney: Its History and Significance for the Development of Linguistic Research.* Dordrecht: Kluwer Academic Publications (1988 preprint of the 1994 publication).

Bohrer, Vorsila L.
- 1979 Bertha Pauline Dutton. In Albert H. Schroeder, ed., *Collected Papers in Honor of Bertha Pauline Dutton,* Papers of the Archaeological Society of New Mexico, 4:1-32. Albuquerque: Archaeological Society of New Mexico.

Bolger, Diane L.
- 1994 Ladies of the Expedition: Harriet Boyd Hawes and Edith Hall at Work in Mediterranean Archaeology. In Cheryl Claassen, ed., *Women in Archaeology,* 41-50. Philadelphia: University of Pennsylvania Press.

Bonta, Marcia Meyers
- 1991 *Women in the Field: America's Pioneering Women Naturalists.* College Station: Texas A&M University Press.

Boule, Marcellin
- 1888 Essai de paléontologie stratigraphique de l'homme. *Revue d'Anthropologie,* 3rd series, 3:129-144, 274-297, 385-411, 647-880.
- 1893 L'homme paleolithique dans Amérique du Nord. *L'Anthropologie* 4:36-39.
- 1894a Exploration de cavernes américaines. *L'Anthropologie* 5:250.
- 1894b Exploration de cavernes américaines. *L'Anthropologie* 5:636.
- 1896 Exploration de cavernes américaines. *L'Anthropologie* 7:499.
- 1900 Review: Henry C. Mercer. The Bone Caves at Port Kennedy, 1894-1896. *L'Anthropologie* 11:752-754.
- 1905 L'origine des éolithes. *L'Anthropologie* 16:257-267.
- 1925 The Anthropological Work of Prince Albert I of Monaco, and the Recent Progress of Human Paleontology in France. (Translated from the French, the 1922 Huxley lecture, *Man* 52:151-162, 1922). *Annual Report of the Smithsonian Institution for 1923,* 485-507.

Boule, Marcellin, and Henri V. Vallois
- 1957/ *Fossil Men: A Textbook of Human Palaeontology.* Trans. Michael Bul-
- 1921 lock for the revised 4th edition. London: Thames and Hudson (Original: M. Boule, 1921. *Les Hommes Fossiles: Éléments de Paléontologie.* Paris: Masson).

Bourque, Bruce J.
- 1992 *Prehistory of the Central Maine Coast.* New York: Garland.

1995   *Diversity and Complexity in Prehistoric Maritime Societies: A Gulf of Maine Perspective.* New York: Plenum Press.

Boyd, Julian P.
1955   *The Papers of Thomas Jefferson, Vol. 12: 7 August 1787–31 March 1788.* Princeton: Princeton University Press.

Bozeman, Theodore D.
1977   *Protestants in an Age of Science: The Baconian Ideal and Ante-Bellum American Religious Thought.* Chapel Hill: University of North Carolina Press.

Brerewood, Edward
1674   *Enquiries Touching the Diversity of Languages and Religions, through the Chief Parts of the World.* 2nd ed. London: Samuel Mearne, John Martyn, and Henry Herringman. (First edition 1614)

Breuil, Abbé Henri
1912   Les subdivisions du Paléolithique supérieur et leur signification. *Congrès International d'Anthropologie et d'Archéologie Préhistorique, Compte Rendu de la XIVe Session, Genève, 1912,* 165–238.
1952   *Four Hundred Centuries of Cave Art.* Trans. Mary E. Boyle. Montignac: Centre d'Etudes et de Documentation Préhistoriques.

Brew, John Otis
1966a *Early Days of the Peabody Museum at Harvard University.* Cambridge: Museum Centennial, Peabody Museum of Harvard University.
1966b *People and Projects of the Peabody Museum, 1866–1966.* Cambridge: Museum Centennial, Peabody Museum of Harvard University.

Bricker, Harvey M.
1989   Comment on: Grave Shortcomings—The Evidence for Neanderthal Burial, by Robert H. Gargett. *Current Anthropology* 30:177–178.

Brinton, Daniel G.
1867   Artificial Shell Deposits of the United States. *Annual Report of the Board of Regents of the Smithsonian Institution for the Year 1866,* 356–358. Washington, D.C.: Government Printing Office.
1885   *The Lenape and Their Legends; With the Complete Text and Symbols of the Walam Olum, a New Translation, and an Inquiry into Its Authenticity.* Brinton's Library of Aboriginal American Literature, No. 5. Philadelphia: Daniel G. Brinton.
1887   A Review of the Data for the Study of Prehistoric Chronology of America. *Proceedings of the American Association for the Advancement of Science* 36:283–301.
1894   Review of "Man and the Glacial Period; G. Frederick Wright." *Science* (o.s.) 20(508):249.

Broca, Paul
1872   The Progress of Anthropology in Europe and America. *Journal of the Anthropological Society of New York* 1:22–42.

Brooks, Henry M.
  1893 A Prefatory Note—Memorial of Doctor Henry Wheatland. In *Essex Institute, Henry Wheatland, Born January 11, 1812, Died February 27, 1893; Founder of the Essex Institute 1847-1848; Its Secretary and Treasurer 1848-1868, Its President 1868-1893*, 1-6. Salem: Essex Institute.

Brower, Jacob V. (editor)
  1902 *Kakabikansing: Memoirs of Explorations in the Basin of the Mississippi*, vol. 5. St. Paul: Minnesota Historical Society.

Browman, David L.
  1997 An Appreciation of Claude Warren and Susan Rose's *William Pengelly's Techniques of Archaeological Excavation. Bulletin of the History of Archaeology* 7(2):31-34.

Browman, David L., and Douglas R. Givens
  1996 Stratigraphic Excavation: The First "New Archaeology." *American Anthropologist* 98(1):80-95.

Bruce, Robert V.
  1987 *The Launching of Modern American Science, 1846-1876*. New York: Knopf.

Bruton, Scott A.
  1992 The Rise of the St. Louis Scientific Community, 1869-1913. Senior Honors thesis, Department of History, Washington University, St. Louis.

Bryant, Jacob
  1774- *A New System, or an Analysis of Ancient Mythology: Wherein an At-*
  1776 *tempt Is Made to Divest Tradition of Fable; and to Reduce the Truth to Its Original Purity*. 3 vols. London: T. Payne, P. Elmsly, B. White, and J. Walter.

Buck, Solon J.
  1936 William Thaw. *Dictionary of American Biography*, 18:396-397. New York: Scribner.

Bull, James Moore
  1909 Dr. Adam Hammer, Surgeon and Apostle of Higher Medical Education. *Journal of the Missouri State Medical Association* 6(3):155-177.

Burgaleta, Claudio
  1999 *José de Acosta, S.J. (1540-1600): His Life and Thought*. Chicago: Loyola Press.

Burke, Luke
  1848 Progress of Ethnology in the United States. *Ethnological Journal* 1(4):170-174.

Byers, Douglas S.
  1939 Warren King Moorehead. *American Anthropologist* 41(2):286-294.

Capes, Katherine H.
  1963 *The W. B. Nickerson Survey and Excavations, 1912-15, of the South-*

ern Manitoba Mounds Region. Anthropological Papers, National Museum of Canada, No. 4. Ottawa.

Carballo, Jesus
- 1931 The American School of Prehistoric Research Visits the Cavern of El Pendo. *Bulletin of the American School of Prehistoric Research* 7:24-27.

Carver, Jonathan
- 1778 *Travels through the Interior Parts of North America (1766-1768).* London: J. Walter.

Catherwood, Frederick
- 1844 *Views of Ancient Monuments in Central America, Chiapas, and Yucatan.* London: F. Catherwood.

Chambers, Robert
- 1844 *Vestiges of the Natural History of Creation.* London: J. Churchill.
- 1845 *Explanations: A Sequel to "Vestiges of the Natural History of Creation."* London: J. Churchill.

Champollion, Jean François
- 1827 *Précis du Système Hiéroglyphique des Anciens Égyptiens, ou Recherches sur Les Élémens Premiers de Cette Écriture Sacrée, sur Leurs Diverses Combinaisons, et sur Les Rapports de ce Système avec Les Autres Méthodes Graphiques Égyptiennes. Revue par l'auteur, et augmentée de la Lettre a M. Dacier, relative à l'Alphabet des hiéroglyphes phonétiques employés par les Égyptiens sur leurs monumens de l'époque grecque et de l'èpoque romaine.* 2nd ed. 2 vols. Paris: Chez Treuttel et Würtz Libraires.

Charlevoix, Pierre F. X.
- 1744 *Histoire et description générale de la Nouvelle France, avec le journal historique d'un voyage fait par ordre du roi dans l'Amérique Septentrionnale.* 3 vols. Paris: Rolins fils.

Chauvenet, Beatrice
- 1983 *Hewett and Friends: A Biography of Santa Fe's Vibrant Era.* Santa Fe: Museum of New Mexico Press.

Cheyney, Edward P.
- 1940 *History of the University of Pennsylvania, 1740-1940.* Philadelphia: University of Pennsylvania Press.

Chinas, Beverly Newbold
- 1999 Zelia Maria Magdalena Nuttall. In John A. Garrity and Mark C. Carnes, eds., *American National Biography,* 16:559-560. New York: Oxford University Press.

Claassen, Cheryl
- 1992 Black and White Women at Irene Mound. *Southeastern Archaeology* 12(2):137-147.

Claassen, Cheryl (editor)
- 1994 *Women in Archaeology.* Philadelphia: University of Pennsylvania Press.

Clarke, Adam
- 1825– *The Holy Bible Containing the Old and New Testaments: The Text*
- 1826 *Printed from the Most Correct Copies of the Present Authorized Translation, Including the Marginal Readings and Parallel Texts.* 6 vols. New York: N. Bangs and J. Emory.

Clavigero, Francesco Saverio
- 1780– *Storia antica del Messico, cavata da' migliori storici spagnuoli, e da'*
- 1781 *manoscritti, e dalle pitture antiche degl' Indiani; divisa in dieci libri e corredata di carte geografiche, e di varie figuri, e dissertazioni sulla terra, sugli animali, e sugli abitatori del Messico.* 4 vols. Cesena: G. Biasini.
- 1789 *Storia della California opera postuma del nob. sig. abate D. Francesco Saverio Clavigero.* Venezia: M Fenzo.

Cogan, Frances B.
- 1989 *All-American Girl: The Ideal of Real Womanhood in Mid-Nineteenth-Century America.* Athens: University of Georgia Press.

Cole, Fay-Cooper
- 1915a A Study of Tinguian Folk-lore. Ph.D. dissertation, Anthropology, Columbia University.
- 1915b Traditions of the Tinguian: A Study in Philippine Folklore. *Field Museum of Natural History, Fieldiana: Anthropology* (o.s.) 14(1).
- 1927 The 1926 Season. *American Anthropologist* 29(2):314–315.
- 1928 The 1927 Season. *American Anthropologist* 30(3):505–506.
- 1929a The 1928 Season. *American Anthropologist* 31(2):344–345.
- 1929b Recent Trends in Anthropology. *Proceedings of the American Philosophy Society* 69:385–390.
- 1931 The 1930 Field Season. *American Anthropologist* 33(3):468.
- 1932 The 1931 (6th) Field Season. *American Anthropologist* 34(3):489–490.
- 1933a The 1932 (7th) Field Season. *American Anthropologist* 35(3):493.
- 1933b Field Methods Employed in Mississippi Valley Archaeology, with Special Reference to the Work in Illinois. *Transactions of the Illinois State Academy of Science* 25(4):82.
- 1936 Frederick Starr. *American Anthropologist* 36(2):271.
- 1943 Chronology in the Middle West. *Proceedings of the American Philosophical Society* 86(2):299–302.
- 1952 Eminent Personalities of the Half Century. *American Anthropologist* 54(2):156–167.
- 1956 Archeology and the Scientific Method. *University of Utah, Anthropological Papers* 26:1–9.

Cole, Fay-Cooper, Robert Bell, John Bennett, Joseph Caldwell, Norman Emerson, Richard S. MacNeish, Kenneth Orr, and Roger Willis
- 1951 *Kincaid: A Prehistoric Illinois Metropolis.* Chicago: University of Chicago Press.

Cole, Fay-Cooper, and Thorne Deuel
  1937   *Rediscovering Illinois.* Chicago: University of Chicago Press.
Comber, Jillian
  1993   The Background and Significance of the Cover Image. In Hillary Du-Cros and Laura-Jane Smith, eds., *Women in Archaeology: A Feminist Critique,* xxi–xxii. Canberra: Australian National University.
Conaway, James
  1995   *The Smithsonian: One Hundred Fifty Years of Adventure, Discovery, and Wonder.* Washington, D.C.: Smithsonian Books.
Conn, Steven
  1998   *Museums and American Intellectual Life, 1876–1925.* Chicago: University of Chicago Press.
Coolidge, Archibald C.
  1918   Oric Bates. *Harvard African Studies* 2:vii–viii.
Coolidge, John Templeman
  1930   Henry Chapman Mercer. *Harvard College, 50th Report, Class of 1879, June 1930:* 444–446.
Cope, Edward D.
  1876   Contributions to the Archaeology of New Mexico. *Proceedings of the American Association for the Advancement of Science* 24:332.
  1879   Report on the Remains of Populations Observed in Northwestern New Mexico. In Frederic W. Putnam, ed., *Report upon United States Geographical Surveys West of the One Hundredth Meridian in Charge of First Lieut. Geo. M. Wheeler, Vol. 7. Archaeology,* 351–361. Washington, D.C.: U.S. Army, Engineer Department.
  1895   The Antiquity of Man in North America. *American Naturalist* 29(342):593–599.
Cordell, Linda S.
  1993   Women Archaeologists in the Southwest. In Nancy J. Parezo, ed., *Hidden Scholars: Women Anthropologists and the Native American Southwest,* 202–220. Albuquerque: University of New Mexico Press.
Cormack, Lesley B.
  1997   *Charting an Empire: Geography at the English Universities, 1580–1620.* Chicago: University of Chicago Press.
Court de Gébelin, Antoine
  1787–   *Monde Primitif: Analyse et comparé avec le monde moderne, ou ori-*
  1788   *gine du langage.* 9 vols. Paris: Chez Durand.
Coye, Noel
  1997   *La Préhistoire en Parole et en Acte: methodes et enjeux de la pratique archéologique (1830–1950).* Paris: L'Harmattan.
Crane, Agnes
  1894   The Noble Life of Mary Hemenway. *The Leisure Hour* 43:708–710.
Croissant, Jennifer L.
  2000   Narrating Archaeology: A Historiography and Notes toward a Sociol-

ogy of Archaeological Knowledge. In Stephen E. Nash, ed., *It's About Time: A History of Archaeological Dating in North America*, 186-206. Salt Lake City: University of Utah Press.

Croly, Jane Cunningham (aka Jennie June)
1898   *The History of the Woman's Club Movement in America.* New York: Henry G. Allen & Co.

Cushing, Stanley Ellis
1997   *The George Washington Library Collection.* Boston: Boston Athenaeum.

Cuvier, Baron Georges
1815   *Essay on the Theory of the Earth.* Trans. Robert Kerr, with Mineralogical Notes, and an Account of Cuvier's Geological Discoveries, by Professor Robert Jameson. 2nd ed. Edinburgh: William Blackwood.

Dall, William H.
1877a On the Distribution and Nomenclature of the Native Tribes of Alaska and the Adjacent Territory, with a Map. *United States Geological and Geographical Survey, Contributions to North American Ethnology,* 1:7–39. Washington, D.C.: Government Printing Office.
1877b On Succession in the Shell-Heaps of the Aleutian Islands. *United States Geological and Geographical Survey, Contributions to North American Ethnology,* 1:41–91. Washington, D.C.: Government Printing Office.
1877c Remarks on the Origin of the Innuit. *United States Geological and Geographical Survey, Contributions to North American Ethnology,* 1:93–109. Washington, D.C.: Government Printing Office.

Daniel, Glyn
1950   *A Hundred Years of Archaeology.* London: Gerald Duckworth.
1967   *The Origins and Growth of Archaeology.* Harmondsworth: Penguin Books.
1968   One Hundred Years of Old World Prehistory. In J. O. Brew, ed., *One Hundred Years of Anthropology,* 54-93. Cambridge: Harvard University Press.

Darnell, Regna
1969   The Development of American Anthropology, 1879-1920: From the Bureau of American Ethnology to Franz Boas. Ph.D. dissertation, Department of Anthropology, University of Pennsylvania, Philadelphia.
1970   The Emergence of Academic Anthropology at the University of Pennsylvania. *Journal of the History of the Behavioral Sciences* 6(1):80-92.
1988   *Daniel Garrison Brinton: The "Fearless Critic" of Philadelphia.* Philadelphia: University of Pennsylvania Publications in Anthropology, No. 3.
1998   *And Along Came Boas: Continuity and Revolution in Americanist Anthropology.* Philadelphia: John Benjamin Publishing Co.

Darwin, Charles
1861   *On the Origin of Species by Means of Natural Selection, or Preserva-*

tion of Favoured Races in the Struggle for Life. 3rd ed. London: John Murray.

Darwin, Erasmus
1801 *Zoonomia; or, The Laws of Organic Life.* 3rd ed. 4 vols. London: J. Johnson.

D'Ault du Mesnil, Geoffroy
1885 Note sur de nouvelles fouilles faites à Thenay (Loir-et-Cher). *Matériaux pour l'Histoire Primitive et Naturelle de l'Homme* 19:241-249.
1886 Nouvelles fouilles faites à Thenay en Septembre 1884. *Association Française pour l'Avancement des Sciences, Compte Rendu de 14e Session* 2:463-466.
1891 Le fabrication moderne des instruments préhistoriques à Abbeville. *Association Française pour l'Avancement des Sciences, Compte Rendu de 19e Session* 1:224.
1896 Note sur le terrain quaternaire des environs d'Abbeville. *Revue Mensuelle de l'École d'Anthropologie (Paris)* 6:284-296.

D'Ault du Mesnil, Geoffroy, et al.
1885 Discussion sur le gisement de Thenay. *Association Française pour l'Avancement des Sciences, Compte Rendu de 13e Session* 2:370-391.

Davis, William M., and Reginald A. Daly
1930 Geology and Geography, 1858-1929. In Samuel Eliot Morison, ed., *The Development of Harvard University since the inauguration of President Eliot, 1869-1929*, 307-328. Cambridge: Harvard University Press.

Dearing, Mary R.
1971 Anita Newcomb McGee. In Edward T. James, Janet Wilson James, and Paul S. Boyer, eds., *Notable American Women, 1607-1950: A Biographical Dictionary,* 2:464-466. Cambridge: Belknap Press of Harvard University Press.

Dechelette, Joseph
1903 *Manuel d'Archaéologie Préhistorique, Celtique et Gallo-Romaine. Tome 1: Archaéologie Préhistorique.* Paris: Librarie Alphonse Picard et fils.

de Laet, Sigfried J.
1981 Philippe-Charles Schmerling (1791-1836). In Glyn Daniel, ed., *Towards a History of Archaeology,* 112-119. London: Thames and Hudson.

De Laguna, Frederica (editor)
1960 *Selected Papers from the American Anthropologist: 1888-1920.* New York: Row, Peterson.

Del Rio, Antonio, and Pablo Felix Cabrera
1822 *Description of the Ruins of an Ancient City, Discovered near Palenque, in the Kingdom of Guatemala, in Spanish America: Translated from the Original Manuscript Report of Captain Antonio del Rio:*

Followed by Teatro Critico Americano; or, a Critical Investigation and Research into the History of the Americans, by Dr. Paul Felix Cabrera. London: Henry Berthoud, and Suttaby, Evance and Fox.

De Mortillet, Gabriel
- 1883 *Le préhistorique: Antiquité de l'homme.* Paris: C. Reinwald.
- 1891 Chronique préhistorique. *Revue Mensuelle de l'École d'Anthropologie (Paris)* 1:249–253.

De Mortillet, Gabriel, and Adrien De Mortillet
- 1900 *Le Préhistorique: Origine et antiquité de l'homme.* Paris: Schleicher Freres, editeurs.

Desmond, Lawrence G.
- 1989 Of Facts and Hearsay: Bringing Augustus Le Plongeon into Focus. In Andrew L. Christenson, ed., *Tracing Archaeology's Past: The Historiography of Archaeology,* 139–150. Carbondale: Southern Illinois University Press.

Desmond, Lawrence G., and Phyllis M. Messenger
- 1988 *A Dream of Maya: Augustus and Alice Le Plongeon in Nineteenth Century Yucatan.* Albuquerque: University of New Mexico Press.

Dethloff, Henry C.
- 1972 Foreword. In Antoine Simon Le Page du Pratz, *The History of Louisiana, or of the Western Parts of Virginia and Carolina, Containing a Description of the Countries That Lie on Both Sides of the River Mississippi.* Baton Rouge: Claitor's.

Deuel, Thorne
- 1935a The Application of a Classificatory Method to Mississippi Valley Archaeology. Ph.D. dissertation, Anthropology, University of Chicago.
- 1935b Basic Cultures of the Mississippi Valley. *American Anthropologist* 37(3):429–445.

Dexter, Ralph W.
- 1965 The "Salem Secession" of Agassiz Zoologists. *Essex Institute Historical Collections* 101(1):27–39.
- 1966a Frederic Ward Putnam and the Development of Museums of Natural History and Anthropology in the United States. *Curator* 9(2):151–155.
- 1966b Contributions of Frederic Ward Putnam to the Development of Anthropology in California. *Science Education* 50(4):314–318.
- 1966c Putnam's Problems Popularizing Anthropology. *American Scientist* 54(3):315–332.
- 1975 The Role of F. W. Putnam in Developing Anthropology at the American Museum of Natural History. *Curator* 19(4):303–310.
- 1978 Guess Who's Not Coming to Dinner? Frederick Ward Putnam and the Support of Women in Anthropology. *History of Anthropology Newsletter* 5(1):5–6.
- 1980 F. W. Putnam's Role in Developing the Peabody Museum of American Archaeology and Ethnology. *Curator* 23(3):183–193.

1982 The Putnam-Metz Correspondence on Mound Explorations in Ohio. *Ohio Archaeologist* 32(4):24-28.
1985 Contributions of F. W. Putnam (1839-1915) to Archaeoethnobiology. *Journal of Ethnobiology* 5(2):135-141.

Dixon, Roland B.
1930 Anthropology 1866-1929. In Samuel Eliot Morison, ed., *The Development of Harvard University since the Inauguration of President Eliot, 1869-1929*, 202-215. Cambridge: Harvard University Press.
1935 Frederic Ward Putnam. *Dictionary of American Biography*, 15:276-278. New York: Scribner.

Dorsey, George A.
1894 The Study of Anthropology in American Colleges. *Archaeologist* 2(12):368-373.
1896 The History of the Study of Anthropology at Harvard University. *Denison Quarterly* 4(2):77-97.

Driscoll, David B.
1996 Henry Chapman Mercer: Technology, Aesthetics, and Arts and Crafts Ideals. In Bert Denker, ed., *The Substance of Style: Perspectives on the American Arts and Crafts Movement*, 243-262. Winterthur, Del.: Henry Francis du Pont Winterthur Museum.

Drooker, Penelope B.
1997 *The View from Madisonville: Protohistoric Western Fort Ancient Interaction Patterns*. Memoirs of the Museum of Anthropology No. 31, University of Michigan.

du Mesnil du Buisson, Comte Robert
1934 *La Technique des Fouilles Archéologiques: Les Principes Généraux*. Paris: Librairie Orientaliste Paul Geuthner.
1968 Un ancienne famille de Normandie: les du Mesnil du Buisson. *Collections d'Archives Familiales, II*. Paris: Édite par l'auteur.

du Ponceau, Peter Stephen
1827 Translator's Preface and Notes. In David Zeisberger, *Grammar of the Language of the Lenni Lenape or Delaware Indians*. Transactions of the American Philosophical Society, n.s., 3(2):65-250.

du Pratz, Antoine Simon Le Page
1758 *Histoire de la Louisiane*. Paris: Chez de Bure, l'Aine, Delaguette, et Lambert.

Dyck, Ian
1998 Toward a History of Archaeology in the National Museum of Canada: The Contributions of Harlan I. Smith and Douglas Leechman, 1911-1950. In Pamela Jane Smith and Donald Mitchell, eds., *Bringing Back the Past: Historical Perspectives on Canadian Archaeology*, 115-133. Hull: Mercury Series, Archaeological Survey of Canada, Paper 158, Canadian Museum of Civilization.

Dyke, Linda F.
   1996   *Henry Chapman Mercer: An Annotated Chronology.* Rev. ed. Doylestown, Pa.: Bucks County Historical Society.
Eastwood, Alice
   1893   Notes on the Cliff Dwellers. *Zoe* 3(4):375-376.
L'École d'Anthropologie de Paris
   1907   *L'École d'Anthropologie de Paris.* Paris: Felix Alcan.
Eggan, Frederick R.
   1962a   Fay-Cooper Cole, Architect of Anthropology. *Science* 135(3502):412-413.
   1962b   Fay-Cooper Cole, 1881-1961. *American Anthropologist* 65(3):641-648.
Encyclopaedia Britannica
   1929   *Encyclopaedia Britannica.* 14th ed. New York: Encyclopaedia Britannica, Inc.
   1999-   *Encyclopaedia Britannica On-Line* (www.Britannica.com).
   2000
Essex Institute
   1893   *Henry Wheatland, Born January 11, 1812, Died February 27, 1893; Founder of the Essex Institute 1847-1848; Its Secretary and Treasurer 1848-1868, Its President 1868-1893.* Salem: Essex Institute.
Fabre d'Olivet, Antoine
   1815/   *The Hebraic Tongue Restored, and the True Meaning of the Hebrew*
   1921   *Words Re-established and Proved by Their Radical Analysis.* 2 parts. Trans. Nayán Louise Redfield. New York: Putnam.
Fackenthal, Benjamin F., Jr.
   1930   Memorial Remarks at the 50th Anniversary Meeting of the Bucks County Historical Society, Doylestown, May 3, 1930. Unpublished typescript, 7 pp.
Fagette, Paul
   1996   *Digging for Dollars: American Archaeology and the New Deal.* Albuquerque: University of New Mexico Press.
Fenichell, Lois F.
   1985   Harriet Arnot Maxwell Converse. In Alden Whitman, ed., *American Reformers,* 189-190. New York: N. W. Wilson.
Fenton, William N.
   1971   Harriet Arnot Maxwell Converse (1836-1903). In Edward T. James, Janet Wilson James, and Paul S. Boyer, eds., *Notable American Women, 1607-1950: A Biographical Dictionary,* 1:375-377. Cambridge: Belknap Press of Harvard University Press.
Fewkes, J. Walter
   1890   A Contribution to Passamaquoddy Folk-lore. *Journal of American Folk-Lore* 3(11):257-281.
Fewkes, Vladimir J.
   1934   Report on the 1933 Summer Course of the American School of Pre-

historic Research. *Bulletin of the American School of Prehistoric Research* 10:21-27.

1935 Explorations in Yugoslavia and Czechoslovakia: A Report on the 1934 Summer Course of the American School of Prehistoric Research. *Bulletin of the American School of Prehistoric Research* 11:7-30.

1939 Report of the 1938 Summer Course of the American School of Prehistoric Research. *Bulletin of the American School of Prehistoric Research* 15:6-12.

Figgins, Jesse D.
1927 The Antiquity of Man in America. *Natural History* 27:229-239.

Fisher, Raymond H.
1977 *Bering's Voyages: Whither and Why.* Seattle: University of Washington Press.

Fitting, James E. (editor)
1973 *The Development of North American Archaeology: Essays in the History of Regional Traditions.* New York: Anchor Books.

Fitzhugh, William W.
2000 Puffins, Ringed Pins, and Runestones: The Viking Passage to America. In William W. Fitzhugh and Elisabeth I. Ward, eds., *Vikings: The North Atlantic Saga*, 11-25. Washington, D.C.: Smithsonian Institution Press.

Fitzhugh, William W., and Jacqueline S. Olin
1993 *Archeology of the Frobisher Voyages.* Washington, D.C.: Smithsonian Institution Press.

Fitzhugh, William W., and Elisabeth I. Ward (editors)
2000 *Vikings: The North Atlantic Saga.* Washington, D.C.: Smithsonian Institution Press.

Fitzpatrick, T. J.
1982 *Fitzpatrick's Rafinesque: A Sketch of His Life with Bibliography.* Rev. and enlarged by Charles E. Boewe. Weston, Mass.: M & S Press.

Flack, J. Kirkpatrick
1975 *Desideratum in Washington: The Intellectual Community in the Capital City, 1870-1900.* Cambridge: Schenkman.

Fletcher, Alice, and Tilly (Matilda) C. Stevenson
1889 Report of the Committee on the Preservation of Archaeological Remains on the Public Lands. *Proceedings of the American Association for the Advancement of Science* 37:35-37.

Fletcher, Maurine S., ed.
1977 *The Wetherills of the Mesa Verde: Autobiography of Benjamin Alfred Wetherill*, edited and annotated by Maurine S. Fletcher. Cranbury, NJ: Associated University Presses.

Fowler, Rev. James
1872 On Shell-heaps. *Annual Report of the Board of Regents of the Smith-*

sonian Institution for the Year 1870, 389. Washington, D.C.: Government Printing Office.

Fox, Jennifer
1993   The Women Who Opened Doors: Interviewing Southwestern Anthropologists. In Nancy J. Parezo, ed., *Hidden Scholars: Women Anthropologists and the Native American Southwest*, 294-310. Albuquerque: University of New Mexico Press.

Fox, Nancy
1976   Marjorie Ferguson Lambert: A Brief Biography. In Albert H. Schroeder, ed., *Collected Papers in the Honor of Marjorie Ferguson Lambert*, 1-18. Albuquerque: Papers of the Archaeological Society of New Mexico No. 3.

Franklin, Michael J.
1995   *Sir William Jones: Selected Poetical and Prose Works*. Cardiff: University of Wales Press.

Freeman, Allen
1996   The Tileman's Castles. *Preservation* 48(6):60-67.

Frisbie, Theodore R.
1974   A Biography of Florence Hawley Ellis. In Theodore R. Frisbie, ed., *Collected Papers in Honor of Florence Hawley Ellis*, 1-11. Albuquerque: Papers of the Archaeological Society of New Mexico No. 2.

Gallagher, James P., and Constance M. Arzigian
1994   A New Perspective on Late Prehistoric Agricultural Intensification in the Upper Mississippi River Valley. In William Green, ed., *Agricultural Origins and Development in the Midcontinent*, 171-188. Iowa City: University of Iowa Press.

Galvano (Galvão), Antonio
1601/   *The Discoveries of the World, from their first original unto the year of*
1862   *Our Lord 1555, by Antonio Galvano, Governor of Ternate, corrected, quoted, and published in England by Richard Hakluyt (1601), now reprinted with the original Portuguese text (1563), and edited by Vice-Admiral Bethune*. Works of the Hakluyt Society, 1st ser., No. 30. New York: B. Franklin.

Garcia, Gregorio
1607   *Origen de los Indios del Nuevo Mundo, e Indias Occidentales*. Valencia: Casa Pedro Patticio Mey.

Gaudry, Albert
1859   Sur les resultats de fouilles géologiques entreprises aux environs d'Amiens. *Comptes Rendus, Hebdomadaires des Seances de l'Académie des Sciences* 49:465-467.

1895   Le gisement de San Isidro près de Madrid. *L'Anthropologie* 6:615-616.

Gentsch, Robert Louis
1963   The Early History of Belleville, Illinois, to 1850. M.A. thesis, Department of History, Washington University, St. Louis.

Gerrodette, Frank Honore
  1892   Map: Linguistic Stocks of the Indians of Mexico and Central America. Cambridge: Harvard College.

Ghent, William James
  1933   John Ledyard. *Dictionary of American Biography* 11:93–94. New York: Scribner.

Gibbs, George
  1862   Instructions for Archaeological Investigations in the United States. *Annual Report of the Smithsonian Institution for 1861*, 292–296.
  1867/ Instruction for Research Relative to the Ethnology and Philology
  1863   of America. *Smithsonian Miscellaneous Collection* 7(11), no. 160. (Separate published in 1863; volume including it published in 1867.) 60 pp.

Gifford, George E., Jr. (editor)
  1978   *Dear Jeffie: Being the Letters from Jeffries Wyman, First Director of the Peabody Museum, to His Son, Jeffries Wyman, Jr.* Cambridge: Peabody Museum Press.

Glenn, James R.
  1991   William H. (William Healey) Dall. In Christopher Winters, ed., *International Dictionary of Anthropologists*, 138–139. New York: Garland.

Gliddon, George Robins
  1844   *Ancient Egypt: A Series of Chapters on Early Egyptian History, Archaeology, and Other Subjects Connected with Hieroglyphical Literature.* New York: J. Winchester.
  1847a Egypt—Mr. Gliddon. *Scioto Gazette*, February 24, March 3, March 31.
  1847b Lectures on Egyptian History and Antiquities. *Scioto Gazette*, May 5.

Goguet, Antoine-Yves, with Alexandre-Conrad Fugere
  1761   *The Origin of Laws, Arts, and Sciences, and Their Progress among the Most Ancient Nations.* 3 vols. Trans. Robert Henry, Alexander Spearman, and D. Dunn. Edinburgh: Alex. Donaldson and John Reid.

Goldstein, Daniel
  1994   "Yours for Science": The Smithsonian Institution's Correspondents and the Shape of Scientific Community in Nineteenth-Century America. *Isis* 84(4):573–599.

Goodell, Abner C.
  1893   Memorial of Henry Wheatland: Address of Vice-President Goodell. In *Essex Institute, Henry Wheatland, Born January 11, 1812, Died February 27, 1893; Founder of the Essex Institute 1847–1848; Its Secretary and Treasurer 1848–1868, Its President 1868–1893*, 9–17. Salem: Essex Institute.

Gossip, William
  1864   On the Occurrence of the *Kjoekkenmoedding*, on the Shores of Nova

Scotia. *Proceedings and Transactions of the Nova Scotia Institute of Science* 1(2):94-99.

Gradwohl, David M.
 1978 Fred H. Sterns: A Pioneer in the Pursuit of Plains Prehistory. *Nebraska History* 59(2):180-209.

Grayson, Donald K.
 1983 *The Establishment of Human Antiquity.* New York: Academic Press.

Greene, John C.
 1996 *The Death of Adam: Evolution and Its Impact on Western Thought.* Ames: Iowa State University Press.

Griffin, James B.
 1955 Review. *Indiana Magazine of History* 51:59-65.
 1976 A Commentary on Some Archaeological Activities in the Mid-Continent, 1925-1975. *Midcontinental Journal of Archaeology* 1(1):5-38.
 1983 George Irving Quimby: The Formative Years. In R. C. Dunnell and D. M. Grayson, eds., *Lulu Linear Punctated: Essays in Honor of George Irving Quimby,* 7-18. Anthropological Papers No. 72, Museum of Anthropology, University of Michigan.
 1985 The Formation of the Society for American Archaeology. *American Antiquity* 50(2):261-271.

Griffin, James B. (editor)
 1952 *Archeology of Eastern United States.* Chicago: University of Chicago Press.

Grotius, Hugo
 1642 *De origine gentium Americanarum dissertatio.* Paris: s.n.

Gruber, Jacob W.
 1965 Brixham Cave and the Antiquity of Man. In Melford E. Spiro, ed., *Context and Meaning in Cultural Anthropology,* 373-402. New York: Free Press.
 1970 Marcellin Boule. In C. C. Gillispie, ed., *Dictionary of Scientific Biography,* 2:346-347. New York: Scribner.

Guthe, Carl
 1939 The Basic Needs of American Archaeology. *Science* 90(2345):528-530.
 1967 Reflections on the Founding of the Society for American Archaeology. *American Antiquity* 32(4):433-440.

Haag, William G.
 1962 The Bering Strait Land Bridge. *Scientific American* 206(1):112-123.

Hakluyt, Richard
 1582 *Divers Voyages Touching on the Discovery of America.* London: Thomas Woodcocke.
 1589/ *Voyages and Discoveries: The Principal Navigations, Voyages, Traf-*
 1972 *fiques and Discoveries of the English Nation.* Edited version, with introduction by Jack Beeching. Penguin Books: Hammondsworth.

Hale, Horatio
  1893 Sketch of Sir Daniel Wilson. *Popular Science Monthly* 44:256-265.
Hall, Gilbert L.
  1927 Minutes of the First Meeting of Incorporators and Trustees of the American School of Prehistoric Research. *Bulletin of the American School of Prehistoric Research* 2:2-3.
Hallowell, A. Irving
  1960 The Beginnings of Anthropology in America. In Frederica de Laguna, ed., *Selected Papers from the American Anthropologist: 1888-1920*, 1-90. New York: Row, Peterson.
Hardy, Gayle J.
  1993 *American Women Civil Rights Activists: Biobibliographies of Sixty-eight Leaders, 1825-1992.* Jefferson, N.C.: McFarland.
Hare, Peter H.
  1985 *A Woman's Quest for Science: Portrait of Anthropologist Elsie Clews Parsons.* Buffalo: Prometheus Books.
Harlow, Alvin F.
  1933 Henry Chapman Mercer. *Dictionary of American Biography*, 12:539-541. New York: Scribner.
Harrisse, Henry
  1896/
  1968 *John Cabot, the Discoverer of North America, and Sebastian, His Son: A Chapter of the Maritime History of England under the Tudors.* New York: Argosy-Antiquarian Ltd.
Haskins, Charles H.
  1930 The Graduate School of Arts and Sciences. In Samuel Eliot Morison, ed., *The Development of Harvard University since the Inauguration of President Eliot, 1869-1929*, 451-462. Cambridge: Harvard University Press.
Haven, Samuel Foster
  1856 *The Archaeology of the United States, or Sketches, Historical and Bibliographical, of the Progress of Information and Opinion Respecting Vestiges of Antiquity in the United States.* Washington, D.C.: Smithsonian Contributions to Knowledge, Vol. 8, Art. 2.
Haynes, Henry W.
  1881 Their Comparison with Paleolithic Implements from Europe. *Proceedings of the Boston Society of Natural History* 21:132-137.
  1893a Palaeolithic Man in North America. *Science* (o.s.) 21(522):66-67.
  1893b Early Man in Minnesota. *Science* (o.s.) 21(540):318-319.
Heckewelder, John
  1819/
  1876 *History, Manners, and Customs of the Indian Nations Who Once Inhabited Pennsylvania and the Neighboring States. Revised Edition, with an Introduction and Notes by the Rev. William C. Reichel.* Philadelphia: Historical Society of Pennsylvania.
  1820 A Comparative Vocabulary of the Algonkin and Delaware Languages.

In Peter Stephen Du Ponceau's "Indian Vocabularies Collected September 1820," 194–200. Manuscript on file at the American Philosophical Society.
1834 Names Which the Lenni Lenape or Delaware Indians, Who Once Inhabited This Country, Had Given to Rivers, Streams, Places, &c., &c., within the Now States of Pennsylvania, New Jersey, Maryland and Virginia: And Also Names of Chieftains and Distinguished Men of That Nation; with the Significations of Those Names, and Biographical Sketches of Some of Those Men. *Transactions of the American Philosophical Society*, n.s., 4(1):351–396.

Heim, Jean-Louis
1984 Les squelettes moustériens de La Ferrassie. In Henri Delporte, ed., *Le Grand Abri de La Ferrassie: Fouilles 1968–1973*, 249–271. Institut de Paléontologie Humaine, Paris.

Helm, June (editor)
1966 *Pioneers of American Anthropology: The Uses of Biography*. Seattle: University of Washington Press.

Hencken, Hugh
1948 George Grant MacCurdy, 1863–1947. *Bulletin of the American School of Prehistoric Research* 16:v–xxii.

Henry, Joseph
1878 Circular in Reference to American Archaeology. *Smithsonian Miscellaneous Collections* 15(9), no. 316. 15 pp.

Herold, Elaine Bluhm (editor)
1971 The Indian Mounds at Albany, Illinois. *Davenport Museum, Anthropological Papers*, No. 1.

Hinsley, Curtis M., Jr.
1981 *Savages and Scientists: The Smithsonian Institution and the Development of American Anthropology, 1846–1910*. Washington, D.C.: Smithsonian Institution Press.
1985 From Shell-Heaps to Stelae: Early Anthropology at the Peabody Museum. In George W. Stocking, Jr., ed., *Objects and Others: Essays on Museums and Material Culture*, 49–74. History of Anthropology, vol. 3. Madison: University of Wisconsin Press.
1992 The Museum Origins of Harvard Anthropology, 1866–1915. In Clark A. Elliott and Margaret W. Rossiter, eds., *Science at Harvard University: Historical Perspectives*, 121–145. Bethlehem: Lehigh University Press.
1994 *The Smithsonian and the American Indian: Making a Moral Anthropology in Victorian America*. Washington, D.C.: Smithsonian Institution Press.
1999 Frederic Ward Putnam. In Tim Murray, ed., *Encyclopedia of Archaeology. Part I: The Great Archaeologists*, 1:141–174. 2 vols. Santa Barbara: ABC-Clio.

Hodge, Frederick W.
  1903a Mary Louise Duncan Putnam. *American Anthropologist* 5(1):173–174.
  1903b Frank Russell. *American Anthropologist* 5(4):737–738.
Holmes, O. W.
  1930 Jonathan Carver. *Encyclopaedia Britannica* 4:954.
Holmes, William Henry
  1892a On the So-Called Palaeolithic Implements of the Upper Mississippi. *Proceedings of the American Association for the Advancement of Science* 40:280–281.
  1892b Modern Quarry Refuse and the Palaeolithic Theory. *Science* (o.s.) 20(512):295–297.
  1893a Vestiges of Early Man in Minnesota. *American Geologist* 11(4):219–240.
  1893b Gravel Man and Palaeolithic Culture: A Preliminary Word. *Science* (o.s.) 21(520):29–30, 519.
  1893c A Question of Evidence. *Science* (o.s.) 21(527):135–136.
  1916 In Memoriam: Matilda Coxe Stevenson. *American Anthropologist* 18(4):552–559.
Hooton, Earnest A.
  1950 George Grant MacCurdy. *Antiquity* 24:187–188.
Hooton, Earnest A., and Charles C. Willoughby
  1920 Indian Village Site and Cemetery near Madisonville, Ohio. *Papers of the Peabody Museum of American Archaeology and Ethnology* 8(1):1–136.
Horapollo
  1993 *The Hieroglyphics of Horapollo.* Trans. George Boas. Princeton: Princeton University Press.
Horn, Georg
  1652 *De originibus Americanis.* Libri Quatuor. Hagae Comitis: Adriani Viacq.
Hough, Walter
  1923 Alice Cunningham Fletcher. *American Anthropologist* 25(2):254–258.
  1935 Charles Rau. *Dictionary of American Biography,* 15:388–389. New York: Scribner.
Hovenkamp, Herbert
  1978 *Science and Religion in America, 1800–1860.* Philadelphia: University of Pennsylvania Press.
Howells, William White
  1995 *Who's Who in Skulls: Ethnic Identification of Crania from Measurements.* Cambridge: Papers of the Peabody Museum of Archaeology and Ethnology, Vol. 82 (whole volume).
Hrdlička, Aleš
  1923 Studies on Early Man in Europe. Smithsonian Explorations, 1923. *Smithsonian Miscellaneous Collections* 76(10):56–66.

Huddleston, Lee Eldridge
  1967 *Origins of the American Indians: European Concepts, 1492-1729.* Austin: University of Texas Press.

Hughes, Hector J.
  1930 Engineering. In Samuel Eliot Morison, ed., *The Development of Harvard University since the Inauguration of President Eliot, 1869-1929*, 413-442. Cambridge: Harvard University Press.

Humboldt, Alexander Von
  1814 *Researches Concerning the Institutions and Monuments of the Ancient Inhabitants of America with Descriptions and Views of Some of the Most Striking Scenes in the Cordilleras!* Trans. Helen Maria Williams. 2 vols. London: Longman, Hurst, Rees, Orme & Brown, J. Murray & H. Colburn.

Imamura, Keiji
  1996 *Prehistoric Japan: New Perspectives on Insular East Asia.* Honolulu: University of Hawaii Press.

Indiana Historical Society
  1954 *Walam Olum or Red Score—The Migration Legend of the Lenni Lenape or Delaware Indians: A New Translation, Interpreted by Linguistic, Historical, Archaeological, Ethnological, and Physical Anthropological Studies.* Indianapolis: Indiana Historical Society.

Irwin-Williams, Cynthia
  1990 Women in the Field: The Role of Women in Archaeology before 1960. In Gabriele Kass-Simon, Patricia Farnes, and Deborah Nash, eds., *Women in Science: Righting the Record*, 1-41. Bloomington: Indiana University Press.

Iversen, Erik
  1961/ *The Myth of Egypt and Its Hieroglyphs in European Tradition.* Prince-
  1993 ton: Princeton University Press.

James, Edward T., Janet Wilson James, and Paul S. Boyer (editors)
  1971 *Notable American Women, 1607-1950: A Biographical Dictionary.* Vols. 1-3. Cambridge: Belknap Press.

Jayanti, Vimala
  1988 Erminnie Adelle Platt Smith. In Ute Gacs, Asiha Khan, Jerrie McIntyre, and Ruth Weinberg, eds., *Women Anthropologists: A Biographical Dictionary*, 327-330. New York: Greenwood Press.

Jefferson, Thomas
  1784 *Notes on the State of Virginia, Written in the Year 1781, Somewhat Corrected and Enlarged in the Winter of 1782, for the Use of a Foreigner of Distinction, in Answer to Certain Queries Proposed by Him, 1782.* Paris: s.n.

Jennings, Jesse D.
  1962 Fay-Cooper Cole, 1881-1961. *American Antiquity* 27(4):573-575.

1994   *Accidental Archaeologist: Memoirs of Jesse D. Jennings.* Salt Lake City: University of Utah Press.

Johnston, John

1820   Account of the Present State of the Indian Tribes Inhabiting Ohio. *Archaeologia Americana: Transactions and Collections of the American Antiquarian Society* 1:269-299.

Jomard, Edme François

1846   Découvertes récentes sur les bords du Scioto. *Bulletin de la Société de Géographie,* 3rd ser., 6:226-234.

1848a Description d'un Ancien Ouvrage Appele le Serpent Situé sur les Bords de la Riviére Brush Creek, État de l'Ohio (Extrait). *Bulletin de la Société de Géographie,* 3rd ser., 9-10:288-290.

1848b Lettré de M. Georges Jomard . . . Sur les Antiquités Américaines et la Montagne Serpent de Brush-Creek. *Bulletin de la Société de Géographie,* 3rd ser., 9-10:283-88.

1848c Sur Les Antiquités Américaines: Récemment Découvertes (Lettré a M. Squier), Paris, December 29, 1847. *Bulletin de la Société de Géographie,* 3rd ser., 9-10:333-337.

Jones, Charles C., Jr.

1873   *Antiquities of the Southern Indians, Particularly of the Georgia Tribes.* New York: D. Appleton.

Jones, J. M.

1864   Recent Discoveries of Kjökkenmoeddings. *Anthropological Review and Journal of the Anthropological Society of London* 2:223-226.

Jones, Sir William

1788a/ On the Gods of Greece, Italy, and India. Written in 1784, and Since
1979a Revised, by the President. *Asiatic Researches Comprising History and Antiquities, the Arts, Sciences, and Literature of Asia,* 1:188-235. New Delhi: Cosmo Publications.

1788b/ The Third Anniversary Discourse, Delivered 2d February, 1786, by
1979b the President, on the Hindus. *Asiatic Researches Comprising History, The Arts, Sciences, and Literature of Asia,* 1:343-355. New Delhi: Cosmo Publications.

1794a/ The Fifth Anniversary Discourse, Delivered 21st February 1788, by
1979c the President, on the Tartars. *Asiatic Researches Comprising History and Antiquities, The Arts, Sciences, and Literature of Asia,* 2:18-34. New Delhi: Cosmo Publications.

1794b/ Discourse the Ninth Anniversary, on the Origin and Families of Na-
1979d tions, Delivered 23rd February 1792, by the President. *Asiatic Researches Comprising History and Antiquities, The Arts, Sciences, and Literature of Asia,* 3:479-492. New Delhi: Cosmo Publications.

Kalm, Pehr (Peter)

1771   *Travels into North America, Containing Its Natural History, and a Circumstantial Account of Its Plantations and Agriculture in Gen-*

eral, with the Civil, Ecclesiastical and Commercial State of the Country, the Manners of the Inhabitants, and Several Curious and Important Remarks on Various Subjects. Trans. Johann R. Forster. 3 vols. London: W. Ayres.

Kass-Simon, Gabriele, and Patricia Farnes (editors)
 1990 *Women of Science: Righting the Record.* Bloomington: Indiana University Press.

Keegan, William F. (editor)
 1987 *Emergent Horticultural Economies of the Eastern Woodland.* Center for Archaeological Investigations, Occasional Paper No. 7. Carbondale: Southern Illinois University.

Kehoe, Alice B.
 1991 The Invention of Prehistory. *Current Anthropology* 32(4):467–476.
 1998 *The Land of Prehistory: A Critical History of American Archaeology.* New York: Routledge.

Keller, Phyllis
 1971 Mary Porter Tileston Hemenway. In Edward T. James, Janet Wilson James, and Paul S. Boyer, eds., *Notable American Women, 1607–1950: A Biographical Dictionary*, 2:179–181. Cambridge: Belknap Press of Harvard University Press.

Kelley, Harper
 1938 Report of the 1937 Summer Course of the American School of Prehistoric Research. *Bulletin of the American School of Prehistoric Research* 14:6–8.

Kelly, John E.
 1993 The Pulcher Site: An Archaeological and Historical Overview. *Illinois Archaeology* 5:434–451.
 1994 The Archaeology of the East St. Louis Mound Center: Past and Present. *Illinois Archaeology* 6:1–57.

Kennedy, R. V., and Company
 1860 *St. Louis Directory 1860: Including, Also, a Business Mirror, Appendix, Co-partnership Directory, &c., &c.* St. Louis: R. V. Kennedy.

Kennedy, Roger G.
 1994 *Hidden Cities: The Discovery and Loss of Ancient North American Civilizations.* New York: Free Press.

Kidder, Lilia, and Homer H. Kidder
 1932 Fouilles du Puy-de-Lacan (Corrèze). Pierres avec signes et autres objets. *Revue Archéologique*, 5th ser., 35:1–21.
 1936a The Cave of Puy-de-Lacan: A Magdalenian Site in South-Central France. *American Anthropologist* 38:439–451.
 1936b Le Puy-de-Lacan et ses gravures magdaléniennes. *L'Anthropologie* 46:17–31.

Kilgo, Dolores A.
1994   *Likeness and Landscape: Thomas M. Easterly and the Art of the Daguerreotype.* St. Louis: Missouri Historical Society Press.

Killian, Gerald
1998   Toward a Scientific Archaeology: Daniel Wilson, David Boyle, and the Canadian Institute, 1852–96. In Pamela Jane Smith and Donald Mitchell, eds., *Bringing Back the Past: Historical Perspectives on Canadian Archaeology,* 15–24. Hull: Canadian Museum of Civilization, Mercury Series No. 158.

Kingsborough, Viscount Edward King
1830–   *Antiquities of Mexico, comprising facsimiles of ancient Mexican*
1848   *paintings and hieroglyphics, preserved in the Royal Libraries of Paris, Berlin and Dresden, in the Imperial Library of Vienna, in the Vatican Library, in the Borgian Museum at Rome, in the library of the Institute at Bologna, and in the Bodleian Library at Oxford.* 9 volumes. London: A Aglio

Kircher, S.J., Athanasius
1987   *China Illustrata.* Trans. Charles D. Van Tuyl. Muskogee, Okla.: Bacon College.

Klein, Kerwin L.
1997   *Frontiers of Historical Imagination: Narrating the European Conquest of Native America, 1890–1990.* Berkeley: University of California Press.

Kohl, Johann Georg
1911   Asia and America: An Historical Disquisition Concerning the Ideas Which Former Geographers Had about the Geographical Relations and Connections of the Old and New World, 1857. *Proceedings of the American Antiquarian Society* 21:284–338.

Kohlstedt, Sally Gregory
1978   Working in from the Periphery: Women in Nineteenth-Century American Science. *Signs* 4(1):81–96.

Kraft, Herbert C.
1986   *The Lenape: Archaeology, History, and Ethnography.* Newark, N.J.: New Jersey Historical Society.
1993   Dr. Charles Conrad Abbott, New Jersey's Pioneer Archaeologist. *Bulletin of the Archaeological Society of New Jersey* 48:1–12.
1996   Mammoth Frauds in Archaeology. *Bulletin of the Archaeological Society of New Jersey* 51:1–11.

Kroeber, Alfred L.
1952   *The Nature of Culture.* Chicago: University of Chicago Press.

Kuklick, Bruce
1996   *Puritans in Babylon: The Ancient Near East and American Intellectual Life, 1880–1930.* Princeton: Princeton University Press.

Kummel, Henry B.
 1898 The Age of the Artifact-Bearing Sand at Trenton. *Proceedings of the American Association for the Advancement of Science* 46:348–352.

Laet, Joannes (Jan) de
 1640 *L'Histoire de Nouveau Monde ou description des Indies Occidentales.* Leyden: Chez Bonaventure & Abraham Elseviers.

Laming-Emperaire, Annette
 1964 *Origines de l'archéologie préhistorique en France, des superstitions médiévales a la découverte de l'homme fossile.* Paris: Editions A. et J. Picard et Cia.

Lawson, John
 1709 *A New Voyage to Carolina; Containing the Exact Description of That Country: Together with the Present State Thereof, and a Journal of a Thousand Miles, Travel'd thro' Several Nations of Indians, Giving a Particular Account of Their Customs, Manners, &c.* London: s.n.

Le Plongeon, Alice Dixon
 1879 Notes on the Yucatan. *Proceedings of the American Antiquarian Society* (o.s.) 72:77–106.
 1885 The New and Old in Yucatan. *Harper's New Monthly Magazine* 70:372–386.
 1886 Yucatan, Its Ancient Temples and Palaces. *Transactions of the New York Academy of Sciences* 5(6):169–189.
 1887 Eastern Yucatan: Its Scenery, People, and Ancient Cities and Monuments. *Transactions of the New York Academy of Sciences* 7:45–48.
 1896 The Potter's Art among Native Americans. *Popular Science Monthly* 49(5):646–655.
 1897 *The Monuments of the Mayach and Their Historical Teachings.* New York: The Albany Institute.

Lessey, Samuel K., W. D. Geiger, Raymond Townsend, and Edward Durell
 1958 Bucks County Historical Society. *Chronicle of the Early American Industries Association* 11(1):1–3, 12.

Levine, Mary Ann
 1991 An Historical Overview of Research on Women in Anthropology. In Dale Walde and Noreen Willows, eds., *Proceedings of the 22nd Annual Chacmool Conference,* 177–186. Calgary: Archaeological Association of the University of Calgary.
 1994a Creating Their Own Niches: Career Styles among Women in Americanist Archaeology between the Wars. In Cheryl Claassen, ed., *Women in Archaeology,* 9–40. Philadelphia: University of Pennsylvania Press.
 1994b Presenting the Past: A Review of Research on Women in Archaeology. In Margaret C. Nelson, Sarah M. Nelson, and Alison Wylie, eds., *Equity Issues for Women in Archaeology,* 23–36. Washington, D.C.: Archaeological Papers of the American Anthropological Association No. 5.
 1999 Women in Americanist Archaeology before the First World War. In

Alice B. Kehoe and Mary Beth Emmerichs, eds., *Assembling the Past: Studies in the Professionalization of Archaeology*, 139-151. Albuquerque: University of New Mexico Press.

Lonergan, David
 1999 Frederick Webb Hodge. In John A. Garrity and Mark C. Carnes, eds., *American National Biography*, 10:909-911. New York: Oxford University Press.

Long, John
 1791 *Voyages and Travels of an Indian Interpreter and Trader, Describing the Manners and Customs of the North American Indians; with an Account of the Posts Situated on the River Saint Lawrence, Lake Ontario, &c. to Which Is Added, a Vocabulary of the Chippeway Language, Names of Furs and Skins, in English and French, a List of Words in the Iroquois, Mohegan, Shawanee, and Esquimaux Tongues, and a Table Shewing the Analogy between the Algonkin and Chippeway Languages*. London: Printed by Robson and others.

Longacre, William A.
 1976 Paul Sidney Martin. *American Anthropologist* 78(1):90-92.

Lovejoy, Arthur O., and George Boas
 1935 *Primitivism and Related Ideas in Antiquity*. Baltimore: Johns Hopkins University Press.

Lubbock, John
 1865 *Prehistoric Times*. London, Williams and Norgate.

Lurie, Edward
 1960 *Louis Agassiz: A Life in Science*. Chicago: University of Chicago Press.

Lurie, Nancy Oestreich
 1966 Women in Early American Anthropology. In June Helm, ed., *Pioneers of American Anthropology: The Uses of Biography*, 29-81. Seattle: University of Washington Press.
 1971a Erminnie Adele Platt Smith. In Edward T. James, Janet Wilson James, and Paul S. Boyer, eds., *Notable American Women, 1607-1950: A Biographical Dictionary*, 3:312-313. Cambridge: Belknap Press of Harvard University Press.
 1971b Matilda Coxe Evans Stevenson. In Edward T. James, Janet Wilson James, and Paul S. Boyer, eds., *Notable American Women, 1607-1950: A Biographical Dictionary*, 3:373-374. Cambridge: Belknap Press of Harvard University Press.

Lyell, Charles
 1830- *Principles of Geology, being an attempt to explain the former changes*
 1833 *of the earth's surface by reference to causes now in operation*. 3 volumes. London: J. Murray.
 1863/ *The Geological Evidence of the Antiquity of Man*. London: J. M. Dent
 1914 & Sons Ltd. (Original 1863, reprint of 1914 cited).

MacCurdy, George Grant
- 1897 Pithecanthropus erectus, by L. Manouvrier [translation]. *American Journal of Science*, 4th ser., 4:213-234.
- 1899 Extent of Instruction in Anthropology in Europe and the United States. *Science* 10(260):910-917.
- 1902a The Teaching of Anthropology in the United States. *Science* 15(371): 211-216.
- 1902b Twenty Years of Section H, Anthropology. *Science* 15:532-534.
- 1905 The Eolithic Problem: Evidences of a Rude Industry Antedating the Paleolithic. *American Anthropologist* 7:425-479.
- 1907 Some Phases of Prehistoric Archeology. *Science* 25:125-139.
- 1909 Ernest Theodore Hamy. *American Anthropologist* 11:145-147.
- 1910 Recent Discoveries Bearing on the Antiquity of Man in Europe. *Smithsonian Report for 1909*, 531-583. Washington, D.C.: Smithsonian Institution.
- 1912 European Prehistoric Man. *Yale Alumni Weekly* 22:177-178.
- 1914 La Combe, a Paleolithic Cave in the Dordogne. *American Anthropologist* 16:157-184.
- 1916 Paleolithic Period. *New International Encyclopedia*, 17:738-743.
- 1917 The Problem of Man's Antiquity at Vero, Florida. *American Anthropologist* 19:252-261.
- 1922 The First Season's Work of the American School in France for Prehistoric Studies. *American Anthropologist* 24:61-71.
- 1924 *Human Origins: A Manual of Prehistory*. 2 vols. New York: Appleton.
- 1925 American School of Prehistoric Research in Europe. Excavations and Researches, 1924. *Art and Archaeology* 19:121-130.
- 1926 The American School of Prehistoric Research. *Art and Archaeology* 21:75-81.
- 1927a Léonce Pierre Manouvrier. *American Anthropologist* 29:340-341.
- 1927b Report by the Director on the Work of the Sixth Season. *Bulletin of the American School of Prehistoric Research* 3:1-22.
- 1928 Report by the Director on the Work of the Seventh Season. *Bulletin of the American School of Prehistoric Research* 4:3-8.
- 1929 Report by the Director on the Work of the Eighth Season. *Bulletin of the American School of Prehistoric Research* 5:5-8.
- 1930 Report by the Director on the Work of the Ninth Summer Session. *Bulletin of the American School of Prehistoric Research* 6:5-7.
- 1931a Report by the Director on the Work of the Tenth Summer Session. *Bulletin of the American School of Prehistoric Research* 7:3-4.
- 1931b The Abri des Merveilles at Castel-Merle, near Sergeac (Dordogne). *Bulletin of the American School of Prehistoric Research* 7:12-23.
- 1932 Report by the Director on Field Work and the Eleventh Summer Session. *Bulletin of the American School of Prehistoric Research* 8:3-5.
- 1933 Report by the Director on Field Work and on the Twelfth Annual Sum-

mer Session. *Bulletin of the American School of Prehistoric Research* 9:3-7.

1934 Report of the Director on the Work of the School, Including the Thirteenth Annual Summer Session. *Bulletin of the American School of Prehistoric Research* 10:3-5.

1935 Report of the Director on the Work of the School, Including the Fourteenth Annual Summer Session. *Bulletin of the American School of Prehistoric Research* 11:3-5.

1938 Report of the Director to the Board of Trustees of the American School of Prehistoric Research. *Bulletin of the American School of Prehistoric Research* 14:3-5.

1939 Report of the Director to the Board of Trustees of the American School of Prehistoric Research. *Bulletin of the American School of Prehistoric Research* 15:3-5.

1946 It Happened in My Time: The Autobiography of George Grant MacCurdy, with a Final Chapter on This Changing World. Typescript, Box 6.7. George Grant MacCurdy Papers (Accession No. 995-3), Peabody Museum Archives, Harvard University, Cambridge. vii + 261 pp.

MacNeish, Richard Stockton

1998 My Life in Canadian Archaeology. In Pamela Jane Smith and Donald Mitchell, eds., *Bringing Back the Past: Historical Perspectives on Canadian Archaeology*, 61-76. Hull: Mercury Series, Archaeological Survey of Canada, Paper 158, Canadian Museum of Civilization.

Macpherson, James (trans.)

1760 *Fragments of Ancient Poetry, Collected in the Highlands of Scotland, and Translated from the Galic or Erse Language.* Edinburgh: G. Hamilton and J. Balfour.

1762 *Fingal, an Ancient Epic Poem in Six Books: Together with Several Other Poems, Composed by Ossian, the Son of Fingal.* London: T. Becket and P. A. De Hondt.

1763 *Temora, an Ancient Epic Poem, in Eight Books, Together with Several Other Poems, Composed by Ossian, the Son of Fingal, Translated from the Galic Language.* London: T. Becket and P. A. De Hondt.

Madeira, Percy C., Jr.

1964 *Men in Search of Man: The First Seventy-Five Years of the University Museum of the University of Pennsylvania.* Philadelphia: University of Pennsylvania Press.

Mann, Horace M.

1945 The Bucks County Historical Society. *Chronicle of the Early American Industries Association* 3(3):23-25, 34.

Mark, Edward L.

1930 Zoology. In Samuel Eliot Morison, ed., *The Development of Harvard University since the Inauguration of President Eliot, 1869-1929*, 378-393. Cambridge: Harvard University Press.

Mark, Joan
- 1980 *Four Anthropologists: An American Science in Its Early Years.* New York: Science History Publications.
- 1988 *A Stranger in Her Native Land: Alice Fletcher and the American Indians.* Lincoln: University of Nebraska Press.

Marquis
- 1966 *Who Was Who in America.* 5th ed. Vol. 1: 1897–1942. Chicago: Marquis Publications.

Marshall, John B.
- 1992 The St. Louis Mound Group: Historical Accounts and Pictorial Depictions. *Missouri Archaeologist* 53:43–79.

Martin, Paul S.
- 1927 Archaeological Survey of Illinois. *Wisconsin Archaeologist* 6(2):56–58.

Martin, Paul S., and John F. Blackburn
- 1926 Illinois Archaeology. University of Chicago Field Expedition Notes with cross references for card index, maps, and photos. [June 27, 1926, to August 28, 1926]. Illinois State Museum Archives, Springfield.

Martin, Paul S., John F. Blackburn, Wilton Krogman, and Robert Redfield
- 1926 Journal of Mound Exploration in Vicinity of Galena, Illinois, in September, 1926. [August 31, 1926, to September 20, 1926]. Illinois State Museum Archives, Springfield.

Mason, J. Alden
- 1956 Henry Chapman Mercer, 1856–1930. *Pennsylvania Archaeologist* 26:152–165.
- 1965 H. Newell Wardle, 1875–1964. *American Anthropologist* 67(6):1512–1513.

Mason, Otis Tufton
- 1883 Report of the American Association for the Advancement of Science, Annual Meeting. *Science* (o.s.) 2(32):369–370.
- 1885 Anthropology. *Annual Report of the Smithsonian Institution for 1883*, 753–763.
- 1888a Anthropology in 1886. *Annual Report of the Smithsonian Institution for 1887*, 523–570.
- 1888b *What Is Anthropology? (A Lecture Given at the U.S. National Museum, 18 March 1885, for the Women's Anthropological Society).* Washington, D.C.: Judd and Detweiler.

McChesney, Lea S.
- 1991 Mary Hemenway. In Christopher Winters, ed., *International Dictionary of Anthropologists*, 281–283. New York: Garland.
- 1999 Mary Hemenway. In John A. Garrity and Mark C. Carnes, eds., *American National Biography*, 10:543–544. New York: Oxford University Press.

McCormack, Thomas J. (editor)
- 1909 *Memoirs of Gustave Koerner, 1890–1896, Life-sketches Written at*

the Suggestion of His Children. 2 vols. Cedar Rapids, Iowa: Torch Press.

McCown, Theodore D.
  1948 George Grant MacCurdy, 1863-1947. *American Anthropologist* 50: 516-524.

McGee, Anita Newcomb
  1889a Historical Sketch of the Women's Anthropological Society of America. In Women's Anthropological Society of America, *Organization and Historical Sketch of the Women's Anthropological Society of America,* 16-22. Washington, D.C.: Women's Anthropological Society of America.
  1889b The Women's Anthropological Society of America. *Science* (o.s.) 13(321): 240-242.
  1897 Anthropology at the American Association for the Advancement of Science. *Science* (n.s.) 6(144):508-513.

McGee, William J.
  1892 Man and the Glacial Period. *Science* (o.s.) 20(513):317.
  1893 Man and the Glacial Period. *American Anthropologist* (o.s.) 6(1):85-95.

McGreevy, Susan Brown
  1993 Daughters of Affluence: Wealth, Collecting, and Southwestern Institutions. In Nancy J. Parezo, ed., *Hidden Scholars: Women Anthropologists and the Native American Southwest,* 294-310. Albuquerque: University of New Mexico Press.

McKenney, Thomas L.
  1827 *Sketches of a Tour to the Lakes, of the Character and Customs of the Chippeway Indians, and of Incidents Connected with the Treaty of Fond Du Lac.* Baltimore: Fielding Lucas, Jun'r.

McNaughton, Douglas
  2000 A World in Transition: Early Cartography of the North Atlantic. In William W. Fitzhugh and Elisabeth I. Ward, eds., *Vikings: The North Atlantic Saga,* 257-269. Washington, D.C.: Smithsonian Institution Press.

Mead, Frances Harvey
  1894 Massachusetts in the Department of Ethnology at the World's Columbian Exposition. In *World's Columbian Exposition, 1893. Report to the Managers Massachusetts Board,* 159-168. Chicago: World's Columbian Exposition.
  1905 The Peabody Museum of Harvard University. *Records of the Past* 4(3):65-79.
  1909 Bibliography of Frederic Ward Putnam. In Franz Boas et al., comps., *Putnam Anniversary Volume: Anthropological Essays Presented to Frederic Ward Putnam,* 601-627. New York: G. E. Stechert.
  1984 *Conejos County, Colorado.* Colorado Springs: Century One Press.

Meek, Ronald L.
- 1976 *Social Science and the Ignoble Savage.* Cambridge: Cambridge University Press.

Meltzer, David J.
- 1983 The Antiquity of Man and the Development of American Archaeology. In Michael Schiffer, ed., *Advances in Archaeological Theory,* 6:1–51. New York: Academic Press.
- 1985 North American Archaeology and Archaeologists, 1879–1934. *American Antiquity* 50(2):249–260.
- 1991 On "Paradigms" and "Paradigm Bias" in Controversies over Human Antiquity in America. In Tom D. Dillehay and David Meltzer, eds., *The First Americans: Search and Research,* 13–49. Boca Raton: CRC Press.
- 1994 The Discovery of Deep Time: A History of Views on the Peopling of the Americas. In Robson Bonnichsen and D. Gentry Steele, eds., *Method and Theory for Investigating the Peopling of the Americas,* 7–26. Corvallis: Center for the Study of the First Americans, Oregon State University.

Meltzer, David J., and William C. Sturtevant
- 1983 The Holly Oak Shell Game: An Historic Archaeological Fraud. In Robert C. Dunnell and Donald K. Grayson, eds., *Lulu Linear Punctated: Essays in Honor of George Irving Quimby.* Anthropological Papers of the Museum of Anthropology, University of Michigan, 72:325–352.

Mendenhall, Susan A.
- 1893 Proceedings of the One Hundredth Meeting. In *Woman's Anthropological Society, Proceedings of the One Hundredth Meeting, January 28, 1893,* 3–9. Washington, D.C.: Gibson Bros.

Mercer, Henry Chapman
- 1885 *The Lenape Stone; or, the Indian and the Mammoth.* New York: Putnam.
- 1892 Pebbles Chipped by Modern Indians as an Aid to the Study of the Trenton Gravel Implements. *Proceedings of the American Association for the Advancement of Science* 40:287–289.
- 1893 Trenton and Somme Gravel Specimens Compared with Ancient Quarry Refuse in America and Europe. *American Naturalist* 27(323):962–978.
- 1894a The Discovery of an Artificially Flaked Flint Specimen in the Quaternary Gravels of San Isidro, Spain. In C. Staniland Wake, ed., *Memoirs of the International Congress of Anthropology,* 61–68. Chicago: Schulte.
- 1894b Indian Jasper Mines in the Lehigh Hills. *American Anthropologist* (o.s.) 7(1):80–92.
- 1894c Re-exploration of Hartman's Cave, near Stroudsburg, Pennsylvania, in 1893. *Proceedings of the Academy of Natural Sciences, Philadelphia* 46:96–104.
- 1894d The Trenton Gravel Discussion. *American Naturalist* 28(328):357–359.

1894e Progress of Field Work of the Department of American and Prehistoric Archaeology of the University of Pennsylvania. *American Naturalist* 28(331):626-628.

1894f Gailenruth Cave in 1894. *American Naturalist* 28(333):821-824.

1894g The Results of Excavating at the Ancient Argillite Quarries Recently Discovered near the Delaware River in Gaddis Run. *Proceedings of the American Association for the Advancement of Science* 42:304-307.

1894h Another Ancient Source of Jasper Blade Material East of the Middle Alleghanies. *Proceedings of the American Association for the Advancement of Science* 42:307-308.

1894i Notes Taken at the Neolithic Flint Quarry of Spiennes, Belgium in March, 1893. *Proceedings of the American Association for the Advancement of Science* 42:331.

1895a Chipped Stone Implements in the Columbian Historical Exposition at Madrid. *Commemoration of the Fourth Century of the Discovery of America (Report of the Madrid Commission, 1892)*, 367-397. Washington, D.C.: Government Printing Office.

1895b A Preliminary Account of the Re-exploration in 1894 and 1895 of the "Bone Hole," Now Known as Irwins' Cave, at Port Kennedy, Montgomery County, Pennsylvania. *Proceedings of the Academy of Natural Sciences, Philadelphia* 47:443-446.

1896a Cave Exploration by the University of Pennsylvania in Tennessee. *American Naturalist* 30:608-611. (Same as 1896, Cave Exploration in the Eastern United States: Preliminary Report. Department of American and Prehistoric Archaeology of the University of Pennsylvania, Philadelphia)

1896b *The Hill-Caves of Yucatan. (A Search for evidence of Man's Antiquity in the Caverns of Central America, Being an Account of the Corwith Expedition of the Department of Archaeology and Palaeontology of the University of Pennsylvania)*. Philadelphia: Lippincott.

1896c Cave Exploration in the Eastern United States. *Scientific American* 75:36-37.

1897a The Finding of the Remains of the Fossil Sloth at Big Bone Cave, Tennessee, in 1896. *Proceedings of the American Philosophical Society* 36:36-70.

1897b On Fossil Bird Bones Obtained by Expeditions of the University from the Bone Caves of Tennessee. *American Naturalist* 31:645-650.

1897c The Antiquity of Man in the Delaware Valley. In Henry C. Mercer, *Researches upon the Antiquity of Man in the Delaware Valley and the Eastern United States, Publications of the University of Pennsylvania Series in Philology, Literature and Archaeology* 6:1-85.

1897d Exploration of an Indian Ossuary on the Coptank River, Dorchester County, Maryland, with a Description of the Human Bones Discovered by Prof. E. D. Cope and an Examination of Traces of Disease in the Bones by R. H. Harte, M.D. In Henry C. Mercer, *Researches upon the Antiquity of Man in the Delaware Valley and the Eastern United States, Publications of the University of Pennsylvania Series in Philology, Literature and Archaeology* 6:87-109.

1897e An Exploration of Aboriginal Shell Heaps Revealing Traces of Cannibalism on York River, Maine. In Henry C. Mercer, *Researches upon the Antiquity of Man in the Delaware Valley and the Eastern United States, Publications of the University of Pennsylvania Series in Philology, Literature and Archaeology* 6:111-137.

1897f The Discovery of Aboriginal Remains at a Rockshelter in the Delaware Valley Known as the Indian House. In Henry C. Mercer, *Researches upon the Antiquity of Man in the Delaware Valley and the Eastern United States, Publications of the University of Pennsylvania Series in Philology, Literature and Archaeology* 6:139-147.

1897g An Exploration of Durham Cave, Bucks County, Pennsylvania, in 1893. In Henry C. Mercer, *Researches upon the Antiquity of Man in the Delaware Valley and the Eastern United States, Publications of the University of Pennsylvania Series in Philology, Literature and Archaeology* 6:149-178.

1897h A New Investigation of Man's Antiquity at Trenton. *Science*, n.s., 6(149):675-680.

1897i A Grooved Axe from the Ohio Drift. *American Naturalist* 31(361):1-3.

1897j The Kabal; or Potter's Wheel of Yucatan. *Bulletin of the Museum, University of Pennsylvania* 1(2).

1897k *Tools of the Nation Maker*. Doylestown, Pa.: Bucks County Intelligencer.

1898 A New Investigation of Man's Antiquity at Trenton. *Proceedings of the American Association for the Advancement of Science* 46:370-380.

1899a The Bone Cave at Port Kennedy, Pennsylvania, and Its Partial Excavation in 1894, 1895, and 1896. *Journal of the Academy of Natural Science of Philadelphia* 11(2):269-286.

1899b *The Decorated Stove Plates of the Pennsylvania Germans*. Doylestown, Pa.: McGinty's Job Press.

1907 The Lenape Stone. *A Collection of Papers Read before the Bucks County Historical Society* 2:492-493.

1914 *The Bible in Iron, or the Pictured Stoves and Stove Plates of the Pennsylvania Germans*. Doylestown, Pa.: Bucks County Historical Society.

1923 The Origin of Log Houses in the United States. *A Collection of Papers Read before the Bucks County Historical Society* 5:568-593.

1926 Recollections of Tennent School. *A Collection of Papers Read before the Bucks County Historical Society* 5:631-641.

1929 *Ancient Carpenters' Tools Together with Lumbermen's, Joiners', and Cabinet Makers' Tools in Use in the Eighteenth Century*. Portland, Maine: Southworth Press.

Metz, Charles L., and Frederic W. Putnam
- 1886 Explorations in Ohio: The Marriott Mound, No. 1, and its Contents. *Nineteenth Annual Report, Peabody Museum of American Archaeology and Ethnology, Peabody Museum, Annual Reports* 3:449-466.

Meyers Lexikon
- 1927 *Meyers Lexikon, siebente Auflage.* Leipzig: Bibliographisches Institut.

Meyerson, Martin, and Dilys Pegler Winegrad
- 1978 *Gladly Learn and Gladly Teach: Franklin and His Heirs at the University of Pennsylvania, 1740-1976.* Philadelphia: University of Pennsylvania Press.

Minvielle, Pierre
- 1972 *Sur les chemins de la préhistoire.* Paris: Éditions Denoel.

Missionaires de Pekin
- 1776 *Mémoires Concernant L'Histoire, Les Sciences, Les Arts, Les Moeurs, Les Usages, &c. Des Chinois.* Vol. 1. Paris: Chez Nyon Libraire.

Mitra, Panchanan
- 1933 *A History of American Anthropology.* Calcutta: University of Calcutta.

Moldow, Gloria
- 1987 *Women Doctors in Gilded-Age Washington: Race, Gender, and Professionalization.* Urbana: University of Illinois Press.

Mondragon, Pat
- 1998 Archaeology at Fonthill Museum: Dig Archaeology. *Abstracts of the 97th Annual Meeting, American Anthropological Association,* 317. Arlington, Va.: American Anthropological Association.

Moorehead, Warren King
- 1910 *The Stone Age in North America.* Boston: Houghton Mifflin Co. 2 vols.
- 1921 Recent Explorations in Texas. *American Anthropologist* 23(1):1-11.
- 1923 A Report on Progress on the Exploration of the Cahokia Group. *University of Illinois Bulletin* 21(6):9-56.
- 1937 Review: Cole and Deuel—*Rediscovering Illinois. Mississippi Valley Historical Review* 24(3):375-376.

Morgan, Lewis H.
- 1985/ *Ancient Society.* Tucson: University of Arizona Press.
- 1877

Morison, Samuel Eliot
- 1971 *The European Discovery of America: The Northern Voyages—A.D. 500-1600.* New York: Oxford University Press.
- 1974 *The European Discovery of America: The Southern Voyages—A.D. 1492-1616.* New York: Oxford University Press.

Morlot, Adolphe von
- 1861 General Views on Archaeology. *Annual Report of the Smithsonian Institution for 1860,* 284-343. Washington, D.C.: Government Printing Office.

1863 An Introductory Lecture to the Study of High Antiquity, Delivered at the Academy of Lausanne, Switzerland, on the 29th of November, 1860. *Annual Report of the Smithsonian Institution for 1862*, 303–317. Washington, D.C.: Government Printing Office.

Morse, Edward Sylvester

1868 Evidences of the Great Antiquity in the Shell Heaps at Goose Island. *Boston Society of Natural History Proceedings* 11:301–302.

1879 *Shell Mounds of Omori*. Tokyo: Memoirs of the Science Department, University of Tokyo, vol. 1, pt. 1.

1915 Frederick Ward Putnam, 1839–1915: An Appreciation. *Essex Institute Historical Collections* 52:3–8.

Morton, Samuel George

1839 *Crania Americana; or, A Comparative View of the Skulls of Various Aboriginal Nations of North and South America*. Philadelphia: J. Dobson.

1844 *Crania Aegyptiaca, or Observations on Egyptian Ethnography, Derived from Anatomy, History, and the Monuments*. (Reprinted from the *Transactions of the American Philosophical Society* 9:1–67.) Philadelphia: J. Pennington.

Movius, Hallam L., Jr.

1995 Inventaire analytique des sites aurignaciens et perigordiens de Dordogne. In Harvey M. Bricker, ed., *Le Paléolithique supérieur de l'abri Pataud (Dordogne): Les fouilles de H. L. Movius Jr.*, 227–314. Paris: Éditions de la Maison des Sciences de l'Homme, Paris.

Murowchick, Robert E.

1990 A Curious Sort of Yankee: Personal and Professional Notes on Jeffries Wyman (1814–1874). *Southeastern Archaeology* 9(1):55–66.

Nadaillac, Jean François Albert de Pouget, Marquis de

1885 *Pre-Historic America*. Trans. N. d'Anvers [pseud.], ed. William H. Dall. London: John Murray.

1895 Congrès International d'Anthropologie, Chicago, 1893. *L'Anthropologie* 6:85–90.

1896 Review: Henry Mercer. The Hill Caves of Yucatan. *L'Anthropologie* 7:69–72.

National Cyclopaedia of American Biography

1929 Matilda Coxe Stevenson. *National Cyclopaedia of American Biography* 20:53–54. New York: James T. White.

National Research Council

1930 *Guide Leaflet for Amateur Archaeologists*. Reprint and Circular Series of the National Research Council No. 93. Washington, D.C.: Committee on State Archaeological Surveys, Division of Anthropology and Psychology, National Research Council.

1932 *Conference on Southern Pre-History*. December 18–20, Birmingham, Alabama. Washington, D.C.: Committee on State Archaeological Surveys, Division of Anthropology and Psychology, National Research Council.

Newcomb, William W., Jr.

1955/ The Walam Olum of the Delaware Indians in perspective. *Texas Jour-*
1974 *nal of Science* 8(1), reprinted in *Bulletin of the Archaeological Society of New Jersey* 30:29-32.

Nickerson, William Baker

1884– Fifty letters between William Baker Nickerson and Frederic Ward Put-
1911 nam, integrated from the Peabody Museum Archives and Pusey Library Archives, Harvard University, Cambridge, and the Illinois State Museum Archives, Springfield. Correspondence from July 14, 1884, to August 22, 1911.

1908a Stone Graves of Northwestern Illinois. *Records of the Past* 7(1):52-58.

1908b Mounds of Northwestern Illinois. *Records of the Past* 7(2):85-95.

1911 The Mound-Builders: A Plea for the Conservation of the Antiquities of the Central and Southern States. *Records of the Past* 10(6):334-338.

1912 The Burial Mounds at Albany, Illinois. *Records of the Past* 11(2):69-81.

1913a Archaeology of Jo Daviess County, Illinois, 1895-1901; Explorations of W. B. Nickerson. Report to the Peabody Museum of American Archaeology, Harvard University. Typescript in the manuscript collection, Illinois State Museum, Springfield. 147 pp.

1913b On an Archaeological Reconnaissance of Manitoba. *Summary Report of the Geological Survey of Canada, Department of Mines, for the Calendar Year 1912*, 504. Ottawa.

1914a Archaeological Evidence as Applied to Southwestern Manitoba. Unpublished report submitted to the National Museum of Canada, 66 pp. National Museum of Canada Archives.

1914b On Archaeological Research in the Valley of the Souris River, Southwestern Manitoba. *Summary Report of the Geological Survey of Canada, Department of Mines, for the Calendar Year 1913*, 387-388. Ottawa.

1921 Explorations in Illinois and Iowa, 1913-1921. Notebook in the manuscript collection, Illinois State Museum Archives, Springfield.

1963 *The W. B. Nickerson Survey and Excavations, 1912-15, of the Southern Manitoba Mounds Region.* Ed. Katherine H. Capes. Ottawa: Anthropological Papers, National Museum of Canada, No. 4.

1988 Archaeological Evidences in Minnesota: Explorations of the Minnesota Historical Society in the Years 1913 and 1916 in the Valley of the Minnesota River by William B. Nickerson under the Direction of Newton H. Winchell and Warren Upham. *Minnesota Archaeologist* 47(2):4-40.

Noll, Mark A.

1994 *The Scandal of the Evangelical Mind.* Grand Rapids, Mich.: Eerdmans.

Nott, Josiah Clark, and George Robins Gliddon
 1854 *Types of Mankind: Or, Ethnological Researches, Based on Ancient Monuments, Paintings, Sculptures, and Crania of Races.* 2nd ed. Philadelphia: Lippincott, Grambo.
 1857 *Indigenous Races of the Earth.* Philadelphia: Lippincott.

Nunn, George E.
 1929 *Origin of the Strait of Anian Concept.* Philadelphia: privately published.

Nutting, Charles C.
 1903 Frank Russell. *Iowa Alumnus* 1(1):1–4.

Obermaier, Hugo
 1924 *Fossil Man in Spain* (translated from *El Hombre Fossil,* 1916, with revision by the author in 1922, by Christine D. Matthew). New Haven: Hispanic Society of America/Yale University Press.

Oestreicher, David M.
 1994 Unmasking the Walam Olum: A Nineteenth Century Hoax. *Bulletin of the Archaeological Society of New Jersey* 49:1–44.
 1995a The Anatomy of the Walam Olum: The Dissection of a 19th-Century Anthropological Hoax. Ph.D. dissertation, Department of Anthropology, Rutgers University, New Brunswick, New Jersey.
 1995b Text Out of Context: The Arguments That Sustained and Created the Walam Olum. *Bulletin of the Archaeological Society of New Jersey* 50:31–52.
 1996 Unraveling the Walam Olum. *Natural History* 105(10):14–21.

Osborn, Henry Fairfield
 1931 *Cope: Master Naturalist: The Life and Letters of Edward Drinker Cope, with a Bibliography of His Writings Classified by Subject.* Princeton: Princeton University Press.

Oviedo y Valdes, Gonzalo Fernandez de
 1535 *Historia general y natural de las Indias Islas y Tierra Firma del mar Oceano.* 4 vols. Seville: Juan Cromberger.

Parezo, Nancy J.
 1993a Anthropology: The Welcoming Science. In Nancy J. Parezo, ed., *Hidden Scholars: Women Anthropologists and the Native American Southwest,* 3–37. Albuquerque: University of New Mexico Press.
 1993b Matilda Coxe Stevenson: Pioneer Ethnologist. In Nancy J. Parezo, ed., *Hidden Scholars: Women Anthropologists and the Native American Southwest,* 38–62. Albuquerque: University of New Mexico Press.
 1999 Matilda Coxe Evans Stevenson. In John A. Garrity and Mark C. Carnes, eds., *American National Biography,* 20:730–731. New York: Oxford University Press.

Parezo, Nancy J., and Susan J. Bender
 1994 From Glacial to Chilly Climate: A Comparison between Archaeology and Socio-cultural Anthropology. In Margaret C. Nelson, Sarah M.

Nelson, and Alison Wylie, eds., *Equity Issues for Women in Archaeology*, 73-81. Washington, D.C.: Archaeological Papers of the American Anthropological Association No. 5.

Parmenter, Ross

1966 *Explorer, Linguist, and Ethnologist: A Descriptive Bibliography of the Published Work of Alphonse Louis Pinart, with Notes on His Life.* Los Angeles: Southwest Museum.

1971 Zelia Maria Magdalena Nuttall. In Edward T. James, Janet Wilson James, and Paul S. Boyer, eds., *Notable American Women, 1607-1950: A Biographical Dictionary*, 2:640-642. Cambridge: Belknap Press of Harvard University Press.

Paton, Lucy A.

1919 *Elizabeth Cary Agassiz: A Biography.* Boston: Houghton Mifflin.

Peabody, Charles

1904 Explorations of Mounds, Coahoma County, Mississippi. *Papers of the Peabody Museum of American Archaeology and Ethnology, Harvard University* 3(2):21-64.

1910 The Exploration of Mounds in North Carolina. *American Anthropologist* 12(3):425-433.

1923 Annual Report of the Director of the American School in France of Prehistoric Studies, 1922-23. *Bulletin of the Archaeological Institute of America* 14:115-118.

Peabody, Charles C., and Warren K. Moorehead

1904 The Exploration of Jacobs Cavern, McDonald County, Missouri. *Phillips Academy, Department of Archaeology, Bulletin* 1.

Pengelly, Hester

1897 *A Memoir of William Pengelly, of Torquay, F.R.S., Geologist, with a Selection of His Correspondence: Edited by His Daughter, Hester Pengelly, with a Summary of His Scientific Work by the Rev. Prof. Bonney.* London: John Murray.

Petit Larousse Illustré

1975 *Petit Larousse illustré.* Paris: Librairie Larousse.

Peyrony, Denis

1923 *Éléments de Préhistoire.* Ussel: G. Eyboulet et Fils.

1939 Le Comté Begouën en Perigord. In *Mélanges de préhistoire et d'anthropologie offerts par ses collégues, amis et disciples au Professeur Comté H. Begouën*, 235-241. Toulouse: Éditions du Muséum.

Pfefferkorn, Ignaz

1794/ *Sonora: A Description of the Province by Ignza Pfefferkorn.* Trans.
1949 Theodore E. Treutlein. Albuquerque: University of New Mexico Press.

1794- *Beschreibung der Landschaft Sonora samt andern merkwürdigen Nach-*
1795 *richten von den innern Theilen Neu-Spaniens und Reise aus Amerika bis in Deutschland, nebst einer Landcharte von Sonora.* 2 vols. Köln am Rhine: Langenenschen Buchhandlung.

Pinsky, Valery
- 1992 Archaeology, Politics, and Boundary-Formation: The Boas Censure (1919) and the Development of American Archaeology during the Inter-war Years. In Jonathan E. Reyman, ed., *Rediscovering Our Past: Essays on the History of American Archaeology,* 179–190. Aldershot: Ashgate.

Powell, Joseph W.
- 1896 Report of the Director. *Thirteenth Annual Report, Bureau of Ethnology, 1891–92,* xxi–lvii. Washington, D.C.: Government Printing Office.

Prestwich, Joseph
- 1859 Sur la découverte d'instruments en silex associés à des restes de mammifères d'espèces perdues dans des couches non remanies d'un formation géologique diluvials. *Comptes Rendus, Hebdomadaires des Seances de l'Académie des Sciences* 49:634–636.
- 1860 On the Occurrence of Flint Implements, Associated with the Remains of Extinct Mammalia, in Undisturbed Beds of a Late Geological Period. *Proceedings of the Royal Society of London* 10:50–59.
- 1874 Report on the Exploration of Brixham Cave, Conducted by a Committee of the Geological Society and under the Superintendence of Wm. Pengelly, Esq., F.R.S., Aided by a Local Committee: With Descriptions of the Animal Remains by George Busk, Esq., F.R.S., and of the Flint Implements by John Evans, Esq., F.R.S. *Philosophical Transactions of the Royal Society of London* 163:471–572.

Preucel, Robert W., and Meredith S. Chesson
- 1994 Blue Corn Girls: A Herstory of Three Early Women Archaeologists at Tecolote, New Mexico. In Cheryl Claassen, ed., *Women in Archaeology,* 67–84. Philadelphia: University of Pennsylvania Press.

Primm, James Neal
- 1983 Missouri, St. Louis, and the Secession Crisis. In Steven W. Rowan, ed. and trans., *Germans for a Free Missouri: Translations from the St. Louis Radical Press, 1857–1862,* 3–22. Columbia: University of Missouri Press.

Prucha, Francis P.
- 1986 *The Great Father: The United States Government and the American Indians.* Abridged ed. Lincoln: University of Nebraska Press.

Purchas, Samuel
- 1625 *Purchas His Pilgrimes, in Five Bookes.* London: William Stansby for Henrie Fetherstone.

Putnam, Elizabeth Duncan
- 1907 Mary Louisa Duncan Putnam, A Memoir. *Proceedings of the Davenport Academy of Sciences,* 10:i–xlii. Davenport.
- 1920 The Life and Services of Joseph Duncan, Governor of Illinois, 1834–

1838. *Transactions of the Illinois State Historical Society for 1919,* Illinois State Historical Library Publication 26:107-187. Springfield.

Putnam, Frederic Ward

1866 On the Indian Grave on Winter's Island, Salem, 1865. *Proceedings of the Boston Society of Natural History* 10:246-247.

1886a *Lectures on American Archaeology.* Cambridge: Peabody Museum of American Archaeology and Ethnology, Harvard University. 6 pp.

1886b On the Methods of Archaeological Research in America. *Johns Hopkins University Circulars* 5(49):89-92.

1886c Report of the Curator. *Nineteenth Annual Report of the Peabody Museum of American Anthropology and Ethnology,* 477-501.

1887 Report of the Curator. *Twentieth Annual Report of the Peabody Museum of American Anthropology and Ethnology,* 535-570.

1887/ Explorations in the Little Miami River Valley. *Twentieth Annual*
1973 *Report, Peabody Museum of American Archaeology and Ethnology.* Reprinted in *The Archaeological Reports of Frederic Ward Putnam—Selected from the Annual Reports of the Peabody Museum of Archaeology and Ethnology, Harvard University, 1875-1903.* Antiquities of the New World: Early Explorations in Archaeology, 8:235-250. New York: AMS Press.

1888 A Collection of Palaeolithic Implements from America and Europe. *Proceedings of the Boston Society of Natural History* 23:421-424.

1891 *Twenty-Fifth Annual Report, Peabody Museum of American Archaeology and Ethnology.* Cambridge: Peabody Museum.

1893 Letter: Memorial to Henry Wheatland. In *Essex Institute, Henry Wheatland, Born January 11, 1812, Died February 27, 1893; Founder of the Essex Institute 1847-1848; Its Secretary and Treasurer 1848-1868, Its President 1868-1893,* 60-63. Salem: Essex Institute.

1898a/ Guide to the Peabody Museum and the Division of American Ar-
1973 chaeology and Ethnology, Harvard University. Reprinted in S. Williams, comp., *The Selected Archaeological Papers of Frederic Ward Putnam.* Antiquities of the New World: Early Exploration in Archaeology, 5:201-227. Cambridge: Peabody Museum.

1898b Editorial Note. In Charles C. Willoughby, Prehistoric Burial Places in Maine. *Archaeological and Ethnological Papers of the Peabody Museum* 1(6):387-388.

1898c Early Man of the Delaware Valley. *Proceedings of the American Association for the Advancement of Science* 46:344-348.

1899 A Problem in American Anthropology. *Proceedings of the American Association for the Advancement of Science* 48:1-17.

Putnam, William Clement

1899 Charles Edwin Putnam, President, Davenport Academy of Natural Sciences. *Proceedings of the Davenport Academy of Natural Sciences* 7:3-13.

Raab, Henry
- 1898 Schools and Teachers in Old Belleville. *Belleville Advocate* 56(12), Friday, December 2.

Rafinesque, Constantine Samuel
- 1820 Oriental Idyls: First Oriental Idyl—The Son of the Hill and the Maid of the Valley; Second Oriental Idyl—The Two Shepards; and Third Oriental Idyl—The Brides of the Hill. *Western Review and Miscellaneous Magazine* 2(4):232–234, 2(5):278–280, 2(6):329–331.
- 1821 *Western Minerva, or American Annals of Knowledge and Literature.* Vol. 1, No. 1. Lexington: Thomas Smith.
- 1824 *Ancient History, or Annals of Kentucky; With a Survey of the Ancient Monuments of North America, and a Tabular View of the Principal Languages and Primitive Nations of the whole Earth.* Frankfort, Ky.: Printed for the Author.
- 1827 Important Historical and Philological Discovery. To Peter Duponceau, Esq. *Saturday Evening Post* 6(285):2.
- 1829 *The Pulmist, or Introduction to the Art of Curing and Preventing the Consumption, or Chronic Phthisis.* Philadelphia: C. Alexander.
- 1832– *Atlantic Journal, and Friend of Knowledge* (in eight numbers). Philadelphia: C. S. Rafinesque.
- 1833
- 1834a Examen analytique des langues Linniques de l'Amérique Septentrionale, et surtout des langues Ninniwak, Linap, Mohigan &c avec leurs dialectes. (Unpublished Prix Volney essay). Archives Institut Royal de France, Paris. 256 pp.
- 1834b Premier Supplement a l'Examen analytique. (Supplement to unpublished Prix Volney essay). Archives Institut de France, Paris, 14 pp. (pp. 257–270).
- 1834c Graphic Systems of America. Manuscript on file at American Philosophical Society.
- 1835 The Chinese Nations and Languages. *The Knickerbocker* 5(5):365–376.
- 1836a *The American Nations; or, Outlines of Their General History, Ancient and Modern: Including the Whole History of the Earth and Mankind in the Western Hemisphere; the Philosophy of American History; the Annals, Traditions, Civilizations, Languages, etc., of All the American Nations, Tribes, Empires, and States.* 2 vols. Philadelphia: C. S. Rafinesque.
- 1836b/ *The World or Instability: A Poem in Twenty Parts.* A facsimile reproduction with an introduction by Charles E. Boewe. Gainesville: Scholars' Facsimiles & Reprints.
- 1956
- 1836c *A Life of Travels and Researches in North America and South Europe.* Philadelphia: F. Turner.
- 1836d *New Flora and Botany of North America or a Supplemental Flora, Additional to All the Botanical Works on North America and the United*

States. Containing 1000 New or Revised Species. 4 pts. Philadelphia: C. S. Rafinesque.

1837 *Safe Banking, Including the Principles of Wealth; Being an Enquiry into the Principles and Practice of Safe and Unsafe Banks, or Monied Institutions in North America, the Defects of the American Banking System and Legislation, &c.* Philadelphia: Divital Institution of North America and Six Per Cent Savings Bank.

1840 *The Good Book, and Amenities of Nature, or Annals of Historical and Natural Sciences.* Philadelphia: Eleutherium of Knowledge.

Rainger, Ronald

1991 *An Agenda for Antiquity: Henry Fairfield Osborn and Vertebrate Paleontology at the American Museum of Natural History, 1890-1935.* Tuscaloosa: University of Alabama Press.

Rau, Charles F.

1859 Die Graeber von Panama. In Otto Ule and Karl Müller, eds., *Die Natur* (Die Natur, ihre Krafte, Gesetze un Erscheinungen im Geiste kosmischer Anschauung), 8:372. Halle.

1864a An Account of the Aboriginal Inhabitants of the California Peninsula, as Given by Jacob Baegert, a German Jesuit Missionary, Who Lived There Seventeen Years during the Second Half of the Last Century. *Annual Report of the Smithsonian Institution for 1864,* 352-369, and *Annual Report of the Smithsonian Institution for 1865,* 378-399. Washington, D.C.: Government Printing Office.

1864b Agricultural Implements of the North American Stone Period. *Annual Report of the Smithsonian Institution for 1863,* 379-380. Washington, D.C.: Government Printing Office.

1865 Artificial Shell-Deposits in New Jersey. *Annual Report of the Smithsonian Institution for 1864,* 370-374. Washington, D.C.: Government Printing Office.

1867a Indian Pottery. *Annual Report of the Smithsonian Institution for 1866,* 346-355. Washington, D.C.: Government Printing Office.

1867b Notes on the Anthropological Congress at Paris. *The Historical Magazine,* October, p. 210. Morisiana, N.Y.

1869a Drilling Stone without Metal. *Annual Report of the Smithsonian Institution for 1868,* 392-400. Washington, D.C.: Government Printing Office.

1869b A Deposit of Agricultural Flint Implements in Southern Illinois. *Annual Report of the Smithsonian Institution for 1868,* 401-407. Washington, D.C.: Government Printing Office.

1872 Ancient Aboriginal Trade in North America. *Annual Report of the Smithsonian Institution for 1872,* 348-394. Washington, D.C.: Government Printing Office.

1875 The Stone Age in Europe. Six parts. *Harper's New Monthly Magazine*

50(299):681–690, 50(300):838–846, 51(301):67–76, 51(302):239–246, 51(303):371–384, 51(304):534–544.
1876 *Early Man in Europe.* New York: Harper and Brothers.
1879 The Palenque Tablet in the United States National Museum, Washington, D.C. *Smithsonian Contributions to Knowledge,* 22(5), Publication No. 331. Washington, D.C.: Government Printing Office.
1882 Indian Stone Graves. *American Naturalist* 17:131–135.
1883 Circular Relative to Contributions of Aboriginal Antiquities to the United States National Museum. *Proceedings of the United States National Museum* 6:479–483. Washington, D.C.: Government Printing Office.
1884 Prehistoric Fishing in Europe and North America. *Smithsonian Contributions to Knowledge* 25(1), Publication No. 509. Washington, D.C.: Government Printing Office.

Reed, Cleota
1987 *Henry Chapman Mercer and the Moravian Pottery and Tile Works.* Philadelphia: University of Pennsylvania Press.

Reinach, Salomon
1922 Edouard-Philippe-Emile Cartailhac, 15 Fev. 1845–25 Nov. 1921. *Revue Archéologique* 15:149–161.

Reyman, Jonathan E.
1998 Review: Pueblo Bonito, by George H. Pepper, Preface by David E. Stuart. 1996. *Bulletin of the History of Archaeology* 8(1):15–17.
1999 Women in Southwestern Archaeology: 1895–1945. In Alice Beck Kehoe and Mary Beth Emmerichs, eds., *Assembling the Past: Studies in the Professionalization of Archaeology,* pp. 213–228. Albuquerque: University of New Mexico Press.

Richard, Nathalie
1999a Gabriel de Mortillet. In Tim Murray, ed., *Encyclopedia of Archaeology. Part 1: The Great Archaeologists,* 93–107. 2 vols. Santa Barbara: ABC-Clio.
1999b Marcellin Boule. In Tim Murray, ed., *Encyclopedia of Archaeology. Part 1: The Great Archaeologists,* 263–274. 2 vols. Santa Barbara: ABC-Clio.

Richling, Barnett
1998 Archaeology, Ethnology, and Canada's Public Purse, 1910–1921. In Pamela Jane Smith and Donald Mitchell, eds., *Bringing Back the Past: Historical Perspectives on Canadian Archaeology,* 103–114. Hull: Mercury Series, Archaeological Survey of Canada, Paper 158, Canadian Museum of Civilization.

Riley, Thomas J.
1987 Ridged-Field Agriculture and the Mississippian Economic Pattern. In William F. Keegan, ed., *Emergent Horticultural Economies of the*

Eastern Woodland, 295-304. Center for Archaeological Investigations, Occasional Paper No. 7. Carbondale: Southern Illinois University.

Romeyn, Sara N.
1999 Harriet Maxwell Converse. In John A. Garrity and Mark C. Carnes, eds., *American National Biography*, 5:360-361. New York: Oxford University Press.

Rossiter, Margaret W.
1982 *Women Scientists in America: Struggles and Strategies to 1940*. Baltimore: Johns Hopkins University Press.

Rowan, Steven W.
1983 The Continuation of the German Revolutionary Tradition on American Soil. In Steven W. Rowan, ed. and trans., *Germans for a Free Missouri: Translations from the St. Louis Radical Press, 1857-1862*, 23-45. Columbia: University of Missouri Press.

Rowbotham, Sheila
1973 *Hidden from History: Rediscovering Women in History from the Seventeenth Century to the Present*. New York: Vintage Books.

Rudwick, M. J. S.
1985 *The Great Devonian Controversy: The Shaping of Scientific Knowledge among Gentlemanly Specialists*. Chicago: University of Chicago Press.

Ruge, Sophus
1873 *Das verhaltnis der erdkunde zu den verwandten wissenschaften. Fretum Anian. (Die Geschichte der Beringstrasse vor ihrer Entdeckung)*. Dresden: H. Henkler.

Ruppel, M. Walter, Oric Bates, and Guenther Roeder
1930 *Der Temple von Dakke. Tome Troisieme: Die Griechischen und Lateinschen Inschriften von Dakke, nach den Aufnahmen von Oric Bates und Guenther Roeder bearbeitet on Walter Ruppel*. Cairo: Imprimé de L'Institut Française d'Archaéologie Orientale.

Russell, Frank
1902 Notes from Frank Russell's *Anth 4:* Prehistoric Archaeology—European Ethnology, Fall Semester, 1902. Peabody Museum Archives, Cambridge. Class notes from an anonymous student.

Sabin, Joseph (editor)
1876 *Catalogue of the Library of E. G. Squier.* New York: Charles C. Shelly.

Sabloff, Paula L. W.
1998 *Conversations with Lew Binford: Drafting the New Archaeology*. Norman: University of Oklahoma Press.

Sackett, James R.
1981 From de Mortillet to Bordes: A Century of French Palaeolithic Research. In Glyn D. Daniel, ed., *Towards a History of Archaeology*, 85-99. London: Thames and Hudson.
1991 Straight Archaeology French Style: The Phylogenetic Paradigm in His-

toric Perspective. In Geoffrey A. Clark, ed., *Perspectives on the Past: Theoretical Biases in Mediterranean Hunter-Gatherer Research*, 108–139. Philadelphia: University of Pennsylvania Press.

Salmon, Philippe, Geoffroy d'Ault du Mesnil, and Louis Capitan
1898   Âges de la Pierre, habitations néolithiques, le Campignien, fouille d'un fond de cabane au Campigny, commune de Blangy-sur-Bresle (Seine-Inférieure). *Revue Mensuelle de l'École d'Anthropologie de Paris* 8:365–408.

Sandford, Joseph E.
1965   The Lenape Stone. *The Historian* (Quarterly Journal of the Bucks County Historical Society) 3(6):1, 44–50.

Sanger, David, and Mary Jo Sanger
1986   Boom and Bust on the River: The Story of the Damariscotta Oyster Shell Heaps. *Archaeology of Eastern North America* 14:65–78.

Sarychev, Gavriil A.
1806/   Account of a Voyage of Discovery to the North-east of Siberia, the Fro-
1969   zen Ocean and the North-east Sea. London: J. G. Barnard for Richard Phillips. (Reprinted in 1969 as by "Gavrila A. Sarychew," Da Capo Press, New York)

Saunders, Bailey
1968   *The Life and Letters of James Macpherson.* New York: Haskell House.

Schmidt, Peter R., and Thomas C. Patterson
1995   Introduction: From Constructing to Making Alternative Histories. In Peter R. Schmidt and Thomas C. Patterson, eds., *Making Alternative Histories*, 1–24. Santa Fe: School of American Research.

Schnapp, Alain
1996   *The Discovery of the Past: The Origins of Archaeology.* London: British Museum Press (translated from the French edition of 1993).

Schoolcraft, Henry Rowe
1845   Observations Respecting the Grave Creek Mound. *Transactions of the American Ethnological Society* 1:369–420.
1849/   Henry R. Schoolcraft's letter to E. G. Squier. In Clinton A. Weslager,
1972   *The Delaware Indians: A History*, Appendix 2, pp. 470–472. New Brunswick: Rutgers University Press.

Schroeder, Albert H. (editor)
1979   *Collected Papers in Honor of Bertha Pauline Dutton.* Albuquerque: Papers of the Archaeological Society of New Mexico, vol. 4.

Schumacher, Paul
1874   Remarks on the Kjökken-möddings on the Northwest Coast of America. *Annual Report of the Board of Regents of the Smithsonian Institution for the Year 1873*, 354–362. Washington, D.C.: Government Printing Office.

Scott, Sir Walter
1816   *The Antiquary.* Edinburgh: Constable.

Seaver, Kirsten
   1996   *The Frozen Echo: Greenland and the Exploration of North America ca. A.D. 1000–1500.* Stanford: Stanford University Press.

Seitz, Don Carlos (editor)
   1911   *Letters from Francis Parkman to E. G. Squier: With Biographical Notes and a Bibliography of E. G. Squier.* Cedar Rapids, Iowa: Torch Press.

Seler-Sachs, Caecilie
   1990   Travels of Dr. Eduard Seler in America. In J. Eric S. Thompson and Francis B. Richardson, eds., *Eduard Seler: Collected Works in Mesoamerican Linguistics and Archaeology* (English translations of German papers from *Gesammelte Abhandlungen zur Amerikanischen Sprach-und Alterthumskunde,* made under the supervision of Charles P. Bowditch), 1:xix–xx. Reprint edition. Labyrinthos, Culver City.

Severin, Timothy
   1967   *Explorers of the Mississippi.* London: Routledge & Kegan Paul.

Shears, Brenda L., Elizabeth C. Welsh, and Margot B. Schevill (editors)
   1989   *The Legacy of Kate Peck Kent: Material Culture Study in the Southwest.* Tempe: Council for Museum Anthropology.

Sigurdsson, Gisli
   2000   The Quest for Vinland in Saga Scholarship. In William W. Fitzhugh and Elisabeth I. Ward, eds., *Vikings: The North Atlantic Saga,* 232–237. Washington, D.C.: Smithsonian Institution Press.

Simpson, James Y.
   1861   *Archaeology: Its Past and Its Future Work.* Edinburgh: Edmonston and Douglas.

Sklenár, Karel
   1983   *Archaeology in Central Europe: The First 500 Years.* New York: St. Martin's Press.

Smith, Harriette Knight
   1898   *The History of the Lowell Institute.* Boston: Lamson, Wolffe.

Smith, Joseph
   1830/   *The Book of Mormon: An Account Written by the Hand of Mormon*
   1977   *upon Plates Taken from the Plates of Nephi.* Salt Lake City: Church of Jesus Christ of Latter Day Saints.

Smith, Philip E. L.
   1966   *Le Solutréen en France.* Publications de l'Institut de Préhistoire de l'Universit de Bordeaux, Memoires, 5. Bordeaux: Imprimeries Delmas.

Snead, James E.
   1999   Science, Commerce, and Control: Patronage and the Development of Anthropological Archaeology in the Americas. *American Anthropologist* 101(2):256–271.

Snyder, Dean H.
   1985   Henry C. Mercer's Archaeological Investigations at Big Bone Cave,

Tennessee. Unpublished student research paper, Center for Cave and Karst Studies, Western Kentucky University Cave Archaeology course.

Sonneville-Bordes, Denise de
- 1960 *Le Paléolithique supérieur en Perigord.* 2 vols. Bordeaux: Imprimeries Delmas.

Spier, Leslie
- 1918 The Trenton Argillite Culture. *Anthropological Papers of the American Museum of Natural History* 22(4):167–226.

Spiess, Arthur E.
- 1985 Wild Maine and the Rusticating Scientist: A History of Anthropological Archaeology in Maine. *Man in the Northeast* 30:101–129.

Squier, Ephraim George
- 1848a Ne-She-Kay-Be-Nais, or the "Lone Bird." *American Whig Review*, n.s., 2(3):255–259.
- 1848b Manabozho and the Great Serpent. *American Whig Review*, n.s., 2(4): 392–398.
- 1849a Historical and Mythological Traditions of the Algonquins; With a translation of the "Walum-Olum," or Bark Record of the Linni-Lenape. *American Whig Review* (n.s) 3(14):273–293.
- 1849b On American Ethnology. *American Whig Review*, n.s., 3(16):385–398.
- 1851a *American Archaeological Researches, No. 1: The Serpent Symbol, and the Worship of the Reciprocal Principles of Nature in America.* New York: George P. Putnam.
- 1851b *Aboriginal Monuments of the State of New York: Comprising the Results of Original Surveys and Explorations, with an Illustrative Appendix.* Washington, D.C.: Smithsonian Contributions to Knowledge, vol. 2, article 9, pp. 9–188.
- 1851c *Antiquities of the State of New York: Being the Result of Extensive Original Surveys and Explorations, with a Supplement on the Antiquities of the West.* Buffalo: George H. Derby.
- 1872 Report. *Journal of the Anthropological Society of New York* 1:16–20.

Squier, Ephraim George, and Edwin Hamilton Davis
- 1848 *Ancient Monuments of the Mississippi Valley: Comprising the Results of Extensive Original Surveys and Explorations.* Washington, D.C.: Smithsonian Contributions to Knowledge, vol. 1.

Stanford, Dennis J., and Jane S. Day (editors)
- 1992 *Ice Age Hunters of the Rockies: Papers Collected in Honor of Marie Wormington.* Denver: Denver Museum of Natural History and University Press of Colorado.

Stanton, William R.
- 1960 *The Leopard's Spots: Scientific Attitudes toward Race in America, 1815–1859.* Chicago: University of Chicago Press.

Starr, Frederick
- 1892   Anthropological Work in America. *Appleton's Popular Science Monthly* 41:289-307.
- 1897   The Davenport Academy of Natural Sciences. *Appleton's Popular Science Monthly* 51:83-98.
- 1903   Mary Louise Duncan Putnam. *Science*, n.s., 17(433):632-633.

Steen, Charlie R., Jr.
- 1979   Introduction. In: Gustav Erik Adolf Nordenskiold. *The Cliff Dwellers of the Mesa Verde, Southwestern Colorado: Their Pottery and Implements*, pp.17-29. D. Lloyd Morgan, trans., from the 1893 Swedish edition. Glorieta, NM: The Rio Grande Press, Inc.

Stein, Julie K.
- 1992   *Deciphering a Shell Midden*. New York: Academic Press.

Stephens, John Lloyd
- 1841   *Incidents of Travel in Central America, Chiapas, and Yucatan.* 2 vols. New York: Harper.
- 1843   *Incidents of Travel in Yucatan.* New York: Harper.

Stevenson, Matilda Coxe
- 1883   The Cliff-Dwellers of the New Mexican Canyons. *Kansas City Review* 6(11):636-639.

Stocking, George W., Jr.
- 1960   Franz Boas and the Founding of the American Anthropological Association. *American Anthropologist* 62(1):1-17.
- 1979   Ideas and Institutions in American Anthropology: Towards a History of the Interwar Years. In George W. Stocking, Jr., ed., *Selected Papers from the American Anthropologist 1921-1945*, 1-53. Washington, D.C.: American Anthropological Association.
- 1985   Philanthropoids and Vanishing Cultures: Rockefeller Funding and the End of the Museum Era in Anglo-American Anthropology. In George W. Stocking, Jr., ed., *Objects and Others: Essays on Museums and Material Culture*, 112-145. History of Anthropology, vol. 3. Madison: University of Wisconsin Press.

Stocking, George W., Jr. (editor)
- 1974   *The Shaping of American Anthropology, 1883-1911: A Franz Boas Reader.* New York: Basic Books.

Stocking, George W., Jr., with Susan P. Montague
- 1979   Interview and Department Focus: George Stocking on Fay-Cooper Cole. *Journal of Anthropology* 1(2):1-17.

Stone, Peter, and Robert MacKenzie
- 1990   Introduction: The Concept of the Excluded Past. In Peter Stone and Robert MacKenzie, eds., *The Excluded Past: Archaeology in Education*, 1-14. London: Unwin Hyman.

Straus, Lawrence Guy
- 1994   The Abbé Henri Breuil: Pope of Paleolithic Prehistory. In Jose A.

Lasheras, ed., *Homenaje al Dr. Joaquin Gonzalez Echegaray*, 189–198. Monografías No. 17. Altamira: Museo y Centro de Investigación de Altamira, Ministerio de Cultura.

Stuckey, Ronald L.
1986 Opinions of Rafinesque Expressed by His American Botanical Contemporaries. *Bartonia* 52:26–41.

Studley, Cordelia A.
1884 Notes upon the Human Remains from the Caves of Coahuila, Mexico. *Sixteenth Annual Report of the Peabody Museum of American Archaeology and Ethnology*, 233–259. Cambridge: Peabody Museum.
1885 Description of the Human Remains Found in the "Intrusive Pit" in the Large Mound of the Turner Group, Little Miami Valley, Ohio, during the Explorations of Messrs. Putnam and Metz. *Proceedings of the American Association for the Advancement of Science* 33:618.

Sullivan, Lynne P.
1984 Madeline Kneberg Lewis: An Original Southeastern Archaeologist. In Cheryl Claassen, ed., *Women in Archaeology*, 110–119. Philadelphia: University of Pennsylvania Press.

Swauger, James L.
1940 A Review of Mr. F. H. Gerrodette's Notes on the Excavation of the McKees Rock Mound. *Pennsylvania Archaeologist* 10:8–10, 23–24.

Talbot, Marion
1910 *The Education of Women*. Chicago: University of Chicago Press.

Tanner, John
1830 *A Narrative of the Captivity and Adventures of John Tanner (U.S. Interpreter at the Sault de Ste. Marie) during Thirty Years Residence among the Indians in the Interior of North America*. Ed. Edwin James. New York: G. & C. & H. Carvill.

Tarabulski, Michael A., and Barry Teicher
1986 Reliving the Past: Alonzo Pond and the 1930 Logan African Expedition. A videotape produced at Beloit College, Beloit, Wisconsin; copy deposited with the Wisconsin State Historical Society.

Tax, Thomas G.
1973 The Development of American Archaeology, 1800–1879. Ph.D dissertation, Department of Anthropology, University of Chicago.

Temkin, Andrea S.
1988 Alice Cunningham Fletcher. In Ute Gacs, Asiha Khan, Jerrie McIntyre, and Ruth Weinberg, eds., *Women Anthropologists: A Biographical Dictionary*, 95–102. New York: Greenwood Press.

Thomas, Cyrus
1889 The Problem of the Ohio's Mounds. *Bulletin of the Bureau of American Ethnology*, No. 8. Washington, D.C.
1890 *The Cherokees in Pre-Columbian Times*. Fact and Theory Papers No. 4. New York: N. D. C. Hodges.

1891 The Story of a Mound; or the Shawnee in Pre-Columbian Times. *American Anthropologist* (o.s.) 4(2):109–159, 4(3):237–273.

Thomas, Dorothy
1933 Exploring the Museum Field. *Independent Woman* 12(7):238–239, 260.

Thompson, J. Eric S.
1957 The First Peopling of the New World. *American Antiquity* 24(2):184.
1958 *Thomas Gage's Travels in the New World*. Edited and introduction by J. Eric S. Thompson. The American Exploration and Travel Series, vol. 58. Norman: University of Oklahoma Press.

Thompson, Raymond H.
1991 Shepard, Kidder, and Carnegie. In Ronald L. Bishop and Fredrick W. Lange, eds., *The Ceramic Legacy of Anna O. Shepard*, 11–41. Boulder: University Press of Colorado.

Tileston, Mary Wilder
1927 *A Memorial of the Life and Benefactions of Mary Hemenway, 1820–1894*. Boston: privately printed.

Tozzer, Alfred M.
1933 Zelia Nuttall. *American Anthropologist* 35(3):475–482.
1936 Frederic Ward Putnam, 1839–1915. *National Academy of Sciences Biographical Memoirs* 16:125–156.

Trevor-Roper, Hugh R.
1984 The Invention of Tradition: The Highland Tradition of Scotland. In Eric Hobsbawm and Terence Ranger, eds., *The Invention of Tradition*, 15–42. New York: Cambridge University Press.

Trigger, Bruce G.
1989 *A History of Archaeological Thought*. Cambridge: Cambridge University Press.
1992 Daniel Wilson and the Scottish Enlightenment. *Proceedings of the Society of Antiquaries of Scotland* 122:55–75.

Trigger, Bruce G. (editor)
1986 *Native Shell Mounds of North America*. New York: Garland.

Troost, Gerard
1845 An Account of Some Ancient Remains in Tennessee. *Transactions of the American Ethnological Society* 1:355–365.

Turner, James
1999 *The Liberal Education of Charles Eliot Norton*. Baltimore: Johns Hopkins University Press.

Tylor, Edward B.
1861 *Anahuac or Mexico and the Mexicans, Ancient and Modern*. London: Longmans, Green, Longman, and Roberts.

Tyndall, John
1970/ Address. Reprinted in George Basalla, William R. Coleman and Robert
1874 H. Kargon, eds., *Victorian Science: A Self-Portrait from the Presiden-*

tial *Addresses of the British Association for the Advancement of Science*, 441–478. Garden City, N.Y.: Doubleday.

Upham, Warren

1888 The Recession of the Ice-Sheet in Minnesota in Its Relation to the Gravel Deposits Overlying the Quartz Implements Found by Miss Babbitt at Little Falls, Minnesota. *Proceedings of the Boston Society of Natural History* 23:436–447.

1894 Early Man in Minnesota. *American Geologist* 13(5):363–364.

1902a Primitive Man in the Ice Age. In Jacob V. Brower, ed., *Kakabikansing: Memoirs of Explorations in the Basin of the Mississippi*, 5:115–119. St. Paul: Minnesota Historical Society.

1902b Man in the Ice Age at Lansing, Kansas, and Little Falls, Minnesota. *American Geologist* 30(3):135–150.

Upham, Warren, and Rose Barteau Dunlop

1912 Minnesota Biographies: 1655–1912. *Collections of the Minnesota Historical Society*, vol. 14. St. Paul: Minnesota Historical Society.

Van Ermen, Eduard

1990 *The United States in Old Maps and Prints*. Wilmington: Atomium Books.

Van Riper, A. Bowdoin

1993 *Men among the Mammoths: Victorian Science and the Discovery of Human Prehistory*. Chicago: University of Chicago Press.

Vanuxem, Lardner

1843 On the Ancient Oyster Shell Deposits Observed near the Atlantic Coast of the United States. *Reports of the First, Second, and Third Meetings of the Association of American Geologists and Naturalists at Philadelphia, in 1840 and 1841, and at Boston in 1842, Embracing Its Proceedings and Transactions*, 21–23.

Villeneuve, Le Chanonine Louis de

1906 *Les Grottes de Grimaldi (Baousse-Rousse)*. Tome I, Fascicule I: Historique et Description. Monaco: Imprimerie de Monaco.

Vincent, Joan

1990 *Anthropology and Politics: Visions, Traditions, and Trends*. Tucson: University of Arizona Press.

Volney, Constantin-François

1804 *View of the Climate and Soil of the United States of America: To Which Are Annexed Some Accounts of Florida, the French Colony on the Scioto, Certain Canadian Colonies, and the Savages or Natives*. Trans. Charles B. Brown. London: J. Johnson.

Walker, S. T.

1880 Report on the Shell Heaps of Tampa Bay, Florida. *Annual Report of the Board of Regents of the Smithsonian Institution for the Year 1879*, 413–422. Washington, D.C.: Government Printing Office.

Wallace, David Reins
  1999 *The Bonehunters' Revenge: Dinosaurs, Greed, and the Greatest Scientific Feud of the Gilded Age.* Boston: Houghton Mifflin.
Warburton, Bishop William
  1741 *Divine Legation of Moses,* Vol. 3. London: T. Tegg.
Warden, David B.
  1827 *Recherchés sur les Antiquités de l'Amérique Septentrionale.* Paris: Imprimerie d'Everat.
Wardle, Harriet Newell
  1901 The Sedna Cycle: A Study of Myth Evolution. *Proceedings of the American Association for the Advancement of Sciences* 49:317-18. (Also published in an expanded version in 1901 in the *American Anthropologist* 3(2):568-579.)
  1903 *Native Spindle Whorls of North America and Adjacent Territory: A Paper Read at the 74th Meeting of the New England Cotton Manufacturers' Association, April 22-23, 1903.* Waltham, Mass.: E. L. Barry.
  1906 The Treasures of Prehistoric Moundville. *Harper's Monthly Magazine* 112(658):200-210.
  1912 Certain Rare West Coast Baskets. *American Anthropologist* 14(2):287-313.
  1919 The Indian Knoll. *American Indian Magazine* 7(4):31-38.
  1920 Iron Ore Artifacts from Alabama. *Proceedings of the Academy of Natural Sciences of Philadelphia* 72:209-213.
Warren, Claude N.
  1998 The Empirical Evidence for the Establishment of Human Antiquity. Paper presented at the 63rd Annual Meeting, Society for American Archaeology, Seattle.
Warren, Claude N., and Susan Rose
  1994 *William Pengelly's Techniques of Archaeological Excavation.* Torquay Natural History Society, Publication No. 5. Torquay, England.
Watkins, Frances E.
  1930 My Experiences as a Field Archaeologist. *Masterkey* 4:13-20.
  1931 Archaeology as a Profession for Women. *Masterkey* 4:173-178.
Wauchope, Robert
  1962 *Lost Tribes and Sunken Continents.* Chicago: University of Chicago Press.
Wayman, Dorothy G.
  1942 *Edward Sylvester Morse: A Biography.* Cambridge: Harvard University Press.
Weeks, Edward
  1966 *The Lowells and Their Institute.* Boston: Little, Brown.
Wertime, Marcia
  1978 Henry Chapman Mercer: Nineteenth-Century Renaissance Man. *Archaeology* 31(4):44-51.

White, Nancy Marie, Rochelle A. Marrinan, and Hester A. Davis
 1994 Early Women in Southeastern Archaeology: A Preliminary Report on Ongoing Research. In Cheryl Claassen, ed., *Women in Archaeology*, 96-109. Philadelphia: University of Pennsylvania Press.

White, Randall
 1992 The History and Research Significance of the Logan Museum French Paleolithic Collections. In Randall White and Lawrence B. Breitborde, eds., *French Paleolithic Collections in the Logan Museum of Anthropology. Logan Museum Bulletin*, n.s., 1(2):1-38.

White, Randall, Kathleen Ehrhardt, and Michael A. Tarabulski
 1992 Extant Research Resources for the Study of North African Archaeological Collections in the Logan Museum of Anthropology, Beloit College. In Lawrence B. Breitborde, ed., *Alonzo Pond and the 1930 Logan Museum Expedition to North Africa: The 1985 Beloit College Symposium. Logan Museum Bulletin*, n.s., 1(1):59-66.

Whitfield, Peter
 1998 *New Found Lands: Maps in the History of Exploration.* London: British Library.

Wilford, Major Francis
 1794/ On Egypt, and Other Countries Adjacent to the CA'LI' River, or Nile
 1979 of Ethiopia—from the Ancient Books of the Hindus. *Asiatic Researches Comprising History and Antiquities, the Arts, Sciences, and Literature of Asia,* 3:295-468. New Delhi: Cosmo Publications.

Wilkins, Thurman
 1971 Alice Cunningham Fletcher. In Edward T. James, Janet Wilson James, and Paul S. Boyer, eds., *Notable American Women, 1607-1950: A Biographical Dictionary,* 1:630-633. Cambridge: Belknap Press of Harvard University Press.

Will, George F., and Herbert J. Spinden
 1906 The Mandans: A Study of Their Culture, Archaeology, and Language. *Papers of the Peabody Museum of American Archaeology and Ethnology, Harvard University* 3(4):79-220.

Willard, Frances E., and Mary A. Livermore (editors)
 1897 *American Women: 1,500 Biographies with over 1,400 Portraits.* 2 vols. New York: Mast, Crowell & Kirkpatrick.

Willey, Gordon R.
 1936 A Survey of Methods and Problems in Archaeological Excavation, with Special Reference to the Southwest. M.A. thesis, Anthropology, University of Arizona.

Willey, Gordon R. (editor)
 1988 *Portraits in American Archaeology: Remembrances of Some Distinguished Americanists.* Albuquerque: University of New Mexico Press.

Willey, Gordon R., and Jeremy Sabloff
- 1974 *A History of American Archaeology.* 1st ed. San Francisco: W. H. Freeman.
- 1980 *A History of American Archaeology.* 2nd ed. San Francisco: W. H. Freeman.
- 1993 *A History of American Archaeology.* 3rd ed. New York: W. H. Freeman.

Williams, Barbara
- 1981 *Breakthrough: Women in Archaeology.* New York: Walker.

Williams, Jeannette Webster
- 1895 The Bandelier Collection of Copies of Documents Relative to the History of New Mexico and Arizona. In Jesse Walter Fewkes, *Catalogue of the Hemenway Collection in the Historico-American Exposition of Madrid,* 305–326. Washington, D.C.: Report of the United States Commission to the Columbian Historical Exposition at Madrid.

Williams, Robert A., Jr.
- 1990 *The American Indian in Western Legal Thought: The Discourses of Conquest.* New York: Oxford University Press.

Williams, Stephen
- 1964 Anthropology 239: Archaeology of Eastern North America. Cambridge: Class Syllabus, Harvard University, Tozzer Library Collection.
- 1969 Harvard Ph.D.'s in Anthropology: 1894–1968. Unpublished manuscript, Peabody Museum, Harvard University. 27 pp.
- 1991 *Fantastic Archaeology: The Wild Side of North American Prehistory.* Philadelphia: University of Pennsylvania Press.
- 1998 A Discussion of the History of Archaeology at Harvard University 1870–1920. Discussion document, Society for American Archaeology's History of Archaeology Committee Biennial Willey Symposium, March 28, 1998. 11 pp.

Williams, Stephen (editor)
- 1973 *The Selected Archaeological Papers of Frederic Ward Putnam.* Antiquities of the New World: Early Explorations in Archaeology, vol. 5. New York: AMS Press.

Williams, Stephen, and John M. Goggins
- 1956 The Long Nosed God Mask in Eastern United States. *Missouri Archaeologist* 18 (3):1–23.

Williston, Sam
- 1936 John Bradley Thayer. *Dictionary of American Biography,* 18:405–406. New York: Scribner.

Willoughby, Charles C.
- 1898 Prehistoric Burial Places in Maine. *Papers of the Peabody Museum of American Archaeology and Ethnology* 1(6):383–486.
- 1923 The Peabody Museum of Archaeology and Ethnology, Harvard University. *Harvard Graduates Magazine Association,* June, 495–503.

Willoughby, Charles C., and Earnest A. Hooton
- 1922 The Turner Group of Earthworks, Hamilton County, Ohio. *Papers of the Peabody Museum of American Archaeology and Ethnology* 8(3):1–132.

Wilmsen, Edwin M.
- 1965 An Outline of Early Man Studies in the United States. *American Antiquity* 31(2):172–192.

Wilson, Carol Green
- 1955 *Alice Eastwood's Wonderland: The Adventures of a Botanist.* San Francisco: California Academy of Sciences.

Wilson, Daniel
- 1851 *The Archaeology and Prehistoric Annals of Scotland.* Edinburgh: Shetland and Knox.
- 1876 *Prehistoric Man.* 3rd ed. 2 vols. London: Macmillan.
- 1878a/ Archaeology. In Thomas Spencer Baynes, Day Otis Kellogg, and
- 1900 William Robertson Smith, eds., *Encyclopaedia Britannica*, 9th edition. American edition, 1900, pp. 333–343, bibliography 367–368. New York: Werner.
- 1878b *Reminiscences of Old Edinburgh*, vol 2. Edinburgh: David Douglas.

Wilson, Rodman
- 1971 Phoebe Apperson Hearst. In Edward T. James, Janet Wilson James, and Paul S. Boyer, eds., *Notable American Women, 1607–1950: A Biographical Dictionary*, 2:170–172. Cambridge: Belknap Press of Harvard University Press.

Wilson, Thomas
- 1889 Address: The Beginnings of the Science of Prehistoric Anthropology. *Proceedings of the American Association for the Advancement of Science* 48:307–353.
- 1890a A Study of Prehistoric Anthropology: Hand-book for Beginners. *Annual Report for the Year Ending June 30, 1888, United States National Museum*, 597–671. Washington, D.C.: Smithsonian Institution, United States National Museum.
- 1890b Results of an Inquiry as to the Existence of Man in North America during the Paleolithic Period of the Stone Age. *Annual Report for the Year Ending June 30, 1888, United States National Museum*, 677–702. Washington, D.C.: Smithsonian Institution, United States National Museum.
- 1890c Report on the Department of Prehistoric Anthropology in the U.S. National Museum. *Annual Report of the U.S. National Museum for 1888*, 123–138. Washington, D.C.: Smithsonian Institution, United States National Museum.
- 1899 Address: The Beginnings of the Science of Prehistoric Anthropology. *Proceedings of the American Association for the Advancement of Science* 48:307–353.

Winchell, Newton H.
- 1893 Some Recent Criticisms. *American Geologist* 11(2):110–112.
- 1902 The Geology of the Mississippi Valley at Little Falls, Minnesota. In Jacob V. Brower, ed., *Kakabikansing: Memoirs of Explorations in the Basin of the Mississippi*, 5:89–104. St. Paul: Minnesota Historical Society.
- 1911 *The Aborigines of Minnesota: A Report Based on the Collections of Jacob V. Brower, and on the Field Surveys and Notes of Alfred J. Hill and Theodore H. Lewis.* St. Paul: The Pioneer Co.

Winegrad, Dilys Pegler
- 1993 *Through Time, Across Continents: A Hundred Years of Archaeology and Anthropology at the University Museum.* Philadelphia: University Museum, University of Pennsylvania.

Winsor, Justin
- 1889a The Progress of Opinion Respecting the Origin and Antiquity of Man in America. In Justin Winsor, ed., *Narrative and Critical History of America*, 1:369–412. Boston: Houghton, Mifflin.
- 1889/ *Justin Winsor: Native American Antiquities and Linguistics. (Narra-*
- 1995 *tive and Critical History of America, Vol. 1: Aboriginal America.)* Ed. Anne and Henry Paolucci. New York: Griffon House.

Winsor, Justin (editor)
- 1889b *Narrative and Critical History of America.* 8 vols. Boston: Houghton, Mifflin.

Wirt, Julia J.
- 1878 Explorations of a Mound near Utah Lake, Utah. *Proceedings of the Davenport Academy of Natural Sciences* 2:28–29, 82.

Wissler, Clark
- 1915 Frederic Ward Putnam. *American Museum Journal* 15:315–317.

Women's Anthropological Society
- 1889 *Organization and Historical Sketch of the Women's Anthropological Society of America.* Washington, D.C.: Women's Anthropological Society of America.

Wormington, Hannah Marie
- 1957 *Ancient Man in North America.* 4th ed. Denver: Denver Museum of Natural History.
- 1981 Foreword. In Barbara Williams, ed., *Breakthrough: Women in Archaeology*, v–vii. New York: Walker.

Worsaae, Jens Jacob Asmussen
- 1849 *The Primeval Antiquities of Denmark.* Trans. by William John Thoms. London: J. H. Parker.

Worthen, Amos H. (editor)
- 1866 Geology. *Geological Survey of Illinois.* Vol. 1. Springfield: Geological Survey.

Wright, George Frederick
  1892a *Man and the Glacial Period.* New York: Appleton.
  1892b Man and the Glacial Period. *Science* (o.s.) 20(510):275–277.
  1893 Mr. Holmes's Criticism upon the Evidence of Glacial Man. *Science* (o.s.) 21(537): 267–268.
  1898 Special Explorations in the Implement-Bearing Deposits on the Lalor Farm, Trenton, N.J. *Proceedings of the American Association for the Advancement of Science* 46:355–364.

Wyman, Jeffries
  1868a An Account of Some Kjoekkenmoeddings, or Shell Heaps, in Maine and Massachusetts. *American Naturalist* 1(11):561–584.
  1868b Recent Examination of Shell Heaps on Goose Island in Casco Bay, Maine. *Boston Society of Natural History Proceedings* 11:288–289.
  1868c On the Fresh-Water Shell-Heaps of the St. Johns River, East Florida. *American Naturalist* 2(8):393–403, and 2(9):449–463.
  1869 Report of the Curator. *Second Annual Report of the Trustees of the Peabody Museum of American Archaeology and Ethnology* 2:5–20.
  1874 Human Remains in the Shell Heaps of the St. Johns River, East Florida: Cannibalism. *American Naturalist* 8(7):403–414.
  1875 Fresh-Water Shell Mounds of the St. John's River, Florida. *Memoirs of the Peabody Academy of Science* 1(4):3–94.

Yule, Henry
  1921 *The Book of Ser Marco Polo, the Venetian, Concerning the Kingdoms and Marvels of the East.* 3rd ed. revised throughout in the light of recent discoveries by Henri Cordier. 2 vols. London.

Zeisberger, David
  1827 *Grammar of the Language of the Lenni Lenape or Delaware Indians.* Trans. Peter Stephen du Ponceau, with a Preface and Notes by the translator. *Transactions of the American Philosophical Society,* n.s., 3(2):65–250.

Contributors

Terry A. Barnhart received his Ph.D. in History from Miami University of Ohio in 1989. His dissertation was entitled "Of Mounds and Men: The Early Anthropological Career of Ephraim George Squier." Currently teaching at Eastern Illinois University–Charleston, he has published on a number of nineteenth-century historical intellectual issues.

Bruce J. Bourque received his Ph.D. in Anthropology from Harvard University in 1971. His dissertation was entitled "Prehistory of the Central Maine Coast." He is currently employed at the Maine State Museum–Orono. His publications include work on isotopic studies of diets, zooarchaeology, a variety of topics on Maine prehistoric and historical archaeology, and museum studies.

Harvey M. Bricker received his Ph.D. in Anthropology from Harvard University in 1973. His dissertation was entitled "The Perigordian IV and Related Cultures in France." He is currently employed at Tulane University. His publications include work on Mayan archaeoastronomy as well as the Upper Paleolithic and Mesolithic of Europe.

David L. Browman received his Ph.D. in Anthropology from Harvard University in 1970. His dissertation was entitled "Early Peruvian Peasants: The Cultural History of a Highland Valley." He is currently teaching at Washington University–St. Louis. His publications include topics on pastoral nomadism, development of Andean agriculture and the complex Andean state, historical archaeology, and history of archaeology.

Hilary Lynn Chester is completing her Ph.D. on labor and subsistence organization during the Mogollon pithouse period, in Anthropology at Southern Methodist University in Dallas, with anticipated graduation date of 2002. She currently is employed part-time doing cultural resource management contract archaeology.

Alice B. Kehoe received her Ph.D. in Anthropology from Harvard University in 1964. Her dissertation was entitled "The Ghost Dance Religion in Saskatchewan: A Functional Analysis." She is currently associated with the University of Wisconsin–Milwaukee. Her publications include work on Native American ethnography, history of archaeology, archaeology of gender, and alternative archaeology.

John E. Kelly received his Ph.D. in Anthropology from the University of Wisconsin in 1980. His dissertation was entitled "The Formative Developments at Cahokia and the Adjacent American Bottom: A Merrell Tract Perspective." He currently splits his time between the Powell Archaeological Research Center and Washington University–St. Louis. His publications include multiple works dealing with Cahokia, as well as the history of archaeological research in the area.

David M. Oestreicher received his Ph.D. in Anthropology from Rutgers–New Brunswick in 1995. His dissertation was entitled "The Anatomy of the Walam Olum: The Dissection of a 19th-Century Anthropological Hoax." He is currently employed as an independent consultant. His publications include several historical views of early-nineteenth-century anthropological issues.

Stephen Williams received his Ph.D. in Anthropology from Yale in 1954. His dissertation was entitled "An Archeological Study of the Mississippian Culture in Southeast Missouri." He is currently Director-Emeritus of the Peabody Museum, and Professor Emeritus of Anthropology at Harvard. His publications include multiple works on the prehistoric and historic archaeology of the Lower Mississippi River region, museum studies, the history of archaeology, and critiques of "Fantastic" archaeology.

Index

References to endnotes include the relevant chapter number in parentheses when the page includes more than one note with the same number.

AAAS (American Association for the Advancement of Science), 210-11, 215, 273-74. *See also* "first generation" (women in archaeology), and the AAAS
Abbott, Charles Conrad, 142, 167-68; and Lenape gorget, 188-89; and Mercer, 186, 198-99. *See also* Paleolithic debate, American
Acosta, José de, 35-37, 55
Adair, James, trader, 44-46, 55
Adam of the Lenape, in the Walam Olum, 70-74
Agassiz, Alexander, 217
Agassiz, Elizabeth Cabot Cary, 222-24, 237
Agassiz, Louis (Jean Louis Rodolphe), 149, 173, 211-14, 217, 300n. 2 (chap. 6)
Albert I of Monaco, influence of, on archaeology, 200-204
Aleuts, and cultural adaptation, 159
amateur scientists, 164-66, 171-74, 181-84; in anthropology, 174-79; in archaeology, 125, 156-57, 164-

70, 179-81, 184, 217-19. *See also* Nickerson, William Baker
American Anthropological Association (AAA), 175-76, 222, 274-75, 279, 304n. 5
American Archaeological Research series (Squier), 105, 298n. 19
American Association for the Advancement of Science. *See* AAAS (American Association for the Advancement of Science)
American Ethnological Society, 88, 90-91, 113-16, 298n. 24
American Indians: Lenape (Delaware), 60-61, 70-74, 77-81, 83-84, 290n. 2, 291nn. 5-7, 295n. 21 (*see also* pictographs); Mound Builders, 87-91, 93, 96-100, 123-24 (*see also* Walam Olum, and origins theories); Ojibwa, 76-77, 103, 138-39, 290n. 1, 295n. 21; Seneca, 239-40
American Naturalist (journal), 196-97, 214-15
American School of anthropology, 88, 92-93, 110-16
American School of Prehistoric Research (ASPR), 277-85, 305n. 10, 306n. 11
Amerindians. *See* American Indians
analogies, cultural: Rau's interest in,

127-31; Squier's interest in, 94-99, 101-4 (*see also* religious systems, Squier's interest in). *See also* ethnology, comparative
Anian, Strait of: appearance of, on maps, 16-20, 32-33; explorations of, 18-25, 40-41, 50-51; use of name, superseded by "Bering Strait," 10, 25-29, 33, 41, 287n. 1 (chap. 1), 288n. 2. *See also* Bering Strait hypothesis; cartography, developments in
animalization, in the Walam Olum, 75-76, 294n. 20
Anin (Chinese province), 12, 14-15
Anthropological Institute of New-York, 88, 113-16
Anthropological Society of Washington, 304n. 4; women excluded from, 165-66, 224
anthropology: professionalization of, 174-76; women in, 164-66, 176-79, 181-84
antiquities protection, efforts at, 222, 230-31, 236-37
Archaeological Institute of America (AIA), 220-21, 226
archaeology: amateurs in, 125, 156-57, 164-70, 179-81, 184, 217-19 (*see also* Nickerson, William Baker); Americanist, histories of, 2-5, 9; "correspondence school" of, 209, 217-19; influence of geology on, 136-37, 141-47, 149-51, 203-4; prehistoric, science of, established (*see* Morlot, Adolphe von; Wilson, Daniel); women in (*see* "first generation" [women in archaeology]). *See also* shell midden archaeology
"Archaeology" (Wilson), 133-36, 142, 146-47
Archaeology and Prehistoric Annals of Scotland (Wilson), 133-34, 137, 141, 146-47
artifacts: "Bust of Isis," 77, 295n. 22; from Folsom, N.Mex., 276, 304n. 6; from La Ferrassie (France), 278, 304n. 7; Lenape gorget, 187-90, 195, 199, 206; from Vero, Fla., 275-76. *See also* collections
Arts and Crafts Movement, and Mercer, 185-86, 204-8
atlases. *See* cartography, developments in
Atwater, Caleb, 89, 295n. 23
avocational archaeologists. *See* archaeology, amateurs in

Babbitt, Frances (Franc) Eliza, 8, 164-72, 178, 184, 223 table 10.2, 225, 300n. 3 (chap. 8)
"Baconian science" (Scottish Common-Sense Realism), 140-41
Bailey, John S., 188
Barentz, Willem, map by, 17
Barrow, John, 72, 294n. 17
Bartlett, John Russell, 90-91, 97, 116
Barton, Benjamin Smith, 51-56, 72-73, 289n. 9; Brerewood quoted in, 38, 288n. 5
Barton, William Paul Crillon, 289n. 9
Bartram, John, 42-43, 56
Bates, Arlo, 160-61
Bates, Oric, 160-62
Belleville, Illinois, Rau in, 121-23
Bennett, John W., and dissemination of Peabody Museum method, 260
Bergen, Fanny D., 223 table 10.2
Bering, Vitus J., explorer, 20, 28, 32-33, 41, 56; map by, 25
Bering Strait. *See* Anian, Strait of; Bering Strait hypothesis
Bering Strait hypothesis, 33-34, 55, 81, 140, 288n. 2; early proponents of, 35-40, 55; eighteenth-century proponents of, 40-49, 55
Berlin, University of, MacCurdy at, 272
Best, George, map by, 16
Bible. *See* ethnology, biblical; Walam Olum
Big Mound (St. Louis), 123-24
Billings, Joseph, explorer, 22-23
Blackburn, John, 258-59
Boas, Franz, 175-76, 177, 219
Boas, George, 145

Book of Mormon, compared to the Walam Olum, 84
Boule, Pierre Marcellin, 185, 191, 199-201, 303n. 2
Bowers, Virginia K., 223 table 10.2
Brerewood, Edward, 37-38, 56, 288n. 5
Breuil, Henri Edouard, 163, 201, 278
Brinton, Daniel C., 158, 189, 227-28
Broca, Paul, 87, 114-15
Bryant, Jacob, and philology, 66-67, 74-75, 294n. 18
Bucks County Historical Society, and Mercer, 187, 205-6
Bureau of American Ethnology (BAE), and American Paleolithic debate, 170-72
Burke, Luke, 87, 92
"Bust of Isis," 77, 295n. 22

Cabot, John (Giovanni Cabato), explorer, 13, 56
Cape Deshnef, 26
Capitan, Louis-Joseph, 202-3, 271, 278
Carey, Arthur Astor, and Mercer, 187, 206
Cartailhac, Émile, 201
cartography, developments in, 287n. 1 (chap. 1); 1500 B.C.-A.D. 1200, 10-11; A.D. 1200-1500, 11-13, 30-31; A.D. 1500-1600, 13-18; A.D. 1600-1800, 18-25; A.D. 1800-1900, 25-27; A.D. 1900-2000, 27-29
Carver, Jonathan, explorer, 47-49, 56, 289nn. 7-8
"Catalan Atlas," 12
cave explorations, Mercer's, 192-95, 197-98, 207
Chambers, Robert, 134, 139, 145, 299n. 1
Champollion, Jean François, 85, 296n. 28
Charlevoix, Pierre, 41-42, 56
Chicago method, 8, 162, 210, 242; Nickerson as source of, 242, 258-64
China: European contacts with, 11-13; influences from, in the Walam Olum, 68-69, 72-73, 79-81, 293n. 13, 294n. 17

Christy, Henry, 149, 163
"cis-Atlantic school of Anthropology," 88, 92-93, 110-16
Clavigero, Francisco Javier, 56-57
codices, Mexican painted, 272, 303n. 3
Cole, Fay-Cooper, 8, 162, 210, 242, 257-58; and dissemination of Peabody Museum method, 259-63
collections: Mercer's, 205-8; Peabody Museum's (Harvard), 202, 239-40; Rau's, 122-27, 130-31
Columbian Exposition (1893), 221, 227, 229, 231-32, 238, 249, 255
Columbus, Christopher, 12, 30-31
Contarini, map by, 13
Converse, Harriet Arnot Maxwell, 239-40
Cook, James, explorer, 21-23, 41, 57
Cope, Edward Drinker, 214; and Mercer, 186, 193, 195-98, 205
"correspondence school" of archaeology, 209, 217-19
Corwith, John White, 193-94
Court de Gébelin, Antoine, and philology, 67, 70-75
Culin, Stewart, 231
Cushing, Frank, 236
Cuvier, Georges, 68, 293n. 15

Dall, William Healey, 158-60
Darwin, Charles (Darwinism), 62, 149, 153, 157, 291n. 8
Darwin, Erasmus, 62-63, 291n. 8
D'Ault du Mesnil, Geoffroy, 203-4
Davenport Academy of Natural Sciences (Iowa), 240-41
Davis, Edwin Hamilton, 88-89, 99. *See also* Squier-Davis investigations
Dee, John, geographer, 16
de Laet, Joannes (Jan), 38-39, 57
Delaware Indians. *See* Lenape (Delaware) Indians
de Mortillet, Louis Laurent Marie Gabriel, 163, 243, 270; and Mercer, 201-3
Deshneva Mys. (East Cape), 26
Deuel, Thorne, 262

Dezhnyov (Deshnef), Semyon Ivanov, explorer, 19–20, 26, 41
Dixon, Roland B., 250–51
Drake, Sir Francis, explorer, 17
du Mesnil du Buisson, Robert, 204
Duncan, Joseph, 240–41
du Ponceau, Peter Stephen, and philology, 67
du Pratz, Le Page, 44, 57

Eastwood, Alice, 223 table 10.2, 234
Eaton, Amos, as women's mentor, 173
École d'Anthropologie (Paris), MacCurdy at, 269–71
Egypt, influences from: and Squier, 98–100, 107; in the Walam Olum, 79–81
Encyclopaedia Britannica, "Archaeology," 133–36, 142, 146–47
England, archaeological researchers from: Christy, 149, 163; Lubbock, 133, 140–43, 145–47, 149; Pengelly, 185, 243–45, 264
"eoliths," 273, 275
Essex Institute, 210–12, 214
ethnology: biblical, 92–93, 106–7, 111, 113–14; comparative, 136–39, 141–47, 150–51, 159 (*see also* analogies, cultural)
etymology. *See* philology
Europe, influences from. *See* pictographs; Rafinesque, Constantine Samuel, influences on; Walam Olum, foreign influences in; *and names of specific countries*
explorations, 23–25, 30–31, 47–49, 56–58, 289nn. 7–8; British, 13, 15–18, 20–23, 31, 41; Norse, 11, 15; Russian, 18–20, 22–23, 26, 28, 32–33, 41; of Strait of Anian, 18–25, 40–41, 50–51. *See also* cartography, developments in

Fabre d'Olivet, Antoine, grammarian, 72, 293n. 16
"Father of Japanese Archaeology" (Morse), 153
Fewkes, Jesse Walter, 160

"first generation" (women in archaeology), 8, 154, 164–70, 232; and the AAAS, 165, 168–69, 173–74, 178–79, 222–27, 229–34, 237–38, 241; and antiquities protection, 222, 230, 236–37; and Columbian Exposition, 227, 229, 231–32, 238; list of, 224–25; mentors of, 172–74, 176–80, 182, 237–39; philanthropists, 235–41; Putnam's assistants, 237–39, 253–57; researchers, 178–81, 183–84, 225–35. *See also* women
Fitting, James E., archaeological historian, 5
Fletcher, Alice C., 177–79, 222, 223 table 10.2, 224–27, 229–30
Folsom (N.Mex.), artifact from, investigated, 276, 304n. 6
Foster, Mary Parke, 233–35
Fowler, James, 158
France, archaeological researchers from, 149, 163, 243, 270–71, 278, 304n. 7; and Mercer, 185, 191–92, 199–204, 207, 303n. 2; and Squier, 87, 92–94, 102
Franklin, Christine Ladd, 223 table 10.2
Frobisher, Martin, explorer, 16, 31
Fulani, Paulo de, map by, 15

Gage, Thomas, 39–40, 57
Gallatin, Albert, 90–91, 113
Galvano, Antonio, Portuguese historian, 18
Gamage, Abram Tarr, 154–56
Garcia, Gregorio, 36–37, 57
Gaudry, Albert: and MacCurdy, 270–71; and Mercer, 185, 191, 199–200, 303n. 2
geography. *See* cartography, developments in; explorations
Geological Survey of Canada, 256–57
geology, influence of, on archaeology, 136–37, 141–47, 149–51, 203–4
Germany, influences from, 121–22, 272. *See also* Humboldt, Alexander von; Rau, Charles
Gibbs, George, 244–45

Gilbert, Sir Humphrey, explorer, 16–17
"glacial man" (Babbitt's term). See Little Falls quartzes
Gliddon, George Robins, 87–88, 91–93, 97–99, 110–12, 297n. 5
Gray, Asa, 217
Grotius, Hugo, 38, 57
Guide Leaflet for Amateur Archaeologists, Chicago method described in, 261–63

Hakluyt, Richard, 37, 57–58
Hall, Edith, 166
Hallowell, Alfred Irving, archaeological historian, 3–4
Hansell, Bernard Z., 187–88
Hardy, Manly, 154
Harvard University: "Harvard Annex" (Radcliffe), 222–24, 237; MacCurdy at, 265–67; Morlot's influence on, 149–57, 162; Museum of Comparative Zoology (MCZ), 149, 212–14; and shell midden archaeology, 148–57, 160–62, 215–17, 232. See also Peabody Museum (Harvard)
Haven, Samuel Foster, archaeological historian, 2, 55, 288n. 6
Hawes, Harriet Boyd, 166
Hawks, Francis L., 106–7
Hearst, Phoebe Apperson, philanthropist, 235
Hebrew, influences from, in the Walam Olum, 68–69, 72, 293n. 16
Heidelberg, University of, Rau at, 120, 130
Hemenway, Mary Porter Tileston, philanthropist, 223 table 10.2, 224, 230, 235–37
Henri-Martin, Léon, 278–79
Henry, Joseph, 141, 244; and Rau, 123, 126–31; and Squier, 100–102
Hewett, Edgar, as women's mentor, 180
hieroglyphs. See pictographs
Hindu, influences from, in the Walam Olum, 69–70
historic material culture, 185–86, 204–8
Hitchcock, Fanny, 223 table 10.2

hoaxes: "Bust of Isis," 77, 295n. 22; Lenape gorget, 187–90, 195, 199, 206; songs of Ossian, 82–84. See also Walam Olum
Hodge, Frederick Webb, 236
Hoernes, Moriz, 269
Holmes, William H., 170–72, 197, 225
Horn, Georg, 38–39, 58
Horner, Eva, 180–81
Horsford, Cornelia, 223 table 10.2, 233
Huddleston, Lee Eldridge, archaeological historian, 4
Human Origins: A Manual of Prehistory (MacCurdy), 275–77
Humboldt, Alexander von, 81–82, 295n. 24, 297n. 6; influence of, on Squier, 87, 94, 102, 106, 110
Hyde, Elizabeth Mead, 233–34

Inuits ("Innuit"), and cultural adaptation, 158–59

James, Sir Edwin, ethnologist, 66
Jefferson, Thomas, 46–47, 58; and John Ledyard, 23–25, 50–51
Jin-wis, in the Walam Olum, 70–74
Jo Daviess County (Illinois), 255–56, 258–60
Jomard, Edme François, 87, 92–94, 102
Jones, Sir William, philologist, 66, 68, 77, 111, 292nn. 11–12, 293n.14

Kalm, Peter, 43–44, 58, 288n. 6
Kelly, Isabel, 180–81
Kennewick man, 55, 290n. 10
Kidder, A. V., as women's mentor, 180
Kidder, Homer, 306n. 11
Kimball, John Cone, 253
King, Ada M., 223 table 10.2
kjoekkenmoeddings (shell middens), 150, 152, 157, 160. See also shell midden archaeology
Kohl, Johann Georg, cartographic specialist, 26–27
Krogman, Wilton, 259–62

La Ferrassie (France), artifacts from, investigated, 278, 304n. 7

languages. *See* philology
Lartet, Edouard, 149, 163
law of variety-production, 134, 139, 145, 299n. 1
Lawrence Scientific School, 212–14
Ledyard, John, explorer, 23–25, 50–51, 58
Lenape gorget, 187–90, 195, 199, 206
Lenape (Delaware) Indians, 60–61, 70–74, 77–81, 83–84, 290n. 2, 291nn. 5–7, 295n. 21. *See also* pictographs
Le Plongeon, Alice Dixon, 227–28
Le Plongeon, Augustus, 227–28
Lewis, Henry Carvill, 188–89
Lilly, Eli, and the Walam Olum, 61–62
linguistics. *See* philology
Linnique peoples, term created by Rafinesque, 60, 290n. 2
Little Falls quartzes, 167–72, 225
Lost Tribes hypothesis, 34, 45–46, 55, 288n. 4
Lubbock, Sir John, 133, 140–43, 145–47, 149

MacCurdy, George Grant, 8–9, 303nn. 1, 3, 304n. 6, 305n. 8; and the AAAS, 273–74; and the American Anthropological Association, 274–75; and American School for Prehistoric Research, 277–85, 305n. 10; education of, in Europe, 267–73; excavations by, 276, 278–82, 304n. 7; at Harvard, 265–67; publications of, 275–77
Macpherson, James, 82–84, 296n. 25
Magellan, Ferdinand, explorer, 12–14
Magill, Emily Tennison, 236
Magill, Margaret Whitehead, 236
maki mani (bad spirit), in the Walam Olum, 74–76
Manes, Roman, 74–76, 294n. 18
Manifest Destiny, ideologues of, 142, 146
maps. *See* cartography, developments in
Mark, Joan, archaeological historian, 5
Marsh, Othniel Charles, 195–96, 266–68
Martin, Paul S., 258–62

Martyr, Peter, 31, 58
Mason, Otis Tufton, 176, 248
Maya: hieroglyphs of, 85, 296n. 27; research on, 227–28
McGee, Anita Newcomb (Mrs. William J.), 165–66, 222, 223 table 10.2, 224–25, 237
McGee, William J., 175–76, 237
Mead, Frances Harvey Teobert, 237–39
mentors, women's, 172–74, 176–80, 182, 237–39
Mercator, Gerardus, map by, 14–15
Mercer, Henry Chapman, 8; American colleagues of, 186–87, 193–99, 205; and Arts and Crafts Movement, 185–86, 204–8; and Bucks County Historical Society, 187, 205–6; cave explorations by, 192–95, 197–98, 207; collections of, 205–8; education of, 186–87; in Europe, 191–92; excavation methodology of, 185–86, 190–95, 199–204, 207–8; French colleagues of, 185, 191–92, 199–204, 207, 303n. 2; and Lenape gorget, 187–90, 195, 199, 206; in Mexico, 193–94, 204–5; publications of, 194, 196–97, 207; and Trenton gravels, 190–92, 195, 197–202, 205; at the University of Pennsylvania, 189–90, 194, 196, 198–99, 205
Mercer Museum (Bucks County, Pa.), 206
methodology, excavation: Mercer's, 185–86, 190–95, 199–204, 207–8; principles of, established, 151–61, 242–45, 264, 277, 306n. 11; Putnam's, 155–56, 160–62, 196, 217–20, 242–43, 246–48 (*see also* Peabody Museum method); Wyman's, 215–17
Metz, Charles L., 220, 253–54
Mexico, research in, 193–94, 204–5, 227–29, 232, 272, 303n. 3
Mitra, Panchanan, archaeological historian, 3, 287 n. 1 (intro.), 288n. 6
monogenesis. *See* monogenist-polygenist debate
monogenist-polygenist debate, 64–68,

92–95, 98–100, 102–7, 109–11, 134, 139–40, 145
Moorehead, Warren K., 251–52
Morgan, Lewis Henry, 139–41, 146
Morlot, Adolphe von, 8, 148, 162–63, 216–17; and Harvard researchers, 149–57, 162; and the Smithsonian, 157–60, 162
Morse, Edwin Sylvester, 149, 152–53
Morton, Samuel George, 88, 139
Mound Builders, 123–24; and Squier-Davis investigations, 87–91, 93, 96–100. *See also* Walam Olum, and origins theories
Murphy, Jeannette Robinson, 223 table 10.2
Museum of Comparative Zoology (MCZ), 149, 212–14
Museum of the Peabody Academy of Sciences (Salem, Mass.), 153, 214–15

Nanabush, in the Walam Olum, 76–77, 295n. 21
national identity, American, need for, 85–86, 103–4
National Museum of Scotland, founding of, 134
Native Americans. *See* American Indians
nature, worship of. *See* sun worship
Neanderthal skeletons, at La Ferrassie, 278, 304n. 7
Nelson, Nels, 201
"Neobagun," term created by Rafinesque, 60, 290n. 1
A New System, or An Analysis of Ancient Mythology (Bryant), 66–67
Nickerson, William Baker: and Peabody Museum method, 252–57; as source of Chicago method, 242, 258–64
Noah, 76–77, 294n. 18
Northeast Passage, search for, 15–18, 31
Northwest Passage, search for, 15–18, 31
Norton, Charles Eliot, and Mercer, 187, 206
Nott, Josiah Clark, 88
Nova Scotia Institute of Natural History, and shell midden archaeology, 157
Nunn, George E., cartographic specialist, 27–28
Nuttall, Zelia Maria Magdalena, 178, 223 table 10.2, 224–25, 228–29

Ohio Valley, mounds in. *See* Squier-Davis investigations
Ojibwa, 76–77, 103, 138–39, 290n. 1, 295n. 21
Olumapies, Rafinesque's meaning of, 83–84
origins theories, 30–34, 54–59, 287n. 1 (chap. 2), 288n. 3, 290n. 10, 292n. 10; A.D. 1500–1600, 34–37; A.D. 1600–1650, 37–40; A.D. 1700–1800, 41–54; and philology, 46–47, 51–54, 66–67, 292n. 12, 293n. 14; and Tartars, 33–34, 81, 288nn. 2, 6; Transpacifican, 34, 140, 288n. 4. *See also* Bering Strait hypothesis; monogenist-polygenist debate; Transatlantean hypothesis; Walam Olum, and origins theories
Ortelius, Abraham, map by, 15
Ossian hoax, 82–84
Oviedo, Fernandez de, 34–35, 58–59

Packard, Alpheus S., 214
Paleolithic debate, American, 167–72, 190–92, 195, 197–202, 205, 225, 303n. 2. *See also* Mercer, Henry Chapman
Patrick, John J. R., 117, 125
Paxson, Albert S., 188
Paxson, Henry D., 188
Peabody, Charles, 251–52, 278–80, 303n. 1
Peabody, George, philanthropist, 149, 153, 214
Peabody, Lucy E., 223 table 10.2, 234
Peabody Museum (Harvard), 7–8, 129; collections of, 202, 239–40
Peabody Museum (Salem, Mass.), 153, 214–15
Peabody Museum method, ii, 7–8;

dissemination of, 259–63; practitioners of, 248–52. *See also* Nickerson, William Baker; Putnam, Frederic Ward, excavation methodology of
Peet, Rev. S. D., 169
Pengelly, William, and excavation methodology, 185, 243–45, 264
Pennsylvania, University of: Mercer at, 189–90, 194, 196, 198–99, 205; and women archaeologists, 231–33
Pepper, George H., 251
Peyrony, Denis, 278, 304n. 7
Pfefferkorn, Ignaz, 42, 59
philanthropists, influence of, in archaeology, 149, 153, 214, 235–41, 265–67
philology, 74–75, 292n. 12, 293n.14, 294n. 18; and origins theories, 46–47, 51–54, 66–67, 292n. 12, 293n. 14. *See also* Rafinesque, Constantine Samuel, linguistic creations of
pictographs, 79–81, 85, 296n. 27; in the Walam Olum, 60–61, 71 fig. 3.1, 77–81, 290n. 1, 291n. 6, 295n. 22
Pinart, Alphonse Louis, 228
Polo, Maffeo, 11, 59
Polo, Marco, 11–13, 30–31, 59; Siberia described by, 12, 32–34
Polo, Niccolò, 11, 59
polygenesis. *See* monogenist-polygenist debate
Pond, Alonzo W., 280, 305nn. 9–10
Pre-Historic America (Nadaillac), Dall's contribution to, 159
prehistoric archaeology, science of, established. *See* Morlot, Adolphe von; Wilson, Daniel
Prehistoric Man (Wilson), 133, 136–37, 139–40, 142, 146–47
Ptolemy, map by, 10
Purchas, Samuel, 37, 59
Putnam, Alice E., 223 table 10.2, 237–39
Putnam, Elizabeth Duncan, 223 table 10.2, 240–41
Putnam, Frederic Ward, 7–8, 178–79, 207, 209–10, 266; and AAAS, 210–11, 215; and the Agassiz family, 149, 211–14, 217, 222–24; and *American Naturalist*, 196, 214–15; assistants of, 237–39, 253–57; and Columbian Exposition, 221, 227, 229, 231–32, 238, 249, 255; "correspondence school" of, 209, 217–19; excavation methodology of, 155–56, 160–62, 196, 217–20, 242–43, 246–48 (*see also* Peabody Museum method); family members, 222–25, 237–41; and institutional development, 220–22; lecture topics of, 217–19, 246–47; pedagogy of, 217–19, 245–46, 250; in Salem, Mass., 153, 214–15; and shell midden archaeology, 153–57, 160–62; and Wheatland, 210–12, 214; and Wyman, 215–17
Putnam, Mary Louisa Duncan, 222, 223 table 10.2, 224–25, 240–41

Raab, Henry, description by, of Rau, 122–23
Radcliffe College ("School for Collegiate Instruction of Women"), 222–24, 237
Rafinesque, Constantine Samuel, 6, 60–62, 188–89; influences on, 62–63, 68, 81–84, 291n. 8, 293n. 15, 295nn. 21–22, 296nn. 25–27; linguistic creations of, 60, 70–77, 83, 290nn. 1–2, 296n. 26; as poet, 62–63, 84, 292n. 8; self-promotion of, 62–63, 84–85. *See also* Walam Olum
Rau, Charles, 7, 118–19, 157; artifacts collection of, 122–27, 130–31; and excavation methodology, 244–45; in Germany, 120, 130; in the Midwest, 121–25, 130–31; in New York, 125–31; previous research on, 117–18, 130; and Smithsonian Institution, 123, 126–31
religious systems, Squier's interest in, 96–100, 103–11

Rudbeck, Olof, 243, 264
Russell, Frank, 196, 249-50
Ruysch, Johannes, map by, 13

Sabloff, Jeremy, archaeological historian, 5
"Salem Secession," 214, 217
Salisbury, Edward Elbridge, philanthropist, 267
Salisbury, Evelyn MacCurdy, philanthropist, 265-67
Sarychev, Gavriil, explorer, 22-23, 25
Schmerling, Philippe-Charles, 119
"School for Collegiate Instruction of Women" (Radcliffe), 222-24, 237
Schumacher, Paul, 157-58
Scotland, influences from, 140-41
Scottish Common-Sense Realism ("Baconian science"), 140-41
Scull, Sarah, 233-34
Seneca tribe, whites adopted by, 239-40
serpent, symbolism of, 97-100, 108-11
Serpent Symbol, The (Squier), 95-96, 105-8, 110
shell midden archaeology: and Harvard researchers, 148-57, 160-62, 215-17, 232; and the Smithsonian, 157-60, 162
Siberia, 12, 25, 32-34
Smith, Erminnie Adelle Platt, 177-78, 222, 223 table 10.2, 224-26, 229-30
Smith, Jennie (Jane), 223 table 10.2, 237-39
Smithsonian Institution: collecting methods of, 219-20, 243-45; Rau's relationship with, 123, 126-31; and shell midden archaeology, 157-60, 162; Squier's relationship with, 100-102, 298n. 18
Society for Arts and Crafts, 206-7
Society of Antiquarians of Scotland, 134
Spice Islands, routes to, sought, 12-13, 15-18
Spier, Leslie, 191
Spinden, Herbert J., 252
Squier, Ephraim George, 6, 297nn. 1, 5, 298n. 19; and the American Ethnological Society, 88, 90-91, 113-16; and biblical ethnology, 92-93, 106-7, 111, 113-14; and cultural analogies, 94-99, 101-4; influences on, 87, 92-94, 102-3, 106, 110 (see also Gliddon, George Robins); and religious systems, 96-100, 103-11; scholarly career of, established, 87-91; and serpent symbolism, 97-100, 108-11; The Serpent Symbol, 95-96, 105-8, 110; and Smithsonian Institution, 100-102, 298n. 18; and sun worship, 97-100, 104-5, 107-8. See also Squier-Davis investigations
Squier-Davis investigations, 87-91, 93, 96-100; end of, 100-101
Steenstrup, Japetus, 149-50
Sterns, Fred H., 252
Stevenson, James, 230
Stevenson, Matilda (Tilly) Coxe, 177, 222, 223 table 10.2, 224-25, 229-31
Stevenson, Sara Yorke (Mrs. Cornelius), 223 table 10.2, 231-32
stratigraphy. See methodology, excavation
Studley, Cordelia A., 154, 223 table 10.2, 232
sun worship, 97-100, 104-5, 107-8
Swanton, John R., 250-51
Switzerland, influences from. See Morlot, Adolphe von

Talbott, Laura O., 223 table 10.2
"Tartaria." See Siberia
Tartars, and origins theories, 33-34, 81, 288nn. 2, 6
Thaw, Mary Sibbet Copley, philanthropist, 223 table 10.2, 237
Thayer, Sophia Bradford Ripley, 239
Thompson, J. Eric S., 39-40
Toronto, University College, Wilson at, 137-38
Transatlantean hypothesis, 34, 140, 288n. 4; proponents of, 34-38, 43-46, 58-59

Transpacifican hypothesis, 34, 140, 288n. 4
travelers. *See* explorations
Trenton gravels, 190–92, 195, 197–202, 205, 303n. 2. *See also* Abbott, Charles Conrad

Upham, Warren, 167–70

Vero (Fla.), artifacts from, investigated, 275–76
Vienna, University of, MacCurdy at, 268–69
Vikings, 11, 15, 233
Volney, Constantin-François, 74–75
Volney Prize, 60–61, 63, 290n. 3

Walam Olum, 6; animalization in, 75–76, 294n. 20; controversy about, 61–64, 85, 291n. 6, 292n. 9; creation accounts in, 61, 67–74; foreign influences in, 68–70, 72–73, 79–81, 293nn. 13, 16, 294n. 17; influence of, on archaeologists, 103, 188–89; *maki mani* (bad spirit) in, 74–76; and origins theories, 61, 64–67, 76–77, 81–82, 86, 292n. 10; supposed sources for, 62, 291n. 7. *See also* pictographs; Rafinesque, Constantine Samuel
Walker, S. T., 159–60
Warburton, William, theologian, 107
Wardle, Harriet Newell, 223 table 10.2, 233–34
Washington, George, 46–47, 59
Watkins, Frances, 180–81
Wetherill, (Benjamin) Alfred, 234
Wetherill, Richard, 234
Wheatland, Henry, 210–12, 214
Will, George F., 252
Willey, Gordon R., archaeological historian, 5, 263

Williams, Jeanette Webster, 236
Willoughby, Charles C., 156–57, 248–49
Wilmsen, Edwin, archaeological historian, 4–5
Wilson, Daniel, 7; "Archaeology" (article), 133–36, 142, 146–47; *Archaeology and Prehistoric Annals of Scotland*, 133–34, 137, 141, 146–47; bibliography by, in *Encyclopaedia Britannica*, 135–36; in Canada, 137–39; and comparative ethnology, 136–39, 141–47; and Lubbock, 133, 140–43, 145–47; papers by, 138–39, 300n. 3 (chap. 6); *Prehistoric Man*, 133, 136–37, 139–40, 142, 146–47; term "prehistoric" introduced by, 133–36
Winchell, Newton, 166–68
Winsor, Justin, archaeological historian, 2–3, 187
Wirt, Julia, 233–35
women, 172–74, 181–84; and the American School of Prehistoric Research, 280–83; in social anthropology, 164–66, 176–79, 181–84. *See also* "first generation" (women in archaeology)
Women's Anthropological Society of America, 165–66, 226, 230–31, 234
Works Progress Administration (WPA), and Chicago method, 263
World's Columbian Exposition. *See* Columbian Exposition (1893)
Wyman, Jeffries, 149–53, 202, 215–17

Yale University, MacCurdy at, 272–73
Yucatán (Mexico), Mercer's investigations in, 193–94, 204–5

Zuckerkandl, Emil, 269